Power, Political Economy, and Historical Landscapes of the Modern World

FERNAND BRAUDEL CENTER
STUDIES IN HISTORICAL SOCIAL SCIENCE

Series Editor: Richard E. Lee

The Fernand Braudel Center Studies in Historical Social Science publishes works that address theoretical and empirical questions produced by scholars in or through the Fernand Braudel Center or who share its approach and concerns. It specifically promotes works that contribute to the development of the world-systems perspective engaging a holistic and relational vision of the world—the modern world-system—implicit in historical social science, which at once takes into consideration structures (long-term regularities) and change (history). With the intellectual boundaries within the sciences/social sciences/humanities structure collapsing in the work scholars actually do, this series offers a venue for a wide range of research that confronts the dilemmas of producing relevant accounts of historical processes in the context of the rapidly changing structures of both the social and academic world. The series includes monographs, colloquia, and collections of essays organized around specific themes.

RECENT VOLUMES IN THIS SERIES:

The *Longue Durée* and World-Systems Analysis
Richard E. Lee, editor

New Frontiers of Slavery
Dale W. Tomich, editor

Slavery in the Circuit of Sugar: Martinique and the World-Economy, 1830–1848
Dale W. Tomich

The Politics of the Second Slavery
Dale W. Tomich, editor

The Trade in the Living
Luiz Felipe de Alencastro

Race and Rurality in the Global Economy
Michaeline A. Crichlow, Patricia Northover, and Juan Giusti-Cordero, editors

Power, Political Economy, and Historical Landscapes of the Modern World: Interdisciplinary Perspectives
Christopher R. DeCorse, editor

Power, Political Economy, and Historical Landscapes of the Modern World

Interdisciplinary Perspectives

Edited by

Christopher R. DeCorse

FERNAND BRAUDEL CENTER
STUDIES IN HISTORICAL SOCIAL SCIENCE

SUNY PRESS

Published by State University of New York Press, Albany

For information, contact State University of New York Press, Albany, NY
www.sunypress.edu

Library of Congress Cataloging-in-Publication Data

Names: DeCorse, Christopher R., editor.
Title: Power, political economy, and historical landscapes of the modern world : interdisciplinary perspectives / edited by Christopher R. DeCorse.
Description: Albany : State University of New York Press, [2019] | Series: Fernand Braudel Center Studies in historical social science | Includes bibliographical references and index.
Identifiers: LCCN 2018020086 | ISBN 9781438473437 (hardcover) | ISBN 9781438473420 (pbk.) | ISBN 9781438473444 (ebook)
Subjects: LCSH: Economic history. | Social evolution. | Social history. | Social change—History.
Classification: LCC HC21 .P688 2019 | DDC 330.9/03—dc23
LC record available at https://lccn.loc.gov/2018020086

10 9 8 7 6 5 4 3 2 1

CONTENTS

ILLUSTRATIONS

Figures

Tables

PREFACE

The impetus for the Fernand Braudel Center colloquium on which this volume is based emerged as a result of the many discussions I have had with Dale Tomich, deputy director of the Fernand Braudel Center for the Study of Economies, Historical Systems, and Civilizations, over the past decade. Our initial connection was made at the School for Advanced Research seminar in Santé Fe in 2008. Apart from our institutional proximity (which somehow seems more distant than it actually is during the Central New York winters), we share a desire to investigate the processes and materialities of the modern world. We bring distinct disciplinary vantage to these endeavors: Dale's grounding in historical sociology and my own in archaeology. We also draw on research on opposite sides of the Atlantic—Dale's primary focus being on the Americas and mine on Africa.

The result of our initial discussions was the formation of the Built Environments of Atlantic Slavery Working Group, an informal, interdisciplinary posse that has hosted several workshops and colloquia at the Fernand Braudel Center. We also shared field trips to coffee plantations in Brazil, as well as other historic sites. Our activities were shaped both spatially and temporarily by concepts of the "Atlantic" world, particularly the Atlantic slave trade. What were the processes that formed the plantation landscapes of Brazil, the Caribbean, and the American South? How did the changes in the coast and hinterlands of West Africa over the past 500 years relate to these Atlantic intersections? I additionally benefited from several graduate seminars on the Atlantic World I held at Syracuse University in 2013 and 2014.

I profited from all of these conversations. However, as our discussions developed, the parameters and utility of the "Atlantic World" as an analytic frame became increasing limiting. While the Atlantic World presents unique historical and geographical connections, it also belays the remarkably global extent of the interconnections that characterized the past five centuries. Many of the intersections and entanglements central to the shaping of the modern world-system began with the advent of European sea trade in the late fifteenth and early sixteenth centuries. Recognizing their distinctive local and regional soundings, the patterns and materialities of the processes that shaped the Atlantic intersections nonetheless shared global interconnections with the worlds of the Indian and Pacific Oceans.

The colloquium that provided the basis for this volume resulted from conversations I had with Dale Tomich and Richard Lee, director of the Fernand Braudel Center, who encouraged me to submit a proposal. The colloquium was fashioned to resonate with the Fernand Braudel Center's commitment to an interdisciplinary perspective, and brought together contributions from historians, archaeologists, sociologists, and geographers from Europe, the United States, and Britain. The colloquium, held at the Center in April 2017, opened an array of wonderfully interdisciplinary discussions. It was an enjoyable time that was one of the best seminars of its kind that I have attended. I am grateful to Dale Tomich, Richard Lee, the volume's contributors, and all of the editorial staff at SUNY Press for their encouragement and continued support throughout this project.

Chapter 1

Historical Landscapes of the Modern World

Christopher R. DeCorse

This volume draws together scholars from varied disciplines to examine the historical encounters, cultural entanglements, and local conditions that shaped the modern world. Research has well demonstrated the extent and complexity of the varied local economic and political systems, and diverse social formations that predated European contact. These preexisting systems confronted the expanding European economy and, in doing so, shaped its emergence. The case studies presented in this volume seek to understand how the intersections of these different regional systems formed unique historical and geographical complexes that structured European-indigene interactions, economic relations, and their materialities. Moving beyond the confines of national or Atlantic histories to examine regional systems and their historical trajectories on a global scale, the studies draw examples from the Caribbean, Mesoamerica, North America, South America, Africa, and South Asia. Collectively they ask how did the diverse political economies of the early modern world collide, mesh, and merge, and to what effect on the engaged populations in different world areas? The studies examine how the new economic, social, and cultural relations of the modern world, nascent European colonialism, and the Atlantic slave trade are revealed in landscapes, settlements, plantations, dwellings, and archaeological assemblages. How and why did these landscapes differ in their expression and in their temporalities? The chapters are by researchers who share an interest in the emergence and interconnections of the modern world, and the utility of interdisciplinary vantage. While the contributions are rooted in substantive studies from different world areas, their overarching aim is to negotiate between global and local frames, to reveal how the expanding world-system entwined the non-Western world in global economies, yet did so in ways that were locally articulated, varied, and often non-European in their expression.

Deep Time and Local Pasts

The studies presented herein build on an extensive body of research across the social sciences that has examined the historical depth and economic interconnections that shaped modernity. The temporal focus is on the economic, cultural, and political entanglements of the past five centuries, a period marked by European expansion across the globe. The emergence of an increasingly Eurocentric global economy drew regional and local economies into new formations that were, if not completely new in their economic structures, (trans)formative in ways that were central to the shaping of the systemic connections, muddles and imbroglios germane to the formation of the modern world.

While the global nature of the connections represented is a central, unifying theme of this volume, the perspective taken in the studies presented is decidedly local. Although varied in their regional and temporal settings, the volume's collective focus is equally on pre-European networks, indigenous social formations, regional economies, and their particularities that are distinctive of the places examined. The contributions are sympathetic to concepts of deep time: local culture histories, traditions, and pasts that shaped indigene-European interactions and ultimately structured the meetings of the capitalist and precapitalist worlds. While the studies presented engage various theoretical frames, they are uniformly accepting of perspectives that situate the changes of the post–fifteenth-century world in the structures, flows, and disjunctures of historical systems. This perspective pushes away from ahistorical perspectives that place societies in static boxes, seemingly unchanging and without agency in the face of European hegemony.

Although the studies engage varied theoretical lenses, they resonate with Fernand's Braudel's view that history should be studied as a long-term process; that understanding of the past ultimately explains the present.[1] Braudel's *longue durée* gives primacy to the long-term historical structures situated in time and place, which have been foundational in the study of the modern world (e.g., Lee 2012, 1–4). Braudel presents this vantage in his classic work *The Mediterranean and the Mediterranean World* (1972a, 1972b). Braudel's focus is on the world of Philip the II of Spain (1527–1598), ruler of an empire that included outposts, trading enclaves, and colonies spanning from Hispaniola and Lima to Goa and Macau—an empire on which the sun never set.[2] Yet Braudel does not remain in the sixteenth century, but rather ranges from classical antiquity to the contours of modernity. In Braudel's view there were many such "Mediterraneans"—particular historical systems that moved from onset and development to decline, and cannot be understood independently from the wider systemic contexts in which they existed. The varied regions of the Americas, Africa, and Asia thus had their own pre-fifteenth-century, pre-European pasts in which the present is intricately imbedded.

The varied patterns, extent, and complexity of many such pre–fifteenth-century, pre-European contact histories have been revealed by a host of scholarship. They have been defined and described in various ways: as cores and peripheries, connectivities, interaction spheres, trading systems, clusters, and world markets. The societies involved evinced varied degrees and manners of socioeconomic formations, political complexity, and cultural confluences. These preexisting regional and inter-regional systems intersected with one another to varying degrees and with varying effects long before the advent of European expansion in the fifteenth century. Indeed, an increasing amount of research has revealed the pre–early modern world to have been far more interconnected than once thought. Demonstrated trade connections between Asia and the East African coast during the first and early second millennia AD (Fleisher et al. 2015), the undeniable Norse settlement in Newfoundland five centuries before the first Columbian voyages to the Americas (Ingstad & Ingstad 2000), and possible genetic evidence for pre–fifteenth-century Polynesian–South American contacts (Moreno-Maynar et al. 2014) hint at deep connections between disparate human populations long before the nascence of the modern world. The cultural confluences represented in some of these meetings may have had limited, transitory effects on the societies involved. For example, Norse–First Nation interactions undoubtedly took place but they may have had negligible impacts on the societies involved. More pointedly, the nuances of these dealings and their consequences are difficult to assess with the data at hand.

Yet if some pre–fifteenth-century cultural contacts were limited in their effects, we can also recognize that long before the era of European expansion the world was divided into economies of varied scope, historical duration, and regional integration. We can also accept that imperialism, hegemony, colonization, slavery, the subjugation of subaltern populations, and the economic underpinnings of these phenomena are not unique to the past five centuries. Many researchers have identified earlier interconnected networks, in some cases suggesting that these were comparable in their complexity and structuring to those of the modern world. In her seminal work *Before European Hegemony: The World System A.D. 1250–1350*, Janet Abu-Leghod (1991) argued that an interconnected network—that is, an economically interconnected network—extended across Eurasia before the advent of Renaissance Europe. She further posited that this earlier system was foundational to Immanuel Wallerstein's (1974) modern world-system and that it was subsequently restructured by it (Abu-Lughod 1991, 361).[3] In a similar vein, in considering Wallerstein's (1974) placement of the long-term economic soundings of the world in the early modern period, Andre Gunder Frank and Barry K. Gills (1993) challenge us to ask if these extend back 500 or 5,000 years.

Researchers from across disciplines have similarly argued for the existence of a multiplicity of "world-systems" of varying durations representing a continuum in size and complexity (e.g., Chase-Dunn & Anderson 2005; Chase-Dunn & Hall 1991, 1997; Kardulias 1999; Pomeranz 2000; Wolf 1982; Wong 2012).[4] These regional systems formed their own unique historical and geographical complexes that intersected with other systems and were of varied import for the societies involved (see fig. 1.1). At times, these junctions were coercive or forcible, involving subjugation and conquest. In other cases, linkages were extended by the formation

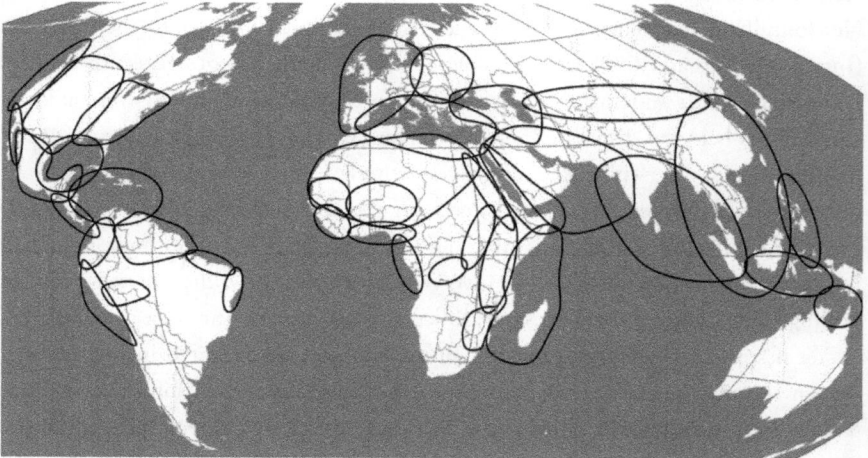

Figure 1.1. Global map with hypothetical, pre-fifteenth-century regional and intraregional networks. Presented here as intersecting circles, the map only hints at the complexity of cultural, social, and economic networks that existed on the cusp of European expansion. (Drawing by Christopher R. DeCorse)

of alliances, treaties, and agreements with indigenous polities, rulers, and emerging elites. In all cases, the participants involved manipulated these convergences to greater and lesser degrees. The fifteenth-century world that Europe encountered was not one of static landscapes, but one populated by preexisting, dynamic societal systems. The crude, hypothetical map in figure 1.1 is only intended to hint at the extent, locations, and multiplicity of regional systems that predated the origins of the modern world.[5] The gaps on the map in some instances represent the lack of available information, rather than an actual absence of pre–fifteenth-century systems, networks, connectivities, and cores.

While pre-European contact pasts can be accepted as a given and the systems that they represented were integral to economic and cultural formations of modernity, in many instances their histories and the histories of Europe's meetings with them are poorly known, only dimly viewed through documentary accounts provided by European colonizers, oral traditions, and archaeological traces. Notably, discussions of premodern world-systems often have not included large portions of sub-Saharan Africa. In part, this is indicative of the lack of available information for many parts of the continent. Nonetheless, placement of post–fifteenth-century developments within the deeper time of indigenous history has long been a characteristic of studies of the African past. Indeed it is particularly striking how many African and Africanist archaeologists and historians focusing on the past two millennia almost imperceptivity move from the first millennium AD through the Atlantic Period.[6]

Yet, in many instances, narratives of European exploration, colonization, and the sociopolitical marginalization of native populations in the past five centuries have overwritten pre-European contact pasts. As Hofman (chapter 3, this volume) observes, while the insular Caribbean was the initial nexus of European–Native American interactions, the indigenous Caribbean became largely unmentioned, undiscussed, and invisible in global history. Stories of European colonial endeavors and the attendant foci on the mineral-rich Aztec, Mayan, and Incan Empires left the histories of the Native peoples of the Caribbean as little more than footnotes in chronicles of the past and only known by names applied by European colonizers.

The contributors to the present volume are sympathetic to the deep soundings of the modern world. Although their focus is on the formulations of the past five centuries, their desire is to recenter study toward local histories that recognize the distinctive aspects and indigeneity of the networks of the Americas, Africa, and South Asia with which Europeans interacted. While recognizing the newness, unique confluences and distinctive structuring of the modern world-system, seeking an unambiguous divide between modern and premodern times creates an artificial boundary that is counterproductive to historical study and presents narratives that marginalize non-European pasts.[7] The studies highlight the diversity of historical contexts and contact settings that underlaid and shaped the formative interactions of the past five centuries, and argue the need to bring this perspective to bear in order to fully understand the processes that shaped the modern world. Despite the dramatic differences in the societies and the culture histories considered, the contours of modernity in these different settings are similarly imbedded in deeper pasts.

Although focused on the period of European expansion, many of the cases considered extend back into the first millennium AD and beyond in order to contextualize and understand the transformations associated with the opening of European economic exchanges. Hence, Corinne Hofman (chapter 3) begins her examination of the "Columbian Turn" in the Insular Caribbean with a review of the eight millennia of history that preceded the arrival of the Europeans. When Martindale and his coauthors (chapter 11) examine nineteenth-century colonial encounters and the tribal identity of the Tsimshian of British Columbia, they consider these formulations within the context of indigenous cultural traditions spanning the past several millennia, and the nuances of the Tsimshian legal system, as well as the changing contours of Tsimshian-European interactions. Similarly, Shanguhyia's (chapter 14) examination of British colonial forest and wildlife man-agement policies in late-nineteenth- and early-twentieth-century East Africa, equally considers the economic basis on which British colonial policy was predicated, along with pre-European indigenous land-use practices, social organization, economic networks, and Indian Ocean circuits of exchange. And, as Johnson (chapter 2) reminds us in his imaginary fifteenth-century journey from Dover to Dublin, the cultures, societies, and economies of Britain and Europe were equally transformed by capitalism and the cultural entanglements of the following centuries.

Beyond Nations, Oceans, and Hemispheres[8]

If the contributors to this volume are well attuned to the indigenous sociopolitical structures, cultural formations, and economic networks that shaped the encounters of the past five centuries, they are equally cognizant of the distinctive aspects of the increasingly Eurocentric, hegemonic nature of many of the interactions and exchanges of the post–fifteenth-century world. In this respect, the contributions resonate with macroscale approaches to social analysis that bridge global and local contexts. Understanding the historical basis of such structural, synergistic interconnections provides a means of examining why such junctures occurred, as well as how changes within one region impact developments across all of the societies and regions involved. This perspective is exemplified by Fernand Braudel's (1972a, 1972b, 1990) view of historically structured systems articulated in *The Mediterranean* and the world-system perspective advanced by Immanuel Wallerstein (1974, 1980, 1989), both of which can be viewed as methodological approaches, as much as conceptual lenses. While some researchers have criticized the use of broad-scale economic models as explanatory frameworks, such models continue to provide a pragmatic means of examining and explaining developments in different, yet structurally interconnected, parts of the world.[9] Social network theory and other "glocal" perspectives of globalization and entanglement have been used increasingly in the social sciences as a way of conceptualizing the complexity of human social interactions, cultural entanglements, and, with particular regard to archaeology, their material expressions and incongruities. They are thus more concerned with the epistemological contemplation of cultural continuities and discontinuities than the material relations that are the core of Braudel's *Mediterranean* and Wallerstein's world-system.[10] Yet, while social theorists have employed a diversity of theoretical and methodological approaches, evincing a great deal of variation in the key tenets represented, the explanatory value in recognizing the systemic, relational nature of the interconnections between the societies is central to understanding the contours of modernity.

If there are similarities between premodern systems and that of the modern world, there are also differences in their structures, margins, and temporalities. The modern world-system is greater in geographical scope than any network or system that preceded it. Its contours and soundings were remarkably well delineated from the initial expansion of Europe into the non–Western World in the fifteenth century. This was a global, pan-oceanic network that from the onset was marked by sea routes, trading posts, and, increasingly in the course of the succeeding centuries, by colonial territories. The Portuguese rounded the Cape of Good Hope in 1488, reaching Western India in 1498, Ceylon in 1505, and China in 1513. Trade began with the initial arrival of the Europeans, and by 1600 Portuguese forts, merchant enclaves, and settlements had been established from West Africa and Brazil, to Asia. The movement of peoples, plants and animals, concepts, cultures, and natural resources between Europe, the Americas, Africa, and Asia began concurrently. Pre-European networks were interconnected in new and unique ways.

The research presented in this volume pushes beyond the confines of both national histories and oceanic boundaries. While the specifics of particular national histories are important in contextualizing individual contact settings, cultural intersections, and colonial projects, it is the economic confluences and their articulations that underlie the studies presented. Recognizing the importance of European contact, trade, and colonization, the contributions herein resite focus to understand how different regional systems formed unique historical and geographical complexes that structured European-indigene relations. Expanding European capitalism and the European-indigene meetings that took place were more characterized by a diversity of situations and outcomes than by unitary phenomena. A unifying theme of the case studies presented here is their grounding in distinctive local histories, economic networks, and sociocultural rhythms. The studies reveal how local exchange networks and sociocultural traditions encountered were shaped by, and shaped, global interconnections.

Many aspects of the research presented resonate with themes that have been central to Atlantic studies, a field that has burgeoned in the past half century. While the geographic and conceptual parameters of Atlantic studies are somewhat diffuse, collectively the research seeks to untangle the complexity of systemic connections that brought together people in a variety of economic, cultural, social, political, and biological interactions in the past five centuries.[11] Research foci such as colonialism, European-indigene interactions, the slave trade, elite-subaltern dichotomies, and their materialities—which have been important foci of Atlantic studies—resonate with the works presented here. Transformations in African settlement patterns in regions impacted by the slave trade (DeCorse 2016a & 2016b) and the colonial landscapes of the Caribbean were consequences of the Atlantic economy and expressive of it. European colonization in many instances created entirely new landscapes, which replaced native topographies. Hence, as Armstrong (chapter 6) illustrates in his study of seventeenth-century Barbados, change in world economy such as the shift from cotton to sugar production are dramatically illustrated in colonial and plantation landscapes (also see Wallerstein 1980, 166–68).

The flows of the Atlantic world are particularly important for understanding the impacts, social transformations, and cultural continuities and discontinuities associated with the emergence, growth, and eventual abolition of the slave trade. The unique historical and geographical complexes of the Atlantic provide a means for understanding the movement and displacement of millions of colonists, enslaved Africans, indigenous populations, and a host of other subaltern populations on both sides of the Atlantic. As Chouin and Olanrewaju (chapter 12) and Kelly (chapter 13) reveal in their studies, Africa was intricately tied to the contours of the Atlantic World, its ebbs and flows represented in African landscapes from the onset of the slave trade to its abolition. These important foci of Atlantic studies are similarly of important in the works presented here.

Yet, although the "Atlantic" has utility in examining specific regional intersections, its constraints as explanatory frame must also be recognized. It is inherently restrictive, failing to trace the wider spatial and temporal articulations of which both European and indigene were part. The varied interconnections of the modern world were global in scope from the beginning of the sixteenth century onward. The impacts of the slave trade in Africa were not confined to the Atlantic margins, nor were they isolated from the boundaries of earlier, pre-Atlantic networks. As Hauser (chapter 15) illustrates, while the Danish enclaves of the Caribbean and South Asia are distinctive in their cultural settings, regional economies, and administrative networks, they were equally expressive of global articulations.

In a similar vein, the Pacific can be examined in terms of its own boundaries, regional histories, and *longue durée*s, and an increasing body of work has sought to delineate the "Pacific World" in manner akin to studies of the Atlantic (e.g., Bentley 2002; Blank & Spier 2002; Gulliver 2011). However, while usefully delineating the distinctive cultural histories, local networks, and regional systems, as in the case of Atlantic Studies, the interconnections of the Pacific extend beyond its shores. As Tolley (chapter 10) demonstrates, the establishment of Franciscan Missions of Alta California and the European-Native entanglements that ensued cannot be divorced from the wider contexts of Spanish, Russian, American, and British rivalries for the fur trade of the western coast of North America, access to Asian markets, and colonial aspirations.

It was the global in nature of the emerging world-system and the varied preexisting systems that it connected that European maritime traders were able to effectively manipulate in new ways with transformative result. Johnson's (chapter 2) imaginary, fifteenth-century travelers would have found London a far different place if they were to have visited it three centuries later. In 1500, London was a medieval city of perhaps of fifty thousand people that retained the traces of its Roman origins. It could be disparagingly compared to the great city-states of Northern Italy and to the ports of the Low Countries. By 1800, however, London's population had increased more than tenfold, a sprawling expression of the industrial revolution. More pointedly, it was the nexus of an ever-extending network of trade routes across the globe. Britain of the modern world had been united by the Acts of Union in 1707, and by 1776 the British Empire in the Americas included a dozen Caribbean colonies, as well as Belize, the thirteen colonies of the nascent United States, and a number of Canadian provinces. The plantations in these colonies were largely dependent on African slave labor and British merchants established far-flung trade networks connecting the Americas, Caribbean, and West Africa.

The eighteenth-century world was a dramatically smaller place than it had been a few centuries earlier. European voyages of exploration sought new lands and opportunities.[12] The accounts of Dampier's (1699), Bougainville's (1771), and Cook's (Hawkesworth 1773) voyages were popular sensations; romantic travelogues with descriptions of exotic peoples and places (see fig. 1.2). The expeditions also

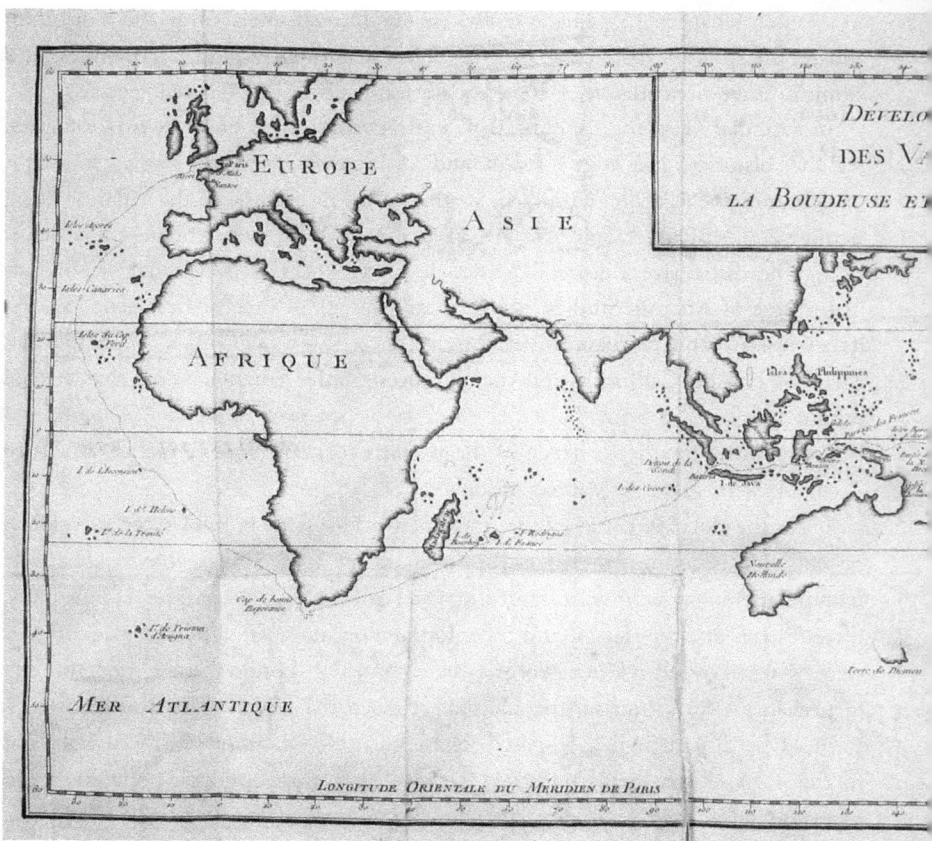

Figure 1.2. Map of Bougainville's circumnavigation of the globe from his "Voyage autour du monde, par la frégate du roi La Boudeuse, et la flûte L'Étoile; en 1766, 1767, 1768 & 1769." (Courtesy of the Biodiversity Heritage Library, https://www.biodiversitylibrary.org/item/127609#page/7/mode/1up)

mapped the lands visited, described the peoples encountered, and documented new species of animals. However, if these voyages of discovery had scientific aims, they were equally economic ventures. The undiscovered corners of the globe with exotic creatures, undiscovered plants, and noble savages were also places that possessed resources to be extracted and economic opportunities. This was a different world indeed from the one Johnson's travelers described in 1492.

If the economic confluences that emerged between the fifteenth and the eighteenth centuries were not completely unlike those of the preceding centuries, the nations of early modern Europe were adept in their ability to insert themselves into these existing economic and social trading networks, fill voids in the networks present, and co-opt existing structures for their own benefit. Products from

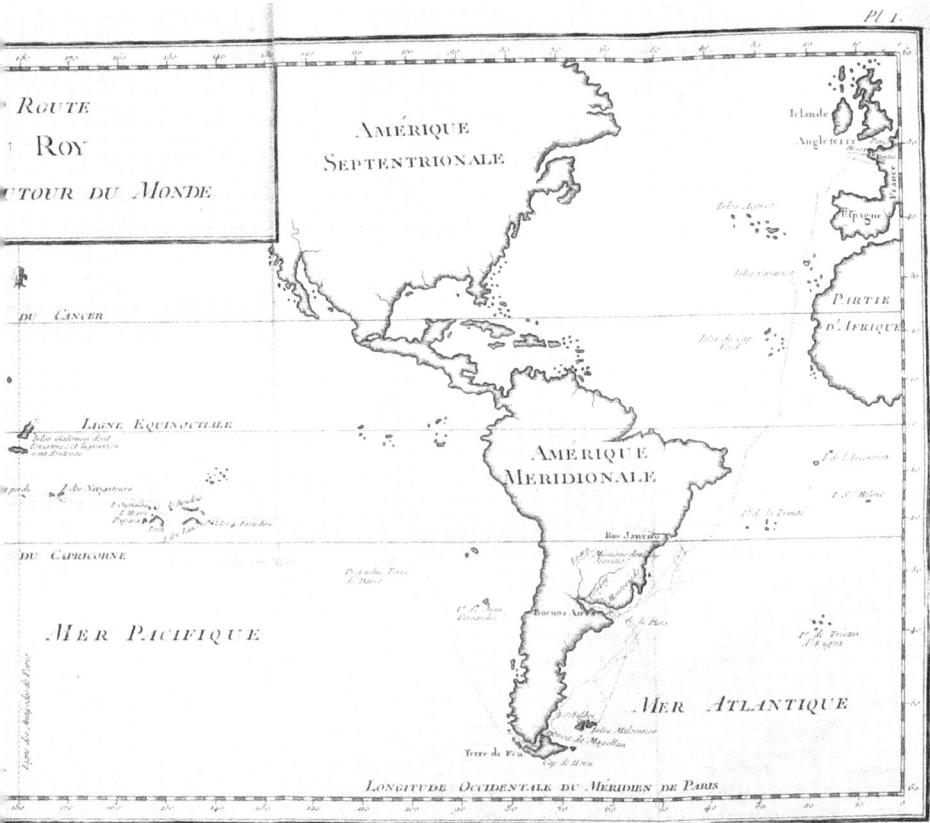

previously unconnected spheres were brought together. As well demonstrated by Sampeck's (chapter 5) discussion of Tacuscalco and Europe's infatuation with cacao, Europeans were shrewd at finding new markets for old products. In doing so they initially co-opted existing social organizations and means of production, but subsequently transformed places such as Tacuscalco into something new. As Pezzarossi (chapter 4) illustrates, colonial Guatemala lacked the mineral wealth of other regions and the Spanish colonial government subsequently sought profit by inserting themselves into precolonial tribute systems reliant on regionally available produce such as cacao. Further to the north in Alta California (in Tolley, chapter 10), the Franciscan missions similarly developed their own mercantile economies, based on their respective hinterlands and wells of Native labor and knowledge. As a counterpoint to prevailing focus on the European quest for mineral wealth, the missions' trade in such mundane products as hides, otter pelts, tallow, locally produced cloth, wine and foodstuffs demonstrates that treasure is where you find it.

The economic structuring and cultural exchanges of the modern world-system are writ large materially, from the presence of trade goods that reflect distant trade relations to dramatic changes in settlement patterns indicative of the restructuring and reorientation of social, political, and economic relations. The establishment of the slave trading emporia of the West African coast neatly mirrored the expansion

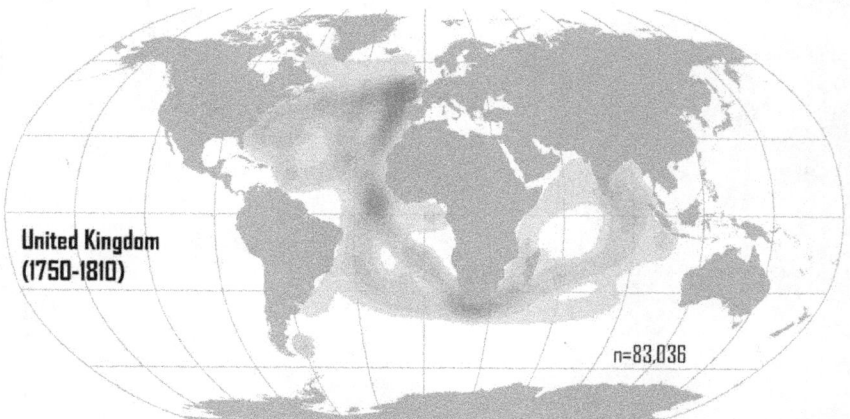

United Kingdom
(1750-1810)

n=83,036

Figure 1.3. Map charting the British shipping as indicated by ship logs. The darkest shading on the image represents a density of more than fifty log entries. (Courtesy of J-P Rodrigue, *The Geography of Transport Systems*, 4th ed., New York: Routledge, 2017)

of the plantation colonies in the Americas (e.g., see DeCorse 2016a & 2016b). Archaeologically, it is remarkable to walk across sites of the past five centuries in Brazil, Curaçao, Sierra Leone, Maryland, and England and find the same artifacts: coarse and refined earthenware, gunflints, glass, and the myriad other trade materials that delineated the margins of the European economic frontier—a readily definable archaeological horizon.[13] The material record does not, however, simply consist of artifacts that provide temporal markers, but also landscapes, buildings, features, and archaeological assemblages that are expressions of unique historical and geographical complexes. They reveal the emerging networks of the early modern world as constellations of strategies, adjustments, and negotiations, rather than fixed-templates of social, cultural, and economic interactions. Europeans and the indigenous populations with whom they interacted pursued varied agendas and strategies, negotiated by local conditions and schema.

Historical Landscapes of the Modern World

The scope of this volume is pointedly broad in temporal and geographic foci to illustrate the scope, depth, and diversity of intersections represented in the historical contours of the modern world.[14] Yet the volume's coverage is unavoidably limited. The largest omissions are the absence of examples of early European-Asian exchanges—the European enclaves of China, Southeast Asia, and the webs of systemic relations of which they were part. The only historic landscapes of the Pacific margins discussed deal with colonial contexts in Peru, Alta California, and northwestern North America on the Pacific's eastern rim. Examination of the economic contours and studies of the *longue durées* of other areas would provide both corollaries and counterpoints to the chapters on early European-Native American, African, and South Asian confluences that are presented. In a similar vein, the historical trajectories of the Iberian Peninsula, France, the Low Countries, Brandenburg-Prussia, Scandinavia, the Apennine Peninsula, and the circum-Mediterranean would afford interesting contrasts with the description of the fifteenth-century British landscape presented in chapter 2.

With the preceding omissions in mind, the studies presented herein nonetheless wonderfully illustrate the varied nature of the entanglements of the modern world and the complexity of the economic, social, and cultural interactions that unfolded. The organization of the chapters is both spatial and temporal, moving across geographical regions and through time within those regions. In chapter 2, Matthew Johnson leads us on an imaginary journey across the British Isles in 1492. He takes us overland from Dover, northeast through London to Caernarvon, then across the Irish Sea to Dublin. Rather that providing a template of nascent capitalism through which to examine European expansion and colonization, the purpose of Johnson's fictional journey is to underscore the transformative nature of the past 500 years for all of the societies involved—Britain and Europe included. The landscapes of the fifteenth-century British Isles were distant in their social, cultural, political, and economic materialities from those that emerged in the following centuries, the seeds of the changes to come at best only hazily seen in the fifteenth century.

Johnson's journey across the British landscape is followed by chapters by Corinne Hofman, Guido Pezzarossi, and Katheryn Sampeck, which examine early European-Native American interactions. Hofman (chapter 3) contextualizes European contact and colonialism in the Americas through the examination of archaeological, documentary, and ethnographic data from across the insular Caribbean. Hofman introduces the richness of Native American social, political, and economic networks that long predated the arrival of the Europeans in the fifteenth century, but were subsequently utilized, transformed, and co-opted by them.

The chapters by Guido Pezzarossi and Kathryn Sampeck, both focusing on colonial Guatemala (including, respectively, modern Guatemala and El Salvador), similarly situate early European colonization within the frame of indigenous, pre-European networks, power dynamics, cultural constructions, and economies. Drawing on his archaeological research in highland Guatemala, Pezzarossi (chapter 4) examines both the frictions and congruencies between emergent European colonialism and earlier Mayan political and economic infrastructures. Rather than presenting the colonized peoples as passive inhabitants of a marginalized periphery, he highlights the colonized as active participants in an integrated, locally articulated system that was integral to the shaping of the colonial world.

In the following chapter, Sampeck (chapter 5) draws on archaeological, ethnographic and documentary data to examine transformations in Tacuscalco, the largest pre-Columbian settlement within the Izalcos polity in what is today western El Salvador. The region's colonial collisions are illustrative of the extreme coercion, violence, population relocation, and hegemonic depredations found in many colonial settings. Following their arrival in the sixteenth century, Spanish colonists vied to divide the region's resources following precolonial boundaries, while the native

Izalcos were forcibly resettled in Spanish-style towns. Tacuscalco was transformed from a major Izalcos settlement and center of native cacao production, into a barrio within a Spanish urban community. Having displaced the Izalcos, colonial cacao plantations relied on enslaved laborers from distant areas with no heritage of cacao cultivation. In recognizing these dramatic changes, Sampeck nonetheless reveals the distinctive local shaping of Tacuscalco's colonial intersections.

The following chapters by Douglas V. Armstrong, Christopher K. Waters, and Erik R. Seeman focus on the varied, colonized landscapes of the American Atlantic world. Drawing on archaeological and documentary sources, Armstrong, in chapter 6, concentrates on the nascence of the plantation system in seventeenth-century Barbados. In the 1620s, the English colony of Barbados was dotted with small-scale farms that grew varied crops, including cotton. Within decades, the island had shifted to sugar plantations dependent on enslaved African labor. Integrating data from the site of Trents Plantation, Armstrong considers the global structuring of the Caribbean economy and its material manifestations on the Barbadian landscape. Waters (chapter 7) affords a different view of the Caribbean colonial landscape through his examination of eighteenth-century Antigua's island-wide defensive system. Often badly planned, shoddily constructed, and ill-suited to meet the island's defense needs, Waters moves beyond simply viewing these defenses as poorly designed military works and reveals them as expressions of colonial power dynamics. In chapter 8, Seeman provides contrasting perspectives of cultural continuity and change through the examination of Jewish graveyards on Curaçao and the African Burial Ground in New York City. He sees these as expressive of power, as well as varying degrees of cultural transformations in the populations represented.

Chapters 9 and 10, by Noa Corcoran-Tadd and Thomas Edward Tolley, illustrate dramatically different examples of Spanish colonies on the Pacific margins. Focusing on the hinterlands of the silver mining centers of the Bolivian Plateau, Corcoran-Tadd examines the integration of pre-European exchange systems, trade routes, and technology into emergent European trade and colonization during the sixteenth century. Extending his focus beyond mineral extraction and agriculture production, he populates the landscape, revealing the importance of seemingly marginal spaces to both pre-Hispanic and colonial political and economic networks as both exchange routes and resource areas. Moving northward to Alta California, and temporally into the late eighteenth and nineteenth centuries, Tolley considers the economic and cultural intersections that stemmed from the founding of missions by the Catholic Church and the regal government of New Spain between 1769 and 1823. Focusing on Mission San Buenaventura, Tolley reframes the missions as native landscapes that were negotiated, exploited, and colonized in varied ways, often not in the manner originally intended.

In chapter 11, Andrew Martindale, George MacDonald, and Sage Vanier focus on European contact and colonization of the Tsimshian territory near Prince Rupert, British Columbia, on the Northwest Coast of North America. The authors complicate perspectives of European-indigene interactions by reconstructing Tsimshian society at the time of contact, in or about 1787, until today. Underscoring the interpretive challenges of the varied sources of data used, they provide a rich ethnography of the Tsimshian, as well as the cultural and economic pressures that European trade and colonization presented. In doing so, Martindale and his coauthors afford a view of a native-lived colonialism, in which Tsimshian people flexed and changed, but were not wholly transformed by the European encounter.

Chapter 12, by Gérard Chouin and Olanrewaju Lasisi, and chapter 13 by Kenneth Kelly shift, attention to West Africa's engagement with the Atlantic World. The chapters provide seminal works that define the scope, temporal depth, and economic framing of the slave trade from its earliest manifestations to its nineteenth-century abolition. European expansion and the nascence of the Atlantic world began in Africa with the development of European trade and the establishment of trading enclaves on the West African coast and the Atlantic Islands of Cabo Verde, São Tomé, Príncipe, and Biagos in the fifteenth and early sixteenth centuries. Thus, some of the sites and African-European interactions discussed predate the first Columbian voyages to the Americas. However, the preceding examination of the early colonial landscapes of the Americas provides necessary context for the understanding the changes in African economies and sociopolitical systems that were intricately tied to European expansion and the subsequent development of the plantation economies of the Americas.

In chapter 12, Chouin and Olanrewaju consider pre-Atlantic sociopolitical developments in the Bight of Benin to assess how the Portuguese, arriving at the end of the fifteenth century, were able to commence a trade that brought enslaved Africans from the Bight of Benin in Nigeria to the Mina coast in present-day Ghana, where they were sold to African merchants. Slaves were only one aspect of the early European trade, which also brought cloth and iron from different regional markets for resale on other parts of the African coast. Focusing the Upper Guinea coast and transformations in the nineteenth century, Kelly's chapter considers the changes in African societies that resulted from the abolition of the slave trade by Britain and other European nations during the nineteenth century. The continuation and expansion of the slave trade in some areas following abolition led to the dramatic reorientation of African political economies and concomitant sociopolitical transformations.

The concluding chapters shift attention to East Africa and South Asia. In chapter 14, Martin S. Shanguhyia deconstructs the political and economic motivations of wildlife conservation efforts in colonial East Africa—Kenya, Tanzania, and Uganda—from the 1890s through the 1930s. Although imbedded in discourses of environmental preservation, Shanguhyia reveals the policies to have been inextricably linked to the economic interests of the colonial governments and settler communities, whose interests often ran counter to those of the indigenous communities that had traditionally occupied, and depended on, the lands on which the game reserves were created. The chapter provides a nuanced example of the different and locally specific ways colonial governments had to identify and exploit local resources as a means of sustaining their economies and the colonial enterprise.

In chapter 15, Mark Hauser brings the volume appropriately to a close with a comparative study of Danish trading enclaves the Indian and Atlantic Oceans that are illustrative of European administrative categories, as much as expressions of global linkages and locally articulated intersections. Drawing comparisons from Tranquebar (Tharnamgambadi) in southern India and the Danish colonial settlements in the Virgin Islands, Hauser illustrates dramatically contrasting cultural encounters. The Danish East India Company acquired Tranquebar through lease from the Thanjavur Nayak kingdom in 1620. It subsequently became the Asian headquarters of the Company and its descendants, a nexus of both regional and global trade networks. St. John, St. Thomas, and St. Croix in the Caribbean, in contrast, were plantation islands established by Danish West India Company. These contrasting settings underscore the extent and complexity of local economic and political systems, the diverse social formations, varied historical encounters, and cultural entanglements of the modern world. Yet, as Hauser suggests, despite the distinctiveness of their settings, these Danish enclaves on opposite sides of the world "rhymed," that is, were linked through material relations and similarly expressive of the Danish colonial enterprise. In this respect, they are exemplary of the volume's themes—counterpoints of an economic system that shaped the contours of modernity.

Notes

1. "The Past Explains the Present" is the subtitle of the final chapter in the English translation of Braudel's (1980, 177–218), *Escrits sur l'histoire* by Sarah Matthews. Also see Braudel (1990, 79–117). This perspective echoes many of the threads expressive of the broader historic turn within the social sciences over the past half-century (e.g., see McDonald 1996).

2. The empire of Philip II resulted from the dynastic union of the crowns of Portugal and Spain following the Portuguese succession crisis of 1580, a union that lasted until 1640. It should, however, be noted that while the entire Iberian Peninsula, as well as Spanish and Portuguese overseas possessions, were brought under one rule, throughout this period Spain and Portugal continued to maintain their respective spheres of influence as laid out in the Treaties of Aláçovas and Tordesillas.

3. Wallerstein (1974, 1980, 1989) situates the genesis of the modern world-system in the sixteenth century, and sees it as a system dominated by a European core and economic peripheries that is fundamentally different from earlier systems. He does not consider world-system theory applicable to premodern societies.

4. Discussion of the details and critiques of these perspectives are not considered here; the more general point is that the existence, if not the specifics and structuring, of such interconnected pre–fifteenth-century systems is well demonstrated.

5. It is impossible to trace the extent and complexity of the varied regional economies, networks and social formations that predated the pre–fifteenth-century world. For general overviews and theoretical framing, see: Abu-Leghod (1991); Braudel (1972a & b); Chase-Dunn and Hall (1991); Chouin and DeCorse (2010); Dietler (2010); Finley (1981); Frank (1998); Frank and Gills (1993); Gosden (2004); Kardulias (1999); Lamberg-Karlovsky (1989); Orser (1996, 2009); Pomeranz (2000); Pomeranz and Topik (2015); Tomich (2012); Stein (1999); Wolf (1982); Wong (2012). For additional examples of premodern regional systems, see Blandon, Kowalewski, and Feinman (1992); Chávez and Spence (2012); Dietler (2010); Fleisher et al. (2015); Howell (2010); Green (2012); Hodos (2017); Keegan and Hofman (2017); Kuznar (1999); LaLone (1994); Malpass and Alconini 2010; Marcus and Williams (2009); Monroe (2013); Pauketat (2004); Persson (2014); Rosenswig (2014); Seetah (2018).

6. For review and discussion, see DeCorse 2014. Notably the recent, substantive treatments of Africa in the Atlantic world by Thornton (2012) and Green (2012) and begin, respectively, in the thirteenth and fourteenth centuries.

7. For example, Braudel (1990, 82–85); Abu-Leghod (1991, 364–73); Kohl (1989, 232–38); and Schmidt and Mrozowski 2013.

8. This heading is adapted from a title used by Jorge Cañizares-Esguerra and Erik Seeman (2007) in their edited volume: *Introduction: Beyond the Line: Nations, Oceans, and*

Hemispheres. This volume similarly pushes away from restrictive national or Atlantic perspectives to a wider conceptual vantage (Cañizares-Esguerra & Seeman 2007, xxiii–xxviii).

9. For example, El-Ojeili 2014; Lee 2012. A major criticism of Wallerstein's world-system perspective has been what some perceive as an overemphasis on the degree to which the European core structured developments in the peripheries. It should be noted, however, that Wallerstein himself underscored the distinctiveness of local systems and the varied nature of connections with the core (see, e.g., Wallerstein 1986, 101–37).

10. See, for example, Martindale et al. and Pezzarossi (this volume). Also see Coronil 2000; Escobar 2001; Ingold 2012; Knappett 2013; Latour 2005; Martindale 2009; Mills 2017; Ortner 2016; Orser 2009; Pezzarossi 2018.

11. See, for example, Bailyn and Denault 2011; Benjamin 2009; Canaries and Seeman 2007; Canny and Pagdan 1987; Crosby 2003; Gilroy 1993; Greene and Morgan 2009; Landers 2011; Nunn and Qian 2010; Ogundiran and Falola 2007; Solow 2001; Tomich 2004; Thornton 2012; Yerxa 2008.

12. By the middle of the eighteenth century, a dozen or so voyages that circumnavigated the globe had been undertaken, including three by William Dampier (Kelsey 2016; Preston & Preston 2005). In Bougainville's case, the economic rationale for the expedition and his intention to identify potential colonial territories of strategic importance were made clear from the outset (Dunsmore 2002, xix–xxiv). Bougainville's circumnavigation is also notable as being the first to include a full complement of naturalists and scientists.

13. The horizon concept in archaeology refers to cultural traits, artifact types, and attributes that are representative of a broad and rapid spread. Archaeological assemblages with features characteristic of a horizon are assumed to be contemporaneous. The horizon concept has been widely used in archaeology and was first applied to the archaeology of European expansion by Stanley South (1978). Horizons can be contrasted with, and are crosscut by, archaeological traditions, which are represented by cultural traits, artifact types, and attributes that extend over long periods.

14. These broad temporal and geographic foci are comparable to those of the original Braudel Center colloquium on which the volume is based. Extensively revised versions of all of the original colloquium papers have been included here, except for two, owing to the authors' commitments elsewhere: one that dealt with Caribbean plantation landscapes and one on South Asia. Two additional papers that could not be presented at the original colloquium are included in the volume; those by Noa Corcoran Tadd on Peru and Thomas Tolley on the Spanish Missions of Alta California.

Works Cited

Abu-Lughod, Janet. 1991. *Before European Hegemony: The World System A.D. 1250–1350.* New York: Oxford University Press.

Bailyn, Bernard, and Patricia L. Denault, eds. 2011. *Soundings in Atlantic History: Latent Structures and Intellectual Currents, 1500–1830*. Cambridge, MA: Harvard University Press.

Benjamin, Thomas. 2009. *The Atlantic World: Europeans, Africans, Indians, and Their Shared History, 1400–1900*. New York: Cambridge University Press.

Bentley, Jerry H. 2002. "Sea and Ocean Basins as Frameworks of Historical Analysis." In *The Pacific World, Volume 1: Defining the Pacific*. Edited by Paul W. Blank and Fred Spier Aldershot: Ashgate Publishing, 1–10.

Blank, Paul W. and Fred Spier. 2002. Introduction. In *The Pacific World, Volume 1: Defining the Pacific*. Edited by Paul W. Blank and Fred Spier. Aldershot, UK: Ashgate Publishing, xiii–xxxiii.

Blandon, Richard E., Stephen A. Kowalewski, and Gary M. Feinman. 1992. The Meso-American World-System. *Review* 15: 419–26.

Bougainville, Louis-Antoine de, Comte. 1771. *Le voyage autour du monde, par la frégate La Boudeuse, et la flûte L'Étoile, en 1766, 1767, 1768, and 1769*. Paris: Saillant and Nyon.

Braudel, Fernand. 1972a. *The Mediterranean and the Mediterranean World in the Age of Philip II*, vol. 1. Translated by Seân Reynolds. New York: Harper and Row.

———. 1972b. *The Mediterranean and the Mediterranean World in the Age of Philip II*, vol. 2. Translated by Seân Reynolds. New York: Harper and Row.

———. 1980. *On History*. Translated by Sarah Matthews. Chicago: Chicago University Press.

———. 1990. *Afterthoughts on Material, Civilization, and Capitalism*. Translated by Patricia Ranum. Baltimore: Johns Hopkins.

Cañizares-Esguerra, Jorge, and Eric R. Seeman, eds. 2007. *The Atlantic in Global History*. Upper Saddle River, NJ: Prentice Hall.

Canny, Nicholas, and Anthony Pagdan, eds. 1987. *Colonial Identity in the Atlantic World, 1500–1800*. Princeton, NJ: Princeton University Press.

Chase-Dunn, Christopher, and E. N. Anderson. 2005. *The Historical Evolution of World-Systems*. New York: Palgrave Macmillan.

Chase-Dunn, Christopher and Thomas D. Hall, eds. 1991. *Core/Periphery Relations in Precapitalist Worlds*. Boulder, CO: Westview.

———. 1997. *Rise and Demise: Comparing World-Systems*. Boulder, CO: Westview.

Chávez, Sergio Gómez, and Michael W. Spence. 2012. "Interaction among the Complex Societies of Classic-Period Mesoamerica." In *The Oxford Handbook of Mesoamerican Archaeology*, 283–300. Edited by Deborah L. Nichols. New York: Oxford University Press.

Chouin, Gerard L., and Christopher R. DeCorse. 2010. "Prelude to the Atlantic Trade: New Perspectives on Southern Ghana's Pre-Atlantic History (800–1500)." *Journal of African History* 51: 123–45.

Coronil, Renando. 2000. "Towards a Critique of Globalcentrism: Speculations on Capitalism's Nature." *Public Culture* 12(2): 351–74.

Crosby, Alfred W. 2003. *The Columbian Exchange: Biological and Cultural Consequences of 1492*. Westport, CT: Greenwood Publishing Co.

Dampier, William. 1699. *A New Voyage Round the World*. London: James Knapton.

DeCorse, Christopher R. 2014. "Postcolonial or Not? West Africa in the Pre-Atlantic and Atlantic Worlds." Keynote Address, 50th Anniversary of the African Studies Center, University of Ibadan. Ibadan, Nigeria: African Studies Center.

———. 2016a. "Tools of Empire: Trade, Resources and the British Forts of West Africa." In *Building the British Atlantic World, 1600–1850*, 165–87. Edited by Bernard L. Herman and Daniel Maudlin. Chapel Hill, NC: University of North Carolina Press.

DeCorse, Christopher R., ed. 2016b. *West Africa during the Atlantic Slave Trade: Archaeological Perspectives*. New York: Bloomsbury Academic.

Dietler, Michael. 2010. *Archaeologies of Colonialism*. Berkeley: University of California Press.

Dunsmore, John. 2002. "Introduction." In *The Pacific Journal of Louis-Antoine de Bougainville, 1767–1768*, xix–lxxvii. Translated and edited by John Dunmore. London: The Hakluyt Society.

El-Ojeili, Chamsy. 2014. "Reflections on Wallerstein: The Modern World-System, Four Decades On." *Critical Sociology* 41(4–5): 1–22.

Escobar, Aturo. 2001. "Culture Sits in Places: Reflections on Globalization and Subaltern Strategies of Localization. *Political Geography* 20: 139–74.

Finley, M. I. 1981. *Economy and Society in Ancient Greece*. Edited with an introduction by Brent D. Shaw and Richard P. Saller. New York: Viking Press.

Fleisher, Jeffrey, Paul Lane, Adria LaViolette, Mark Horton, Edward Pollard, Eréndira Quintana Morales, Thomas Vernet, Annalisa Christie, and Stephanie Wynne-Jones. 2015. "When Did the Swahili Become Maritime?" *American Anthropologist* 117(1): 100–15.

Frank, Andre Gunder. 1998. *ReORIENT: Global Economy in the Asian Age*. Berkeley: University of California Press.

Frank, Andre Gunder, and Barry Gills, eds. 1993. *The World System: Five Hundred Years or Five Thousand?* New York: Routledge.

Gosden, Chris. 2004. *Archaeology and Colonialism: Culture Contact from 5000 BC to the Present*. New York: Cambridge University Press.

Green, Toby. 2012. *The Rise of the Trans-Atlantic Slave Trade in Western Africa, 1300–1589*. New York: Cambridge University Press.

Greene, Jack P., and Philip D. Morgan, eds. 2009. *Atlantic History: A Critical Appraisal*. New York: Oxford University.

Gulliver, Katrina. 2011. "Finding the Pacific World." *Journal of World History* 22(1): 83–100.

Hawkesworth, John. 1773. *An Account of the Voyages Undertaken by the Order of His Present Majesty, for Making Discoveries in the Southern Hemisphere, and Successively Performed* by Commodore Byron, Captain Wallis, Captain Carteret, and Captain Cook, in the Dolphin, the Swallow, and the Endeavour: Drawn up from the Journals which Were Kept by the Several Ccommanders and from the Papers of Joseph Banks, Esq. London: W. Strahan and T. Cadell.

Hodos, Tamar. 2017. *The Routledge Handbook of Archaeology and Globalization.* New York: Routledge.

Howell, Martha C. 2010. *Commerce before Capitalism in Europe, 1300–1600.* New York: Cambridge University Press.

Ingold, Tim. 2011. *Being Alive: Essays on Movement, Knowledge and Description.* London: Routledge.

Ingstad, Helge, and Anne Stine Ingstad. 2000. *The Viking Discovery of America: The Excavation of a Norse Settlement at L'Anse aux Meadows, Newfoundland.* St John's, Newfoundland: Breakwater.

Kardulias, P. Nick, ed. 1999. *World-Systems Theory in Practice: Leadership, Production, and Exchange.* New York: Rowman and Littlefield.

Kelsey, Harry. 2016. *The First Circumnavigators: Unsung Heroes of the Age of Discovery.* New Haven: Yale University Press.

Keegan, William F., and Corinne L Hofman. 2017. *The Caribbean before Columbus.* Oxford: Oxford University Press.

Knappett, Carl. 2013. *Network Analysis in Archaeology: New Approaches to Regional Interaction.* Oxford, UK: Oxford University Press.

Kohl, Philip L. 1989. "The Use and Abuse of World Systems Theory: The Case of the 'Pristine' West Asian State." In *Archaeological Thought in America.* Edited by C. C. Lamberg-Karlovsky, 218–40. New York: Cambridge University Press.

Kuznar, Lawrence A. 1999. "The Inca Empire: Detailing the Complexities of Core/ Periphery Interactions." In *World-Systems Theory in Practice. Leadership, Production, and Exchange*, 223–40. Edited by P. Nick Kardulias. Lanham: Rowman and Littlefield Publishers.

LaLone, D. 1994. "An Andean World-System: Production Transformations Under the Inca Empire." In *The Economic Anthropology of the State*, 17–42. Edited by Elizabeth Brumfiel, 17–42. Lanham, MD: University Press of America.

Landers, Jane Gilmer. 2011. *Atlantic Creoles in the Age of Revolutions.* Cambridge, MA: Harvard University Press.

Latour, Bruno. 2005. *Reassembling the Social: An Introduction to Actor-Network Theory.* Oxford, UK: Oxford University Press.

Lamberg-Karlosky, C. C. 1989. *Archaeological Thought in America.* New York: Cambridge University Press.

Lee, Richard E., ed. 2012. *The Longue Durée and World-Systems Analysis.* Albany: State University of New York Press.

Malpass, Michael, and Sonia Alconini. 2010. *Distant Provinces in the Inka Empire*. Iowa City: University of Iowa Press.

Marcus, Joyce, and Patrick Ryan Williams. 2009. *Andean Civilization: A Tribute to Michael E. Moseley*. Los Angeles: Cotsen Institute of Archaeology.

Martindale, Andrew. 2009. "Entanglement and Tinkering: Structural History in the Archaeology of the Northern Tsimshian." *Journal of Social Archaeology* 9: 59–91.

McDonald, Terrance J., ed. 1996. *The Historic Turn in the Social Sciences*. Ann Arbor: University of Michigan Press.

Mills, Barbara J. 2017. "Social Network Analysis in Archaeology." *Annual Review of Anthropology* 46(1): 379–97.

Monroe, J. Cameron. 2013. "Power and Agency in Precolonial African States." *Annual Review of Anthropology* 42: 17–35.

Moreno-Maynar, J. Victor, Simon Rasmussen, Andaine Seguin-Orlando, Morten Rasmussen, Mason Liang, Siri Tennebø Flåm, Benedicte Alexandra Lie, Gregor Duncan Gilfillan, Rasmus Nielsen, Erik Thorsby, Eske Willerslev, and Anna-Sapfo Malaspinas. 2014. "Genome-wide Ancestry Patterns in Rapanui Suggest Pre-European Admixture with Native Americans." *Current Biology* 24(21): 2518–25.

Nunn, Nathan, and Nancy Qian. 2010. "The Columbian Exchange: A History of Disease, Food, and Ideas." *Journal of Economic Perspectives* 24(2): 163–88.

Ogundiran, Akinwumi, and Toyin Falola, eds. 2007. *Archaeology of Atlantic Africa and the African Diaspora*. Bloomington: Indiana University Press.

Orser, Charles E. 1996. *A Historical Archaeology of the Modern World*. New York: Plenum.
———. 2009. "World-Systems Theory, Networks, and Modern World Archaeology." In *The International Handbook of Historical Archaeology*, 253–67. Edited by Teresita Majewski and David Gaimster. New York: Springer.

Ortner, Sherry B. 2016. "Dark Anthropology and Its Others: Theory since the Eighties." *Journal of Ethnographic Theory* 6(1): 47–73.

Pauketat, Timothy R. 2004. Ancient *Cahokia and Mississippians*. New York: Cambridge University Press.

Persson, Karl Gunnar. 2014. Markets and coercion in medieval Europe. In *The Cambridge History of Capitalism Volume I: The Rise of Capitalism: From Ancient Origins to 1848*, 225–66. Edited by Larry Neal and Jeffrey G. Williamson. Cambridge, UK: Cambridge University Press, 2014.

Pezzarossi, Guido. 2019. "Rethinking the Archaeology of Capitalism: Coercion, Violence, and the Politics of Accumulation." *Historical Archaeology* 53(3).

Pomeranz, Kenneth. 2000. *The Great Divergence: China, Europe, and the Making of the Modern World Economy*. Princeton: Princeton University Press.

Pomeranz, Kenneth, and Steven Topik. 2015. *The World That Trade Created: Society, Culture, and the World Economy—1400 to the Present*. New York: Routledge.

Preston, Diana, and Michael Preston. 2005. *A Pirate of Exquisite Mind: The Life of William Dampier*. New York: Penguin.

Rosenswig, Robert M. 2014. *The Beginnings of Mesoamerican Civilization Inter-Regional Interaction and the Olmec*. New York: Cambridge.

Schmidt, Peter R., and Stephen A. Mrozowski, eds. 2013. "The Death of Prehistory: Reforming the Past, Looking to the Future." New York: Oxford University Press.

Seetah, Krish. 2018, ed. *Connecting Continents: Archaeology and History in the Indian Ocean World*. Athens: Ohio University Press.

Solow, Barbara L. 1991. *Slavery and the Rise of the Atlantic System*. New York: Cambridge University Press.

South, Stanley. 1978. "Evolution and Horizon as Revealed in Ceramic Analysis in Historical Archaeology. In *Historical Archaeology: A Guide to Substantive and Theoretical Contributions*, 68–82. Edited by Robert L. Schuyler. Farmingdale, NY: Baywood Publishing.

Stein, Gil. 1999. Rethinking World-Systems: Power, Distance, and Diasporas in the Dynamics of Interregional Interaction. In *World-Systems Theory in Practice. Leadership, Production, and Exchange*, 153–78. Edited by Nick P. Kardulias. Lanham, MD: Rowman & Littlefield Publishers.

Thornton, John. 2012. *A Cultural History of the Atlantic World, 1250–1820*. New York: Cambridge University Press.

Tomich, Dale. 2004. "Atlantic History and World Economy: Concepts and Constructions." *Proto Sociology* 20: 102–21.

———. 2012. Fernand Braudel, the Longue Durée, and World-Systems Analysis. In *The Longue Durée and World-Systems Analysis*, 1–7. Edited by Richard E. Lee. Albany: SUNY Press.

Wallerstein, Immanuel. 1974. *The Modern World-System, vol. I: Capitalist Agriculture and the Origins of the European World-Economy in the Sixteenth Century*. New York: Academic Press.

———. 1980. *The Modern World-System, vol. II: Mercantilism and the Consolidation of the European World-Economy, 1600–1750*. New York: Academic Press.

———. 1986. *Africa and the Modern World*. Trenton, NJ: Africa World Press.

———. 1989. *The Modern World-System, vol. III: The Second Era of Great Expansion of the Capitalist World-Economy, 1730s–1840s*. New York: Academic Press.

Wolf, Eric R. 1982. *Europe and the People without History*. Berkeley: University of California Press.

Wong, bin R. 1997. *China Transformed: Historical Change and the Limits of European Experience*. Ithaca, NY: Cornell University Press.

Yerxa, Donald A., ed. 2008. *Recent Themes in the History of the Atlantic World: Historians in Conversation*. Columbia, SC: University of South Carolina Press.

Chapter 2

1492: A Different Kind of "Discovery"

Matthew Johnson

The aim of this chapter is very simple. I describe a journey through a group of landscapes and seascapes as they existed in 1492. The journey is through the British Isles, the archipelago that in the three following centuries was to be the earliest setting for the unfolding of "nascent capitalism," however defined, the place of the earliest Industrial Revolution in Europe and the world, the setting for processes of state formation and internal colonialism that have been the subject of intense discussion by archaeologists and historians. This journey is conceived of as a fictional one, but its basis is in evidence—what we know from archaeology, historical geography, and landscape history.

The ultimate objective of the paper is to delineate some of the ways in which the stage was set, at the end of the fifteenth century, for the unfolding of capitalism, colonialism, and modernity across the British Isles—however little contemporaries might have forecast such developments. It describes some of the geographical, material, and cultural preconditions for subsequent developments, and also lays out some of the ways past histories and antecedent material patterns formed settings and infrastructures that played a critical role in subsequent developments.

I see this journey as a kind of "field trip" (see figs. 1 and 2). We will travel over 500 years back in time to the year 1492, and set off to see some sights. We will meet some people along the way, including a young Thomas More, as well as other local interlocutors, but our responses to what we see will be modern, and we will occasionally discuss how twentieth- and twenty-first-century scholarship offers explanations for what we are seeing in the landscape, explanations that would not necessarily be fully understood or shared by people in the 1490s. I ask

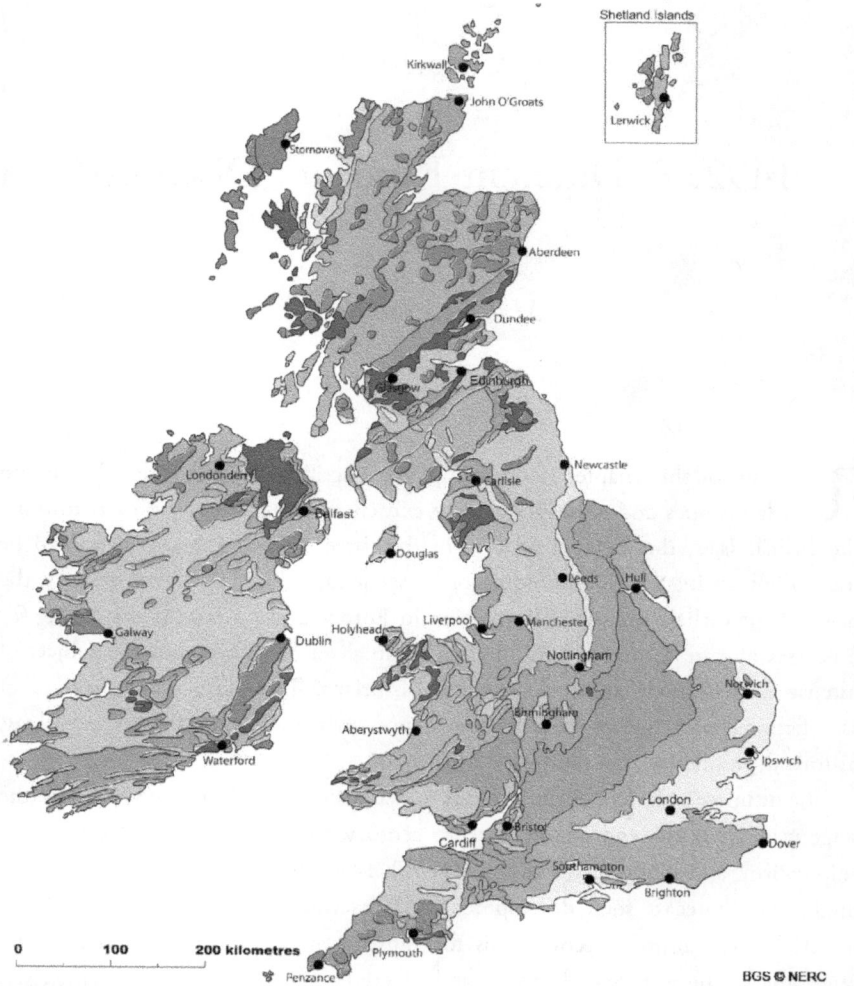

Figure 2.1. Simplified geology of the British Isles. (Courtesy of the British Geological Service, @NERC 2017)

Sedimentary rocks

| Quaternary, Neogene and Palaeogene | Cretaceous | Jurassic | Triassic | Permian | Carboniferous | Devonian |

| Silurian | Ordovician | Cambrian | Neoproterozoic |

Metamorphic rocks

| Lower Palaeozoic and Upper Proterozoic | Lower Proterozoic and Archaean |

Igneous rocks

| Intrusive | Volcanic |

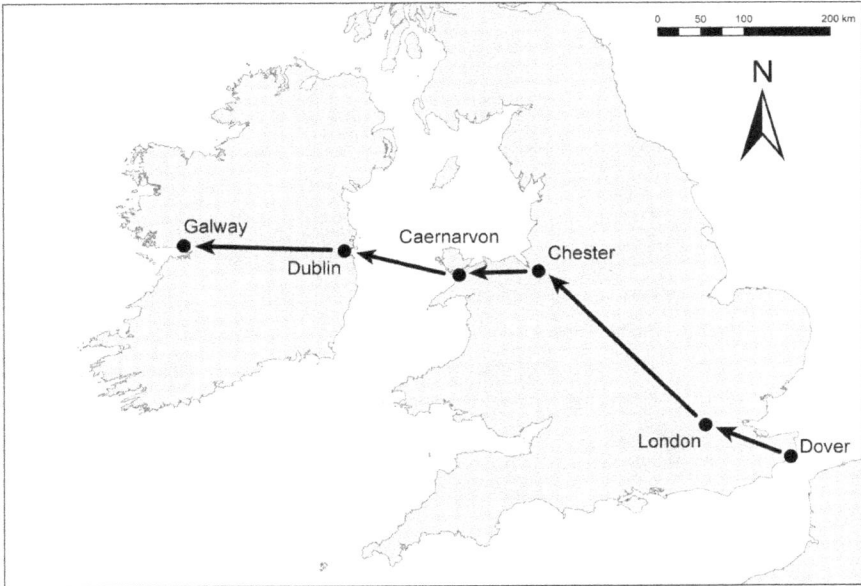

Figure 2.2. Location map of routes taken and places visited in the text. (Map by Kathryn A. Catlin)

the reader to engage with this exercise in a very simple and pedagogical spirit; to momentarily set aside the myriad evidential, epistemological and ontological issues and problems such a thought-exercise raises.[1]

I have called this journey a "discovery," to act as a counterpoint to the traditional but problematic term used for Columbus's voyage across the Atlantic in the same year. In the English language, around 1500, the term *discovery* had a series of specific meanings that were in flux. *The Oxford English Dictionary* indicates that in the fifteenth century, to "discover" was to disclose or expose to view something previously covered up. By the 1550s the term *discovery* could refer more generally to the action of bringing to light what was previously unknown; by the 1770s, it could be applied to geographical exploration or reconnaissance. Written texts could be titled "discoveries," not just of foreign lands, but of localities, regions, and human actions: thus, for example, *The Discoverie of Witchcraft*, published by Reginald Scot in 1584, was a book setting out, and in part expressing skepticism about, what was "known" of witches and their practices (Almond 2015).

My account draws inspiration from Braudel's initial description of, and emphasis on, the different ecological zones and infrastructures to be found across Europe, that he sets out in the first book of *The Mediterranean and Mediterranean World in the Age of Philip II* (Braudel 1972). I am also thinking of the famous journey set out in the conclusion of Sir Cyril Fox's *Personality of Britain: Its Influence on Inhabitant and Invader in Prehistoric and Early Historic Times* (Fox 1932). Fox's short book was written in the 1930s, and gave an account of British prehistory centered on a series of distribution maps, in which archaeological material (findspots, artifacts, and site types) was plotted and set against physical geography, climate, and other factors. The result was an understanding that stressed the importance of geography and environment without (in my reading) being narrowly determinist. Fox defined "highland" and "lowland" zones of Britain, based in part on the underlying geology, with older and harder rocks in the north and west and younger and softer rocks in the south and east (see fig. 2.2); but these zones were cultural as well as physical, and defined also in terms of communications (southeastern proximity to Continental Europe; northwestern links across the Irish Sea and Atlantic Coast).

Fox ended his book with the memorable image of a journey from southeast to northwest, across what he called "the essential Britain, in which Man [*sic*] ensconced himself so snugly," a country so densely covered in forest that "without emerging from its canopy a squirrel could traverse the country from end to end." Fox's traveler "steered his way along the ridges, past barrow and cairn and stone circle, by the sight of successive mountain tops. So guided he reached his goal, the shore of a forgotten harbour, and saw against the sunset—like blackbeetles—the barks of the Irish" (Fox 1932, 82–83[2]).

Like Fox, our fictional journey will move from southeast to northwest, though unlike Fox, we will then cross the Irish Sea and venture across Ireland. So let us start by dressing appropriately, in high-status garb, so as to command respect and avoid being classified as vagrants or worse, and arriving without incident at Dover, at the southeast corner of the British Isles, across the English Channel from France (see fig. 2.1).

Dover to London, Chalk and Clay

We may well, as "strangers" with no coherent explanation of what we are doing here, immediately be in trouble with the officials of the King of England, Henry

VII. This is a tense time in dynastic and territorial politics—Henry defeated and killed Richard III just seven years ago, his grip on the throne is still uncertain, and a series of rebellions continue to break out (Schrimes 1992). In the summer and fall of 1492 the English conducted a siege of the French coastal port of Boulogne, on the adjacent French coast. The aim, which was achieved in the subsequent peace treaty, was to secure Calais as an English possession and further to dissuade the French from interfering in English dynastic politics. There is a wider point here: that to contemporaries, the to and fro of Continental European politics and warfare was far more important than colonial entanglements. Fifty years later, in 1544–46, Henry's son Henry VIII launched a much larger-scale military action in continental Europe that consumed much more of his financial and other resources than any contemporary colonial endeavor (James 2007).

Assuming that we are not immediately imprisoned or worse, we acquire a pair of horses—and then get out of town as quickly as we can, en route to Canterbury and then London. We pause briefly to admire the famous white cliffs, above them the great royal castle of Dover, and, in particular, the tower of the church of St Mary in Castro. I explain to you that this tower is actually the old Roman lighthouse, of polygonal form and with distinctive banded masonry of Roman bricks (Wheeler 1929).

Over the next few weeks, on horseback, we make perhaps thirty miles a day or more, depending on the terrain. I want you to note the relative ease of travel here: the route from Dover to London runs along open chalk ridges, "downs." It was these routes that Fox identified as important for prehistoric traffic, and it was the areas that we can see to our left and south, that he saw as dense and impassable forest. In the twenty-first century, Fox's powerful vision has been abandoned—empirically, the blank areas of his maps that he saw as indicators of dense forest avoided by human settlement have often now been filled in by subsequent finds made by a later generation of archaeologists, while it is also clear that his vision of human settlement penetrating into uninhabited areas is ideologically loaded (both in a postcolonial sense and also, for example, as the inspiration for Tolkien's "Wild Wood": Johnson 2002, 47–48; Johnson 2017, 186–87).

The easiest way for us to travel to London would be to stay on the chalk downs, the clear straight route flanked by expansive, open fields and sheep runs, made famous between Canterbury and London as the route traveled by the pilgrims heading to the shrine of St. Thomas à Becket in Chaucer's *Canterbury Tales*. But I want to show you the area we can see to the south, called the Weald, from the

Old English -*walda* or woodland. Turning left and south, coming down off the ridges we are immediately in *clayland*. The narrow roads now twist and turn, and can be sunken into the landscape; let's hope it doesn't rain, for if it does, they will become impassable quagmires. On the few occasions we can see through the dense hedges along the roads, around us are patchworks of small, enclosed fields. Some are arable, mostly wheat and a little barley and oats; others are lush grass, pastured for sheep and cattle. Fringing the fields are numerous patches of woodland. We encounter very few nucleated villages. Instead, we see isolated churches, small hamlets, and isolated substantial timber-framed, plastered and thatched houses (see fig. 2.3).[3]

We stop and talk to a middle-aged woman who calls herself the "huswife" or mistress of a household, consisting of her husband, sons and daughters, and two or three live-in servants. She refers to her husband as a "plowman," but a century later the more common term will be *yeoman* or *husbandman*. These are socially middling households. Master and male servants work in the fields; the women of the household produce dairy products for local markets. Perhaps also she describes some involvement in local rural industry—the woodlands provide charcoal for

Figure 2.3. A house of late medieval origins, surrounded by fields and patches of woodland, in the Wealden landscape, Kent. (Photograph by Matthew Johnson)

glassmaking and iron production. The area is also well known for its wool; previous generations have exported the raw wool to the Low Countries, but more recently finished cloth has been produced locally (Zell 2000; Mate 2010).

Legally, socially and politically, these households have a strong ethic of independence. This area of Kent has seen "peasant revolts" over and over again in the last century, that is, after the most famous revolt of Wat Tyler in 1381. Many of these revolts have been put down by force, but lords have learned to tread very carefully, and have acquiesced in older manorial practices of rent extraction going out of use (Hilton 1973; Zell 2000; Grummit 2010).

London: Streetscapes, Strangers

We return to the high road to London, and approach the city via the south bank of the river Thames. We pass a number of buildings and institutions that were generally placed outside the city walls in the later Middle Ages—smaller monastic institutions; some noxious and water-driven industries like fulling (the cleansing of cloth), banished from the city; and next to the river, royal and baronial palace sites at a distance from the urban throng. We pass the Tabard, the inn made famous by Chaucer, and find ourselves in Southwark, the suburb of London south of the Thames, dominated by the great church of Southwark Priory. But before we arrive at the church itself, we turn right and north to the River Thames; London itself, in the sense of the area defined by London city walls lies on the north side of the river. We cross the river by the fortified London Bridge; its gatehouse and drawbridge were rebuilt in the 1460s, as part of a more general refurbishment of the city walls.

Our first impression of 1490s London is the smell. Our second impression is that the city is nothing special (see fig. 2.4 on page 32). There are cities across Europe that are larger at this date, from the great city-states of Northern Italy to the ports of the Low Countries. London does have extensive suburbs such as that of Southwark, with almost as many people living outside the city walls as inside, but the walled area itself is small, traversable from its eastern to its western extremity by foot in less than half an hour. The church of St Paul's is much longer, but not nearly as high, as the great French cathedrals, and its vault is timber, not stone.

Our third impression is of a place whose form and location owes much to its Roman antecedents. The city walls follow the Roman line; as we pass the city

Figure 2.4. London in the mid-sixteenth century, by Wyngaerde, detail taken from Mitton 1908. Not all the details are accurate in this nineteenth-century transcription. The view is from the south bank of the Thames with Southwark in the foreground. Across the river, St Paul's stands at one end of Cheapside. The city walls can be seen farther out. Above and to the northeast of St Paul's, a sharp kink represents a topographic trace of two walls of the old Roman fort at Cripplegate. (Courtesy of Wikimedia Commons)

walls we see, in patches, the same distinctive bands of brick masonry we saw at the Pharos of Dover. Above these bands, patching the Roman fabric, are successive medieval rebuilds. The gridded Roman street plan has been almost entirely lost (it is possible that the market street of Cheapside is one topographical element that survives). City gatehouses are now great medieval towers proclaiming the city's independence through their battlements, heraldry, and elaborate gate arrangements, but their locations are Roman. The distinctive "kink" in the city walls at the northwestern corner is a topographical trace of the old Cripplegate fort, two sides of the distinctive playing-card pattern such forts followed as standard Roman practice. London Bridge was rebuilt five centuries ago, but again on the location of the Roman bridge. Londoners might not consciously recognize these Roman antecedents, but medieval historians identified London as the capital of Roman Britain, and locals identify the great White Tower at the center of the royal castle, the Tower of London, as Roman. They attribute it to Julius Caesar (as it will be attributed ninety years later, in Shakespeare's *Richard II* and *Richard III*).

London is the only place until we get to the Irish Sea and to Galway where we may encounter numbers of *strangers*, the contemporary term for City dwellers of foreign origin. Merchants and their families from across the Baltic, Europe, and the Mediterranean worlds form distinct communities and "language worlds" (Hsy 2013), and many of the small cluster of printers and booksellers around St Paul's Cathedral are of non-English birth. William Caxton returned from continental Europe and founded the first English printing press in the western suburb of Westminster in 1476, in the Almonry of the Abbey there; but when we go to visit him, we are told he has been dead for six months. His successor Richard Pynson has a print shop in St Clement Danes; he is a Frenchman, later naturalized as an Englishman (Gillespie 2006).

London to Chester: Midland England

We leave the city by Newgate, and head west and north, out of the Thames Valley, along Watling Street—a Roman road, one of a series of roads to and from London that radiate like spokes of a wheel to the corners of the former Roman province of *Britannia* (see fig. 2.5 on page 34). The first night we stop at the Abbey of St Albans (27 miles, that is, one day's journey, from London, built of reused Roman brick and the shrine of a Roman martyr). There, as is customary for

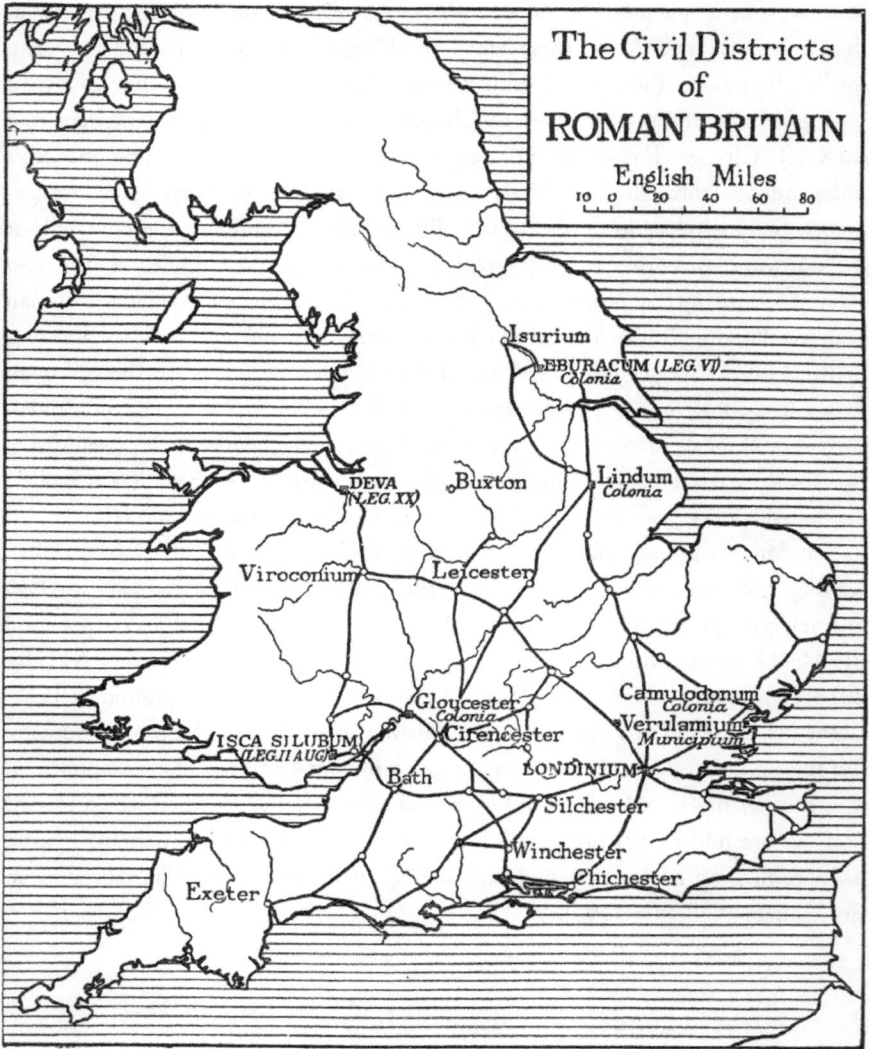

The Civil Districts
of
ROMAN BRITAIN

English Miles

10 0   20   40   60   80

Isurium

EBURACUM (LEG. VI)
Colonia

DEVA
(LEG. XX)

Buxton

Lindum
Colonia

Viroconium

Leicester

Camulodonum
Colonia

Gloucester
Colonia

Cirencester

Verulamium
Municipium

ISCA SILUBUM
(LEG. II AUG)

Bath

LONDINIUM

Silchester

Winchester

Chichester

Exeter

Figure 2.5. Cyril Fox's diagram of "civil districts" (this page) and "military districts" (opposite page) of Roman Britain, broadly corresponding to his definition of Highland and Lowland Zones. (After Fox 1932, figs. 13 and 14, courtesy of Amgueddfa Genedlaethol Cymru, National Museum of Wales)

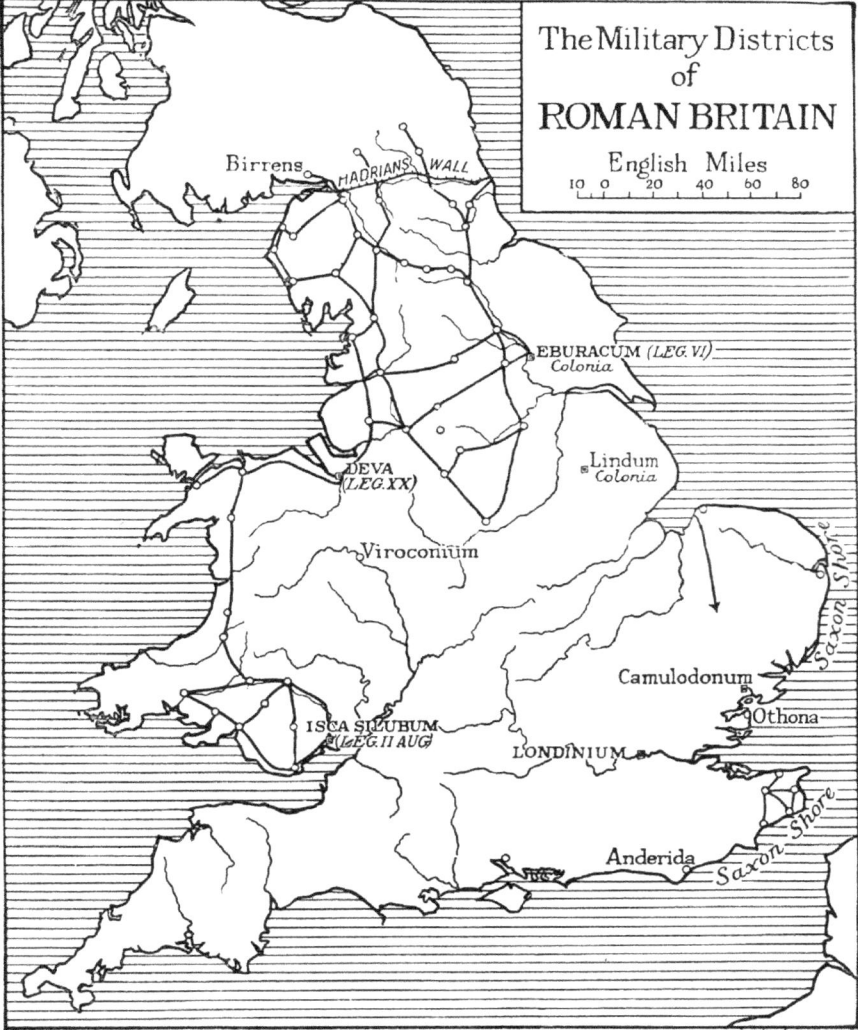

The Military Districts
of
ROMAN BRITAIN

English Miles

10 0   20   40   60   80

Birrens

HADRIANS WALL

EBURACUM *(LEG. VI)*
Colonia

DEVA
(LEG. XX)

Lindum
Colonia

Viroconium

Camulodonum

Othona

ISCA SILUBUM
(LEG. II AUG)

LONDINIUM

Saxon Shore

Anderida   *Saxon Shore*

travelers arriving at monastic institutions, we are offered hospitality—a bed for the night and a meal at the abbot's table. Over dinner we talk to a young student on his way to Oxford, Thomas More, and ask him what we will see on our journey northwest to Chester. This is perhaps a mistake, for More has a great deal to say, and he gets quite angry about it. The landscape, he says, will be dominated by sheep, and he goes on to denounce the reason for this as he sees it: greed of the landowners who in his view are evicting tenants and depopulating the countryside in order to profit from the wool and cloth industry.

> . . . your sheep . . . that commonly are so meek and eat so little, now . . . they have become so greedy and so fierce that they devour human beings themselves. They devastate and depopulate fields, houses and towns. For in whatever parts of the land sheep yield the finest and thus the most expensive wool, there the nobility and gentry, yes, and even a good many abbots—holy men—are not content with the old rents that the land yielded to their predecessors . . . For they leave no land free for the plough; they enclose every acre for pasture; they destroy houses and abolish towns, keeping the churches—but only for sheep-barns. And as if enough of your land were not already wasted on [parks] and forests for hunting wild animals, these worthy men turn all habitations and cultivated fields back to wilderness . . .

More explains that the profits of the wool trade make it financially attractive to landlords to forcibly depopulate villages, hedge and enclose the land, and turn it over to sheep runs. He ignores the visible discomfort of his host, the abbot, and continues to bemoan the fate of the evicted poor.

> Thus, so that one greedy, insatiable glutton, a frightful plague to his native country, may enclose thousands of acres within a single fence, the tenants are ejected; and some are stripped of their belongings by trickery or brute force, or, wearied by constant harassment, are driven to sell them. One way or another, these wretched people, men, women, husbands, wives, orphans, widows, parents with little children and entire families (poor but numerous, since farming requires many hands)—are forced to move out . . . Since they must leave at once without waiting for a proper buyer, they sell for a pittance all their household goods . . . what finally remains for them but to steal, and so be hanged, justly, no doubt—or to wander and beg?

Figure 2.6. Hamilton, Leicestershire: earthworks of a deserted medieval village, surrounded by traces of arable agriculture turned over to pasture by the 1490s. (Courtesy of Historic England Archive)

More links this new spirit of acquisitiveness and profit to the moral decay not just of the landlords, but of the whole nation, pointing to the decline of values of hospitality and general disorder and moral turpitude in the populace, even changes in fashion.

So [England] will be ruined by the crass avarice of a few . . . the high cost of living causes everyone to dismiss as many retainers as he can from his household; and what, I ask, can these men do but rob or beg? . . . To make this miserable poverty and scarcity worse, they exist side by side with wanton luxury. The servants of noblemen, tradespeople, even some farmers—people of every social rank—are given to ostentatious dress and gourmandizing. Look at the cook-shops, the brothels, the bawdy houses and those other places just as bad, the wine-bars and alehouses. (Logan ed. 2016, 19–20)

Next morning, somewhat shaken by this tirade, we set out again and discuss More's views. These are familiar to us both, from our knowledge of the historiography of the period (the extracts above are taken from More's 1516 *Utopia*). More's condemnation of acquisitive landowners formed part of the evidence for Richard Tawney's view of "the agrarian problem of the 16th century." More broadly, the origins of capitalism as seen in the countryside have been located by many twentieth-century scholars in these processes of depopulation and enclosure, which led, for example, in the thought of Robert Brenner, to growing class division in the sixteenth and seventeenth centuries (Tawney 1912; Aston & Philpin 1986).

I explain, however, that this view, though strongly held by More, and following him Tawney and Brenner, is out of academic fashion in the twenty-first century: that later scholars have found very little primary evidence of forced evictions or organized depopulations of villages. Where More saw abandoned villages and arable fields given over to pasture, this is the result of not of forcible eviction but of population shrinkage and piecemeal enclosure in the 150 years after the Black Death of 1348–49, leading to a halving of the medieval population; that the climatic deterioration known as the "Little Ice Age" has to be factored in; and that tenants were actually quite successful in defending their rights. You keep your own counsel; whatever the empirical evidence, this reframing offered by some later scholars, attributing change to environment and market forces rather than to class and human agency, sounds pretty neoliberal to your ears (Wrightson 2011, 102–4, summarizes the present state of this debate; Whittle 2016 offers a balanced but ultimately positive assessment of Tawney 1912 as "a great book").

This landscape we see over the next week or so as we ride on horseback through the Midlands on our way to Chester certainly does not appear on the brink of catastrophe. It may well be more familiar to you if you have read idealized accounts of the feudal system, or indeed watched any BBC historic drama set in the countryside: one of nucleated villages, each with its own church, peasant houses, tofts, crofts, and manor house; and we see the occasional watermill or windmill. The building materials, and, hence, the building style and external appearance, of these buildings varies; as we are traveling southeast to northwest, we are cutting across the grain of the underlying geology (see fig. 2.1). These villages are characteristically surrounded by large "open" fields, or more accurately large unbounded fields growing wheat, barley and oats, or lying fallow, subdivided into long, narrow strips, each strip held and worked by a different household. We also see other areas of land: "commons," under pasture, in which the whole community has rights; areas of uncultivated land referred to by contemporaries as "waste" or even "wilderness" as More does, but which we observe being used in different ways, for example, rough pasture. There are frequent patches of woodland, not so much as in the Weald, but nevertheless important; these are not the primeval forests of Fox's vision, but rather managed and subject to different use rights. We see pigs roaming freely in the woods, grazing on acorns; peasants gathering firewood; and foresters cutting down mature trees for building timber.

However, we also see signs of change, the changes More saw as being driven by acquisitive landlords. In many areas we see long, narrow ridges, identical in form to the strips of the extant open fields we have seen, but now under grass; these are indeed where open arable fields have been converted to pasture. We also see signs of recent enclosure in the landscape, smaller fields demarcated by hedges and ditches, or by stone walls. And there are deer parks, enclosed by banks and ditches or by walls, though these may either be quite recent or of great antiquity.

And occasionally, we do see traces of abandoned or shrunken villages: a church standing on its own in a field, or gaps in the tenements or property boundaries of a village, like missing teeth. We might even see places that are completely deserted, humps and bumps in fields, with sheep grazing (see fig. 2.6). However, we do not see the large numbers of vagrants and indigent poor that More made so much of. And so we are still arguing about More's views and the evidence for them in the landscape around us when we arrive at Chester.

Chester to Caernarvon: Uplands

Chester, like London, bears the marks of its Roman past: we see traces of Roman work in the reused city walls, particularly on the north and west sides, where they follow the playing-card pattern of the old Roman fortress (Deva) on which Chester was built. Inside the walls, the main streets are flanked by impressive half-timbered, multistoried urban shops and dwellings organized in two tiers or "rows" (Brown 1999). Chester sits on the River Dee, leading out to the Irish Sea. If we wanted to get to Ireland quickly, it would be best to take passage on a boat from here, hugging the North Wales coast before setting out across the Irish Sea. I want us to see some sights in North Wales, however, so we set out west, overland.

The landscape now is different from anything we have seen: we have just crossed Fox's boundary between lowland (southeast) and highland (northwest) zones. We travel along a strip of lower ground, with the coast to the north and the great mountains of Snowdonia to the south. We do not cross a "national" boundary; the area has been under English administration since its conquest by Edward I in the 1280s, apart from a brief period of 1400–1415, during the rebellion of Owain Glyndwr. We might observe the ancient traces of Offa's Dyke, a bank-and-ditch earthwork seven centuries old, built by King Offa as a western frontier to his kingdom of Mercia; the language spoken by common people changes quite quickly from English to Welsh, and place-names change also (Hawarden to Penarlâg, Anglesey to Ynys Môn, Newtown to Drenewydd). We have left behind the nucleated villages of the Midlands with their open arable fields. Fields are once again smaller and more of a patchwork, with a greater emphasis on pastoral agriculture. Farmsteads are isolated or in small hamlets or clusters, and we see distinct forms, for example "longhouses" with provision for cattle and humans under one continuous roof (Johnson 2010, 74 and plate 10).

We travel between a series of small towns, strung out along the coast or situated on estuaries. The size of these towns is not impressive, but the castles that dominate them are. We have seen many castles before in our journey, more often than not ruined or derelict, and most of them "private" or owned by the nobility. These Welsh castles, however, are royal rather than private. West of Chester, the first we encounter is Hawarden, then Rhuddlan and Flint, and then Conway and Caernarvon. Conway and Caernarvon are on an even larger scale altogether (we do not have time to visit the other two in this group of "mega-castles," Harlech & Beaumaris).

I explain that these castles were built two centuries ago, toward the end of the thirteenth century, as part of Edward I's conquest of North Wales. Edward established not only the castles but the associated towns, laid out like so many other small planned towns during the economic growth of the twelfth and thirteenth centuries, but ringed with masonry walls. As established by Edward, the walls were intended to shelter English-speaking merchants and others, with Welsh speakers excluded from the walled area. However, as we walk through the streets of Conway, we notice a fair amount of Welsh being spoken; it would appear that the strict rules of segregation have broken down somewhat in the past two centuries. Much of Conway in particular is now occupied by Welsh-speaking merchants and traders.

Most striking is Caernarvon (see fig. 2.7). The towers of Caernarvon Castle are polygonal, rather than circular as with the others, and the masonry is banded. The effect is strongly reminiscent of the banded masonry of the Roman walls we have seen. We recall also the polygonal tower of the Roman lighthouse at Dover, at the other end of the kingdom, and we note also the carved eagles adorning the great Eagle Tower at one end of the castle. Caernarvon is on the site of a Roman fort (Caer-narvon means fort on the River Arfon), and the site is associated with an ancient legend about a Roman emperor of Britain—the *Dream of Macsen Wledig*.

We will take passage on a ship to Ireland the next day, but while we wait for the tide we reflect on what we have seen in a tavern under the walls of the great

Figure 2.7. The Edwardian castle of Caernarvon. Note polygonal towers and banded masonry. (Photograph by Matthew Johnson)

castle. Edward's thirteenth-century castles and towns appear to us as evidence of a strategy of nascent colonialism. Welsh were excluded, and the scale and massing of the castle and town walls speaks of an ideological attempt to overawe and dominate. Edward sought to legitimate his territorial conquest of Wales, and his (ultimately unsuccessful) ambitions in Scotland, by presenting himself as emperor of Britain rather than simply as king of England. "Britain," of course, included the territories of Wales and Scotland. This is the logic behind the Roman architectural and landscape references at Caernarvon: they seek to establish the Imperial nature of Edward's claim, and its wider scope, spanning the whole of Britain.

Edward failed to complete his castles; we notice that the interior of Caernarvon appears unfinished, and were we to go to the nearby castle of Beaumaris on the island of Anglesey, we would see another unfinished structure. Edward did however establish his son as "prince of Wales," and the practice of designated the eldest son and heir to the throne as such is now established. However, as we have seen from the growing presence of Welsh speakers within the towns, times are changing. The current king, Henry VII, is of Welsh descent (the "Tudor" surname being an Anglicization of the patronymic name ap Tudur, of Penmynydd on Anglesey). Six years ago Henry named his newborn son and heir Arthur, in a deliberate reference back to the ancient King of the Britons. A year ago, Arthur was installed as prince of Wales, and while in the 1490s he has not yet actually been to Wales, Arthur is being brought up at court in the company of Welsh and Irish noblemen.

As with More's analysis, we disagree about what we are seeing. You see clear evidence of nascent colonialism and even apartheid (and you would be supported by, for example, Christopher's 1983 article "From Flint to Soweto"). It doesn't surprise you to learn that much of the cost of Edward's castles was met by revenues from English Crown's estates in Ireland (O'Keeffe 2011). I counter that it's much more complex than that—that Wales never existed as a kingdom prior to Edward's conquest; that models of "nascent colonialism" are arguably inappropriate or anachronistic in a medieval context; that the towns we have passed through in 1492 have evidence of the growth of a Welsh-speaking middle class; that while we are seeing profound inequalities on the basis of status and identity, a concept of "race" is anachronistic. You remark that the monk Gerald of Wales was already writing about the inferiority of the Welsh in the 1200s . . . and we continue arguing as we make passage for Dublin.

Dublin to Galway: Toward an Atlantic World

The sea passage to Dublin is not easy. The prevailing winds are "westerlies," which mean that it is relatively easier to sail to Ireland from Spain and the west coast of France than it is to get there from England. Dublin is another city of middling rather than great size; it does have another grand royal castle, built by King John in the early thirteenth century. Like Dover, the political atmosphere may be tense. Five years previously, Lambert Simnel, pretending to be the lost Prince Edward, was "crowned" Edward VII in Christ Church Cathedral as part of an abortive attempt to depose Henry VII. This very year, the streets of Dublin have seen fighting between the men of Gerald Fitzgerald, Eighth Earl of Kildare and Lord Deputy of Ireland, and his rival the Earl of Ormond, ending in a standoff in Christ Church Cathedral and eventual reconciliation between the two parties.

Where North Wales is securely within the control of the English Crown, King Henry's power and authority over Ireland is much more tenuous. Locals tell us that local power is actually wielded by Gerald Fitzgerald. Henry's lack of power in Ireland was confirmed when he was forced to reappoint Fitzgerald as lord deputy, notwithstanding Fitzgerald's blatant disloyalty to the Crown on repeated occasions, for example, his previous support for Simnel. Fitzgerald's surname is an indication of his origins (Fitz being Norman French for "son of"), part of a dynasty of old Norman landowners who, having been part of the original Anglo-Norman invasion of the 1160s, carved out land for themselves, married Irish partners, adopted the language, and became in the words of contemporary commentators "more Irish than the Irish themselves" (O'Keeffe 2016, 224).

Setting off from Dublin westward, we are traveling through "the Pale," the area of Anglo-Norman settlement and (at least notionally) under direct English control. Locals tell us of the derivation of the name, from the idea of a "pale" or boundary fence and ditch that demarcates the area from Irish settlement outside the authority of the Crown (hence, the origin of the phrase, "beyond the Pale"). However, we may not actually see any such physical boundary. A statute passed in 1488 specified a bank and ditch to be (re)built, and the line along which it should be constructed; but it is unclear that a continuous bank and ditch was ever completed.

We experience the Pale as a land of a few villages, with a patchwork of fields around them of different kinds including a variety of forms of open fields and strip fields. Rapidly, we hear less and less English being spoken and, within one or two days travel out of Dublin, little but Irish until we get to Galway. We can see the landscape clearly because we are traveling along the top of an esker, a linear glacial deposit, that affords a view of the surrounding countryside and which itself is an important pilgrim route from east to west across Ireland. As we leave the Pale, we see hamlets and isolated farmsteads rather than villages, a mixture of arable and pastoral husbandry within enclosed fields with wider open areas beyond, patches of woodland and areas of bog, and the occasional monastery and castle.

We particularly see scores of tower houses. These are smaller and much more numerous than castles, though the dividing line between small castle and large tower-house is quite unclear. Most are square in plan, and have an attached enclosure or bawn with outbuildings (see fig. 2.8). We receive hospitality overnight at several of these places, a memorable experience that is described over a century later thus:

Figure 2.8. Tower house with remains of its enclosure or bawn to the left, Srah, Ireland. (Photograph by Matthew Johnson)

. . . But we will go to the gentleman that dwells in the castle. See the company yonder, they are riding to a coshering [wedding] let us strike in among them . . . The castles are built very strong, and with narrow stairs, for security. The hall is the uppermost room, let us go up, you shall not come down again till tomorrow . . . The lady of the house meets you with her train. I have instructed you before how to accost them. Salutations paste, you shall be presented with all the drinks in the house, first the ordinary beer, then aquavitae, then sack, then old-ale, the lady tastes it, you must not refuse it. The fire is prepared in the middle of the hall, where you may solace yourself till supper time . . . By this time the table is spread and plentifully furnished with variety of meats, but ill cooked, and without sauce. Neither shall there be wanting a pasty or two of red deer . . . They feast together with great jollity and healths [toasts] around; towards the middle of supper, the harper begins to tune and singeth Irish rhymes of ancient making. If he be a good rhymer, he will make one song to the present occasion. Supper being ended, it is at your liberty to sit up, or to depart to your lodging, you shall have company in both kind. When you come to your chamber, do not expect canopy and curtains. It is very well if your bed content you, and if the company be great, you may happen to be bodkin in the middle. In the morning there will be brought unto you a cup of aquavitae . . . You may drink a knaggin without offence, that is the fourth part of a pint. Breakfast is but the repetitions of supper. When you are disposing of your-self to depart, they call for *Dogh a dores*, that is, to drink at the door, there you are presented again with all the drinks in the house, as at your first entrance. Smace them over, and let us depart. (Gernon c. 1620, cited in Falkiner, ed. 1904, 345–62)[4]

Somewhat under the weather after this experience, we follow the esker westward across the Irish midlands until we get to the ancient monastery of Clonmacnoise, on the River Shannon. To cross the Shannon, we have to either use a boat or head north to the bridge at Athlone. Once across the Shannon, we find to our consternation that there is no clear route or high road west, just a patchwork of tracks and paths across an increasingly pastoral, stonewalled landscape. Navigating this patchwork with difficulty, we eventually end up on the west coast of Ireland, and at the town of Galway. Galway is a small town by the standards of London and Dublin, but strikingly cosmopolitan—a mix of people identifying as English,

Irish, Scots, Bretons, French, Spaniards, and Portuguese (Hartnett 2010). These people are stunned to hear that we have arrived overland from Dublin; any sane person would have made the journey around the island by boat.

Talking to this mix of people, it comes as a surprise to us to realize that they do not think of themselves as being on the western extremity of a European world. Rather, their world runs from north to south; it is a seascape, a maritime network running from Spain, Portugal, and France northward along the Atlantic Seaboard to Scotland, Iceland, and beyond to Newfoundland. One person who has recently traveled along this network is Christopher Columbus, who probably visited Galway in 1477 on his way to, or from, Iceland. Columbus made a marginal note in his copy of Pierre d'Ailly's Imago Mundi, referring to his observation of corpses washed up at Galway, bodies he speculated had come from "Cathay" (Quinn 1992, 284).

General Reflections over a Glass of Wine

We retire to a Galway tavern, to end our journey and reflect on what we have learned, over a glass of wine (wine was traded to Galway, Dublin and beyond into Ireland from France and Spain; it was generally reckoned to be of poor quality; Hartnett 2010, 117).

Our subjective experience has been shaped in various ways. A person in the 1490s would not have had a modern cartographic perception, but rather would have visualized the journey as a series of strip maps, navigating by asking directions to the next town on the itinerary, and would not necessarily have perceived the journey in Cartesian terms but in terms of travel time between the towns. Our ability to make such a journey in the first place has also been shaped by expectations of gender and social class. The majority of those who traveled during that time period were men, and in groups of some size. Of Chaucer's twenty or so pilgrims traveling at the end of the fourteenth century, only four are women, and to state the obvious, while critics frequently comment on Chaucer's mix of social classes, there is almost no one who might be termed a farmer and no landless laborers in the group. Nevertheless, travel by solitary women was known; the religious mystic Margery Kemp frequently traveled alone in the 1430s (Evans 2016, 28). Finally, we have chosen to take a route that avoids the southwest and north of England and the entirety of Scotland; we would have had a very different impression of the British Isles had we traveled from northeast to southwest.

We have traveled across a landscape that, as Cyril Fox observed, has offered a set of geographical affordances, without necessarily being determinist. The first and most obvious factor is geology. In traveling from southeast to northwest, we have cut across the grain of the surface geology. The relatively gentle chalk ridges of Kent and the Downs give way to the Midlands *claylands*, which in turn give way to the older and harder rocks of North Wales and the glacial landscapes of Ireland. The variation in underlying geology has afforded, first, a strong sense of regional difference, manifested in a very different set of vernacular building materials. Peasant houses have varied in style and appearance, and the variations have often been quite sudden. Second, the geology, combined with the climate, has afforded different kinds of agricultural practice. The highland zone is more suited to pastoral than to arable agriculture. At the end of the fifteenth century, market relations have not yet deepened, and most family farms practice a mixture of subsistence agriculture and market production, with an emphasis on the former. Consequently, regional specialization is still relatively limited compared to subsequent centuries; pretty much wherever we have gone, we have seen an interdependence of arable and pastoral, with the manure from sheep and cattle fertilizing the fields. As we have traveled, we have seen a very broad shift from richer to poorer, from a more to a less fertile countryside, from relatively dense to relatively dispersed settlement. We have seen less wheat, and more oats and barley, as we have traveled northwest.

The climate of course has been colder and wetter as we have traveled northwest toward the Atlantic Coast. The weather also has geopolitical consequences. The prevailing westerlies made invasion of Ireland from France or Spain a relatively easy proposition, and contributed to the constant English fear of a "backdoor" invasion and consequent perceived need to maintain control of the island of Ireland up to and including the Second World War. The Little Ice Age will continue until the 1800s. By 1492, the colder climate has caused shifts in North Atlantic ocean currents, leading to movement in the location of fishing grounds, prompting in its turn longer voyages and more sustained exploration of the North Atlantic.

The routes we have taken are frequently ancient. Most obviously, as Fox observed, water travel along the coast or across the Irish Sea has always been important, linking to extensive systems of inland river transport (Martin 2016). Overland, roads were constantly the subject of maintenance and repair through the Middle Ages (Allen 2016). The ridgeways, for example along the North Downs, are often of prehistoric origin, while pilgrim routes are very often at least three or four centuries old (Wells 2016). Most fundamentally, medieval roads were heavily influenced by the Roman road system, with Roman roads radiating out like the spokes of a wheel from the provincial capital of Londinium.

Roman settlement in Britain followed Fox's highland/lowland zone distinction. Roman villas, the majority of towns, and the road system are concentrated in the lowland zone. In the highland zone, in Wales and Northern England up to Hadrian's Wall, we find roads, fortifications, and military installations (the Roman legionary fortresses of Chester/Deva and York/Eboracum stood at the junction of highland and lowland zones; see fig. 2.5). Roman settlement, in turn, prefigured cultural boundaries in the early and high medieval period, most obviously between Anglo-Saxon and Celt and then between English, Welsh, Scots, and Irish. At the same time, the Roman Empire has cast a heavy ideological shadow, from building forms and practices to conceptions of an imperial identity that could be mobilized to legitimate territorial conquest and nascent colonialism.

Some elements of human settlement have remained constant across this changing landscape. First, and most obviously, is the Catholic Church, and its buildings and institutions (again, Roman in origin). Most obviously, in 1492, every community has its parish church. The building material and particular size and form varies, but the "Perpendicular" (late Gothic) architectural style is remarkably constant across a broad swath of these buildings. A peasant on the west coast of Ireland might well be quite familiar with the form and layout of a parish church in Kent. As we travel, we know the time of day by the tolling of the church bell; in most of lowland England, very few places would be outside this aural range.

A network of monastic institutions of different orders and rules is scattered across the landscape, as it is across late medieval Europe as a whole. Monasteries are laid out to a standard plan, though they can be large and small, and architectural styles show variation. Our journey might well not have been possible without reliance on the customs of hospitality at these institutions, as we saw at St Albans. And every few miles on our journey we have encountered elements of a religious landscape—shrines, holy wells, chapels on bridges.

A second constant is the network of castles and great houses. Where no local monastery was available, we have often sought hospitality at these places (and More's warnings notwithstanding, have received it). In the southeast and Midlands, many of these buildings have been derelict or even ruined for some decades or even centuries. Writing fifty years later in the 1540s, the early topographer John Leland noted time and again the decay of castles and other houses that he visited (Johnson 2002, 126–27).

Our first conclusion, then, is that if we want to understand the British Isles in 1492, and the landscapes beyond of Europe, our first thought must be to attend to geology and physical geography; and our second must be to attend to "second nature" (Cronon 1992) and to enduring structures, the limits of the possible (Braudel 1981). Following, of course, many of Braudel's critics, we can see that the full suite of these enduring structures includes cultural and ideological patterns and continuities as well as physical ones; indeed, following the insights of mere recent political ecology, we must see natural and social as dialectically related (Robbins 2012).

Elements of Change

Our primary interest on this trip, however, has been to identify incipient change—to identify what we can of changes in the landscape that historians see unfolding over the next several centuries, leading to capitalism, colonialism, and modernity, however defined.

We have seen dramatic changes in the landscape of the English Midlands, and been struck by More's account of the reasons for it. Over the next three centuries, these changes will continue to unfold (Whittle 2017). Farmers will grow, and urban markets will consume, new crops, the most obvious and infamous being the introduction of the potato to Ireland (Aalen, Whelan, & Stout, 2011). The landscape will move from being dominated by small family farms to a more polarized landlord-tenant–landless laborer hierarchy. More's description of the poor wandering from parish to parish may not have been a balanced picture when he wrote, but it certainly was a century later (Boulton 2017).

We have seen little hint, however, of several key and interrelated changes that have all, in different ways, been cited by historians as key to the development of capitalism: population rise, urban growth, and religious reformation. It is very difficult, surveying the scene in 1492, to point to clear signs that the British Isles will be the earliest instance of agrarian and industrial capitalism or the seat of global empire.

The first sign is population: in 1492, the British Isles, and Europe generally, is at the low point of a population curve. The population has declined from the Black Death of 1348–39 into the later fifteenth century, and in 1490s stands at about half what it had been at pre–Black Death levels. In the next few decades, the population will start rising, reaching pre–Black Death levels by circa 1600 before plateauing in the mid- to later seventeenth century, and then rising again (Wrigley & Schofield 1989).

The second sign pertains to the rise of London. In 1492, London is just another North European city. From the sixteenth century onward London will grow exponentially. Its growth, and that of other urban centers, will fuel the rise of national and regional markets, and this in turn will motivate farmers to specialize and provide food for these urban markets. The economy of Kent in particular will be transformed by this "pull" of London. London will also change and diversify culturally and socially very soon after the 1490s, if it has not done so already. There has been an African presence in Britain since the Roman period, and in our travels we may have encountered an individual of African birth or ancestry. The trumpeter John Blanke probably arrived in nine years later, in 1501, as part of Katherine of Aragon's household. However, the first records of numbers of Africans in London date to the 1560s (Walvin 1971).

The third sign applies to religious reformation. It is possible that we may have met one or two dissenters from the established beliefs of the Catholic Church. The doctrines of Wycliff and the Lollards were popular around 1400, but religious historians differ strongly over the extent to which they were effectively repressed in the following decades. Henry VIII's Reformation and the Dissolution of the Monasteries are over forty years away. A century from 1492, however, England will be a securely Protestant nation, while parts of Scotland and most of Ireland will remain Catholic. The effect of this Reformation will be to add an important religious element to conceptions of cultural difference and identity between different elements of the British Isles.

Any scholar engaging the study of religion and capitalism first thinks of Weber's Protestant ethic thesis; but here, in this Galway tavern, I emphasize the future impact of reformation on the landscape. By 1550 St Albans, and most monasteries of its kind, will be dissolved, its fabric destroyed or reused and adapted for other purposes. A couple of decades later, the shrines, holy wells, and chapels will be gone also, and the interior of every parish church in England and Wales stripped of much of its interior in accordance with new practice. The everyday landscape of every English person will have been secularized (Ryrie 2017), one element of a move away from a landscape of custom and practice and toward a landscape of acquisition and profit.

We have argued, as we rode along, about whether *colonial* is an appropriate term for medieval English policy in Ireland and Wales, but we would have no such argument were we to repeat the exercise a century after 1492. In 1494 King Henry will establish the Englishman Edward Poynings as deputy in Ireland; "Poynings' Law" will codify the supremacy of the English Parliament; Henry VIII and then Queen Elizabeth will establish ever tighter colonial control over the island of Ireland in the face of successive rebellions; and in the 1580s, the English will attempt wholesale reorganization and "plantation" of the landscape in the Irish province of Munster. Wales is to lose any national identity and be "shired" and absorbed into the administrative structure of England in the 1530s. In 1601 Elizabeth will authorize the deportation of "Negroes and blackamoors" (Aubrey 1993), and in 1603 the banks of the River Thames will be thronged with Londoners observing Amerindians paddling their canoes. There will a community of African descent in London of some thousands by 1700, many of them enslaved until the Somerset decision of 1772. Many of the "masterless men" moving across the landscape from the later sixteenth century onward will be of Welsh, Irish, and Roma descent.

How much of this future has been predetermined, in the enduring structures already in place in 1492? How much is the inexorable unfolding of history, and how much a matter of contingency—what if there were no Reformation, what if Henry VII rather than the King of Spain had commissioned Columbus? We have finished our wine, and our time machine awaits us; we can discuss these and other matters on the journey home.

Acknowledgments

I thank all the participants in the symposium, particularly Chris DeCorse for the invitation, and Mark Hauser. Rebecca Johnson, Jessica Winegar, and Andy Wood who kindly commented on earlier drafts. I am grateful to Tadhg O'Keeffe for general advice, and guidance with the Irish section.

Notes

1. Of course, much of the documentary evidence I have used to construct this fictional account is in and of itself an artifact of change: printed maps, travel narratives, "discoveries," topographies, population surveys, tax records. The century after 1492 saw an explosion of materials of these kinds, and this explosion is of course an artifact of nascent capitalism,

colonialism, and modernity itself—the urge to describe, classify, list, and render taxable, are artifacts themselves of state formation.

2. Fox edited this passage in later editions in revealing ways, for example, changing *barks* to *black ship*s.

3. I review the archaeological evidence for this landscape in Johnson (2017, 183–89).

4. The spelling has been modernized for this paper. The picture of hospitality that this passage paints is compelling, and has been used by several scholars, including the author, as an entry into tower-house life (Sherlock 2011; O'Keeffe 2015, 271–75). It should be noted, however, that it comes from a source over a century later; it includes elements that would not have been present in the 1490s, for example, tobacco; and that the source needs to be ideologically situated, as written by a self-identified Irishman seeking to inform an English audience of the "true" nature of the country, in the context of recent rebellion, violence, and English prejudice toward the Irish.

Works Cited

Aalen, F. H. A., Kevin Whelan, and Matthew Stout. 2011. *Atlas of the Irish Rural Landscape*, 2d rev. ed. Cork, Ireland: Cork University Press.

Allen, V. 2016. "When Things Break: Mending Roads, Being Social." In. *Roadworks: Medieval Britain, Medieval Roads*. Edited by V. Allen R. and Evans. Manchester, UK: Manchester University Press, 74–96.

Allen, V., and R. Evans, eds. 2016. *Roadworks: Medieval Britain, Medieval Roads*. Manchester, UK: Manchester University Press.

Almond, Philip C. 2015. *England's First Daemonologist: Reginald Scot and the Discoverie of Witchcraft*. New York: Tauris.

Aston, T. H., and C. H. E. Philpin, eds. 1985. *The Brenner Debate: Agrarian Class Structure and Economic Development in Pre-Industrial Europe*. Cambridge, UK: Cambridge University Press.

Aubrey, James R. 1993. "Race and the Spectacle of the Monstrous in Othello." *Clio* 22(3): 221–39.

Boulton, Jeremy. 2017. The 'Meaner Sort': Laboring People and the Poor. In. *A Social History of England 1500–1750*. Edited by Keith Wrightson. Cambridge, UK: Cambridge University Press, 310–29.

Braudel, Fernand. 1972. *The Mediterranean and the Mediterranean World in the Age of Philip II*. Translated by Sian Reynolds. Berkeley: University of California Press.

———. 1981. *Civilization and Capitalism, 15th–18th Century*. London: Collins.

Brown, Andrew 1999. *The Rows of Chester: The Chester Rows Research Project*. London: English Heritage.

Christopher, C. 1983. "From Flint to Soweto: Reflections on the Colonial Origins of the Apartheid City." *Area* 15(2): 145–49.

Cronon, W. 1991. *Nature's Metropolis: Chicago and the Great West*. New York, Norton.

Evans, R. 2016. "Getting There: Wayfinding in the Middle Ages." In *Roadworks: Medieval Britain, Medieval Roads*. Edited by V. Allen and R. Evans. Manchester, UK: Manchester University Press, 127–56.

Falkiner, C. Litton, ed. 1904. *Illustrations of Irish History and Topography, Mainly of the 17th[h] Century*. London: Longman.

Fox, Cyril. 1923. *The Archaeology of the Cambridge Region*. Cambridge, UK: Cambridge University Press.

———. 1932. *The Personality of Britain: Its Influence on Inhabitant and Invader since Prehistoric and Early Historic Times*. Cardiff: National Museum of Wales.

Gillespie, Alexandra. 2006. *Print Culture and the Medieval Author: Chaucer, Lydgate, and Their Books 1473–1557*. Oxford, UK: Oxford University Press.

Grummit, D. 2010. "Kent and National Politics, 1399–1461." In *Later Medieval Kent 1220–1540*. Edited by S. Sweetinburgh, 235–50. Woodbridge, UK: Boydell.

Hartnett, A. B. 2010. "Legitimation and Dissent: Colonialism, Consumption and the Search for Distinction in Galway, Ireland, c. 1250–1691." PhD thesis, University of Chicago. http://search.proquest.com/openview/e4efe1eb8b0165d367e0a41e5e994 7a6/1?pq-origsite=gscholar&cbl=18750&diss=y.

Hilton, Rodney H. 1973. *Bond Men Made Free: Medieval Peasant Movements and the English Rising of 1381*. London: Temple Smith.

Hsy, J. 2013. *Trading Tongues: Merchants, Multilingualism, and Medieval Literature*. Columbus: Ohio State University Press.

James, Raymond. 2007. *Henry VIII's Military Revolution: The Armies of 16th Century Britain and Europe*. London: Tauris.

Johnson, Matthew H. 2002. *Behind the Castle Gate: From Medieval to Renaissance*. London: Routledge.

———. 2007. *Ideas of Landscape*. Oxford, UK: Blackwell.

———. 2010. English *Houses 1300–1800: Vernacular Architecture, Social Life*. London: Pearson.

Johnson, Matthew H., ed. 2017. *Lived Experience in the Later Middle Ages: Studies of Bodiam and Other Elite Landscapes in South-East England*. Southampton, UK: Highfield Press.

Logan, George M. (ed.) 2016. *More: Utopia*. Cambridge, UK: Cambridge University Press.

Martin, C. A. 2016. London: The Hub of an English River Transport Network, 1250–1550. In *Roadworks: Medieval Britain, Medieval Roads*. Edited by V. Allen and R. Evans, 249–76. Manchester, UK: Manchester University Press.

Mate, M., 2010. The Economy of Kent, 1200–1500: The Aftermath of the Black Death. In *Later Medieval Kent 1220–1540*. Edited by S. Sweetinburgh, 11–24. Woodbridge, UK: Boydell.

O'Keeffe, Tadhg. 2011. "Landscapes, Castles and Towns of Edward I in Wales and Ireland: Some Comparisons and Connections." *Landscapes* 11(1): 60–72.

———. 2015. *Medieval Irish Buildings*. Dublin, Ireland: Four Courts Press.

———. 2017. "Kilcolman Castle, Co. Cork: A New Interpretation of Edmund Spenser's Residence in Plantation Munster." *International Journal of Historical Archaeology* 21(1): 223–39.

Quinn, D. B. 1992. "Columbus and the North: England, Iceland and Ireland." *William and Mary Quarterly* 49(2): 278–97.

Robbins, Paul. 2012. *Political Ecology: A Critical Introduction*. 2d ed. Malden, MA: Blackwell Publishing.

Ryrie, Alex. 2017. "Reformations." In *A Social History of England 1500–1750*. Edited by Keith Wrightson, 107–28. Cambridge, UK: Cambridge University Press.Schrimes, S. B. 1999. *Henry VII*. New Haven, CT: Yale University Press.

Sherlock, Rory. 2011. "The Evolution of the Irish Tower-House as a Domestic Space." *Proceedings of the Royal Irish Academy* 111C: 115–40.

Tawney, Richard. 1912. *The Agrarian Problem in the 16th Century*. London: Longman.

Thirsk, J. 2000. "Agriculture in Kent, 1540–1640." In *Early Modern Kent 1540–1640*. Edited by Zell, Michael. Woodbridge: Boydell Press.

Walvin, James. 1971. *The Black Presence: A Documentary History of the Negro in England, 1555–1860*. London: Orbach and Chambers.

Washburn, Wilcomb E. 1962. "The Meaning of 'Discovery' in the 15th and 16th Centuries." *American Historical Review* 68(1): 1–21.

Wells, Emma J. 2016. *Pilgrim Routes of the British Isles*. London: Hale.

Wheeler, M. 1929. "The Roman Lighthouses at Dover." *Archaeological Journal* 86(1): 29–46.

Whittle, Jane 2017. "Land and People." In, *A Social History of England 1500–1750*. Edited by Keith Wrightson, 152–73. Cambridge, UK: Cambridge University Press.

Whittle, Jane, ed. 2013. *Landlords and Tenants in Britain, 1440–1660: Tawney's Agrarian Problem Revisited*. Woodbridge, UK: Boydell Press.

Wrightson, Keith. 2011. *Earthly Necessities: Economic Lives in Early Modern Britain*. New Haven, CT: Yale University Press.

Wrightson, Keith, ed. 2017. *A Social History of England 1500–1750*. Cambridge, UK: Cambridge University Press.

Wrigley, E. A., and Schofield, R. S. 1989. *The Population History of England 1541–1871: A Reconstruction*. Cambridge, UK: Cambridge University Press.

Zell, M. 2000. "Landholding and the Land Market in Early Modern Kent." In *Early Modern Kent 1540–1640*. Edited by Zell, Michael, 39–74. Woodbridge, UK: Boydell Press.

Chapter 3

Indigenous Caribbean Networks in a Globalizing World

Corinne L. Hofman

At the time of the European invasion, the insular Caribbean was already well settled by indigenous societies whose ancestors had entered the archipelago around 6000 BC from different parts of Coastal South and Central America. By AD 1000 a mosaic of culturally diverse island societies had developed (Keegan & Hofman 2017; Wilson 2007). The indigenous Caribbean networks were flexible, robust, inclusive, and outward-looking systems, and Europeans arriving in the late fifteenth century encountered a web of interlocking networks that spread across the region (Hofman & Bright 2010; Hofman et al. 2007, 2011, 2014; Mol 2014) (see fig. 3.1 on page 56). Being the nexus of the first encounters between the Old and the New World, the Caribbean was the initial space of intercultural Amerindian-European-African dynamics leading to the formation of new identities and social and material worlds (Anderson-Córdova 2017; Curet & Hauser 2011; Deagan 2004; Hofman et al. 2012, 2018b). European settlement and colonization of the Caribbean was not a single event, but rather a series of processes with some islands in the Lesser Antilles resisting European control until the 1800s.

Between the sixteenth and the eighteenth centuries, the indigenous Caribbean became largely invisible in global history, and emphasis was laid on the Aztec, Maya, and Inca empires. The neglect of the Caribbean region as the first port of entry to the Americas can to a great extent be considered as a direct consequence of the European eagerness for dominance and its quest for gold, as well as the decimation of indigenous Caribbean populations due to imported diseases, enslavement, and sociopolitical marginalization (Ulloa Hung & Valcárcel Rojas 2016). Marginalized ethnically and politically, indigenous peoples were either no longer allowed to be "indigenous" or

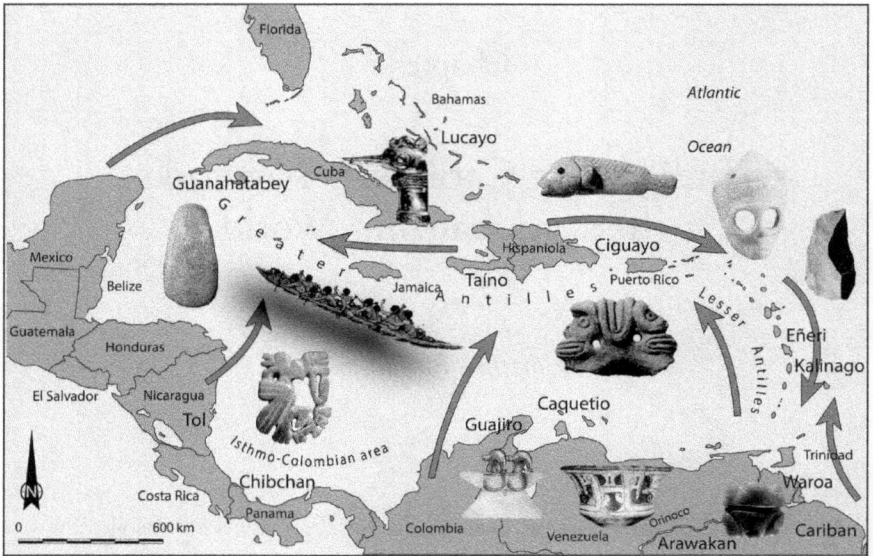

Figure 3.1. Map of the Caribbean with hypothetical precolonial networks of human mobility and the exchange of goods and ideas from 6000 BC–1492. (Map by Corinne Hofman and Menno Hoogland)

they themselves wished no longer to be perceived as "indigenous" by the colonizers. Over time they came to blend into newly formed mixed, "hybrid" (sensu Bhabha 1994), or "transculturated" (see Ortiz 1995) cultures, gradually losing their indigenous identities, and their presence in historical texts and colonial administration.

In this chapter, I take a long-term historical perspective (sensu Braudel's [1949] *longue durée*) to review the transformations of social, cultural, political, and economic relationships of the indigenous Caribbean communities on multiple temporal and spatial scales. After considering the precolonial Caribbean contexts, I focus on a period of 300 years, between AD 1492 and 1800, in which the transformations and responses of the indigenous societies to the changing cultural, social, and political environments triggered by colonialism are archaeologically traceable. The first episode concentrates in northern Hispaniola, where the first Spanish incursions into the interior of the island were made and where intensive confrontations took place between indigenous peoples and the European invaders. The second episode entails the establishment of the first Spanish forts in the Cibao Valley of what is now the Dominican Republic and the initial exploitation of gold in this area, as well as that of the pearling grounds offshore the Venezuelan island of Cubagua. These enterprises entailed massive translocation of indigenous peoples and the beginnings of slavery. Indigenous and African slaves were put to work in the gold mines and pearl fisheries. For the third episode I examine the early-sixteenth-century mixed encomienda cemetery at El Chorro de Maíta in northeastern Cuba. The funerary practices and associated material culture were profoundly affected by Christianization. The fourth and last episode describes the resistance to European hegemony among the indigenous populations of the Lesser Antilles. This was the *Kalinago* society in the Lesser Antilles, a regrouping of peoples from other islands to the North as well as the South American mainland in a landscape otherwise invaded by the Spanish Main. Amerindian cultural and religious traditions became entangled with African and European practices during the first centuries of European invasion and colonization and still prosper in today's multiethnic and multicultural Caribbean society.

The Precolonial Caribbean

The first colonization of the insular Caribbean took place around 8000 years ago, with peoples moving from the surrounding continental areas of South and Central America (Hofman et al. 2011). The first islands to be colonized were those closest to the mainland(s), including Trinidad (7800 BP) in the south and Cuba in the north (5500 BP). The Venezuelan offshore islands were first settled between 7000 and 4500 years ago (Antczak et al. 2018), and some of the islands of the Lesser and Greater Antilles between 5000 and 3000 years ago (Keegan & Hofman 2017). The settlement of Jamaica and the Lucayan islands present a void as no Archaic Age sites have yet been found (Keegan & Hofman 2017). Most of the Windward Islands of the Lesser Antilles also lack firm archaeological evidence, but recent paleoenvironmental research indicates the occurrence of anthropogenic fires on several of the islands dating to this period (Siegel et al. 2015, 2018).

Seasonal campsites and more permanent habitation sites in various environmental settings (mangroves, riverbanks, and mountains) resulted in transformations of the pristine island landscapes early in the settlement history of the Caribbean (Fitzpatrick & Keegan 2007). Large conch middens are the product of intensive *Lobatus gigas* exploitation on many of the lower limestone islands and islets (Antczak et al. 2018; Bonnisssent 2013; Hoogland & Hofman 2015). In later periods conch fishing was a prominent mode of existence and often the meat and shells, which were worked into tools, were transported over hundreds of kilometers (Antczak & Antczak 2006; Hofman et al. 2019a). Flint, another important commodity, was similarly transported over long distances early on from the few sources in the Lesser and Greater Antilles (Hofman et al. 2019a; Hofman & Hoogland 2011; Knippenberg 2007; Rodríguez Ramos 2010).

Resource procurement during the Archaic is suggestive of yearly mobility cycles during which communities island hopped on a seasonal basis (Hofman et al. 2006, 2019a; Rivera Collazo 2011). The toolkit included stone, shell, coral, and bone tools with multifunctional uses (Gijn et al. 2008). The neolithization of the insular Caribbean should be seen as a gradual process starting during the Archaic Age (Hofman et al. 2018a). Domesticates like manioc, beans, maize, sweet potato, and arrowroot, together with wild yam, palm, arrowhead, renealmia, and wild bean, suggest that these were cultivated by 6000 BC, while various Antillean wild plants and crops were also used and exploited (Pagán Jiménez 2011; Pagán Jiménez et al. 2015). Maize and zamia have been revealed to have been much more important in the precolonial Caribbean than previously thought, and also more important than manioc in many cases (Mickleburgh & Pagán Jiménez 2012, Pagán Jiménez 2011). Pottery was also produced in Late Archaic Age contexts on some of the Greater Antilles and the offshore islands of the Venezuelan coast (Hoogland & Hofman 2015; Ulloa Hung & Valcárcel Rojas 2002; Rodríguez Ramos et al. 2008).

The diversity of human agency reflected in the archaeological record, is the result of complex fissions and fusions of peoples (Hofman et al. 2019a). Between the fourth and first millennia BC a new wave of immigrants from the South American mainland established large and relatively permanent settlements on the islands between Trinidad and Puerto Rico. The sea route taken to Puerto Rico is not yet clear, but in the space of a few centuries the entire Lesser Antillean archipelago became a dynamic landscape with peoples moving between the islands and the mainland shores (Fitzpatrick 2013; Hofman et al. 2007). The great environmental variety, the diversified distribution of natural resources, the seaward orientation of the indigenous communities, and the complexities of social interaction—friendly or warlike—formed the basis for a dynamic, highly interconnected island world. Long-lasting social relationships with mainland communities as well as among near and more distant islanders of varied sociopolitical complexities (ranging from local groups to hierarchical societies) both consolidated and shifted over time.

The Bahamas as well as the islands of the Greater Antilles west of Puerto Rico (Hispaniola, Jamaica, & Cuba) were increasingly populated by AD 600–800 and some developed around AD 1000 into what the Spanish interpreted as a sociopolitical organization headed by leading personalities or *caciques*. Based on the European chroniclers, five *cacicazgos* are thought to have existed in Hispaniola at the time of contact (Wilson 1990). In the northwestern Dominican Republic, villages at the time consisted of round houses (between 4 and 9 meters in diameter) with two rows of posts and surrounded by earthworks and multifunctional mounds or *montículos* sometimes two meters in height, reflecting the domestic and ritual activities of each household (Hofman & Hoogland 2015). Some sites include small circular *montones*, which were for the planting of root crops (López Belando 2012). Plots of land with hundreds of *montones*, irrigation channels, and terracing are mentioned in early colonial European sources (Newsom & Wing 2004; Oviedo y Valdéz 1851). Paleoenvironmental records in the central Cibao valley show the impact of these economic activities in the island's ecology (Castilla-Beltrán et al. 2018). Intercommunity gatherings were organized in ceremonial centers with large plazas or ball courts, as known from Puerto and Hispaniola (Curet & Torres 2010; Oliver 1998; Wilson 1990, 2007).

As a result of the misinterpretation of varied historical, anthropological and archaeological information, the peoples of the Greater Antilles and the Bahamian archipelago became known as Taíno, Macorige, Lucayo, Ciboney, and Guanahatabey. Many of these labels are now contested (Keegan & Hofman 2017; Petitjean Roget 2015). The Lesser Antilles were pictured to be inhabited by a different, much more fierce people, known as Caribes (Hofman et al. 2008). But also other peoples such as Igneri or Eñeri were recorded, and French chroniclers introduced the term Island Carib (Caraïbe Insulaire) to differentiate the Lesser Antillean islanders from the mainland Carib (Breton 1665, 1666). The Kalinago still inhabiting some of these islands are likely the descendants of a regrouping of peoples that took place as a result of the Spanish conquest and attacks in the region (Mans 2018; Taylor & Hoff 1980).

Genomic reconstruction of a 1,000-year-old Bahamian individual from Eleuthera points to northern South America as the place of origin of the indigenous peoples inhabiting the Bahamas during precolonial times (Schroeder et al. 2018). Long-distance migration from northern South America is evident in some individuals (Laffoon 2012), indicating that the connections with the homeland were maintained over the centuries. Isotope data from burial assemblages of the Greater and Lesser Antilles indicate that immigrants were common at most sites and that the proportion of immigrants was substantial. Isotopic and chronological data are consistent with the migrations of individuals from disparate origins over several generations (Laffoon & de Vos 2011). Immigrants were also found more likely than locals to be interred with exotic, imported, or unique grave goods, which in several cases were found exclusively with immigrant females (Hoogland et al. 2010). The practice of intentional cranial modification—or head shaping—first appears in the Caribbean Amerindian societies in the skeletal material and iconography of the first Ceramic

Age communities, suggesting that the practice was introduced to the islands at the time of the grand-scale migrations from northern South America between 400 and 200 BC (Duijvenbode 2017; Pina Peña 1972; Crespo Torres 2005). From its introduction, the practice spread across the entire Caribbean and was prevalent in many populations at the time of the first European encounters, when it rapidly declined (Duijvenbode 2017). The practice of modifying the skull at childhood is most likely associated with the expression of a shared group identity.

Burial practices reflect a complex, diversified pattern, with single and composite burials, primary and secondary internments and manipulation of skeletal remains (Hoogland & Hofman 2013; Mickleburgh et al. 2019). The distribution patterns of ceramic, lithic, shell, coral, and bone objects, as well as plants across the islands suggest the integration of the precolonial archipelagic communities into a millennia-old network of local, regional and pan-regional interaction spheres (e.g., Hofman & Bright 2010; Hofman & Hoogland 2011; Knippenberg 2007; Laffoon et al. 2014). These networks, incorporating varied settlement locations and resource bases, were likely important in providing security in periods of environmental, climatic or social challenges. Ceramic repertoires similarly reflect a high degree of heterogeneity between circa 400–200 BC and European contact (Keegan & Hofman 2017; Rouse 1992; Wilson 2007). This heterogeneity is indicative of intensive social interaction, cross marriage, and the exchange of goods and ideas (Hofman 2013; Hofman & Hoogland 2011; Ulloa Hung 2014).

Other materials also speak to extensive interregional connections. Materials and finished objects that were exchanged include ornamental beads and pendants of semiprecious stones, green stone (blue schist, jadeitite), celts, polishing implements, paraphernalia, and raw lithic material. Geochemical signatures of lithic material point to transport over long distances throughout the Ceramic Age (García-Casco et al. 2013). *Guanín*, a gold/copper alloy, was exchanged through networks extending from Colombia and other parts of northern South America into the islands (Siegel & Severin 1993; Cooper et al. 2008; Valcárcel Rojas & Martinón Torres 2013). Gold and *guanín* played central roles in social interaction and in negotiating power relations, and are one expression of increasing social complexity (Oliver 2000).

The Columbian Turn: Exploitation and Enslavement

The precolonial networks were disrupted by the arrival of the Europeans in 1492. Spanish colonizers took advantage of indigenous networks and knowledge in a rapid dispersion across the Caribbean Sea and into the rest of the Americas. Northern

Hispaniola was one of the first areas in the Americas where extensive confrontations between the Amerindians and Europeans took place (Hofman et al. 2018b). It was here that they fashioned practices of subjugation and enslavement of indigenous peoples. Following Columbus's second voyage in 1493, the Spanish promoted and intensified the exchange of goods with the indigenous peoples in the interior of Hispaniola (Hofman et al. 2018b; Keehnen 2019). For the Europeans, these exchanges were mechanisms to establish alliances with indigenous *caciques*. They obtained favors and information on sources of gold, while attempting to maintain a favorable image for the communities that they encountered. More than 300 archaeological sites have recently been recorded in northern Hispaniola (Hofman et al. 2018b). The settlement patterns, management of space, and the material culture allude to the social and cultural diversity of the region that Europeans experienced at the time of contact (Herrera-Malatesta 2018; Hofman & Hoogland 2015; Sonnemann et al. 2016; Ulloa Hung 2014). The archaeological record provides a view of a connected and interactive landscape that subsequently provided the foundation for colonial domination. Amerindian-European encounters led to the creation of new social identities and material culture repertoires (Deagan 2004; Hofman et al. 2012, 2018b; Samson et al. 2016; Valcárcel Rojas et al. 2014). The Amerindians received beads, bells, broken bowls, glass, metals, canvas shirts, and colored cloths in exchange for gold ornaments, foodstuffs, cotton, and exotic birds. These items are in some instances associated with local ritual paraphernalia,

Figure 3.2. Late-fifteenth to early-sixteenth-century Spanish materials mixed with indigenous objects in Amerindian sites in Hispaniola. (Drawing by Erick van Driel. Photographs by Corinne Hofman and Menno Hoogland)

suggesting integration of foreign items into existing sociocultural practices and existing value systems (Ernst & Hofman 2015; Keehnen 2011, 2019; Samson 2010) (see fig. 3.2). The number of such European objects at indigenous sites is very low (ratio of 100 to 40,000) (Keegan pers. communication 2016). In contrast, bones of European animal species like the domesticated pig and rats are found in significant numbers (Deagan 2004). Domesticates were incorporated into the local cuisine, representing a key marker indicating changes in social and cultural identity (Beaudry 2013; Ernst & Hofman 2019; van der Veen 2006).

Turning to Columbus's third and fourth voyages (1498–1502), the remaining areas of the Caribbean were sighted, while the first expeditions to the Pearl Coast of northern Venezuela were made. The early sixteenth century saw the massive forced movement of indigenous populations across the Caribbean and adjacent mainland(s), and their enslavement (Sued Badillo 1995; Valcárcel Rojas 2016[b]). They were put to work in the goldmines and on the sugar estates of Hispaniola, Cuba, and Puerto Rico, and in the pearl fisheries of Cubagua. In the Greater Antilles the *encomienda* system institutionalized a pattern of intensive exploitation that disarticulated indigenous societies and transformed their sociocultural practices. The early sixteenth-century site of El Chorro de Maíta in northeastern Cuba was likely an *encomienda* village, in which an indigenous community headed by an indigenous leader in charge of mobilizing the assessed tribute and labor was put under European control (Arranz Márquez 1991; Valcárcel Rojas 2016[a]). More than 120 individuals were found buried in a graveyard, presumably next to the village. Isotopic and genetic studies indicate that the burials include individuals of Amerindian, European, and African descent, as well as immigrants from Central America (Laffoon 2012). The mortuary practices attest to a mixture of Amerindian and European traditions. A decline in traditional cranial modification in the nonadult individuals buried in the cemetery is probably the result of significant changes in indigenous identity in the early colonial period (Duijvenbode 2017). Contrary to the late precolonial practice of internment in a flexed position, the Europeans buried their dead in a stretched position with the arms crossing the chest, as the Christian belief system demanded (Valcárcel Rojas 2016a). The latter practice is found in nearly 10 percent of the Chorro de Maíta burials, including Amerindians. Several Amerindian individuals were interred with European metal objects, such as brass aglets, indicating that they were probably dressed in European clothing. Others were buried with European brass implements as well as local Caribbean or Colombian gold ornaments (Cooper et al. 2008; Valcárcel Rojas et al. 2011; Valcárcel Rojas 2016[a]). The encomienda at El Chorro de Maíta is exemplary of the transformative situation during the early sixteenth century when Amerindian settlements were subordinated by the Spanish and supplemented by nonlocal Amerindian and African slaves. Coerced by European colonizers, they were forced to accept Christian customs and traditions and provide labor for Spanish colonial enterprises. The interregional interactions are indicative of a cross-Caribbean and cross-Atlantic reorientation of earlier indigenous networks (Hofman et al. 2014; Valcárcel Rojas et al. 2013). The site represents an encounter in which Caribbean societies and cultures were radically changed but where indigenous agents (re)negotiated aspects of their preencounter identities and their material expressions (Hofman et al. 2014).

Gold and Pearls

The main centers of Amerindian enslaved labor were the Spanish towns of Nueva Cádiz de Cubagua, located off the coast of Venezuela, and the towns of La Concepción de la Vega, and Cotuí on Hispaniola (Antczak et al. 2019; Olsen Bogaert 2015). Nueva Cádiz de Cubagua was a hub of pearl extraction, while Cotuí was the site of one of the first gold mines and La Concepción de la Vega a gold-processing center (Olsen Bogaert 2015).

The material culture in these sites reflects Amerindian, Spanish, and African intercultural dynamics (Ernst & Hofman 2019). The production and use of local and regional pottery continues, though in new ways (see also Cusick 1991 for similar observations at En Bas Saline, Haiti). Major changes are apparent in vessel forms, decorative patterns, surface treatment, and function. New vessel shapes resembling Spanish, African, and Central or South American prototypes emerged, sometimes made using traditional coiling techniques and in other instances using the newly introduced European potter's wheel (see fig. 3.3 on page 64). The influx of various nonlocal peoples after the foundation of the Spanish towns impacted the developmental trajectories of the indigenous populations and forged new forms of socio-material interactions (Deagan 2004; Ortega & Fondeur Ortega 1978; Ting et al. 2018).

The presence of locally made, Spanish-style vessels may reflect an attempt to maintain an Iberian lifestyle in the colonies. Vessels with both Amerindian and African influences are predominantly found in kitchen and cooking areas, both spaces were of high importance for the creation of early colonial transcultural sociality (Deagan 2004; Ernst & Hofman 2019).

Figure 3.3. Intercultural ceramics at the sixteenth-century site of La Vega, Dominican Republic. (Photographs by Marlieke Ernst, Corinne Hofman and Menno Hoogland)

Kalinago Strongholds

The Kalinago society in the Windward Islands of the Lesser Antilles presents another example of colonial encounter. Most of the islands of the Caribbean were settled by the Spanish in the course of the sixteenth century, but their lack of interest in the Lesser Antilles and their failed ventures at settlement left these islands beyond their control (see fig. 3.4). Columbus first heard of on the man-eating Caribes in the fearsome accounts of the indigenous peoples he encountered in Hispaniola. They mentioned the repeated pillaging of their settlements by Caribes living to the southeast (Allaire 2013; Hofman & Hoogland 2012, 2018; Hofman et al. 2019b; Hulme 1986; Hulme & Whitehead 1992; Keegan & Hofman 2017). During the early years of the conquest, the Spanish raided the Lesser Antilles for slaves and from 1503 Real Cédulas were issued by the Spanish Crown, legally permitting the capture of indigenous slaves in these *islas inútiles* or "useless islands." The Lesser Antilles, though, also functioned as a refuge for peoples from islands to the North, as well as the South American mainland, who then in some cases served as "middlemen" in trade between the Spanish Caribbean and continental South America (Hofman & Hoogland 2018; Hofman et al. 2019b).

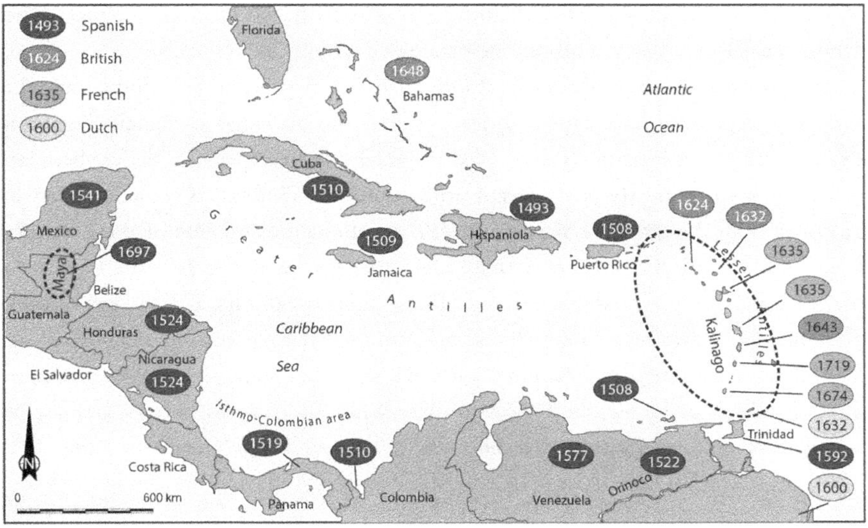

Figure 3.4. Initial European colonization and settlement of the insular Caribbean and adjacent parts of coastal Central and South America. (Map by Corinne Hofman and Menno Hoogland)

Approximately 130 to 150 years passed until other European nations permanently settled in these small islands despite fierce Kalinago resistance. The latter claimed origin from the mainland and lived in a series of strongholds between Tobago and St. Christopher (St. Kitts). St. Kitts was the first island of the Lesser Antilles to be settled by Europeans, initially the English in 1623, and then by the French in 1625. Subsequently, Guadeloupe and Martinique were occupied by the French in 1643, while Grenada was only settled by the French in 1649. St. Vincent and Dominica were not officially colonized as these islands were designated as "neutral" and left in the possession of the Kalinago until the eighteenth century (Hofman & Hoogland 2018; Hofman et al. 2019b). Archaeologically, the existence of the Kalinago has long been contested because of the lack of evidence. It was only in the late 1980s and early 1990s that archaeologists identified the Cayo ceramic complex with links to the Guianas on the South American mainland. The location, and chronological and cultural associations of the Cayo sites allows them to be associated with the historically known Kalinago (Boomert 1986; Hofman 2013; Hofman & Hoogland 2012; Keegan & Hofman 2017). Of the approximately twenty known Cayo sites, the majority is located on St. Vincent, Grenada, and Dominica (Bright 2011; Hofman & Hoogland 2012) (see fig. 3.5).

Recent excavations at the early colonial sites of Argyle on St. Vincent and La Poterie on Grenada, have provided new insights into Kalinago settlement organization, burial practices, and its associated material culture repertoire dating between the late fifteenth and the early seventeenth centuries (Hofman & Hoogland 2018; Hofman et al. 2019b). The sites are located on the windward side of these islands, facing the Atlantic Ocean, on elevated plateaus near water courses. The layouts of the settlements are very similar to early European descriptions of Kalinago villages. They include a communal men's house and family dwellings around a central plaza. Several small rectangular structures were scattered between the houses (Boomert 2009; Hofman & Hoogland 2012; Hofman et al. 2015). Cayo pottery was largely locally produced, suggesting that this was not an exchange item but rather that

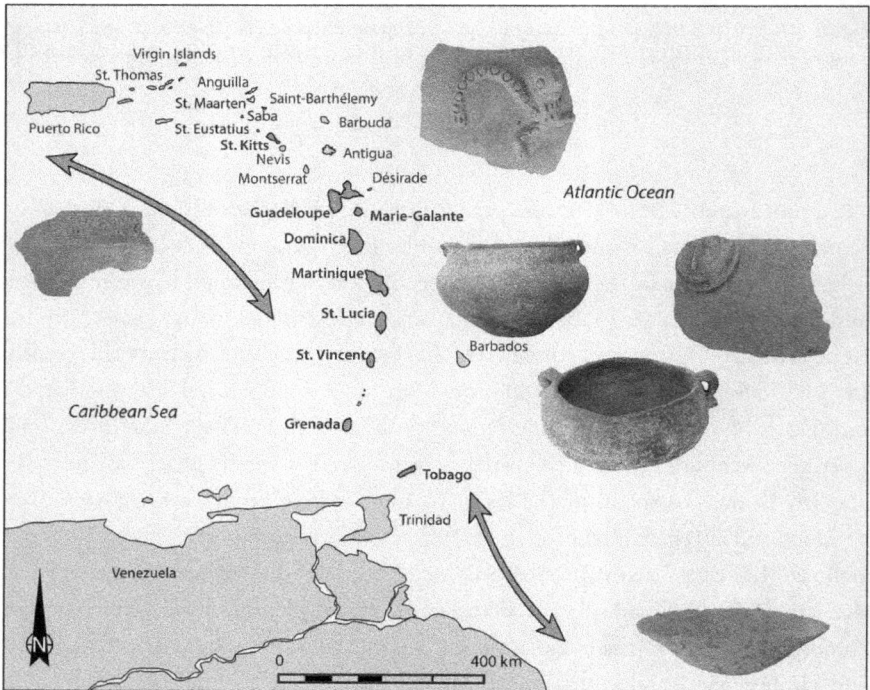

Figure 3.5. Kalinago strongholds in the Lesser Antilles based on archaeological evidence and historic documents. (Figure by Corinne Hofman and Menno Hoogland)

potters moved from the mainland bringing with them their knowledge (Scott et al. 2018). The presence of nonlocal, perforated peccary and tapir teeth, which were used as pendants, as well as flutes from deer bone, attest for continuing exchange with South America. In the late sixteenth century, a pattern of exchange developed between the Kalinago and several European nations. Most of this trade took place with Spanish ships, or along the coast of the Guianas, known as the Wild Coast, where the Dutch had settled since the early 1600s. Goods imported from Europe were integrated in the indigenous assemblages and there is evidence of mixing of local and nonlocal practices within one single object. The Kalinago strongholds participated in a complex trans-Atlantic system that started from the combination of new colonial and trade strategies with preexisting indigenous exchange and alliance networks (Hofman et al. 2014; Shafie et al. 2017). Kalinago communities were surrounded by the expanding territories of the new European colonial powers, but enjoyed a high degree of local autonomy and the ability to renegotiate new colonial realities (Hofman et al. 2014). Portions of the Lesser Antilles participated in the last phase of indigenous resistance to the colonial powers. By 1800, the remaining indigenous populations became a marginalized group, but they retained an important though underestimated role in the plantation economy of the islands (Hauser 2015). Today, descendants of the Kalinago live throughout the Lesser Antilles, notably on Dominica, St. Vincent, and Trinidad, where they actively claim their Amerindian origins as an integral part of their identity in Caribbean society (Boomert 2016; (Hofman & Hoogland 2018; Hofman et al. 2019b; Honychurch 2000).

Amerindian-African-European Intercultural Dynamics

Escaped African slaves were also absorbed into indigenous communities in varied ways. On St. Vincent, increasing numbers of escaped Africans led to the formation of villages with a Black Carib identity next to Kalinago communities that remained purely Amerindian (Yellow Carib). After several wars with the English, many Black Carib were deported to Central America in 1791, where they still identify as Garifuna. They retain strong links with the Garifuna of St. Vincent. Kalinago on other islands of the Lesser Antilles such as Grenada are known to have taken both Africans and Europeans as captives, shaving their hair and piercing their ears as signs of enslavement. The intercultural nature of Kalinago communities is illustrated by the ceramic assemblage from the site of La Poterie, Grenada.

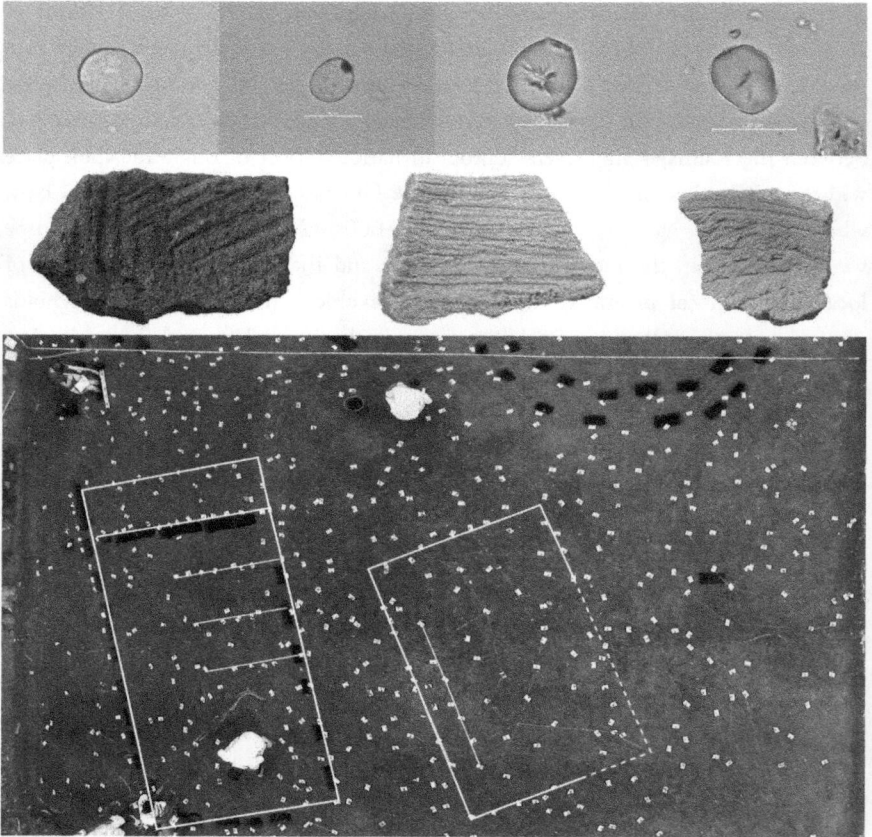

Figure 3.6. Rectangular structures, pottery, and starch grains indicative of indigenous–Afro-Caribbean–European interactions at the archaeological site of La Poterie, Grenada, around AD 1700. The pottery fragments are possibly from a grinding pot, with starches of manioc, peppers, and wheat/barley. (Photographs of ceramics and floorplan by Corinne Hofman and Menno Hoogland. Photographs of starch grains by Jaime Pagán Jiménez)

The pottery appears to be a blend of Amerindian and African cultural traditions within a setting of the eighteenth-century European plantation economy. Indigenous continuity in the ceramics is indicated by the selection of clays, temper, and use of the coiling technique, but major changes are shown in vessel forms, decoration motifs, surface treatment, and function. Starch grain analysis, by Jaime Pagán Jiménez, on a ceramic piece, identified as a pepper grinding pot, revealed the combination of chili pepper, manioc, and wheat (possibly barley) starches, thus reflecting a true blend of such cultural traditions (see fig. 3.6).

Conclusion:
Continuity and Change in the Indigenous Caribbean

This deep history of the Caribbean reviewed provides a broad sketch of the transformations of the island networks, cultures, and societies across the prehistorical/historical divide. Our studies reveal the existence of a complex and diverse sociocultural landscape on the eve of the colonial encounters. The spheres or lines of social interaction among the indigenous communities, from precolonial moments on, cemented a regional history marked by coexistence, interaction, and transculturation. Caribbean networks of mobility and exchange were shaped by expanding and contracting group territories, fission and fusion of local communities, variable degrees of sociopolitical integration, and differential responses to the colonial encounter, all of which were fundamental in the shaping of modern society. The persistence of indigenous cultural traditions and knowledge in present-day Caribbean society strongly counters the idea of substitution, displacement, or disappearance, as is suggested by traditional historiographies. Amerindian-African-European intercultural dynamics are still mirrored in today's locally produced Afro-Caribbean earthenware (Hauser & Handler 2009; Hofman & Bright 2004). Indigenous elements are also visible in the extensive use of forms of traditional agriculture (slash-and-burn, *conucos*), house building, an array of cultural traditions, ritual practices, as well as in the intensive use of indigenous plant species for economic and curative purposes, all aspects that constitute an important part of everyday life in the Caribbean today (Hofman et al. 2018b; Pesoutova & Hofman 2016).

Acknowledgments

The research leading to these results has received funding from the Netherlands Organization for Scientific Research (Island Networks project grant nr. 319020) and the European Research Council under the European Union's Seventh Framework Programme (FP7/2007-2013)/ERC-NEXUS1492 grant agreement no. 319209. I wish to acknowledge the NEXUS1492 team members and members of the Caribbean Research Group at Leiden for their contributions, which led to many of the publications cited in this text. I especially thank Menno Hoogland, with whom I have conducted all the fieldwork in the Caribbean over the past thirty years. He is the codesigner and producer of all the figures in this paper. I would like to express my gratitude to my BA, MA, and PhD students, who participated in the different excavations and laboratory work since 1987, but above all to the indigenous and local communities in the various islands for collaborating in our projects and exchange of knowledge. I would like to thank Arie Boomert, Alvaro Castilla-Beltrán, and Finn van der Leden for their editorial help. The finalizing of this chapter was supported by a fellowship from The Netherlands Institute for Advanced Study in the Humanities and Social Sciences (NIAS).

Works Cited

Allaire, Louis. 2013. "Ethnohistory of the Caribs." In *The Oxford Handbook of Caribbean Archaeology*. Edited by William F. Keegan, Corinne L. Hofman, and Reniel Rodríguez Ramos, 97–108. New York: Oxford University Press.

Anderson-Córdova, Karen F. 2017. *Surviving Spanish Conquest. Indian Fight, Flight, and Cultural Transformation in Hispaniola and Puerto Rico*. Tuscaloosa: University of Alabama Press.

Antczak Andrzej T. 2019. Marlena M. Antczak, and Oliver Antczak. "Rancherías: Historical Archaeology of Early Colonial Campsites on Margarita and Coche Islands, Venezuela." In *Material Encounters and Indigenous Transformations in the Early Colonial Americas*. Edited by Corinne L. Hofman and Floris W. M. Keehnen, 144–172. Leiden, the Netherlands/New York: Brill.

Antczak, Andrzej T., Jay B. Haviser, Menno L. P. Hoogland, Arie Boomert, Raymundo A. C. F. Dijkhoff, Harold J. Kelly, Marlena M. Antczak, and Corinne L. Hofman. 2018. "Early Horticulturalists of the Southern Caribbean." In *Early Farmers of the Caribbean and Circum-Caribbean*. Edited by Basil A. Reid, 113–46. London: Routledge.

Antczak, Marlena M., and Andrzej T. Antczak. 2006. *Los Ídolos de las Islas Prometidas: Arqueología Prehispánica del Archipiélago de Los Roques*. Caracas, Venezuela: Editorial Equinoccio.

Arranz Márquez, Luis. 1991. *Repartimientos y Encomiendas en la Isla Española (El Repartimiento de Alburquerque de 1514)*. Madrid, Spain: Ediciones de la Fundación García Arévalo.

Bhabha, Homi K. 1994. *The Location of Culture*. London: Routledge.

Beaudry, Mary C. 2013. "Mixing Food, Mixing Cultures: Archaeological Perspectives." *Archaeological Review from Cambridge* 28(1): 285–97.

Bonnissent, Dominique. 2013. *Les gisements précolombiens de la Baie Orientale. Campements du Mésoindien et du Néoindien sur l'île de Saint-Martin (Petites Antilles)*. Paris: Documents d'archéologie française 17. Editions de la Maison des Sciences de L'homme.

Boomert, Arie. 1986. "The Cayo Complex of St. Vincent: Ethnohistorical and Archaeological Aspects of the Island-Carib Problem." *Antropológica* 66: 3–68.

———. 2009. "Searching for Cayo in Dominica." *Proceedings of the XXIIIrd Congress of the International Association of Caribbean Archaeology*, Antigua.

———. 2016. *The Indigenous Peoples of Trinidad and Tobago: From the First Settlers until Today.* Leiden, The Netherlands: Sidestone Press.

Braudel Fernand. 1949. *La Méditerranée et le monde méditerranéen à l'époque de Philippe II.* Paris: Armand Colin.

Breton, Raymond. 1665. *Dictionnaire caraibe-françois.* Auxerre, France: Gilles Bouquet.

———. 1666. Dictionnaire françois-caraibe-. Auxerre, France: Gilles Bouquet.

Bright, Alistair J. 2011. "Blood Is Thicker than Water: Amerindian intra- and inter-insular relationships and social organization in the pre-Colonial Windward Islands." PhD dissertation. Leiden, The Netherlands: Sidestone Press.

Castilla-Beltrán, Alvaro, Henri Hooghiemstra, Menno L. P. Hoogland, Jaime Pagán-Jiménez, J., Bas van Geel, Mike H. Field, Maarten Prins, Timme Donders, Eduardo Herrera Malatesta, Jorge Ulloa Hung, Crystal McMichael, Will Gosling, and Corinne L. Hofman. 2018. Columbus' Footprint in Hispaniola: A Paleoenvironmental Record of Indigenous and Colonial Impacts on the Landscape of the Central Cibao Valley, northern Dominican Republic. *Anthropocene* 22: 66–80.

Cooper, Jago, Marcos Martinón-Torres, and Roberto Valcárcel Rojas. 2008. "American Gold and European Brass: Metal Objects and Indigenous Values in the Cemetery of el Chorro de Maíta, Cuba." In *Crossing the Borders: New Methods and Techniques in the Study of Archaeological Materials from the Caribbean.* Edited by Corinne L. Hofman, Menno L. P. Hoogland, and Annelou L. van Gijn, 34–42. Tuscaloosa: Alabama: Alabama University Press.

Crespo Torres, Edwin F., ed. 2005. *La cultura huecoide y su conexión con la introducción de la práctica de la deformación cefálica intencional en las antillas.* San Juan: Universidad de Puerto Rico, Recinto de Río Piedras.

Curet, Luis A., and Joshua M. Torres. 2010. "Plazas, Bateys, and Ceremonial Centers: The Social and Cultural Context of Tibes in the Ancient History of Puerto Rico." In *Tibes: People, Power, and Ritual at the Center of the Cosmos.* Edited by Luis A. Curet and Lisa, 261–86. M. Stringer. Tuscaloosa: University of Alabama Press.

Curet, Luis A., and Mark W. Hauser. 2011. *Islands at the Crossroads: Migration, Seafaring, and Interaction in the Caribbean.* Tuscaloosa: University of Alabama Press.

Cusick, James G. 1991. Culture Change and Pottery change in a Taino Village, *Proceedings of the XIIIth International Congress for Caribbean Archaeology,* Curaçao, 446–61.

Deagan, Kathleen A. 2004. "Reconsidering Taino Social Dynamics after Spanish Conquest: Gender and Class in Culture Contact Studies." American Antiquity, 69(4): 597–626.

Duijvenbode, Anne van. 2017. "Facing Society: A Study of Identity through Head Shaping Practices among the Indigenous Peoples of the Caribbean in the Ceramic age and Colonial Period. PhD dissertation, Leiden University, Leiden.

Ernst, Marlieke, and Corinne L. Hofman 2015. "Shifting Values: A Study of Early European Trade Wares in the Amerindian Site of El Cabo, Eastern Dominican Republic." In

Global Pottery 1: Historical Archaeology and Archaeometry for Societies in Contact. Edited by J. Buxeda, M. M. I. Fernández, and J. G. Iñañez, 195–204. Oxford, UK: BAR publishing.

———. 2019. "Breaking and Making Identities: Transformations of Ceramic Repertoires in Early Colonial Hispaniola." In *Material Encounters and Indigenous Transformations in the Early Colonial Americas.* Edited by Corinne L. Hofman and Floris W. M. Keehnen, 122–143. Leiden, The Netherlands/New York: Brill.

Fitzpatrick, Scott M., and William F. Keegan. 2007. "Human Impacts and Adaptations in the Caribbean Islands: An Historical Ecology Approach." *Royal Society of Edinburgh Scotland Foundation* 98(1): 29–45.

———. 2013. "Seafaring Capabilities in the Pre-Columbian Caribbean." *Journal of Maritime Archaeology* 8(1): 101–38.

Garcia-Casco, Antonio, Sebastiaan Knippenberg, Reniel Rodríguez Ramos, George E. Harlow, Corinne L. Hofman, José Carlos Pomo, and Idael F. Blanco-Quintero. 2013. "Pre-Columbian Jadeitite Artifacts from the Golden Rock Site, St. Eustatius, Lesser Antilles, with Special Reference to Jadeitite Artifacts from Elliot's, Antigua: Implications for Potential Source Regions and Long-Distance Exchange Networks in the Greater Caribbean." *Journal of Archaeological Science* 40: 3153–69.

Gijn, Annelou L. van, Yvonne Lammers-Keijsers, and Iris Briels. 2008. "Tool Use and Technological Choices: An Integral Approach toward Functional Analysis of Caribbean Tool Assemblages." In *Crossing the Borders: New Methods and Techniques in the Study of Archaeological Materials from the Caribbean.* Edited by Corinne L. Hofman, Menno L. P. Hoogland, and Annelou L. van Gijn, 101–14. Tuscaloosa: University of Alabama Press.

Hauser, Marks. W. 2015. "The Infrastructure of Nature's Island: Settlements, Networks and Economy of Two Plantations in Colonial Dominica." *International Journal of Historical Archaeology* 19 (3): 601–22.

Hauser, Mark W., and Jerome Handler. 2009. "Change in Small Scale Pottery Manufacture in Antigua, West Indies." *African Diaspora Archaeology Newsletter* 12 (4): 1.

Herrera Malatesta Eduardo N. 2018. *Una isla, dos mundos: estudio arqueológico sobre el paisaje indígena de Haytí y su transformación al paisaje colonial de La Española (1200–1550).* Leiden, The Netherlands: Sidestone Press.

Hofman, Corinne L. 2013. "The Post-Saladoid in the Lesser Antilles (A.D. 600/800–1492)." In *The Oxford Handbook of Caribbean Archaeology.* Edited by William F. Keegan, Corinne L. Hofman, and Reniel Rodríguez Ramos, 205–20. New York: Oxford University Press.

Hofman, Corinne L., Arie Boomert, Alistair J. Bright, Menno L. P. Hoogland, Sebastiaan Knippenberg and Alice V. M. Samson. 2011. "Ties with the Homeland(s): Archipelagic Interaction and the Enduring Role of the South and Central American Mainlands in the Pre-Columbian Lesser Antilles." In *Islands at the Crossroads: Migration, Seafaring and Interaction in the Caribbean*, 73–86. Edited by Luis A. Curet and Mark W. Hauser. Tuscaloosa: University of Alabama Press.

Hofman, Corinne L., Lewis Borck, Emma Slayton, and Menno L. P. Hoogland. 2019a. "Archaic Age Voyaging, Networks, and Resource Mobility around the Caribbean Sea." In *Early Settlers of the Caribbean. Dearchaizing the Archaic*. Edited by Corinne L. Hofman and Andrzej T. Antczak, 356–381. Leiden, The Netherlands: Sidestone Press.

Hofman, Corinne L., and Alistair J. Bright. 2010. "Towards a Pan-Caribbean Perspective of Pre-Colonial Mobility and Exchange: Preface to a Special Volume of the Journal of Caribbean Archaeology." *Journal of Caribbean Archaeology*, Special Publication 3: 1–3.

———. 2004. "From Suazoid to Folk Pottery: Pottery Manufacturing Traditions in a Changing Social and Cultural Environment on St. Lucia." *New West Indian Guide/ Nieuwe West-Indische Gids* 78(1–2): 73–104.

Hofman, Corinne L., Alistair J. Bright, Arie Boomert, and Sebastiaan Knippenberg. 2007. "Island Rhythms: The Web of Social Relationships and Interaction Networks in the Lesser Antillean Archipelago between 400 B.C. and A.D. 1492." *Latin American Antiquity* 18(3): 243–68.

Hofman, Corinne L., Alistair J. Bright, Menno L. P. Hoogland. 2006. Archipelagic Resource Procurement and Mobility in the Northern Lesser Antilles: The View from a 3000-Year-Old Tropical Forest Campsite on Saba. *Journal of Island and Coastal Archaeology* 1(2): 145–64.

Hofman, Corinne L., Alistair J. Bright, Menno L. P. Hoogland, and William F. Keegan. 2008. "Attractive Ideas, Desirable Goods: Examining the Late Ceramic Age Relationships between Greater and Lesser Antillean Societies." *Journal of Island and Coastal Archaeology* 3(1): 17–34.

Hofman, Corinne L., Gareth R. Davies, Ulrik Brandes, and Willem J. H. Willems. 2012. NEXUS 1492: New World Encounters in a Globalising World. ERC-Synergy Grant, Research Proposal, unpublished manuscript (NEXUS1492.eu).

Hofman, Corinne L., and Menno L. P. Hoogland. 2011. "Unravelling the Multi-Scale Networks of Mobility and Exchange in the Pre-Colonial Circum-Caribbean." In *Communities in Contact: Essays in Archaeology, Ethnohistory and Ethnography of the Amerindian Circum-Caribbean*. Edited by Corinne L. Hofman and Anne V. Duijvenbode, 14–44. Leiden, The Netherlands: Sidestone Press.

———. 2012. "Caribbean Encounters: Rescue Excavations at the Early Colonial Island Carib Site of Argyle, St. Vincent." *Analecta Praehistorica Leidensia* 43–44: 63–76.

———. 2015. "Investigaciones arqueológicas en los sitios El Flaco (Loma de Guayacanes) y La Luperona (Unijica)." *Informe pre-liminar. Boletin del Museo del Hombre Dominicano* 46 (42): 61–74.

———. 2018. *Arqueología y patrimonio de los Kalinago en las islas de San Vincente y Granada.* In *Arqueología y patrimonio de los Kalinago en las islas de San Vincente y Granada.* In De la desaparición a la permanencia. Indígenas e Indios en la Reinvencion del Caribe. Edited by Roberto Valcarcel Rojas and Jorge Ulloa Hung, 227–245. Instituto Tecnológico de Santo Domingo with Intec y Fundación García Arevalo.

Hofman, Corinne L., Menno L. P. Hoogland, John Angus Martin, and Arie Boomert. 2019b. "Colonial Encounters in the Southern Lesser Antilles: Indigenous Resistance, Material Transformations, and Diversity in an Ever-Globalizing World." In *Material Encounters and Indigenous Transformations in the Early Colonial Americas: Archaeological Case Studies.* Edited by Corinne L. Hofman and Floris Keehnen. Leiden, The Netherlands/New York: Brill.

Hofman, Corinne L., Menno L. P. Hoogland, and Benoit Roux. 2015. "Reconstruire le táboüi, le manná et les pratiques funéraires au village caraïbe d'Argyle, Saint-Vincent. » In *À la recherche du Caraïbe perdu : Les populations amérindiennes des Petites Antilles de l'époque précolombienne à la période coloniale.* Edited by Bernard Grunberg, 41–50. Paris: L'Harmattan.

Hofman, Corinne L., Angus A. A. Mol, Menno L. P. Hoogland, and Roberto Valcárcel Rojas. 2014. "Stage of Encounters: Migration, Mobility and Interaction in the Pre-Colonial and Early Colonial Caribbean." *World Archaeology* 46(4): 590–609.

Hofman, Corinne L., Reniel Rodríguez-Ramos, and Jaime R. Pagán-Jiménez. 2018a. "The 'Neolithisation' Process in the Northeastern Caribbean: Mobility and Social Interaction." In *Early Caribbean farmers.* Edited by Basil A. Reid, 71–97. London, UK: Routledge.

Hofman, Corinne L., Jorge Ulloa Hung, Eduardo Herrera Malatesta, Joseph S. Jean, and Menno L. P. Hoogland. 2018b. "Indigenous Caribbean Perspectives: Archaeologies and Legacies of the First Colonised Region in the New World." *Antiquity* 92(361): 200–16.

Honychurch, Lennox. 2000. *Carib to Creole: A History of Contact and Culture Exchange.* Roseau, Dominica: Dominica Institute.

Hoogland, Menno L. P., and Corinne L. Hofman. 2013. "From Corpse Taphonomy to Mortuary Behavior in the Caribbean." In *The Oxford Handbook of Caribbean Archaeology.* Edited by William F. Keegan, Corinne L. Hofman, and Reniel Rodríguez Ramos, 452–69. New York: Oxford University Press.

———. 2015. "Archaeological Assessment in Compliance with the Valetta Treaty, at Spaanse Water, Curaçao." In *Managing Our Past into the Future.* Edited by Corinne L. Hofman and Jay B. Haviser. Leiden, the Netherlands: Sidestone Press, 183–94.

Hoogland, Menno L., Corinne L. Hofman, and Raphael G. A. M. Panhuysen. 2010. "Inter-island Dynamics: Evidence for Human Mobility at the Site of Anse à la Gourde, Guadeloupe." In *Island Shores, Distant Pasts: Archaeological and Biological Approaches to the Pre-Columbian Settlement of the Caribbean*. Edited by Scott M. Fitzpatrick and Ann H. Ross, 148–62. Gainesville: University Press of Florida.

Hulme, Peter. 1986. *Colonial Encounters: Europe and the Native Caribbean*, 1492–1797. London, UK and New York: Methuen.

Hulme, Peter, and Neil L. Whitehead, eds. 1992. *Wild Majesty: Encounters with Caribs from Columbus to the Present Day—An Anthology*. Oxford, UK: Clarendon Press.

Keegan, William F., and Corinne L. Hofman. 2017. *The Caribbean before Columbus*. New York: Oxford University Press.

Keehnen, Floris W. M. 2011. "Conflicting Cosmologies: The Exchange of Brilliant Objects between the Taíno of Hispaniola and the Spanish." In *Communities in Contact: Essays in Archaeology, Ethnohistory and Ethnography of the Amerindian Circum-Caribbean*. Edited by Corinne L. Hofman and Anne van Duijvenbode, 253–68. Leiden, The Netherlands: Sidestone Press.

———. 2019. "Treating 'Trifles': The Indigenous Adoption of European Material Goods in Early Colonial Hispaniola (1492–1550)." In *Material Encounters and Indigenous Transformations in the Early Colonial Americas: Archaeological Case Studies*. Edited by Corinne L. Hofman and Floris W. M. Keehnen, 58–81. Leiden, The Netherlands/ New York: Brill.

Knippenberg, Sebastiaan. 2007. "Stone Artefact Production and Exchange among the Northern Lesser Antilles." ASLU series, Leiden, The Netherlands: Leiden University Press.

Laffoon, Jason E. (2012). Patterns of Paleomobility in the Ancient Antilles: An Isotopic Approach. PhD dissertation, Leiden University.

Laffoon, Jason, and Bart de Vos. 2011. "Diverse Origins, Similar Diets: An Integrated Isotopic Perspective from Anse à la Gourde, Guadeloupe." In *Communities in Contact: Essays in Archaeology, Ethnohistory and Ethnography of the Amerindian Circum-Caribbean*. Edited by Corinne L. Hofman and Anne van Duijvenbode, 187–204. Leiden, The Netherlands: Sidestone Press.

Laffoon, Jason E., Reniel Rodríguez-Ramos, Luis Chanlatte Baik, Yvonne Nargenes Storde, Miguel Rodríguez Lopez, Gareth R. Davies, and Corinne L. Hofman. 2014. "Long-Distance Exchange in the Precolonial Circum-Caribbean: A Multi-Isotope Study of Animal Tooth Pendants from Puerto Rico." *Journal of Anthropological Archaeology* 35: 220–33.

López Belando, Adolfo J. 2012. "El sitio arqueológico de Playa Grande, Río San Juan, María Trinidad Sánchez: Informe de las excavaciones arqueológicas campaña 2011–2012." Santo Domingo: Museo Del Hombre Dominicano.

Mans, Jimmy L. J. A. 2018. Centros indígenas de conexión en las islas occidentales de Sotavento (1493–1631). In De la desaparición a la permanencia. Indígenas e Indios en la Reinvencion del Caribe. Edited by Roberto Valcarcel Rojas and Jorge Ulloa

Hung, 145–174. Instituto Tecnológico de Santo Domingo with Intec y Fundación García Arevalo.

Mickleburgh Hayley L., Menno L. P. Hoogland, Jason E. Laffoon, Darlene A. Weston, Roberto Valcárcel Rojas, Anne van Duijvenbode, and Angus A. A. Mol. 2019. "Defining Non-normative Practices in a Diverse Funerary Record: Insights from the Caribbean." In *A Bioarchaeological Perspective of Atypical Mortuary Practices: A Geographic and Temporal Investigation*. Edited by Tracy K. Betsinger, Amy B. Scott, and Anastasia Tsaliki, vols. I and II. Gainesville: University Press of Florida.

Mickleburgh, Hayley L., and Jaime R. Pagán-Jiménez. 2012. "New Insights into the Consumption of Maize and Other Food Plants in the Pre-Columbian Caribbean from Starch Grains Trapped in Human Dental Calculus." *Journal of Archaeological Science* 39(7): 2468–78.

Mol, Angus. A. A. 2014. *A Socio-material Metwork Approach to Patterns of Homogeneity and Diversity in the Pre-colonial Period*. Leiden, The Netherlands: Sidestone Press.

Newsom, Lee A., and Elisabeth S. Wing. 2004. *On Land and Sea: Native American Uses of Biological Resources in the West Indies*. Tuscaloosa: University of Alabama Press.

Oliver, José R. 1998. El centro ceremonial de Caguana, Puerto Rico. Oxford, UK: British Archaeological Reports.

———. 2000. "Gold Symbolism among Caribbean Chiefdoms: Of Feathers, Çibas and Guanín Power among Taíno Elites." In *Pre-Columbian Gold in South America: Technology Style and Iconography*, 196–219. Edited by Colin McEwan. London, UK: British Museum Press.

Olsen Bogaert, Harold. 2015. "Arqueología en Cueva Balaguer: Pueblo Viejo de Cotuí." *Museo del Hombre Dominicano* 42(46): 109–40.

Ortega Elpidio, and Carmen Fondeur Ortega. 1978. *Estudio de la cerámica del período Indo-Hispánico de la Antigua Concepción de La Vega*. Santo Domingo, Dominican Republic: Taller, 1978.

Ortiz, Fernando. 1995. *Cuban counterpoint, tobacco and sugar*. Durham, NC: Duke University Press.

Oviedo y Valdez, Fernando de G. 1851. *Historia general y natural de las Indias, Islas y Tierra Firme del Mar Océano*. Madrid, Spain: Real Academia de la Historia.

Pagán-Jiménez, Jaime R. 2011. "Early Phytocultural Processes in the Precolonial Antilles: A Pan-Caribbean Survey for an Ongoing Starch Grain Research." In *Communities in Contact: Essays in Archaeology, Ethnohistory and Ethnography of the Amerindian Circum-Caribbean*. Edited by Corinne L. Hofman and Anne van Duijvenbode, 87–116. Leiden, The Netherlands: Sidestone Press.

Pagán-Jiménez, Jaime R., Reniel Rodríguez Ramos, Basil A. Reid, Martijn van den Bel, and Corinne L. Hofman. 2015. "Early Dispersals of Maize and Other Food Plants into the Southern Caribbean and Northeastern South America." *Quaternary Science Reviews* 123: 231–46.

Pesoutova, Jana, and Corinne L. Hofman. 2016. "La contribución indígena a la biografía del paisaje cultural de la República Dominicana: Una revisión preliminar." In *Indígenas e Indios en el Caribe Presencia, legado y studio*. Edited by Jorge Ulloa Hung and Roberto Valcárcel Rojas, 115–50. Santo Domingo, Dominican Republic: Instituto Tecnológico de Santo Domingo.

Petitjean Roget, Henri. 2015. *Tainos et Callinas des Antilles. Tome 1*. Basse-Terre, Guadeloupe: Association internationale d'archéologie de la Caraïbe.

Pina Peña, Plinio F. 1972. "Los períodos cronológicos de las culturas aborígenes en las Antillas Mayores." *Revista Dominicana de Antropología e Historia* 1(1): 165–79."

Rivera-Collazo, Isabel C. 2011. "Palaeoecology and Human Occupation during the Mid-Holocene in Puerto Rico: The Case of Angostura." In *Communities in Contact: Essays in Archaeology, Ethnohistory and Ethnography of the Amerindian Circum-Caribbean*. Edited by Corinne L. Hofman and Anne van Duijvenbode, 407–20. Leiden, The Netherlands: Sidestone Press.

Rodríguez-Ramos, Reniel. 2010. *Rethinking Puerto Rican Precolonial History*. Tuscaloosa: University of Alabama Press.

Rodríguez-Ramos, Reniel, Elvis Babilonia, Luis A. Curet, and Jorge Ulloa-Hung. 2008. "The Pre-Arawak Pottery Horizon in the Antilles: A New Approximation." *Latin American Antiquity* 19(1): 47–63.

Rouse, Irving B. 1992. *The Tainos: Rise and Decline of the People Who Greeted Columbus*. New Haven, CT: Yale University Press.

Samson, Alice V. M. 2010. "Renewing the House: Trajectories of Social Life in the Yucayeque (Community) of El Cabo, Higüey, Dominican Republic, AD 800 to 1504." Leiden, The Netherlands: Sidestone Press.

Samson, Alice V. M., Jago Cooper, and Josué Caamano-Dones. 2016. "European Visitors in Native Spaces: Using Palaeography to Investigate Religious Dynamics in the New World." *Latin American Antiquity* 27(4): 443–61.

Hannes, Schroeder, Martin Sikora, Skyan Gopalakrishnan, Lara M. Cassidy, Pierpaolo Maisano Desler, Marcela Sandoval Velasco, Joshua G. Shraiber, Simon Rasmussen, Julian R. Homburger, Maria D. Ávila-Arcos, Morton E. Allentoft, José V. Moreno-Mayar, Gabriel Renaud, Alaberto Gómez-Carballa, Jason E. Laffoon, Rachel J. A. Hopkins, Thomas F. G. Higham, Robert S. Carr, William C. Schaffer, Jane S. Day, Menno L. P. Hoogland, Anotonio Salas, Carlos D. Bustamante, Rasmus Nielsen, Daniel G. Bradley, Corinne L. Hofman, and Eske Willerslev. 2018. "Origins and Genetic Legacies of the Caribbean Taino." *Proceedings of the National Acadamy of Sciences of the United States of America*: 1–6.

Scott, Rebecca, Bert Neyt, Corinne L. Hofman, and Patrick Degryse. 2018. "Determining the Provenance of Cayo Pottery from Grenada, Lesser Antilles, Using Portable X-Ray Fluorescence Spectrometry. *Archaeometry*. https://doi.org/10.1111/arcm.12359.

Shafie, Termeh, David Schoch, Jimmy L. J. A. Mans, Corinne L. Hofman, and Ulrik Brandes. 2017. "Hypergraph Representations: A study of Carib Attacks on Colonial Forces, 1509–1700." *Journal of Historical Network Research* 1: 3–17.

Siegel, Peter E., ed. 2018. *Island Historical Ecology: Socionatural Landscapes of the Eastern and Southern Caribbean.* Oxford, UK and New York: Berghahn.

Siegel, Peter E., John G Jones, Deborah M. Pearsall, Nicholas P. Dunning, Pat Farrell, Neil A. Duncan, Jason H. Curtis, and Sushant K. Singh. 2015. "Paleoenvironmental Evidence for First Human Colonization of the Eastern Caribbean." *Quaternary Science Reviews* 129(1): 275–95.

Siegel Peter E., and Kenneth P. Severin. 1993. "The First Documented Prehistoric Gold-Copper Alloy Artefact from the West Indies." *Journal of Archaeological Science* 20: 67–79.

Sonnemann, Till F., Jorge Ulloa Hung, and Corinne L. Hofman. 2016. "Mapping Indigenous Settlement Topography in the Caribbean Using Drones." *Remote Sensing* 8(10): 791.

Sued Badillo, Jalil. 1995. "The Island Caribs: New Approaches to the Questions of Ethnicity in the Early Colonial Caribbean. In *Wolves from the Sea*. Edited by Neil L. Whitehead, 61–89. Leiden, The Netherlands: KITLV Press.

Taylor, Douglas R., and Berend J. Hoff. 1980. "The Linguistic Repertory of the Island-Carib in the Seventeenth Century: The Men's Language: A Carib Pidgin?" *International Journal of American Linguistics* 46(4): 301–12.

Ting, Carmen, Jorge Ulloa Hung, Corinne L. Hofman, and Patrick Degryse. 2018. "Indigenous Technologies and the Production of Early Colonial Ceramics in Dominican Republic." *Journal of Archaeological Science: Reports* 17: 47–57.

Ulloa Hung, Jorge. 2014. *Arqueología en la Línea Noroeste de La Española. Paisajes, cerámicas e interacciones.* Santo Domingo, Dominican Republic: Instituto Tecnológico de Santo Domingo.

Ulloa Hung, Jorge, and Roberto Valcárcel Rojas. 2002. *Cerámica temprana en el centro oriente de Cuba.* Santo Domingo, Dominican Republic: Ediciones Impresos View Graph.

———, eds. 2016. *Indígenas e Indios en el Caribe. Presencia, legado y estudio.* Santo Domingo, Dominican Republic: Instituto Tecnológico de Santo Domingo.

Valcárcel Rojas, Roberto. 2016a. *Archaeology of Early Colonial Interaction at El Chorro de Maíta, Cuba.* Gainesville: University Press of Florida.

———. 2016b. Cuba: "Indios después de Colón." In *Indígenas e Indios en el Caribe: Presencia, legado y studio.* Edited by Jorge Ulloa Hung and Roberto Valcárcel Rojas, 7–48. Santo Domingo, Dominican Republic: Instituto Tecnológico de Santo Domingo.

Valcárcel Rojas, Roberto, Menno L. P. Hoogland, and Corinne. L. Hofman. 2014. "Indios: Arqueología de una Nueva Identidad." In *Indios en Holguín*. Edited by Roberto Valcárcel Rojas and Hiram Perez, 20–42. Holguín, Cuba: Editorial La Mezquita.

Valcárcel Rojas, Roberto, and Marcos Martinón Torres. 2013. "Metals in the Indigenous Societies of the Insular Caribbean." In *The Oxford Handbook of Caribbean Archaeology* Edited by Keegan William F., Hofman Corinne L., Reniel Rodríguez Ramos, 504–24. New York: Oxford University Press.

Valcárcel Rojas Roberto, Alice V. M. Samson, and Menno L. P. Hoogland. 2013. "Indo-Hispanic Dynamics: From Contact to colonial Interaction in the Greater Antilles." *International Journal of Historical Archaeology* 17(1): 18–39.

Valcárcel Rojas, Roberto, Darlene A. Weston, Hayley L. Mickleburgh, and Jason E. Laffoon. 2011. "El Chorro de Maíta: A Diverse approach to a Context of Diversity." In *Communities in Contact: Essays in Archaeology, Ethnohistory and Ethnography of the Amerindian Circum-Caribbean*. Edited by Corinne L. Hofman and Anne van Duijvenbode, 225–52. Leiden, The Netherlands: Sidestone Press.

Van der Veen, James M. 2006. "Subsistence Patterns as Markers of Cultural Exchange: European and Taíno Interactions in the Dominican Republic." PhD dissertation, Indiana University, Bloomington.

Wilson, Samuel M. 1990. *Hispaniola: Caribbean chiefdoms in the age of Columbus*. Tuscaloosa: University of Alabama Press.

———. 2007. *The Archaeology of the Caribbean*. Cambridge, UK: Cambridge University Press.

Chapter 4

Rethinking Colonial Maya Peripherality

Colonial Frictions, Salvaged Value, and the Production of Modernity in Highland Guatemala

Guido Pezzarossi

The archaeology of colonialism and capitalism in early modern colonial contexts can at times get locked into what Tsing (2013)—in reference to globalization—calls following the Western "engineers" and their plans, and in the process losing sight of the unexpected worlds that emerged. Colonial narratives of "Conquest" and dominance, as well as historiographies of capitalism and colonialism that presume power differentials in advance can gloss encounters as the unmodified *imposition* of will, ideology, or plans on populations and environments.

While archaeologies of capitalism and colonialism have done well in highlighting how native/colonized populations were active agents within and against these imposed plans, within such framings, the colonized, and the exploited, are limited in their actions to only being able to react or resist in relation to an imposed structure, system, or regime. The argument against colonization-as-imposition seems appropriate when no clear-cut evidence of domination is available. DeCorse (2018) provides examples of West African English forts beholden to local polities that dictated the terms and structure of trade, as well as the very presence of the forts in the region. Richard White's (1991) concept of the "middle ground" provides a related approach to seventeenth-century French and native engagements generative of novel and unexpected social, and material arrangements within and between engaged communities, while Jordan's (2009) conception of cultural entanglement strikes a similar chord.

In many other cases, colonization frequently relied on violence and coercion to compel individuals into any number of economic, social, political, and religious projects. As a result, responsible analyses of such contexts require ample attention to the effects of these violent impositions on colonized communities or risk minimizing their effects and recasting colonialism in a much more favorable light. Silliman (2005) has argued this point by critiquing the use of "culture contact" as a more innocuous descriptor of New World colonial contexts that elides the violence of colonial engagements and long-term processes of colonization. Moreover, contact rather than colonialism serves to minimize native people's creative tactics of "residence" within the harsh and foreign colonial worlds thrust on them.

Between these models of colonialism, the assumption or expectation of more or less equal power is required for a more robust consideration of mutually consti-tuting encounters, generative of the social, political, and material formations and transformations on all colonial populations. However, even in contexts of more overt violence, and coercion, greater recognition is needed of the contributions, role, presence, influence, and participation of colonized/native communities, their materialities and knowledges in shaping and dictating encounters and engagements, rather than just reacting to or residing in them. Discourses of domination and imposition reify binary classifications of colonizer and colonized, as an agent-patient relationship that ends with the embedding of native worlds within the colonial, or early modern world, albeit as still separate wholes buffeted by the world around them, but never fully enmeshing itself with it. Such framings—intended or not—have the effect of casting the colonized as always exterior to a world that is not theirs, but one that they must engage from native spaces, or refuges, or "navigate," resist, refuse, or reside in, without ever fully "dwelling" or being-in it.

Heidegger's notion of "being-in" provides a foundation for a critique of this kind of relationship to the colonial world from a position of exteriority, given that such a relationship is only possible by belonging in and to that world: "It is not the case that man 'is' and then has, by way of an extra, a relationship-of-Being towards the 'world'—a world with which he provides himself occasionally" (Heidegger 1962, 84).

I argue that what is needed is a shift from colonized and/or native people's spatial proximity or location within or in relation to the colonial world, to thinking through how they dwelled and continue to dwell in the modern world emerging from colonial encounters. This notion of dwelling in the colonial world extends beyond disembedded location, such that to dwell "is not merely to be inside it spatially . . . Rather, *it is to belong there*, to have a familiar place there" (Wheeler 2011; emphasis mine). Within colonial contexts, Mary Louise Pratt (1992, 6–7) punctures notions of "separateness" (such as that implied by the spatially moored discourse and political framework of the Two Republics—one Indian and one Spanish—of Spanish colonies), and instead see colonial relationships as defined by "copresence, interaction, interlocking understandings and practices."

Rather than further marginalizing the "periphery," I look for a way to highlight how colonized people dwelled within the emerging colonial world as co-constituents, active participants and integral producers of it; essentially as individuals and communities with a claim to and stake in the modern world, as being-in and belonging there (and thus here). In no way am I arguing for a minimization of perceptions of the harshness of colonization and of detrimental effects suffered by colonized populations. Rather, I seek to challenge the primacy of colonists and their plans, and of the completeness of domination, crystallized in the discourse of conquest, by exposing the contingency of these colonial entanglements on the contributions and influences of the colonized. I follow Enrique Dussel in this line of reasoning, as he has posited the importance of the colonial periphery to the emergence of modernity, given its essential contributions to the emergence of the Western European core/center as a locus of power in part through the generation of value in the periphery, captured in the core (Dussel 2001, 104; Sellers-Garcia 2014, 4–5). For Dussel, the encounter with the New World is a "constitutive fact of modernity" both in its literal contributions, as well as in its role as foil for the discursive construction of Europe as the center, through the identification of the periphery as constitutive outside (echoing Said's notion of the Orient and Occident; Said 1979).

Dussel provides a way to conceptualize how in even assuredly violent colonial contexts, the periphery plays a constitutive role, such that the characteristics and effects of exploitative relations, and violent practices emerge in the encounter, a product of the colonized's agency, or extant material and social practices, settlement patterns, or responses to the encounter that shape all aspects of colonial projects and the contexts they cogenerate,. In this light, colonization is never carried out exactly according to an abstract plan and simply applied to a passive landscape and population either piecemeal or in full. It is a move from the imposition of fully formed colonial plans, toward the imposition of violence in the pursuit of particular projects, albeit of unexpected and contingent forms and arrangements. In doing so, it forces a reconsideration of how colonist's agency, intentions, and expected outcomes are tempered, rerouted, transformed, or rebuffed by their "friction" (see Tsing 2005) with the social and material contours of particular contexts and the actions of those living in them. However, these frictions are more than just obstacles or bumps in the road that slow down the imposition of a fully formed plan; they are instead a generative force giving shape and substance to social, political, and cultural structures, as well as the material arrangements of such contexts of interaction and engagement.

In this chapter, I build up from these issues and look to provide a framework for the archaeology of colonialism/capitalism that refocuses on a context driven account of how new and old power relations, meanings, values, identities, and practices were negotiated, and emerged for all engaged populations within newly shared social and economic fields (Bourdieu 1993). Part of this requires a shift in perspective away from colonization as Spanish, English, or Portuguese exploitative structures as simply stamped into local contexts; essentially deforming the local into

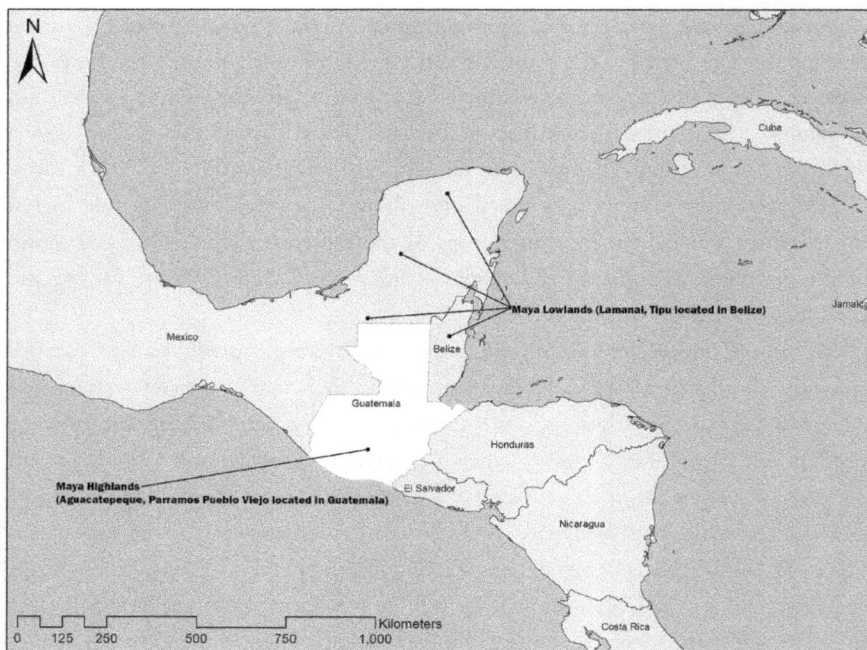

Figure 4.1. Location of sites and regions mentioned in chapter 4. (Map by Guido Pezzarossi, based on US National Park Service, USGS, East View Cartographic)

and around configurations and arrangements desired and imposed by colonists, the emerging global capitalist economy and/or the world system. Instead, a lens is placed on identifying how the colonized, or the periphery, contributed to the literal composition of the colonial world, staked a claim to it, and came to dwell in it, through these contributions.

Framed by Anna Tsing's theorizing of global connections, I draw on archaeological and archival material to highlight how Spanish colonial Guatemala (see fig. 4.1) and their global economic entanglements remained embedded in and constituted by Maya/Mesoamerican political economic practices, power relations, infrastructures, and knowledge(s), as well as the material affordances of the landscape and laboring bodies. Maya communities in the "periphery" of highland Guatemala provided more than just unskilled alienated labor and raw materials to Spanish colonial projects of accumulation; rather, they were integral in shaping the contours of the Guatemalan colonial context and the broader early modern world they dwelled in and actively produced.

Generative Frictions, Salvage, and the Complexes of Conjuncture

Anthropologies of globalization have led the way in theorizing local/global connections in the present, and have provided helpful insights for rethinking colonial entanglement beyond domination/imposition. These approaches have tuned analyses to the mutual and cross-cutting interdependence, influence, and participation of various actors in globalized contexts. Their contributions have provided critical appraisals of place based and bounded notions of culture, while relations of dominance are destabilized in the search for the articulation of local practices and global, transcultural, and transnational flows at a variety of scales, in the production of new arrangements and relations (Inda & Rosaldo 2002; Rouse 2002; Appadurai 1996; Tsing 2005; Marcus 1995).

Anna Tsing's work (2005; 2015) provides a useful framing for the articulations and intersections of early modern colonial/capitalist encounters, specifically in terms of their generative and coconstituting engagements. Tsing's concept of "friction" challenges conceptions of capitalism, globalization (and I argue, colonialism) as a homogenizing force substituting one order with an entirely new one. Instead, Tsing emphasizes the encounter as a generative friction that does not impede, but rather provides traction ("where the rubber meets the road" and movement ensues) for the particular social and material arrangements of capital accumulation projects that are carried out in place, in particular ways. What emerges is not the effects of the global on the local, but new arrangements coconstituted by their engagements, albeit informed by *longue durée* ontologies and structures. Bhabha's (2004; Rutherford & Bhabha 1990) notion of the "Third Space" extends a similar perspective into contexts of unequal power and "domination." The always already liminal Third Space, as the locus and outcome of processes of hybridity, is the space "which enables other positions to emerge . . . it displaces the histories that constitute it, and sets up new structures of authority, new political initiatives" that are only partially understandable from standpoints that came before (Rutherford & Bhabha 1990, 210–11). In a sense, the Third Space recasts colonial interactions of any sort as generative processes that transform identities, ontologies, political economic practices, and materialities in novel and unexpected ways, simply due to their performance in relation to, and/or informed by the "new" otherness of encountered Others. These perspectives draw our analyses to the more illuminating and interesting questions of how the arrangements of a given context came together in complex fashion, what was generated (and extracted) and how, and to what effects on all those engaged.

In a recent publication, Tsing (2015) introduces the concept of "salvage accumulation" to further expand out the forms of value and wealth captured/accumulated in capitalist/colonial contexts, beyond coerced labor and surplus value capture. Tsing notes that: "Accumulation is the amassment of wealth under capitalism; [and salvage] refers to the conversion of stuff with other histories of social relations (human and not human) into capitalist wealth." Salvage accumulation applies to human labor, albeit to the "harvesting" of value from immaterial skills and knowledge not provided or trained for. As an example, "where factories employ women workers to sew, knit, or process food, owners rarely train their employees; they assume that women already know how to do this work from growing up as women. It is *salvage accumulation* to harvest the value of this training in making capitalist commodities" (Tsing 2015). Moreover, Tsing considers how other forms of productive "labor" can be salvaged, including that of flora (e.g., photosynthesis), and fauna (e.g., reproduction, etc.). In all these examples, wealth/value is generated for "free" outside of capitalist relations, or coerced colonial labor regimes, and then captured and translated into capital, in concert with the usual forms of surplus value capture from exploited labor (Tsing 2015).

What Tsing provides is a method or framework for considering how people, from particular standpoints, produce capitalism through situated "worldly encounters" (Tsing 2005, 4), and not through the abstract imposition of a plan unchanged from place to place. As a result, this generative process introduces incredible diversity into the modes of capitalism, given their contingency on the social, political, and material affordances of different encounters, and the disparate culturally, politically, and economically informed goals, values, and actions undertaken in the encounter.

Given the acknowledged entanglements between the emergence of capitalism, and Western European colonial projects (see Pezzarossi 2014, 2019, for a discussion), and the robust approach to thinking through generative encounters and engagements, I extend Tsing's approach to frame an archaeology of colonial frictions and salvage accumulation in highland Guatemala. This approach facilitates an analysis of how *longue durée* Maya prestige, power, knowledge, practices, materialities, aesthetics, skills, and, of course labor, contributed to and remained indelibly present in the emerging complexes of the colonial and early modern world, its global economic networks, and the value circulating through them. These Maya contributions of value, coerced from laboring bodies, as well as salvaged from the landscape and the accreted histories, abilities, materialities, and knowledges of Maya people, leave tendrils and trails (Tsing 2013) that shoot through and continue to constitute the emergent complexes of the (early) modern world within which Maya people dwell(ed).

In the following sections, I seek more than more than just an account of agency as resistance or ability to survive. Rather, I look to a more expansive consideration of agency in this colonial context that positions the Maya, their complexes and landscapes as constituent members of, and multifaceted contributors to, the emergence and persistence of modernity. Spanish colonial use of Maya concepts, infrastructures, economic landscapes, knowledge, and more did not fully evacuate and replace all Maya meanings and relations, as tendrils and traces remained present, allowing Maya people to find themselves advantageously positioned within structures and practices of persisting value and necessity.

Native Allies and Mythical Conquistadors

Spanish colonial projects are commonly cast as the imposition of a fully formed colonial "plan" developed during the Reconquista of the Iberian Peninsula in the fifteenth century, onto the Mesoamerican landscape. However, even the initial incursions into Aztec Central Mexico by Hernan Cortes and 500 soldiers in 1519 immediately relied on native skills and knowledge through the use of translators and intermediaries, like the enslaved bilingual Maya/Nahutal woman La Malinche, as well as a bevy of native warriors, scouts, spies, cooks, porters, and more drawn from communities, like Tlaxcala, that had chafed under Aztec imperial control.

The importance of native allies in structuring these initial encounters cannot be understated; both in terms of the labor and fighting potential they provided a vastly outnumbered and poorly supplied colonial force, as well as the knowledge and abilities salvaged through their use as guides, procurers of food and supplies, and seasoned soldiers. Moreover, native communities similarly profited from these uneasy alliances with colonists, and the martial abilities they proffered, entangling Spanish colonists into their feuds with ancestral rivals, and even salvaging sacred power from the alterity of Spanish colonists and their material culture, as Timothy Pugh has demonstrated for seventeenth-century lowland Peten Itza and Kowoj Maya communities (Pugh 2009).

Colonists' entrance into highland Guatemala in 1524 was similarly made possible by the contributions of a diverse invading army of Spanish "partners" in this joint business venture (Restall & Asselbergs 2007, 7–8) led by Pedro Alvarado, Central Mexican allies numbering into the thousands, and free and enslaved Africans (see also Restall 2003). Indeed, "Indian conquistadors" from Central Mexico and elsewhere went to great pains to emphasize their alliances with Spanish forces, and their roles in the "Conquest" of Guatemala, albeit as still independent communities with their own identities, and not as colonized people (Asselbergs 2007, 73). The contributions of Central Mexican Nahuatl speakers—and their knowledges—to the invasion of Guatemala remain tangible in the present landscape of Guatemala. Nahuatl place-names persist from these early encounters and mark the landscape with residues of the knowledges that made colonization possible.

The Guatemalan invading force was joined in 1524 by Kaqchikel Maya allies from Guatemala, who had attempted to broker an alliance with the Spanish as early as 1522 to fulfill their own expansionistic political agenda against rival groups in the region. As a result, early colonial encounters in Guatemala were largely dictated by the Kaqchikel, as they directed the invading army to attack in stepping-stone fashion, their ancestral enemies—the K'iche, Tzutujil, and Pipil—in what was essentially a move to consolidate their own power and position in the region (Restall & Asselbergs 2007, 10–11). However, this alliance would last only months, as Spanish demands for labor and tribute made of the Kaqchikel undermined their supposed standing as allies and equals given their contributions to the colonist's incursions. Spanish labor and tribute demands were not simply imposed, but instead faltered and were unevenly carried out as Alvarado's violation of native mores and values related to the breaking of the alliance led to widespread Kaqchikel revolts that lasted six or more years, complicating attempts at colonial control (see Lovell et al. 2013).

However, colonization was not solely carried out through the violent repression and "conquest" of Maya communities, afforded by indispensable native contributions to these efforts. Spanish colonization would also come to rely on pathways and regimes of Maya value and prestige to create a legitimization or at least justification for colonial control in explicitly Maya terms (see more on tribute below). Colonists frequently leveraged themselves into extant native hierarchies and "salvaged" prestige, positioning, and obligations through violence, through the capture and execution of native rulers (Hill 1992, 21–22), as well as by marrying into elite or noble families to cement alliances and/or ensure acquiescence, such as Pedro de Alvarado did when he married (or was "given") Luisa Xicotencatl, a member of Tlaxcala's royal family (Restall & Asselbergs 2007, 8).

However, even these marriage alliances were not a novel tool of colonization, but rather an established practice in Mesoamerica, stretching well into the Classic Period. Lowland Maya political histories tell of victorious Maya ajaws/kings marrying into noble families of subordinate polities as a means of "cementing" alliances and ensuring peaceful relations between previously warring factions, as well as a means of increasing political capital and status by connecting to important dynasties (see Munson & Macri 2009, 429–30; Josserand 2002, 139). While such colonial elite intermarriage did not persist for long in parts of the Maya region (Patch 1994, 24), colonists clearly acknowledged the persisting value of Mesoamerican and Maya noble prestige and status, and the mechanism of marriage as a means of connecting to it. It's viability as a source of power drew colonists to salvage its benefits through marriage, highlighting the utility or necessity of navigating extant native social structures and regimes of value from which colonists claims to authority and power could be made.

Colonial Site Planning and Territoriality

By 1541, colonists had established the capital of the Audiencia of Guatemala at Santiago de Guatemala, known today at Antigua, Guatemala. Santiago, as were many other Spanish colonial towns, was planned and built according to a series of requirements eventually codified in the Laws of the Indies of 1573 (Kinsbruner 2005; Low 1995). This grid plan is argued to be, "one of the central devices of colonization" (Fowler 2009, 434), as well as "an architectural representation of colonial control and oppression" (Low 1995, 749). In general, the site form consists of a central plaza ringed by the church and administrative buildings, with higher-status colonist's homes located in proximity to the plaza. From the plaza a rectilinear street grid extended outward, dividing uniform lots (*solares*). Historically, this form is argued to have derived from Renaissance-era ideas of rationality (Low 1995, 750) or to be based on the plan for the siege-city of Santa Fe de Granada used in the conquest of Granada during the Reconquista (Fowler 2009, 434–35). Protocols for the construction of the grid city, and consideration of its location in healthful and economically viable places (e.g., along trade routes, etc.) emerged more uniformly as early as 1513 (Kinsbruner 2005, 11).

However, scholars have found that town plans in early contexts do not conform to the grid plan consistently or even absolutely, as much variability is evident in early town plans, implying this city-plan emerged out of the colonial encounter, rather than transplanted to the colonies fully formed (Fowler 2009, 434). Citing archaeological and ethnohistorical data, Low (1995) has argued that precolonial town plans and their plazas, as well as outdoor mass ritual observations in Central Mexico, and the Maya region were important influences in the development of the Spanish grid-plan and its centralized plaza as a center of religious, administrative, and economic activity (see Voss 2008, 870). The Caribbean itself, the first landings of Spanish colonists, may also be an influence on the centralized plaza design as Taino houses frequently ringed a central ball-court or plaza-like structure associated with the homes of caciques (Low 1995). While it is difficult to identify exactly how and how much such New World influences had on the Spanish grid-form, documentary, and archaeological evidence points to interpenetrating influences (Low 1995) and thus as a product emerging from the "Third Space" of colonial encounters that makes disentangling the entangled impossible. As Voss (2008, 870) notes, given the evidence pointing to New World influences: "Attributing the colonial town plan exclusively to colonial men forecloses consideration of the syncretic genesis of new social landscapes in the Spanish Americas."

Moreover, colonists frequently "founded" or based their colonial capitals in and on extant Maya and Aztec settlements and their plazas, most visibly in the Aztec capital of Tenochtitlan in Central Mexico, but also at the Kaqchikel Maya site Iximche in Guatemala, where the first iteration of Santiago de Guatemala was located before being burned by colonists in the aftermath of the Kaqchikel rebellion in 1524 (Restall & Asselbergs 2007, 12). However, this pattern was repeated across the Maya region with smaller *"pueblos de indios"*—"indian" towns founded by colonists by resettling dispersed communities as part of the practice of *"congregación."* These resettlement practices are generally glossed as the outcome of "logical" and efficient Spanish colonial labor extraction strategies by essentially creating a more concentrated laborer pool, in more easily administered locations. However, such a characterization does not fully explain the observed association of the colonial *pueblos de indios* with precolonial Maya settlements and features, including those of ritual and religious importance, and thus does not account for how these institutions and policies emerged from the frictions of Spanish colonial desires, and extant Maya social, material, and cultural complexes.

In Belize, the Maya towns of Tipu and Lamanai reveal early churches built on Post-Classic–era buildings and "temples" (Low 1995, 754). In the Yucatan, sites for monumental Franciscan church and convent construction were explicitly evaluated in part for their extant "religious prominence" for Maya populations; allowing the new religious buildings to draft off of the value already accorded to the site. In highland Guatemala, the Kaqchikel Maya site of San Pedro Aguacatepeque—just to the south of the Antigua Valley—yielded evidence of a colonial-era brick plaza, and building collapse rubble (likely associated with a colonial church) directly over a prepared stone and clay precolonial platform surface or plaza, indicating a persistence of public-use of this part of the site (fig. 4.2 on page 92; Pezzarossi 2014). In addition, the main habitation area of the site was located on a terraced, plaza-like area near a series of Late Classic mound groups built into natural topography, a common pattern among Late Classic highland Maya sites. At the Kaqchikel Maya colonial site of Pueblo Viejo, Parramos, the standing remains of the colonial church similarly abut a Late Classic terrace built into the hillside, and both are located within fifty or so meters of an additional complex of Late Classic mound and plaza groups (fig. 4.3 on page 92; Pezzarossi & Montejo 2017).

A similar practice is borne out at a regional scale in highland Guatemala, particularly in the Antigua valley (around the former Spanish capital). Of twenty-four securely dated Late Post-Classic settlements identified by Robinson's (1997) survey of the valley, nineteen contained a colonial-era component indicating the persistence of settlement location despite the disruptions of colonization by disease, violence, and *congregación* policies. Colonial sites mainly clustered on lower elevations, in

Figure 4.2. Excavation Unit 20 at San Pedro de Aguacatepeque, Guatemala. On the left, a colonial-era brick plaza (Feature 15) with wall-fall debris overlaying. On the right, Feature 17, a clayey platform constructed over a large rock "bedding," likely dating to precolonial occupation of the site. Both features were not associated with domestic refuse, and appeared very "clean," indicating some form of public-use of space. (Photos by G. Pezzarossi)

Figure 4.3. Pueblo Viejo Parramos, Guatemala. Note proximity of Colonial church (and town center), location of Late Classic terraced Hill and Late Classic mound complex. (Map by G. Pezzarossi; figure imagery source: ESRI, DigitalGlobe, GeoEye, i-cubed, Earthstar Geographics, CNES/Airbus DS, USDA, USGS, AEX, Getmapping, Aerogrid, IGN, IGP, swisstopo, and the GIS User Community)

more accessible locations (Robinson 1997, 70), a product of Spanish resettlement away from defensive positions to more easily controlled and accessed extant sites on valley bottoms, nearer to expanses of arable land (see next section for economic landscape discussion). However, resettlement did not entail the founding of towns in new locations determined solely by colonists, as the location of extant communities in valley bottoms, likely due to their nearness to water sources, fields, roads/paths, as well as economic and ritual importance appears to have influenced, if not determined, which Maya towns in the region were maintained.

Determining the exact boundaries of these resettled Maya towns was also not entirely in Spanish colonial hands, but instead largely informed by precolonial boundaries and settlement practices and colonial-era native and nonnative voices and perspectives. Echoing the central point of this chapter, Sampeck argues that colonial map and boundary-making practices that instantiated colonial power "was the product of a messy debate and rather haphazard consensus-building of many actors [including numerous native community members] rather than a unilateral pronouncement" (Sampeck 2014, 201). The continued valence of these boundaries is obvious in contexts like Sampeck's where they continue to serve as boundaries for present-day municipalities (Sampeck 2014).

The construction of churches on Maya mounds, temples, and ritual spaces and towns on extant settlements should not be thought of as a simple "conquest metaphor" or the imposition of order on disorder (Hanks 2010). Following Hanks' work on colonial *reduccion*, or the "convincing" and conversion of Maya people to adopt a Christian colonial order in the Yucatan region (2010, 3), such practices are better conceptualized as an acknowledgment of the debauched, yet nevertheless valid (and still powerful) Maya order that required respect and reordering rather than obliteration (Hanks 2010, 3). As part of this, the "ordering" of Mayan languages through the production of grammatical structures and dictionaries to describe and codify language was not primarily a descriptive/academic exercise undertaken by missionaries. Rather, it was foremost a critical avenue for reconfiguring Mayan languages and worldviews along Christian and Western concepts and perspectives, such that the foreignness of Christianity was mitigated by the reframing of its concepts in Mayan languages, expressions, and perspectives (Hanks 2010).

However, colonists recognized that working with what preexisted "involved creating and redefining Mayan terms according to the meanings of their European counterparts. This redefinition involved suppressing the division between the languages and obscuring thereby the European history of the meanings" (Hanks 2010, 15). The unintended consequences of this process destabilized the meaning and made it multiple, allowing for Christian doctrine to take on new, or coexist with other meanings simultaneously. Mayan terms (or indeed, places and things), persisting in a Mayan system of language concepts used to explain the Christian universe, did not fully evacuate all other meanings. Rather, Maya meanings and structures continued to frame Christian ones, and persist in these new colonial productions as neither Mayan nor Spanish, but as new languages, materialities, and regimes of value. Colonists recognized, that despite the effectiveness in convincing and converting individuals, "The challenge was to do so without fostering the persistence of the old world from which the parts had come. The result was pervasive ambiguity, ambivalence, and an almost morbid fear of the unseen and the insincere hiding beneath the appearance of truth" (Hanks 2010, 3–4).

In a similar light, settlement-related practices and policies described above represent colonist's attempt to draw on or "salvage" extant Maya uses of space, including knowledge of settlement desirability (e.g., access to water, arable land, etc.) as well as the sacredness, histories, and cosmological orientations of sites to bolster the legitimacy, acceptance and convince Maya people of the "rightness" of the desired colonial order through such connections to the past. Despite its effectiveness, Low (1995, 758) notes that "the spatial relationships maintained by building on ruins, using the same stones and foundations, allowed elements of the indigenous politico-religious system to remain. These latent meanings were not necessarily acted upon publicly, but they may have been useful in reinforcing aspects of indigenous identity, self-esteem, and spiritual power that helped to preserve indigenous folkways, beliefs, and practices." (Low 1995, 758). Beyond preserving past practices, I point to these instances to highlight the central, and thoroughly enmeshed role of the "peripheral" Maya; in the literal constitution of the colonial landscape, in shaping the Spanish colonial presence on it, and in helping inscribe the boundaries experienced by Maya and Pipil people into the colonial archive and modern-day municipal holdings.

Economic Landscapes and Infrastructures of Tribute and Prestige

Spanish colonial resource, labor, and value extraction in highland Guatemala relied almost exclusively on Maya labor, practices, hierarchies, infrastructures, and economic landscapes for their viability. In large part, Spanish colonial wealth capture was carried out through various forms of coerced labor: from enslavement (briefly), to tribute demands in kind, and in currency and *repartimiento* mandatory labor drafts. Chamberlain (1951) has argued that Spanish tribute assessments were directly built on extant craft and agricultural production specialties of native communities in Mesoamerica, some of which may have already been providing the fruits of their labor to native elites and/or lineages as tribute. The Soconusco region, or modern-day Chiapas, had become a tribute-paying outpost of the Aztec Triple Alliance, providing mainly cacao to Central Mexico, as well as a series of other regionally available goods indicated in a detailed accounting of quantities and types recorded in the Codex Mendoza. The K'iche and Kaqchikel also controlled small outposts and towns on the Pacific Coast of Guatemala that likely paid tribute in cacao to rulers located in the highlands (see Berdan et al. 2003, 105; Orellana 1995, 40–41). As a result, tribute payments were not an imposition of the Spanish, but emerged through the heavy-handed influence of precolonial complexes already funneling prized luxury, as well as subsistence goods into elite hands. The overt reliance on this tribute payment/collection framework is attested to by royal decrees, such as one in 1553, that requested what Mumford (2012) refers to as "colonial ethnographies" detailing the "tribute system that existed among the Indians at the arrival of the Spanish" and any account or records of tribute owed to help determine appropriate quantities to demand (see Matas Oria 1999).

As discussed previously, colonial practices of *congregación* and *reducción* brought together spatially dispersed communities, and centralized them, in part in order to efficiently control, convert, and exploit their labor. Hill (1992) provides a detailed accounting of highland Maya social organization at colonization, that I will only briefly discuss here. Among the highland Maya, the *chinamit* served as territorial unit, and consisted of an elite/aristocratic family, from which the head of the group was elevated, while the rest of the *chinamit* population served as "commoners" and laborers (Hill 1992, 39). These *chinamit* could become bundled together into confederations of *chinamit* known as *amaq*, which in turn could become bundled together into broader confederations (such as when the Kaqchikel & Tukuche were allied; Hill 1992, 39). The leader of a *chinamit* would be responsible for various administrative, judicial, and economic tasks, including the likely collection of tribute. The *chinamit* would also serve as social unit used in *congregación* policies, essentially leading to colonial towns as groupings of potentially unconnected Maya social and territorial units (Hill 1992, 43). These distinct groupings would become the *parcialidades* or territorial units controlled by distinct *chinamit* of colonial Maya towns, divided out as barrios or neighborhoods with their own landholdings and a leader drawn from the aristocratic family that helped govern and, most importantly, collect the share of tribute requirements from their *parcialidad* for the *audiencia*, the church, and for town and *parcialidad* projects (see Hill 1992, 42–44; Matthew 2012, 166–68). A similar arrangement existed in the Yucatan, as "the newly created pueblos reducidos, both *visitas* and *cabeceras*, often reproduced at the barrio level relations that had previously obtained between distinct named places" dispersed on the landscape (Hanks 2010, 48–49). These newly congregated communities made up of bundles of self-governing *chinamit/parcialidades* officially interfaced with one another, and with Spanish colonial administration through the *cabildo* (town council) usually composed of two *alcaldes* (mayors) and a variable number of *regidores* (councilmen) elected to office on a year-to-year basis (Hill 1992, 43). In addition, a *governador*, drawn from the elites in town, was appointed by the Spanish and was ultimately responsible for the collection and payment of tributes twice a year (as it was charged to the town) under threat of beatings and incarceration, albeit by working through the *cabildo*, and in turn through the *parcialidad* leadership (at times referred to as *indios principals*).

Hill (1992, 46) argues that the official positions were nothing more than "fronts" needed to meet Spanish requirements, as the "parcialidad leaders remained the true authority in the pueblos"; a situation attested to by colonial observers in the seventeenth and into the late eighteenth centuries that maintained Maya autonomy—to a degree—as far as day to day life and some of the economic practices pursued by the town as a whole, and *parcialidades* within. On the other hand, colonists largely left intact some of these power structures in order to lean on Maya *principales*, who were exempted from tribute demands and maintained their status, to collect tribute from their communities as before. This approach salvaged traditional and historical relations of obligation, and recognitions of authority to do the "dirty work" of tribute collections, without micromanagement of the organization of labor, and the production of tribute goods, however it depended on and maintained power structures that became codified into the broader structure of the Spanish colonial economy.

Spanish colonial tribute demands were made according to the specialties—both manufactured and agricultural goods—of the communities in Guatemala located within unique horizontally and vertically differentiated ecological and geological niches. Tribute assessments were predominantly built on extant craft and agricultural production specialties of native communities with the skills and knowledge to work these disparate regions. Feldman (1992; 1985) provides an accounting of the various tribute items demanded from native communities in *encomienda* in the 1549 Cerrato Assessments.

Guatemala presented an obstacle to colonial desire for high value minerals (more readily available in the mines of Mexico and Bolivia), as the region boasted little in the way of easily worked placer deposits (Hill 1992, 22). Instead, the focus in Guatemala quickly shifted to bioprospection, or a search for valuable export commodities and other resources from biological matter. Recent work by Londa Schiebinger (2004) and others in the field of colonial science studies, have detailed the economic, political, and embodied importance of bioprospection and "applied" botany in the Atlantic world. The search for "green gold" as well as treatments for tropical ailments intensively relied on accumulating salvaged native knowledge of useful local flora, medicinal (and other) preparations of potential use as food, luxuries, or medicine.

As one of the densest value goods circulation in Mesoamerica, cacao quickly became central to colonial accumulation in Guatemala. Prior to Spanish colonization (and into the colonial period), cacao had served as a critically important exchange resource for its potential use in making ritualized chocolate drinks, but also due to cacaos use as a form of currency with which to facilitate market transactions and accumulate wealth (Gasco 1996; Millon 1955; Reents-Budet 2006, 220). The importance of cacao prior to colonization was not always readily apparent to Spanish colonists, however, it quickly became the focus of colonial labor and tribute demands given its prominent role in preexisting tribute systems (Norton 2006, 676).

The delicate, care-intensive nature, and particular growing conditions of cacao required skilled agricultural labor, such that Spanish colonial wealth accumulation through coerced cacao tribute demands also depended on salvaged practical Maya knowledges, and the "labor" of extant fixed biotic capital (e.g., the cacao orchards) in generating new capital and commodity flows within and between regions via cacao. In 1593, San Pedro Aguacatepeque petitioned the *audiencia* that they be excluded from *repartimiento* labor drafts, due to the fact that they cultivated and paid tribute in highly valued cacao, and should be left to this work given its importance to the colonial economy (Sherman 1979, 203). In a different context, eighteenth-century Maya communities in the Verapaz region of the Audiencia drove brisk commerce in feathers and cotton that generated sufficient revenue for their tribute obligations (Patch 2013, 93), while other communities near the capital at Santiago Guatemala argued against their resettlement by noting the "fixed" capital that their fruit orchards represented, and noted the loss to tribute that would result from abandoning them (Patch 2013, 93).

The cacao paid as tribute to colonists was distributed via markets and trade routes throughout Guatemala, colonial Mesoamerica (especially in New Spain/Mexico where abundant demand existed; Herrera 2003, 38–40), and more modestly to Spain (see Simpson 1959). While colonization transformed these networks in various ways, colonial supply lines and markets in Guatemala and surrounding areas were clearly established on extant trade routes and market towns, feeding the new demands of colonists—both in the New World, and increasingly in the Old—and of native consumers (Herrera 2003, 40; Hill 1992, 80–82). In the process, precolonial Maya recipes, and the economic value of cacao served as the foundation on which new global tastes, desires, and markets for cacao emerged; an inversion of the traditional notion of Spanish "improvement" of cacao, given the "internalization" of Mesoamerican aesthetics and recipes, and their proliferation throughout the world (Norton 2006).

These examples indicate that while the knowledge of cacao cultivation and other value-dense crops or lucrative native-run commerce made some Maya communities central to colonial tribute collection and salvage accumulation, this knowledge also afforded communities a measure of insulation and autonomy from some of the more damaging colonial institutions, such as *repartimiento* forced labor drafts, given the persisting value of Maya knowledge and its products to the colonial economy (Sampeck 2014, 183).

The persisting commercial entanglements of the Mesoamerican "World System" (see Smith & Berdan 2003) created other opportunities for colonists to salvage value and wealth from extant practices and infrastructures. Maya marketplace and itinerant commerce within and outside highland Guatemala became an important source of wealth capture, given its foundational role in the colonial economy, and to the subsistence of the region and its people. Underlining the importance of native commerce to the colonial project, in 1549 the Audiencia decreed that native towns should all have markets, so that residents, travelers, and itinerant merchants should have all they need (Matas Oria 1999, 84). In addition to supplying native towns—and thus their laborer pool—with necessities, this commerce in daily subsistence (rather than high-value goods like cacao) created ample opportunities for profiting off the needs and abilities of Maya people, in particular.

Herrera (2003, 40) reveals how Spanish merchants and dealers frequently insinuated themselves into extant Maya trade and commercial networks as middlemen connecting native producers and consumers, in large part displacing (but not eliminating) Maya merchants. As an example, in Santiago, Spanish merchants became involved in acquiring and selling Mixtec textiles from southern Mexico that were in high demand among Maya people in and around Santiago both prior to and after colonization, essentially profiting from Maya demand by controlling supply (Herrera 2003,40). Similarly, colonial sources indicate that Dominican clergy played an active role in controlling some of the production and distribution (and thus profit) of Chinautla-type polychromes to regional markets and communities (Paredes & Romero 2008, 85–86). Obviously, power played a key role, as the use of coerced colonial labor allowed Spanish merchants and traders the opportunity to buy low and sell high, increasing the value captured in these transactions. Other practices, like the *derrama*, saw colonists acquire raw material, like cotton, and then salvage Maya weaving knowledge and skill—for free or poor wages as part of *repartimiento*—to produce native textiles for sale at market (see MacLeod 1983, 195; Pezzarossi 2014 for other such "antimarket" practices).

These various colonial labor regimes shared a dependence on Maya tribute demands, products, labor relations, distribution mechanisms, and "taskscapes," with colonists essentially slotting into the receiving end of extant labor and tribute obligations, albeit with some onerous intensifications of labor/tribute demanded, violence, and the reordering of settlements and space, as described above. The complexes that emerge from Spanish and Maya engagements around the economic landscape so crucial to colonial goals of accumulation, served as the literal mechanisms by which the uneven contours of power of the early modern and modern world were constructed through the disproportionate accumulation of wealth generated by native labor, and "salvaged" from knowledge, skill, infrastructures and the biological "labor" of Mesoamerican crops.

Ambivalent and Anxious Landscapes: Inhabiting the Differently Familiar

Expanding out the range of Maya contributions to the colonial world beyond simple labor and raw material—the usual wheelhouse of the periphery—pushes our analyses to better consider the contingencies of the Spanish colonial world on the "local" contributions of Maya people, communities, and materialities. I have argued that a more robust consideration of how Maya labor, but also politics, power, knowledge, and materiality literally shaped and even dictated central aspects and historical trajectories of the encounter, and its legacies in the present. While the violent and coercive extraction of value via labor remains in focus, as it should, Tsing's notion of salvage accumulation allows for a simultaneously more expansive, and higher resolution perspective on the various means of harvesting and profiting from *other* value-generating relations and the unpaid and salvaged knowledges and labor of humans and nonhumans (e.g., skills, meanings and values, photosynthesis, infrastructure, etc.). As a result, what sneaks in is an acknowledgement of the extensive *dependencies* of colonists and colonial structures in Guatemala on Maya knowledges, values and materialities already present at Spanish arrival, such that an argument for the Spanish colonial superimposition of their world on the Maya is difficult to support.

In some cases, the importance of Maya economic practices, and production of economically valuable goods restricted to particular microclimates—such as cacao—created an opportunity for Maya people to inhabit a differently familiar world in which overt forms of labor control were mitigated by the persisting value of knowledge, skills, and crafts in particular places. As a result, some communities and individuals—such as elite and aristocratic Maya families—found themselves insulated from some of the more pernicious colonial labor policies that reduced Maya people to manual labors. Beyond the economic landscape, the entwined historical and cosmological valences of the landscape and its newly built spaces also endured in colonial settlement's entanglement with precolonial places, of ritual, economic, and/or ancestral importance. As Hanks (2010, 4) notes for processes of conversion and *reducción*, such entanglements—while effective—were also generative of a "nervous landscape" (see Byrne 2003) never fully dominated and controlled that led to a "pervasive ambiguity, ambivalence, and an almost morbid fear of the unseen" for colonists, as Maya people continued to inhabit—or dwell in—legible social/material fields and a world they were decidedly more knowledgeable of, despite important transformations and reconfigurations of power. Through this framework, a different perspective on the periphery, and peripherality, emerges; shifting the colonized Maya from the margins of colonial history, and into the generative milieu at the center of modernity.

Works Cited

Appadurai, Arjun. 1996. *Modernity At Large: Cultural Dimensions of Globalization*. Minneapolis: University of Minnesota Press.

Berdan, F., Marilyn A. Masson, J. Gasco, and Michael Ernest Smith. 2003. "An International Economy." In *The Postclassic Mesoamerican World*. Edited by G. C. Smith and F. Berdan, 96–108. Salt Lake City: University of Utah Press.

Bhabha, Homi K. 2004. *The Location of Culture*. London: Routledge.

Bourdieu, Pierre. 1993. *The Field of Cultural Production: Essays on Art and Literature.* Cambridge: Polity Press.

Byrne, Denis R. 2003. "Nervous Landscapes: Race and Space in Australia." *Journal of Social Archaeology* 3(2): 169–93.

Chamberlain, Robert S. 1951. *The Pre-Conquest Tribute and Service System of the Maya as Preparation for the Spanish Repartimiento-Encomienda in Yucatan*. Coral Gables, FL: University of Miami Press.

DeCorse, Christopher. 2018. "Landlords and Strangers: British Forts and Their Communities in West Africa." In *British Forts and Their Communities: Archaeological and Historical Perspectives*. Edited by Christopher DeCorse and Beier Zachary. Gainesville, FL: University Press of Florida.

Dussel, Enrique. 2001. "The 'World System': Europe as 'Center' and Its 'Periphery,' beyond Eurocentrism." In *Latin America and Postmodernity: A Contemporary Reader*. Edited by Pedro Lange-Churion and Eduardo Mendieta, 93–122. Amherst, NY: Humanity Books.

Feldman, Lawrence H. 1985. *A Tumpline Economy: Production and Distribution Systems in Sixteenth Century Eastern Guatemala*. Culver City, CA: Labyrinthos.

———. 1992. *Indian Payment in Kind: The Sixteenth-Century Encomiendas of Guatemala*. Culver City: Labyrinthos.

Fowler, Williman R. 2009. "Historical Archaeology in Yucatan and Central America." In *International Handbook of Historical Archaeology*. Edited by Teresita Majewski and D. Gaimster, 429–47. New York: Springer.

Gasco, Janine. 1996. "Cacao and Economic Inequality in Colonial Soconusco, Chiapas, Mexico." *Journal of Anthropological Research* 52(4): 385–409.

Gasco, Janine, and Frances F. Berdan. 2003. "International Trade Centers." In *The Mesoamerican World System*. Edited by G. C. Smith and F. Berdan, 109–16. Salt Lake City: University of Utah Press.

Hanks, William F. 2010. *Converting Words: Maya in the Age of the Cross*. Berkeley: University of California Press.

Heidegger, Martin. 1962. *Being and Time*. Edited by J. Macquarrie and E. Robinson. New York: Harper and Row.

Hill, Robert M. 1992. *Colonial Cakchiquels: Highland Maya Adaptations to Spanish Rule, 1600–1700*. Fort Worth, TX: Harcourt Brace Jovanovich.

Inda, Jonathan Xavier, and Renato Rosaldo. 2002. *The Anthropology of Globalization*. Edited by Jonathan Xavier Inda and Renato Rosaldo. Malden, MA: Blackwell.

Jordan, Kurt A. 2009. "Colonies, Colonialism, and Cultural Entanglement: The Archaeology of Postcolumbian Intercultural Relations." In *International Handbook of Historical Archaeology*, 31–49. New York: Verlag.

Josserand, J. Kathryn. 2002. "Women in Classic Maya Hieroglyphic Texts." In *Ancient Maya Women*. Edited by Traci Arden, 114–51. Walnut Creek, CA: AltaMira Press.

Kinsbruner, Jay. 2005. *The Colonial Spanish American City: Urban Life in the Age of Atlantic Capitalism*. Austin: University of Texas Press.

Lovell, W. George, Christopher Lutz, Wendy Kramer, and William Swezey. 2013. *Strange Lands and Different Peoples: Spaniards and Indians in Colonial Guatemala*. Norman: University of Oklahoma Press.

Low, Seth M. 1995. "Indigenous Architecture and the Spanish American Plaza in Mesoamerica and the Caribbean." *American Anthropologist* 97(4): 748–62.

MacLeod, Murdo J. 1983. "Ethnic Relations and Indian Society in the Province of Guatemala Ca. 1620–ca. 1800." In *Spaniards and Indians in Southeastern Mesoamerica: Essays on the History of Ethnic Relations*. Edited by Murdo J. MacLeod and Robert Wasserstrom, 189–214. Lincoln: University of Nebraska Press.

Marcus, George E. 1995. "Ethnography in/of the World System: The Emergence of Multi-Sited Ethnography." *Annual Review of Anthropology*: 95–117.

Matas Oria, Arturo Francisco. 1999. "Los Efectos de la Legislación Indígena Aplicada en la Provincia de Guatemala en la Estructuración de los Pueblos Del Valle de Chocojol Juyú 1530–1601." Report by Universidad de San Carlos de Guatemala, Dirección General de Investigación, Programa Universitario de Investigación en Historia de Guatemala. Guatemala City: Instituto de Investigaciones Históricas, Antropológicas y Arqueológicas

Matthew, Laura E. 2012. *Memories of Conquest: Becoming Mexicano in Colonial Guatemala*. Chapel Hill: University of North Carolina Press.

Millon, René Francis. 1955. When Money Grew on Trees: A Study of Cacao in Ancient Mesoamerica. PhD dissertation. New York: Columbia University.

Mumford, Jeremy Ravi. 2012. *Vertical Empire: The General Resettlement of Indians in the Colonial Andes*. Durham, NC: Duke University Press.

Munson, Jessica L, and Martha J. Macri. "Sociopolitical Network Interactions: A Case Study of the Classic Maya." *Journal of Anthropological Archaeology* 28, no. 4 (2009): 424–38.

Norton, Marcy. 2006. "Tasting Empire: Chocolate and the European Internalization of Mesoamerican Aesthetics." *American Historical Review* 111(3): 660–91.

Orellana, Sandra. 1995. *Ethnohistory of the Pacific Coast*. Lancaster, CA: Labyrinthos.

Paredes, Jose Hector, and Luis A. Romero. 2008. "La Ceramica Tipo Chinautla Del Convento de Santo Domingo." In *Investigaciones Arqueologicas En El Convento de Santo Domingo, Antigua Guatemala*, vol. 2. Edited by Zoila Rodriguez Giron. Guatemala City: Asociacion Tikal.

Patch, Robert. 1994. *Maya and Spaniard in Yucatan: 1648–1812.* Stanford, CA: Stanford University Press.

———. 2013. *Indians and the Political Economy of Colonial Central America, 1670–1810.* Norman: University of Oklahoma Press.

Pezzarossi, Guido. 2014. A New Materialist Archaeology of Antimarkets, Power and Capitalist Effects in Colonial Guatemala. PhD dissertation. Stanford, CA: Stanford University.

———. 2019. "Rethinking the Archaeology of Capitalism: Coercion, Violence, and the Politics of Accumulation." *Historical Archaeology,* Vol. 53, Issue 3, Special Issue, Guido Pezzarossi (guest editor).

Pezzarossi, Guido, and Mauro Montejo. 2017. "Proyecto Arqueológico Colonial Parramos, Pueblo Viejo Parramos: Informe Anual No. 1." Report for the Instituto de Antropologia e Historia de Guatemala, Guatemala City.

Piñero, Eugenio. 1994. "The Town of San Felipe and Colonial Cacao Economies." *Transactions of the American Philosophical Society* 84(3).

Pratt, Mary Louise. 1992. *Imperial Eyes: Travel Writing and Transculturation.* London: Routledge.

Pugh, Timothy W. 2009. "Contagion and Alterity: Kowoj Maya Appropriations of European Objects." *American Anthropologist* 111 (3): 373–86.

Reents-Budet, Dorie. 2006. "The Social Context of Kakaw Drinking among the Ancient Maya." In *Chocolate in Mesoamerica : A Cultural History of Cacao.* Edited by Cameron L. McNeil, 202–23. Gainesville: University Press of Florida.

Restall, Matthew. 2003. *Seven Myths of the Spanish Conquest.* Oxford, UK: Oxford University Press.

Restall, Matthew, and Florine Asselbergs. 2007. *Invading Guatemala: Spanish, Nahua and Maya Accounts of the Conquest Wars.* University Park: The Pennsylvania State University Press.

Robinson, Eugenia. 1997. "Proto-Historic to Colonial Settlement Transition in the Antigua Valley, Guatemala." In *Approaches to the Historical Archaeology of Mexico, Central and South America.* Edited by Janine Gasco, Greg Charles Smith, and Patricia Fournier-Garcia, 59–70. Los Angeles: The Institute of Archaeology, University of California.

Rouse, Robert. 1991. "Mexican Migration and the Social Space of Postmodernism." *Diaspora: A Journal of Transnational Studies* 1(1): 8–23.

Rutherford, Jonathan, and Homi K. Bhabha. 1990. "The Third Space: Interview with Homi Bhabha." In *Identity: Community, Culture, Difference.* Edited by Jonathan Rutherford, 207–21. London: Lawrence & Wishart.

Said, Edward W. 1979. *Orientalism.* New York: Vintage Books.

Sampeck, Kathryn E. 2014. "From Ancient Altepetl to Modern Municipios: Surveying as Power in Colonial Guatemala." *International Journal of Historical Archaeology* 18(1):175–203.

Schiebinger, Londa L. 2004. *Plants and Empire: Colonial Bioprospecting in the Atlantic World*. Cambridge, MA: Harvard University Press.

Sellers-García, Sylvia. 2013. *Distance and Documents at the Spanish Empire's Periphery*. Palo Alto, CA: Stanford University Press.

Sherman, William L. 1979. *Forced Native Labor in Sixteenth-Century Central America*. Omaha: University of Nebraska Press.

Silliman, Stephen. 2005. "Culture Contact or Colonialism? Challenges in the Archaeology of Native North America." *American Antiquity* 70(1): 55–75.

Simpson, Lesley Byrd. 1959. "A Seventeenth-Century Encomienda: Chimaltenango, Guatemala." *The Americas* 15(4): 393–402.

Tsing, Anna Lowenhaupt. 2005. *Friction : An Ethnography of Global Connection*. Princeton, NJ: Princeton University Press.

———. 2013. "Sorting out Commodities: How Capitalist Value Is Made through Gifts." *HAU: Journal of Ethnographic Theory* 3(1): 21–43.

———. 2015. *The Mushroom at the End of the World: On the Possibility of Life in Capitalist Ruins*. Princeton, NJ: Princeton University Press.

Voss, Barbara. 2008. "Gender, Race, and Labor in the Archaeology of the Spanish Colonial Americas." *Current Anthropology* 49(5): 861–93.

Wheeler, Michael. 2017. "Martin Heidegger." *The Stanford Encyclopedia of Philosophy*, fall 2017 ed. https://plato.stanford.edu/archives/fall2017/entries/heidegger/.

White, Richard. 1991. *The Middle Ground: Indians, Empires and Republics in the Great Lakes Region, 1650–1815*. Cambridge, UK: Cambridge University Press.

Chapter 5

Early Modern Landscapes
of Chocolate

The Case of Tacuscalco

Kathryn Sampeck

This study examines the birth pangs of early modern social, political, and economic relationships by tracing changes in the cultural landscape of one small area in colonial Guatemala, a place known as Tacuscalco. Tacuscalco was one of several crucial communities that were part of a powerful Mesoamerican polity known as the Izalcos, located in what is today Western El Salvador (see fig. 5.1 on page 106). The Izalcos was swept up into the vortex of colonial change—one could say even took center stage for a short while—because of its pivotal role in the development of chocolate as a colonial commodity. The unusual social, political, and economic role of the Izalcos in the early modern world of chocolate and cacao, the tree seed that is the vital ingredient in chocolate, makes logical and indeed possible an examination of intersections of different political economies on a global scale and over centuries by focusing on one small place. The historical trajectory of Tacuscalco illustrates a recasting of lives and livelihood, including technological change, reorientation of spatial regimes, and reconfiguring labor sources and relationships that supported astronomical production to feed increasingly common consumption on both sides of the Atlantic. Deep, pervasive, and observable transformation of cultural landscapes of Tacuscalco had perniciously mundane consequences for the early modern world.

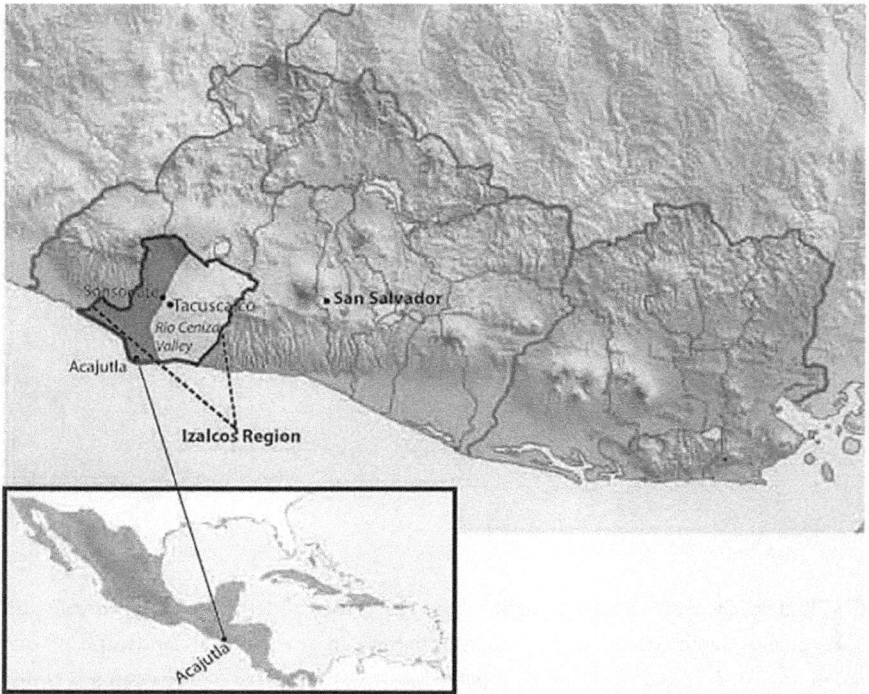

Figure 5.1. Map of the Izalcos region showing the location of Tacuscalco. (Map by Kathryn Sampeck)

Places of Chocolate

Fernand Braudel (1992, 227) includes chocolate in his discussion of drinks, stimulants, and drugs, recognizing that drinks "have always served as drugs." His focus, as is the case with much chocolate-related research, is on the consumer end of the commodity chain, particularly European consumers. Focusing on Tacuscalco offers an opportunity to examine the entire chain: agricultural production, processing, distribution networks, and American consumption, as well as the recursive effects of this small place with expanding global consumption and production.

How early did chocolate cross the Atlantic, and how quickly did Europeans adopt it into their foodways? The very first description by Europeans of cacao was of the seed. This first encounter with cacao happened during the 1502 (fourth) voyage of Christopher Columbus, when the expedition chanced upon a trading canoe off the coast of the Yucatán peninsula. The Maya vessel held a dizzying array of goods. Ferdinand Columbus, a son of Christopher, described the finely embroidered clothing, food, and drink. Most notable was how the canoe held "many of those almonds [cacao seeds] that those of New Spain have for money, which they seemed to hold in high esteem, because when these things of theirs were placed in our ship, I noticed that if just one of these almonds dropped, they all immediately bent to recover it, as if an eye had fallen out, in that moment it seemed that they did not remember themselves, being taken away from their canoes as prisoners into the ships amid people so ferocious and strange as we are compared to them" (Colombo 1563, 200r–200v; translation by Sampeck and Matteo Binasco; see fig. 5.2 on page 108). Cacao first arrived in Spain in the 1520s, then the Spanish Netherlands in 1606 (Norton 2008). Braudel (1992) traces the first arrival of cacao to Europe in the form of loaves and tablets—already processed, but solid.

European early modern chocolate initially took many forms, with a frothy beverage becoming most common over time. Braudel (1992, 249) credits Cardinal Richelieu with the first use of cacao in France; in fact, it was Richelieu's older brother, who took it sometime before 1642 for splenetic vapors (Wheaton 1983, 87). When Philip IV of Spain's daughter, Maria Teresa, married Louis XIV in 1660 she brought with her to France her taste for chocolate, and the maid skilled at preparing it (Franklin 1893, 157–58); Wheaton (1983, 87) comments that chocolate was one of the princess's "few pleasures." Chocolate reached England from France about 1657, a favorite at times of a fickle French court. The earliest recipe using chocolate as an ingredient in French cooking is in François Massialot's *Cuisinier roïal et bourgeois* (1691) for widgeon (*macreuse* or dabbling duck) in a ragout with chocolate (Wheaton 1983, 87). The directions include first seasoning a plucked, cleaned, eviscerated, and scalded widgeon with salt, pepper, bay leaf, and a bouquet garni. The next step is awfully casual: "you make a little chocolate which you throw in. Prepare at the same time a ragout, with the livers, mushrooms, morels, truffles, and a quarteron of chestnuts" (Massialot 1691, 285). The recipe carefully describes how to season and prepare the bird, but does not explain how to make chocolate, only that after the widgeon is cooked and arranged on its dish, "you pour your ragout over it, and serve it garnished with whatever you wish" (Massialot 1691, 286). Chocolate occurred as a pleasant and apparently unremarkable addition in savory European cuisine at this early date. The late-seventeenth to early-eighteenth centuries witnessed a remarkable expansion of the chocolate-consuming public. From England to Hungary and beyond, choco-

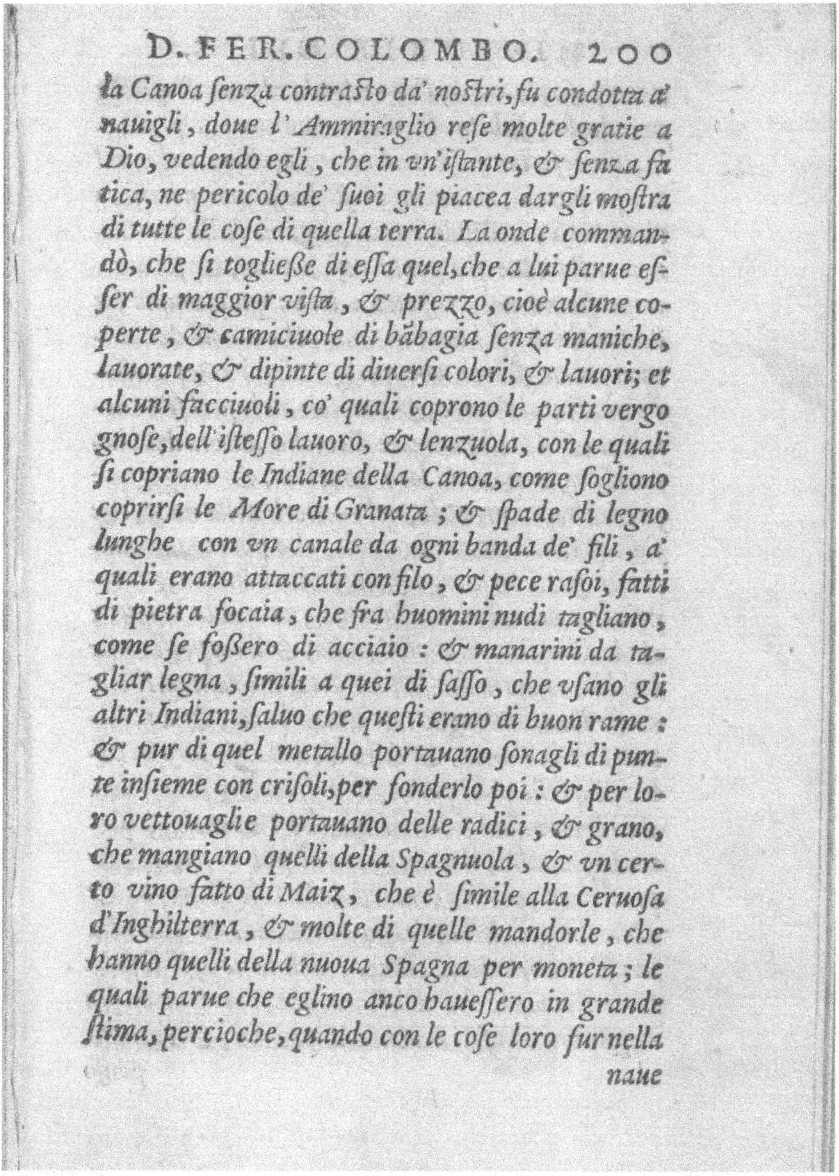

la Canoa senza contrasto da' nostri, fu condotta a'
nauigli, doue l' Ammiraglio refe molte gratie a
Dio, vedendo egli, che in vn'istante, & senza fa
tica, ne pericolo de' suoi gli piacea dargli mostra
di tutte le cose di quella terra. La onde comman-
dò, che si togliesse di essa quel, che a lui parue es-
ser di maggior vista, & prezzo, cioè alcune co-
perte, & camiciuole di bābagia senza maniche,
lauorate, & dipinte di diuersi colori, & lauori; et
alcuni facciuoli, co' quali coprono le parti vergo
gnose, dell'istesso lauoro, & lenzuola, con le quali
si copriano le Indiane della Canoa, come sogliono
coprirsi le More di Granata ; & spade di legno
lunghe con vn canale da ogni banda de' fili, a'
quali erano attaccati con filo, & pece rasoi, fatti
di pietra focaia, che fra huomini nudi tagliano,
come se fossero di acciaio : & manarini da ta-
gliar legna, simili a quei di sasso, che vsano gli
altri Indiani, saluo che questi erano di buon rame :
& pur di quel metallo portauano sonagli di pun-
te insieme con crisoli, per sonderlo poi : & per lo-
ro vettouaglie portauano delle radici, & grano,
che mangiano quelli della Spagnuola, & vn cer-
to vino fatto di Maiz, che è simile alla Ceruosa
d'Inghilterra, & molte di quelle mandorle, che
hanno quelli della nuoua Spagna per moneta ; le
quali parue che eglino anco hauessero in grande
stima, percioche, quando con le cose loro fur nella

naue

Figure 5.2. The first mention of cacao in any European text. (Page 200 recto, from the description by Ferdinand Columbus. In *Historie Del S.D. Fernando Colombo; Nelle quali s' ha particolare, & vera relatione della vita, & de' fatti dell'Ammiraglio D. Christoforo Colombo, suo padre* . . . [1571] [US 2313.2*] Houghton Library, Harvard University)

late became part of people's daily lives, not just in royal courts, but in common households as well. As Sidney Mintz (1985) argues, a change in consumption is a sign of transformed production strategies. To understand chocolate's extraordinary global career requires looking at growing grounds.

Changing Places

The reshaping of political, social, and labor relationships in zones of production that brought chocolate into a wide world of consuming publics operated at what the performance scholar and artist Mike Pearson and archaeologist Michael Shanks (2001, 142) phrase as the "lived experience of landscape." People's engagement with place relies on perception and belief, neither of which are neutral processes. Rather than an objective observation of "the way things are," perception is instead tied to political strategy and structures of inequality, a point vividly illustrated by the phrase "our land, not yours" (Pearson and Shanks 2001, 155). Furthermore, the lived experience of the landscape is not just broad brushstrokes and major distinctions, but is also deeply personal. Pearson (2006, 14) offers an example of this interconnected, discursive and recursive social, political, economic, and subjective geography with the Welsh concept of *y filltir sgwar*—the square mile of intimate landscape of childhood, the patch we know in detail, a web of favorite places, others to avoid; neighbors and their stories. The lived landscape is thus constitutive of the beginnings of geography, history, and society as well as difference and similitude (Pearson 2006, 19, 23). This intimate landscape experience and understanding is a routine concept for archaeologists, as part of our work is to know about small patches in extraordinary detail, including soil types, settlement history, and seemingly minor variations in deposits and constructions that give clues about past activities. From an archaeological, lived landscape perspective, an effective way of understanding the trajectory of change is to understand meticulously the intricacies of one place.

This knowledge built from thorough familiarity shows dramatic changes in Tacuscalco's cultural landscape. The place had a career that went from being a pre-Columbian center of social and political power, a site of decisive battles, and extraordinary agricultural production of cacao, to a racially segregated neighborhood in a growing city, and finally, a lingering place-name, seemingly with no place. These transitions are tied to shifts in the cacao economy and politics, decisions made and acted on in Tacuscalco that then recalibrated far-reaching networks and processes. Comparing the kinds of changes in regimes of space and material life provides a view into critical large-scale and short- and long-term processes. Tacuscalco is a window into the early modern, to Spanish America, as much as it is into one small corner of colonial Guatemala.

Pipil Tacuscalco: Spatial Regimes

Although it would be possible to begin with the first evidence of human settlement and each stage in pre-Columbian dynamics, this summary will focus on a just a few elements especially relating to the fifteenth century (for evidence from earlier periods, see Fowler 1987; Sampeck 2007, 2014b; Verhagen 1997). The residents of this area in the fifteenth century were actually relatively recent arrivals, coming to the region sometime around 1200 ACE, a period known archaeologically as the inception of the Late Postclassic. The archaeological evidence demonstrates a striking change that emphasized spatial organization and material culture informed by practices of Central Mexico (Fowler 1989; Sampeck 2007, 2010a). The earliest colonial accounts record that the people spoke Nahuat, a sister language to the Nahuatl of the Aztecs, and called themselves by the ethnic name of Pipil (Alvarado 1924[1525]). Archaeological and documentary evidence also indicate that the pre-Columbian and early colonial residents in this region were superproducers of cacao (Fowler 1987, 1994, 2006; MacLeod 1973; Sampeck 2007). Cacao was a pre-Columbian means of sustenance, and even fueled the state through tribute demands in cacao (Fowler 1989). Cacao has a long history of use in Mesoamerican ritual practice, but its use as small currency in the pre-Columbian economy was a late development that fostered a system of state-supported inequality (Sampeck 2010b, 2018). The "minting" of a stable money supply required cultural and environmental conditions that in the Izalcos was accomplished through communal agricultural production of phenomenal amounts of cacao (Fowler 1994; MacLeod 1973; Sampeck 2007).

The Place of Tacuscalco

Tacuscalco was one of the largest and most complex pre-Columbian settlements in the entire Izalcos region. The cultural landscape of pre-Columbian Tacsucalco exhibited hierarchical order through plaza groupings, temples, and other public spaces and works (see fig. 5.3). This was the largest Preclassic (400 BCE–400 ACE) site in the Department of Sonsonate and during the Late Classic (400–800 ACE), people continued to build large mounds there. The range structures (long, low mounds) appear to be Late Postclassic (1200–1500 ACE) in date, the last pre-Columbian addition to this accumulation of high-investment structures. The impressive architecture and the consistent attention across pre-Columbian generations to this public and ceremonial core accentuate the enduring importance of the place.

The spatial arrangement of pre-Columbian Tacuscalco consists of large structures arranged around seven plazas. Plazas, as much as the buildings that surround them, are central design elements of community planning and intrasite spatial organization (Kidder 2004). Plazas provide space for large groups of people to gather, and in an urban environment, such space is at a premium. The clear space of plazas is a choice for public gathering, rather than more administrative, domestic, commercial, or other kinds of buildings, an effort to bring people together who do not necessarily live in that immediate area. The continued accretion of plaza space in pre-Columbian Pipil spatial regimes at Tacuscalco can be taken as a campaign to prioritize public spaces. That access to plazas became ever more common suggests

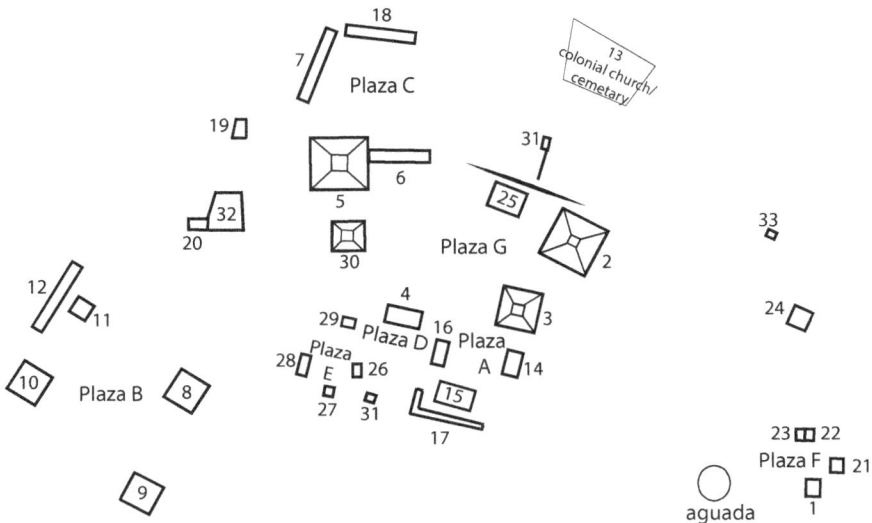

Figure 5.3. Plan map of the plazas and structures in pre-Columbian Tacuscalco. (Map by Kathryn Sampeck)

political change by increasing integration of lordly and commoner populations. Nahua peoples have particular forms of social and political integration that in fact are attested in Izalcos region toponyms; the toponyms and archaeological remains together provide a view into the political flavor of the lived landscape experience of Tacuscalco.

It is likely that some of the structures on these plazas were temples for religious ceremonies, others were for political administration, and yet others were domestic residences for nobility. In addition to the remains of monumental structures, the existence of palaces is inscribed on the place through names in the Izalcos region: one settlement was regularly referred to in different kinds of documents as "Tecpán Izalco." Just as the physical remains of plazas have political and social implications, the use of the term *tecpán* has important political implications, as well. *Tecpán* means "palace"; the literal translation is "where a lord is" (Lockhart 1992, 104). Another important political institution for Nahua nobility was the *tecalli*. In some regions, every *teuctli* (lord) was the head of a *tecalli* and every *pilli* (noble) was a member of one. Lords administered their dependents and lands through the *tecalli*. The integration of such political administrative functions and land tenure varied regionally, however. In the eastern Nahua area of central Mexico, the *tecalli* functioned independently of the *altepetl*, the ethnic state, and its constituent sub-units, the *calpolli*. In this system, *calpolli* members owned land and dependents of lords of tecalli did not (Lockhart 1992: 106). For western Nahuas, the *tecpán* was integrated into the calpolli in that lords were also heads of the *calpolli* and he and his followers were one of several wardlike sets of people and land within his *calpolli* subdivision (Lockhart 1992, 105). The use of the term *tecpán* to identify Izalco could indicate the more integrated form of lordly houses that in fact emphasized ethnicity.

Lockhart proposes that

[t]he two types of description [*tecalli* versus *tecpán*] . . . could be two ways of looking at almost exactly the same thing, the western view emphasizing ethnicity, with the lords seen primarily as officers and leaders of the ethnic group, the eastern view emphasizing noble lineages, with the broader ethnic group relegated to the background and imagined as dependent on the lineages. Place names suggest not only the political division of territories, but also the form of political organization. (1992, 108)

These observations well serve the instance of the Izalcos and further emphasize the geographic nature of political organization—that people were bound to the polity through place, and place-based distinctions brought into sharper relief priorities within the flow of power in Nahua states. From a western Nahua view, priorities were the ethnic ties of those people to each other as well as to the tenure of land.

Natural and cultural features indicate the importance of the locale of Tacuscalco within the Izalcos region. Tacuscalco sits at a ford at the south end of another settlement, Nahulingo, with which the place had a historically close association, perhaps at some point in the fourteenth to fifteenth century forming a single political unit, an *altepetl* (Lockhart 1992). This close association between Tacuscalco and Nahulingo does not necessarily mean that relations were always cordial, and ethnohistoric data suggest that Tacuscalco may have begun to fission from Nahulingo to form an independent altepetl before colonial intervention (Sampeck 2015). The site is also located at a point where the Nahulingo municipal boundary widens considerably and this may mark an ancient dividing line (Sampeck 2016). A 1560 document of the *audiencia* (circuit court) cites ". . . los pueblos de los yzalcos y los tacuscalcos . . ." that underscores the union of Nahulingo and Tacuscalco as one unit while Izalco and Caluco were another unit (Escalante 1992, 1: 55). Izalco and Tacuscalco may have been fissioning or had fissioned by the 1520s, forming two independent *altepetl*. Furthermore, Nahulingo and Tacuscalco were not given two-part names like Caluco Izalco and Tecpán Izalco, also indicating that they were probably different divisions, at least, or perhaps independent *altepetl*. These geopolitical arrangements had much to do with the way that trans-Atlantic colonists first experienced the place; Tacuscalco was a turning point in colonization efforts in the region.

Sixteenth-Century Tacuscalco: A Battlefield

As a reward for his service in the conquest of Mexico, the Spanish king granted Pedro de Alvarado permission to conquer Guatemala. During his 1524 expedition, Alvarado fought a major battle at Tacuscalco (Alvarado 1924[1525]; Lovell et al. 2017). In his letters, Alvarado (1924[1525]) identified the battle place as Tacuscalco, but it is doubtful that the indigenous army was mustered from residents of Tacuscalco alone. The army size of several thousand indicates that soldiers were also drawn from the other Izalcos region settlements. The naming of the battle site—Tacuscalco—also reinforces a spatial division of the region by the Rio Ceniza: west of the river was Tacuscalco, while east of the river was Nahulingo. Tacuscalco is mentioned in court cases against Alvarado, as a place where some Indians came in war, and that "for the good of the land they castigated them (. . . para le bien de la tierra hazer en ellos algund castigo)" (Libro Viejo 1943, 203, 204). Testimony in a 1532 case against Alvarado states that upon hearing the cruelties done by Alvarado to those who came in peace as well as those in war, those of "Tlacusqualco" (Tacuscalco) decided to die in battle, and they were all killed (Libro Viejo 1934. 142). War and death was a better choice than living through atrocities.

The illustrations in *Historia de Tlaxcala* written in 1582 by Diego Muñoz Camargo includes graphic scenes of battles, one of which is "La Guerra de Tlacochcalco" (Tacuscalco). George Lovell, Christopher Lutz and Wendy Kramer (2017) published reproductions of images from the *Historia*, and figure 5.4 is a redrawing

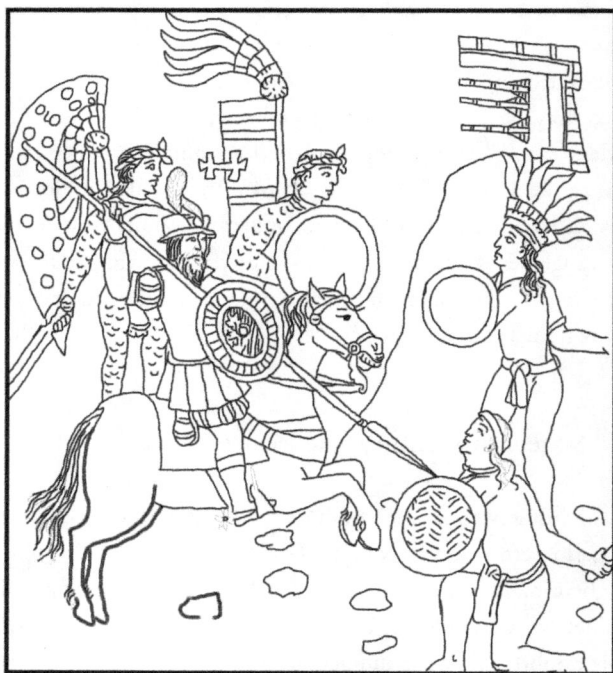

Figure 5.4. The Battle of Tacuscalco. (Illustrated by Diego Muñoz Carmargo. After Lovell et al. 2017, fig. 10. Drawing by Kathryn Sampeck)

of the published image. All of the scenes in the *Historia* usually feature Alvarado wielding a spear while astride a horse in a levade position. In the background but near Alvarado are trusty Tlaxcaltec warriors. Also in the background, to the right of the Tlaxcallans, is the place-name. That it is a place-name is indicated by a hill, a convention in Nahua graphemes. At the summit of the hill are the rebus-like/hieroglyphic elements of the name. For Tacuscalco, three darts (arrows) are within a house. The darts are *tlacochtli*, long flexible arrows typically tipped with obsidian projectile points and thrown with the aid of an *atlatl* or spear thrower. Altogether, the graphic elements and their linguistic counterparts are *tlacoch*-(dart/arrow)-*cal*-(house, *calli*)-*co* (an affix designating a place). Taken together, this group of graphemes (graphic linguistic meaning units) forms the word Tlacochcalco (Tacuscalco), which means "Place of the House of Arrows."

In the foreground on the right side are two warriors, one about to be impaled by Alvarado's spear. Although this warrior is on one knee, seemingly a gesture of defeat, he is holding a weapon in his right hand, which is drawn back perhaps to strike. The warrior standing between him and the place name hill wears an elaborately feathered headdress and likewise has his arm drawn back, though what his hand may hold is cut off from the picture. Both local warriors carry shields, but the patterns on the shields do not match, perhaps indicating different ranks or polities. The scene is not as grisly as the ones just before (Acajutla) and after (Miahuatlan), which show dismembered native bodies. Taken in the context of the other illustrations, the one of Tacuscalco especially emphasizes fierce defiance and perhaps regional mustering or military hierarchy associated with this place. The image is a distilled view of the place as a battlefield.

After dealing with tough resistance in Tacuscalco, Alvarado had few problems traveling through the rest of the valley. This lack of resistance adds credence to the idea that the army in Tacuscalco was pooled from settlements across the Izalcos. Once that battle was over, Alvarado marched east through a relative void until reaching Miahuatlan, likely the large archaeological site on the principal pass north of the formidable Balsam Range, near the present-day town of Armenia (Sampeck 2007).

Tacuscalco's role as a battlefield did not end in 1524. Tacuscalco became a battleground of different sorts across the sixteenth century, coercion and violence with the aim of extracting wealth in the form of cacao. The Izalcos was a shining example of extreme abuse and depredation in the sixteenth century, shown in severe depopulation, prison-like systems to manage cacao producers, and other forms of state-sponsored collective violence that played out in geographic, spatial modes.

Tacuscalco and Colonial Order

The beginning of colonial Tacuscalco in the 1520s to 1550s was actually a case in which Spaniards lived within indigenous lifeways and spatial orders. James Lockhart (1992) demonstrated that Spanish divisions of Nahua altepetl followed indigenous territorial boundaries and formed divisions that were relatively equal in economic output. In other words, altepetl with high tribute yields were subdivided more than ones with lower yields. In this way, Spanish geographic divisions were economic leveling grounds so that rewards could be dealt out in comparable units.

In the case of cacao, the criteria for divisions, the economic output, were determined by native production strategies. In the Izalcos region, native residents managed cacao production and retained control over those lands, with most land held communally; the Spanish siphoned off indigenous wealth rather than radically change production methods or activities (Fowler 2006).

The divvying of Tacuscalco is thus a view into processes typical across colonial Guatemala and even New Spain. Dividing Tacuscalco into four encomiendas actually merged Nahulingo and Tacuscalco together and was a relative measure of the production levels of that community versus others in the region. Izalco, Tacuscalco, and Nahulingo thus produced cacao at about the same level. A larger implication of this practice of building colonial economic and political programs on the foundation of native practices is that Spanish policies, despite other tumultuous kinds of changes, provided some stability and preservation of native practices, especially spatial regimes, if it fostered increased wealth. Furthermore, newcomer laborers and entrepreneurs such as Afrodescendants learned to work within and replicate these regimes for fostering economic productivity. A large-scale implication of this small place was that native Izalcos forms of production shaped the colonial market and Spanish statecraft and set precedents for official policies.

Archaeological evidence of the size and distribution of settlements in the mid-sixteenth century indicate a rapid depopulation compared to the numbers and sizes of settlements in the fifteenth century, yet those settlements had arrangements and kinds of structures clearly of the style and likely the function of pre-Columbian Izalcos settlements (see fig. 5.5; Sampeck 2007, 2010a). Archaeological survey also has shown that the municipal boundaries in the region of Tacuscalco follow pre-Columbian dividing lines (Sampeck 2014a, b). When we look at a map of Western El Salvador today, we see the remnants of pre-Columbian politico-economic spatial organization. Maintaining the pre-Columbian economic geography made colonists

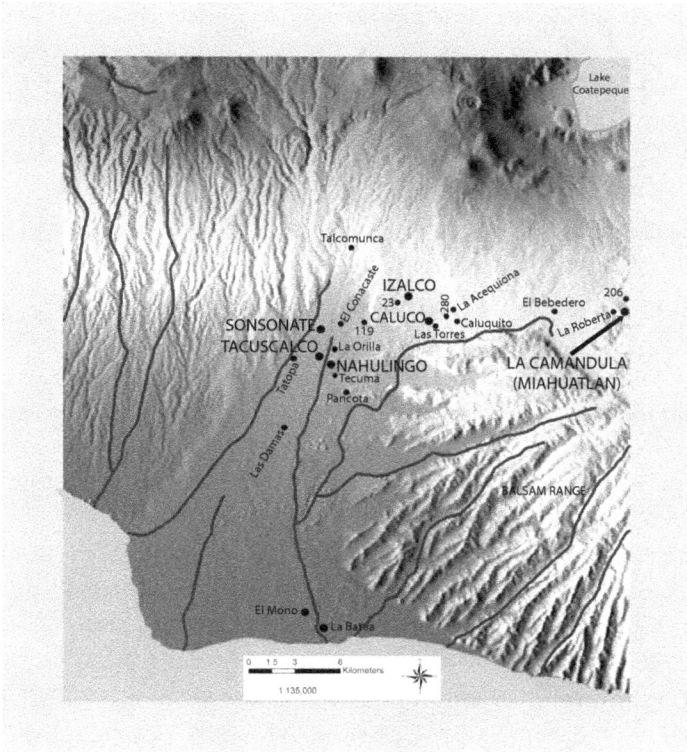

Figure 5.5. Map of sixteenth-century settlements in the Izalcos region. (Map by Kathryn Sampeck)

rich by maintaining flows to royal coffers, lining pockets illegally, and creating vitality in the intercolonial market.

The Economic and Political Place of Colonial Tacuscalco

Two important questions to gauge the relative place of Tacuscalco in the local and transcolonial market are its population size, and that population's relative productivity. Two mid-sixteenth-century censuses to establish tribute levels give a view of the relative population of Tacuscalco compared to other settlements in the Izalcos region. The first tribute assessment, the Cerrato *tasación* of 1548–1551, lists several principal settlements and their tributary populations: Icolco (Izalco or Caluco), 400—Icolco listed a second time with no figure; Naolingo (Nahulingo), 200; Cacaluta, 100; Tacuscalco, 100; Acaxutla, 20; Miaguatlan, 6. Tacuscalco's 100 tributaries had to give 400 xiquipiles to the encomendero Francisco Calderón, worth about 2,000 pesos in 1550 (Escalante 1992, 2:7, 17). In 1572, Tacuscalco had a population of 400 according to the count of the vicar Juan Arias de Vera (Escalante 1992, 2:18). López de Velasco replicated Cerrato's count, finding 200 tributaries in Nahulingo and 100 in Tacuscalco in 1574 (Escalante 1992, 2:17; Fowler 1985, 164). The precipitous rise then fall in the counts could be due to differences in the manner of counting, with Arias recording indigenous population rather than tributary units (a single unit was usually a married couple), or perhaps differences in determining tributary units (such as counting a widow as one unit, rather than a half), or even a combination of differences in assessment and real changes in population due to migration and disease.

A relative idea of how extraordinary Tacuscalco's tributary demand was is to compare it to the rate of other places famous for abundant cacao production: Soconusco, Suchitepequez, and Escuintla, which gave from 10 to 15 zontles (a count of 200, so 2,000–3,000 beans) to 1 *xiquipil* (8,000 beans) per tributary unit. The residents of Tacuscalco gave at least four times more cacao than the next-closest high-producing area, a difference between 1 *xiquipil* at most of these other regions versus 32,000 beans of Tacuscalqueños each year per tributary unit, a demand that lasted for decades. This place had an astoundingly abundant and stable flow of wealth.

This stability in native productivity ratcheted up tensions among different Spanish social and political factions and encouraged reconsideration of domains of control for the Crown. Francisco de Morales in a letter to Phillip II in 1562 claimed that *oidores* (circuit judges) and other royal officials as well as *vecinos* (official residents) were all engaged in cacao trade, such that the Crown should consider ". . . Acaxutla, Içalcos, Tacuscalco, Naolingo, Ateos, Santana, Cuscatan . . ." to be royal property because the Izalcos region represented one of the richest and most prosperous territories in the Indies (Escalante 1992, 1:47–48). Morales's argument was that if the Crown assumed direct ownership, the tribute would reside in the Crown rather than enlarging the capital of an oligarchic group who "were not even conquistadors" (Escalante 1992, 1:48).

The Moral Place and Urban Spaces of Tacuscalco

The verdant wealth of Tacuscalco also fostered what seen by some to be a scandalous and morally degrading mixing. In 1552, Francisco del Valle de Marroquín succeeded Gonzalo de Alvarado as *alcalde mayor* of Acajutla and acted on an order of the *audiencia* to evict forcibly Spanish merchants not just living in the indigenous settlements of Izalco, Nahulingo, and Tacuscalco, but also entering into the homes of native residents and "vexing and molesting" them (Escalante 1992, 1:35, citing Gall 1963, 374). Unfair demands and trade were such that Spaniards needed to be banned from the Indian pueblos to protect indigenous residents from the colonists and to impose moral order among a wayward group of Christians. The Bishop of Guatemala, Francisco Marroquín, complained in 1547 that "in this city there are two pueblos, one named Izalco, which is in the power of two vecinos, and the other Tacuscalco, in the power of four; they are of great interest and in them there is no justice or reason" (Escalante 1992, 1:30, 220).[1]

The Spanish cure for dangerously mixed communities was spatial segregation. The first Spanish settlement in the Izalcos region was called Espiritu Santo. Gonzalo de Alvarado, brother of Pedro, founded the town in 1552 by the banks of the Río Ceniza, very near Tacuscalco and Nahulingo. Alvarado was the *alcalde mayor* of Acajutla, the port town, so he had authority over Acajutla only. The new settlement fell in the jurisdiction of Santiago de Guatemala in the area of what today is called Antigua Guatemala. Santiago de Guatemala was the seat of regional government, but geographically well to the west and outside of the Izalcos region, across a substantial mountain range inhabited by several different Highland Maya groups (Escalante 1992, 1:34). The case of being too intimate with native populations in the Izalcos before the founding of the town shifted to one of absentee governance. The lessened oversight due to physical distance facilitated abusive and illegal situations in Tacuscalco.

This first Spanish town in the Izalcos lasted only a few years, until the Crown issued royal orders to found a town even farther away from native settlements. About 100 Spaniard merchants relocated to La Trinidad de Sonsonate in 1555, in a location established by Pedro Ramirez de Quiñónez and farther north of Tacuscalco than Espiritu Santo. This movement northward suggests movement toward a relative void in Izalcos political geography, a place that perhaps offered a better chance for Spanish order to dominate regimes of movement, commerce, and urban geometry.

William Hanks (2010) argued that Spanish colonists, missionaries, and officials colonized to implement *reducción* (ordering), create a Christian colonial order by altering space, language, and conduct. Scholars often conflate *reducción* with *congregación*, the forced resettlement of people. *Congregación* was one, but not the only, way that colonial officials enacted the policy of *reducción*. Hanks (2010, 3) demonstrated that colonial sources defined the term as "persuade" rather than the modern dictionary sense of "reduce." For example, Covarrubias (1995[1611]: 854) glossed *reducido* as "convencido y vuelto a mejor orden" (convinced and turned into a better order), a program that affected social space, the human body, and everyday social conduct (Hanks 2010, 3).

The goal of missionaries and Crown representatives was to make the moral order of *reducción* a habit in their daily life: "the idea of policía was to instill ways of perceiving, experiencing, and behaving, rooted in the little details of the body in its social life and in the disposition to reproduce them" in multiple practices and material forms, such as written doctrines, built spaces, and gestural repertoires (Hanks 2010, 114). An intimate element of the lived landscape experience at Tacuscalco was the agenda of *reducción*. Because the agenda was a practice, people could put it to use in new ways. In the name of accessibility, ease, or intelligibility, indigenous and other subaltern actors could frame the practices and materials of *reducción* according to their own canons of style and modes of expression. As was the case with assigning municipal boundaries, such actions resulted in the appearance of complicity with the norms of colonial governance. The appearance of compliance offered a chance at subversion, however (Hanks 2010, 57, 287), a key point in the specific case of Tacuscalco.

The attractiveness, perhaps even tenaciousness, of indigenous economic organization subverted the moralizing goals of Spanish resettlement and spatial redesign. The ordinances for Sonsonate and the Izalcos were established not long after the founding of the villa in 1555 (Escalante 1992, 1:213). Many of the ordinances governed trade, both in the city and in the Izalcos pueblos. The *tiangue* (market) was authorized to happen in Tacuscalco on Mondays, in Nahulingo on Tuesdays, in Izalco on Wednesdays, and in Caluco on Thursdays, with Friday, Saturday, and Sunday available for any pueblo (Escalante 1992, 1:213). The ordering of populations and practices was temporal and spatial at the same time.

Despite the establishment of a new, official market in Sonsonate, much of the commerce continued to be conducted in the indigenous towns, with Tacuscalco a magnet for migrant wage laborers for cacao farming. A 1560 document of the *audiencia* depicts how this centripetal power of native economic hubs caused market reorientation and reorganization as well as tremendous disruption in individual lives and families across a very wide region

> The towns of the Izalcos and Tacuscalcos . . . next to the port of Acajutla, is land Rich and of great abundance of cacao which is what the Indians most want and what they spend the most and value from the outskirts of the city of San Salvador which it borders and the land of Gracias a Dios of Honduras, and the city of San Miguel of Guatemala and of many other parts come a great quantity of people to those towns to be hired and to sell their corn, hens, and fruits and other things and to rent themselves to work in the cacao orchards; this land is in general a tomb of all the Indians that come there, because a great number of them die and others forget their wives who they leave in the towns where they were born. . . . (Escalante 1992, 1:55)[2]

The lure of the native settlements was both economic and coercive: to have direct access to and control over cacao commerce. Tacuscalco during this time was one of the central places for reordering not just Crown political and economic priorities, but also in reshaping the trajectory of people's social and economic lives across a broad region.

While Spanish-style urban organization directly controlled people's mobility, segregating them into containable units to control mixing and its consequence, corruption, in the case of Tacsucalco, the plan both failed and succeeded. Residential segregation did not stop Spaniards from engaging in unethical practices that affected cacao cultivation. The first alcalde mayor of Sonsonate, Francisco de Magaña, permitted Gomez Diáz de la Reguera, an unofficial resident of Sonsonate, to pay indigenous residents of Tacuscalco to divert *acequias* (irrigation canals) destined for Nahulingo (Escalante 1992, 1:65).

Trying to establish *policía*, Christian moral practices, in Tacuscalco was shaped by profit concerns. In 1553 Izalco, Nahulingo, Tacuscalco, and Acajutla had their own *curas* (curates, regular clergy) (Escalante 1992, 1:26). That same year, fray Tomás de la Torre wrote to the king that it would be best to have a Dominican or Franciscan convent in the Izalco region and expulse the secular clerics. The annual tribute of the market (*tributo de la comarca*) amounted to about 8,000 pesos, which he argued was too high to leave without permanent infrastructure and dedicated professionals (Escalante 1992, 1:56). Economy provided the impetus for the location of convents.

These merchant-clergy had networks that penetrated Tacuscalco. More than just economic transactions, clergy reinforced status hierarchies with economic practices. The cleric of Izalco in 1540s, Juan Juárez, bought cacao at a cheaper price than merchants: if dealing with *principales* (native political leaders), he paid eight *tostones* per *xiquipil*, if it were a *macehual* (commoner), no more than six. He also sold wine, transported by the black (Afrodescendant) Baltazar, and this business stretched as far as Tacuscalco (Escalante 1992, 1:54).

What eventually became church land in Tacuscalco was gained through native debt. The vecino Alejo López de Bilches was the owner of one *caballería* (a land measurement that varied according to climate and soil quality, typically about 105 acres) of land on the other side of the Río Grande from Sonsonate, in the territory of Tacuscalco. Bilches had received this land in payment from the residents of Tacuscalco for having constructed an acequia that watered their cacao orchards (Escalante 1992 1:167). Bilches erected buildings and plantations on the plot (Escalante 1992, 1:168).

As part of the ceremony for the Dominicans to become owners of the land, the vicar Juan de Bobadilla, the *alguacil* (sheriff), along with three friars, evicted the squatters in the buildings of the donated land, then walked the perimeter of the plot to the intersection of the roads to Tacuscalco and Izalco, then walked farther, to the ford of the Barrio de los Mexicanos of Sonsonate (Escalante 1992, 1:168). On the same day, in the "pueblo de naolingo de los ysalcos," that is, to the east, across the Río Ceniza from Tacuscalco, the *oidor* formally recognized the ownership of the land by the Dominicans (Escalante 1992, 1:169). Taking ownership was a lived experience, made possible by repeated divestment of indigenous peoples from land. This single instance in Tacuscalco is emblematic of policies, suites of actors, and procedures for usurping property and establishing domain: from indigenous domain to private Spanish property and indigenous squatting, followed by opportunistic clerical control abetted by the strong-arm of the state.

From Pueblo to Barrio

In the mid-sixteenth century, Cerrato found one hundred tributary units in Tacuscalco. By the seventeenth century, Tacuscalco witnessed precipitous native population decline. In 1679, Tacusalco had only fifteen tributary units according to the census of Vázquez de Campos (Escalante 1992, 2:137). By 1684, the tribute of *maravedis* amounted to one and a half *reales* from seven family heads (Escalante 1992, 2:137). The situation continued to decline in the eighteenth century, with a total of 10 *tostones* in 1734, a payment one-tenth that of nearby Caluco. Not long after this assessment, officials began to refer to the place as a barrio (urban neighborhood). A 1737 document noted the extinction of the Indian pueblo: only one Indian remained, a parishioner of the church of Nuestra Señora (Escalante 1992, 2:138).

What does this mean? Tacuscalco changed form, but continued to exist. It is less important that Tacuscalco changed, than what it turned into: a suburb of the city. The integration of residents was no longer as an independent entity within the municipal or tribute system, but instead subsumed into the growth of the villa of Sonsonate. By the eighteenth century, Sonsonate had four barrios surrounding the urban core: San Miguel Sonzacate, Santo Domingo (San Angel), Santa Isabel de los Mexicanos, and San Francisco Tacuscalco (see fig. 5.6; Escalante 1992, 2:137). A suburb slightly farther away, to the north, was Sonzacate, a small indigenous

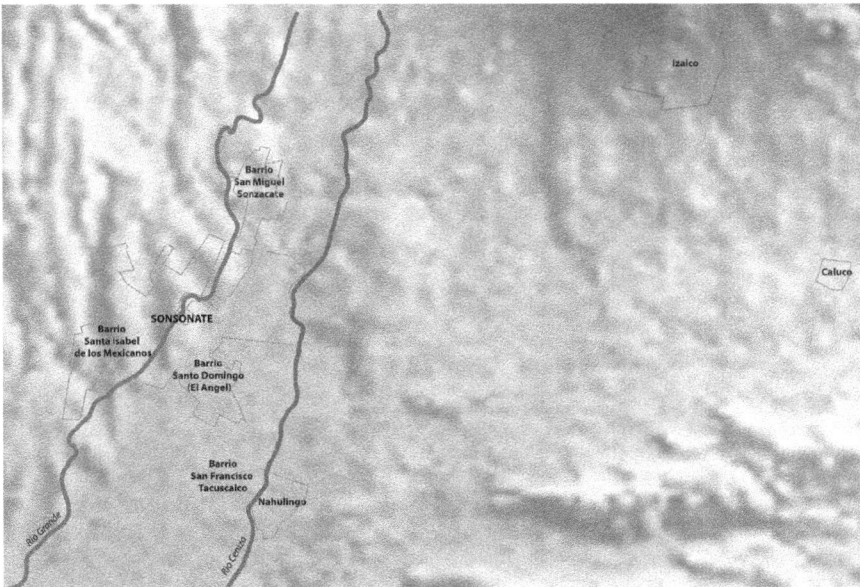

Figure 5.6. Map of neighborhoods (barrios) of Sonsonate in the eighteenth century. (Map by Kathryn Sampeck)

settlement in lands that may have belonged to the encomendero Gómez Díaz de La Reguera (Escalante 1992, 2:128). After the Dominican monks moved their location to the city in 1726, some indigenous families and many ladinos formed the barrio Santo Domingo, later called the barrio El Angel (Escalante 1992, 2:138). On the north side of the barrio San Angel, near the road to Sonzacate, was the small Barrio del Rosario, also in Dominican lands, populated by Indians and *mulatos*. This small barrio eventually merged with Barrio El Angel.

Santa Isabel was a gift to its residents, but also the site of illegal, or at least unethical practices. Even though a royal *cédula* (royal decree) in 1552 prohibited giving Mexican and Tlaxcallan populations in *encomienda* (royal grant of rights of a colonist to demand tribute and forced labor) as labor, in 1547 (before the establishment of the barrio in the villa), residents complained that they were having to pay tribute and were being divvied up as slaves (Escalante 1992, 2:138). In response to these complaints, Crown officials suspended tribute requirements and Cerrato dedicated land to them. That place of refuge was the barrio of Santa Isabel de los Mexicanos, founded in the outskirts of Sonsonate (Escalante 1992, 2:138). This reprieve, however, was short-lived: in 1572 the seventy tributaries of the barrio resumed tribute obligations. Even after nearly one hundred years (in 1659), the tribute requirement ceased only for dead or absent Mexicans (Escalante 1992, 2:139).

The final barrio of Sonsonate, San Francisco Tacuscalco, was the lingering remnant of the Pipil settlement of Tacuscalco. The *mestizaje* of Sonsonate that had increased in the seventeenth century clearly dominated by the eighteenth century. Sonsonate was described by a *vecino* in 1765 as having few Spanish residents, but many *zambos* and *mulatos*, two barrios with few Indians, twenty pueblos de indios (including Dolores and Asunción Izalco, Nahulingo, Guaymoco, and Caluco), and one pueblo of mulatos, San Francisco Tacuscalco (Escalante 1992, 2:151–53).

These observations of Tacuscalco as a *mulato* stronghold occur also in the survey of Cortés y Larráz, who in 1768 noted that many *mulatos* and some Spanish were in the area: Altogether, Cortés y Larráz found 28 families with 115 members, all *mulatos* or Spanish (Escalante 1992, 2:138). The data provided by Cortés y Larráz in table 5.1 indicate that the family size was highly consistent from one barrio to the next. The villa and San Miguel Sonsonate had families with about 4.5 people, while the smallest family size was in Santa Isabel Mexicanos, with 4 members per family. The consistent family size did not seem to relate to ethnicity. Cortés y Larráz (1958 [1], 76) stated that the people of Sonsonate and San

Francisco were Spanish and *mulatos*, while those of San Miguel, San Antonio, and Santa Isabel were Indians.

This consistency in Sonsonate stands in contrast to the variability seen in family size from one settlement in the region to another. This consistency may indicate that the local conditions were affecting all subgroups relatively equally, while conditions were very different from one town to another.

Did the difference in lifeways, the lived experience of one pueblo versus another translate into differences in material culture? A comparison of the patterning of ceramics in Tacuscalco with Izalco and Caluco provides one way to evaluate the "small details" of *policía* in daily life. The relative amount of Spanish style tin-enameled earthenware, *maiolica*, from Guatemala, follows a general pattern of being most abundant in the late fifteenth to mid-seventeenth century, and of the three towns, this early phase of creole Spanish wares is especially abundant in Tacuscalco. This was the time of forced resettlement into Spanish pueblos de Indios, and the daily material practices were observably Spanish.

The next hundred years tends to have a proportionally small amount, but Tacuscalco swings entirely the other direction. Tacuscalco residents simply did not use certain Spanish forms, yet they definitely had resources enough to have other valued serving wares, including Chinese porcelains. The life of the place as a *barrio de mulatos* also marks the return of low levels of Guatemalan *maiolica*.

A wider context for evaluating these shifts in a material culture associated with social sharing is by including other ceramics that were commonly available. By replicating some, most, or all of Spanish ceramic attributes, local potters took over a market share and had some say about when and how those attributes would be used, co-opting the element by reconfiguring it for their own goals that may have been entirely different from the uses and practices conceived by colonizers. One attribute of Guatemalan *maiolicas* is an undulating or "wavy" rim, also called a "pie-crust" rim. Pie-crust rims appear in low frequencies in utilitarian earthenware of Spanish tradition and thus are not limited to decorated serving or display wares. This rim form, however, was not present in pre-Columbian ceramics of the region, so it is an easily recognizable element of Spanish style in local coarse earthenware. Potters of the Izalcos created fluted rims on a variety of serving forms, such as hemispherical and wide, low, straight-walled bowls as well as Spanish forms of brimmed plates and *lebrillos* (flat-bottomed, slant-sided bowls). In other words, pie-crust rims occurred on local tradition pottery forms rather than solely on Spanish ones (Sampeck 2015). What region utterly rejected fluted rims? Tacuscalco. The lived experience of Tacuscalco's most intimate form of social sharing, the consumption of food and drink, defined a geography of subversion.

This refusal of Spanish style in material culture by residents of Tacuscalco occurred during the transition from being a center of cacao production to a subset of a Spanish urban community, a system of production far more reliant on Spanish oversight and determination. How did this happen precisely at the time that chocolate was booming internationally? It was precisely due to this shift in productive environments. The leading cacao producers in the seventeenth to eighteenth century changed from the Izalcos, under native direction, to plantations of enslaved laborers in areas with little or no heritage of intensive cacao cultivation: Venezuela, Costa Rica, and Ecuador, and by the nineteenth century, sub-Saharan Western Africa (MacLeod 1973; Martin & Sampeck 2016).

The spatial regime of Tacuscalco in the eighteenth century exemplifies this change in the career of chocolate. What were indigenous spaces of livelihood became Afro–Latin American ones, a shift that facilitated Spanish oversight. The shift was not one of just personnel. In other words, Afro–Latin Americans did not merely take the place of native peoples in existing cacao orchards. Expanding cacao production was achieved by creating more locales of production in new places, even if of lower quality and relatively lower individual production volume. Escaping areas of deep heritages with cacao was the strategy for French, Dutch, and English cacao cultivation, yet those very practices for caring for cacao must have first been learned in native orchards. The potency of Tacuscalco in the transcolonial marketplace then made it vulnerable to selective rejection, a change shown in native flight and depopulation and new economic and political roles for new residents in a new spatial environment.

The lingering legacy of Tacuscalco is as a name loosely attached to a place. The area of large mounds is now known as Los Cerritos, and the barrio of Sonsonate is now known as San Francisco. Social and economic power now resides in places other than Tacuscalco, and much of the chocolate available in the area is made by large multinational corporations using African cacao.

Change in Place

This survey of Tacuscalco's changing landscape challenges ideas about the early modern development of monocrop plantation economies, regimes of coerced or enslaved labor, racial ideologies, and asserting and subverting rural-urban spatial order. The agents of colonialism, whether space, practice, or object, the pueblo, cacao cultivation, or chocolate, in small and large ways had the potential to become vectors of resistance as well; far-reaching relations and forces had roots in the small place of Tacuscalco.

Notes

1. "[e]n esta cibdad hay dos pueblos, el uno se llama içalco, que está en poder de dos vecinos, y otro tacuscalco, en poder de cuatro: son de mucho interese y en ellos no hay justicia ni razón."

2.

> [L]os pueblos de los y çalcos y tacuscalcos . . . junto al puerto de acaxutla, es tierra rica y de grande abundancia de cacao que es lo que más los yndios quieren y lo que más se gasta y vale de los terminos de la cibdad de sant salvador que por allí confinan, y de la tierra de gracias a dios de honduras y villa de sant miguel de guatimala y de otras muchas partes viene grand cantidad de gente a aquellos pueblos a contratar y vender su maíz, gallinas, y frutos y otras cosas y alquilarse para labrar los cacaguatales; esta tierra es general sepultura de todos dichos yndios que allí vienen, porque se mueren grand cantidad dellos y otros olvidan sus mugeres que dejan en los pueblos donde son naturales. . . ."

Works Cited

Alvarado, Pedro de. 1924[1525]. *An Account of the Conquest of Guatemala in 1524*. Edited by Sedley J. Mackie, with a facsimile of the Spanish original. New York: The Cortes Society.

Braudel, Fernand. 1992. *Civilization & Capitalism, 15th–18th Century, Volume 1. The Structures of Everyday Life: The Limits of the Possible*. Los Angeles: University of California Press.

Colombo, Fernando. 1563. *Historie del S.D. Fernando Colombo: Nelle quali s' ha particolare, & vera relatione della vita, & de' fatti dell'Ammiraglio D. Christoforo Colombo, suo padre: et dello scoprimento, ch'egli fece dell'Indie Occidentali, dette mondo nvovo, Hora possedute dal Sereniss*. Venice, Italy: Appresso Francesco de' Francheschi Sanese.

Cortés y Larráz, Pedro. 1958. *Descripción geográfico-moral de la Diocesis de Goathemala*. Guatemala City: Sociedad de Geografía e Historia de Guatemala.

Covarrubias Orozco, Sebastián de. 1995[1611]. *Tesoro de la lengua castellana o española*. Edited by Felipe C. R. Maldonado. Madrid, Spain: Editorial Castalia.

Escalante Arce, Pedro Antonio. 1992. *Códice Sonsonate: Crónicas Hispánicas.* 2 vols. San Salvador, El Salvador: Consejo Nacional Para La Cultura y El Arte, Dirección General De Publicaciones e Impresos.

Fowler, William R. 1987. "Cacao, Indigo, and Coffee: Cash Crops in the History of El Salvador." *Research in Economic Anthropology: An Annual Compilation of Research* 8: 139–67.

———. 1989. *The Cultural Evolution of Ancient Nahua Civilizations: The Pipil-Nicarao of Central America.* Norman: University of Oklahoma Press.

———. 1993. "La region de Izalco y la villa de la Santísima Trinidad de Sonsonate." In *Dominación Española: Desde la conquista hasta 1700.* Volume II, edited by Ernesto Chinchilla Aguilar, 601–9, in *Historia General de Guatemala.* 1993–1999. Series edited by Jorge Luján Muñoz. 6 Volumes. Guatemala City: Asociación de Amigos del País, Fundación para la Cultura y el Desarrollo.

———. 2006. "Cacao Production, Tribute, and Wealth in Sixteenth-Century Izalcos, El Salvador." In *Chocolate in Mesoamerica: A Cultural History of Cacao.* Edited by Cameron McNeil, 307–21. Gainesville: University Press of Florida.

Franklin, Alfred. 1893. *La Vie privée d'autrefois: Arts et métiers, modes, moeurs, usages de parisiens du XIIe au XVIIIe siècle d'aprés des documents originaux et inédits, vol. 13: Le Café, le thé et le chocolat.* Paris: Librairie Plon.

Hanks, William F. 2010. *Converting Words: Maya in the Age of the Cross.* Berkeley: University of California Press.

Kidder, Tristram R. 2004. "Plazas as Architecture: An Example from the Raffman Site, Northeast Louisiana." *American Antiquity* 69(3): 514–32.

Libro Viejo. 1934. *Libro Viejo de la fundación de Guatemala, papeles relativos a D. Pedro de Alvarado.* Guatemala City: Sociedad de Geografía e Historia.

Lockhart, James. 1992. *The Nahuas after the Conquest: A Social and Cultural History of the Indians of Central Mexico, Sixteenth through Eighteenth Centuries.* Stanford, CA: Stanford University Press.

Lovell, W. George, Christopher Lutz, and Wendy Kramer. 2017. *Atemorizar la tierra: Pedro de Alvarado y la conquista de Guatemala, 1520–1541.* Guatemala City: F & G Editores.

MacLeod, Murdo J. 1973. *Spanish Central America: A Socioeconomic History, 1520–1720.* Berkeley: University of California Press.

Martin, Carla D., and Kathryn Sampeck. 2016. "The Bitter and Sweet of Chocolate in Europe." *Socio.hu* 3, http://dx.doi.org/10.18030/socio.hu.2015en.37.

Massialot, François. 1691. *Le Cuisinier roïal et bourgeois: Qui apprend a ordonner toutes sorte de repas en gras at en maigre, et la meillure maniere des ragoûts les plus delicats et les plus à la mode.* Paris: C. de Sercy.

Mintz, Sidney W. 1985. *Sweetness and Power: The Place of Sugar in Modern History.* New York: Penguin Books.

Norton, Marcy. 2008. *Sacred Gifts, Profane Pleasures: A History of Tobacco and Chocolate in the Atlantic World*. Ithaca, NY: Cornell University Press.

Pearson, Mike. 2006. *"In Comes I": Performance, Memory and Landscape*. Exeter Performance Studies. Exeter, UK: University of Exeter Press.

Pearson, Mike, and Michael Shanks. 2001. *Theatre/archaeology*. New York: Routledge.

Sampeck, Kathryn E. 2007. "Late Postclassic to Colonial Landscapes and Political Economy of the Izalcos Region, El Salvador." PhD diss., Tulane University.

———. 2010a. Late Postclassic to Colonial Transformations of the Landscape in Western El Salvador. *Ancient Mesoamerica* 21(2): 261–82.

———. 2010b. "Comments on Kaufman and Justeson: 'The History of the Word for Cacao in Ancient Mesoamerica.'" *Ancient Mesoamerica* 21(2): 430–32.

———. 2014a. "From Ancient Altepetl to Modern Municipio: Surveying as Power in Colonial Guatemala." *International Journal of Historical Archaeology* 18(1): 175–203.

———. 2014b. "Making the Municipio: Political Geographies in Colonial Guatemala." *Journal of Latin American Geography* 13(2): 153–79.

———. 2015. "Chronology and Use of Guatemalan Maiolica: Ceramics as Reducción in the Izalcos Region of El Salvador." *Historical Archaeology* 48(4): 18–49.

———. 2018. "Cacao and Violence: Consequences of Money in Colonial Guatemala." *Historical Archaeology* 53(3), 000.

Verhagen, Inez. 1997. "Caluco, El Salvador: The Archaeology of a Colonial Indian Town in Comparative Perspective." PhD diss., Vanderbilt University.

Wheaton, Barbara Ketcham. 1983. *Savoring the Past: The French Kitchen and Table from 1300 to 1789*. Philadelphia: University of Pennsylvania Press.

Chapter 6

Early-Seventeenth-Century Settlement in Barbados and the Shift to Sugar, Slavery, and Capitalism

Douglas V. Armstrong

The initial years of English settlement in Barbados, beginning in 1627, involved the establishment of small-scale farms with a mixed array of crops, including potatoes, tobacco, and cotton. During this period planters and laborers lived in close quarters with relatively scarce supplies and material accompaniment. By the 1640s, some farmers were generating surplus capital based on the production of cotton. However, beginning with the first successful sugar crop in 1643, Barbados underwent a rapid shift to industrial production of sugar resulting in huge profits, rapid expansion, and a shift to slavery, and capitalism. This chapter explores two themes. First, the rise of agro-industrial–based capitalism in the Barbados and the Caribbean; and second, the confluence of multinational funding in the mid-seventeenth century that ensconced capitalism, as a means of financing and empowering agro-industrial sugar production and a slave-based labor regime. Most specifically, I will focus on Dutch and English interactions and the implications of capital finance resulting from globally based public trading companies and ungoverned capital investment in sugar and slavery.

Sugar in Barbados

This chapter draws from archaeological and historical data from Trents plantation, St. James, Barbados. It examines a revolutionary change from small-scale presugar farms (1627–1640s) to sugar producing plantations (1640s and on) that has local, regional, and global implications. This study is an important counter to recent histories of the early period of colonial settlement in Barbados like Larry Gragg's "Englishmen Transplanted" (2003). Gragg projects a static transplantation of English forms of religious and civil governance in the new colony, virtually ignoring the abundant evidence of new economic and social systems, including the emergence of slavery and capitalism.[1] More broadly, the study makes a case for the critical role of the emergence of globally oriented private trading companies in the early seventeenth century in the generation of capital and the production of profits in colonial settings. In Barbados, and settings, "Beyond the line" of formal regulation by nations like England, new and exploitive investment and labor schemes, involving unfettered capitalism and the formalization of enslavement, emerged and spread (Bridenbaugh & Bridenbaugh 1972, 2; Armstrong & Reilly 2014).

In reviewing the argument for the role of capitalism in the shift to sugar and slavery, I was surprised at the silence that I found related to capitalism in the telling of the region's early history (Armstrong forthcoming). Michel-Rolph Trouillot's in *Silencing the Past* (1995) addresses the ways in which underlying power structures shape our understanding of history and our understanding of social relationships. In this case, historical constructs of the eighteenth and nineteenth centuries have tended to overshadow the formative nature of seventeenth-century capitalism and the role it played in transforming social relations, landscapes, and perceptions.

There is general agreement among socially conscious scholars related to the deleterious impacts of slavery and colonialism on past and present societies in the Caribbean. Moreover, scholars societies in the Caribbean acknowledge the traumatic role of slavery and colonialism and the importance of understanding Caribbean societies (Dunn 1972; Beckles 2006; Higman 2011; 53, 2005; Mintz 1985; Williams 2005[1944]; and others). Not surprisingly, the colonial enterprise is framed as invasive and associated with dramatically negative impacts on native peoples, enslaved laborers, and regional biota (Watts 1987). However, an understanding of the impacts of early capitalism and capitalists tends to be historically truncated. Many have avoided applying these terms to the actual period of dramatic shift to capitalism in the mid-seventeenth century.

Even Eric Williams and Sidney Mintz stopped short of directly correlating it to capitalism. Each saw the seventeenth-century shift to sugar in the Caribbean as a revolutionary change. William's, *Capitalism and Slavery*, set a foundation for the study of colonialism, imperialism, and capitalism in the Caribbean (2005[1944]).

However, he only addresses capitalism, and capitalists, in relation to wage laborers and the "new industrial order" of the postemancipation era (Williams 2005[1944]).[2] In *Sweetness and Power*, Sidney Mintz asserts that "most students of capitalism (though not all) believe that capitalism became a governing economic form in the late eighteenth century and not before" (Mintz 1985, 55). However, in relation to the dramatic economic and social changes of the early seventeenth century, he does obliquely comment that "If it is not 'capitalism,' it was still an important step towards capitalism" (Mintz 1985, 55). I argue that the shift to sugar and slavery in the seventeenth century was not only an important step toward capitalism; it was both capitalistic and capitalism.

Capitalism is defined as, "an economic system characterized by private or corporate ownership of capital goods, by investments that are determined by private decision, and by prices, production, and the distribution of goods that are determined mainly by competition in a free market" (*Merriam-Webster* 2015).[3] The term "*capitalism*" is often conceived in relation to eighteenth-century economist Adam Smith's (1937[1776]) notion of capital accumulation associated with a rising class of financially and politically powerful industrialists in mid-eighteenth-century Europe. Critical use of the term "*capitalist*" is most often associated with mid- to late-nineteenth century political economists Karl Marx and Frederick Engels (Marx 1972[1867]; Marx & Engels 2004[1888]).[4] The fact that these writers described the eighteenth and nineteenth century does not preclude application of the term "*capitalism*" to the seventeenth century or twenty-first centuries.

The convergence of factors leading to the shift to sugar, slavery, and capitalism in Barbados occurred during a period of political turmoil in England that resulted in laissez-faire governance and a void in administrative oversight in the West Indies (Armstrong & Reilly 2014). The individual elements that combined to make sugar and slavery so profitable were not unique. They included plantation-based sugar production, enslavement of laborers, and industrial innovations that were applied to sugar processing. What was new in the early seventeenth century was the confluence of a new privately funded capitalistic financial system based on differential commodity prices and an ability to engage in global trade. This financial system produced profits that allowed protection of base capital and profits, and fed a desire to reinvest profits to generate new capital. Capitalist investors, flush with profits, were eager to invest and profit from this convergence—and, then to reinvest the profits in the emerging plantation systems and in broader fabrics of society, finance, and governance.

Setting the Stage: Emergent Agro-Industrial Capitalism in the Seventeenth Century

Sugar had a long history as a domesticated crop in South and East Asia, and it had been produced in the Mediterranean since the seventh century (Galloway 1989, 50). Sugar production involved enslaved laborers as early as the tenth century, and by the fourteenth century the Portuguese had established colonial holdings in the islands off the North African coast, in places like Madeira, and the Azores, and both the Spanish and Portuguese had influence in the Canary Islands.[5] Christopher Columbus brought sugar cane with him on his second Atlantic voyage, in 1493 (Morison 1942).[6] An outcome of the Treaty of Tordesillas in 1494 was a division of Iberian control in the Americas, with the Portuguese gained control of large expanses of land suitable for agricultural production, while Spain retained rights what gold and silver producing western regions of South America. The fifteenth century saw the beginning of an ever-increasing demand for sugar in Europe and the Portuguese applied their knowledge of sugar production (Galloway 1989, 64).[7]

In Brazil, Portuguese sugar plantations, or *engenhos* (mills), expanded from the 1520s through the sixteenth century, and labor gradually shifted from wage and contract laborers to enslaved laborers from Africa. As late as 1583, two-thirds of the laborers working in Pernambuco remained indigenous peoples, with the remainder enslaved Africans (Galloway 1989, 77). However, as indigenous peoples began to resist, the Portuguese came to rely on Africans in Brazil, and by 1600, the sugar *engenhos* were dependent on enslaved laborers from Africa. Much of the shift to African labor in Brazil occurred in the last quarter of the sixteenth century.

Technology was also on the cusp of dramatic change. In the early seventeenth century planters began converted from the old horizontal, two-roller mills (as practiced in the Mediterranean), to three roller vertical mills system driven by cattle. By 1618, this type of cattle mill was widespread, and by 1628 it was the predominant form of mill used in Brazil.[8] When brought to Barbados, sugar production incorporated the newest technological change, an elaborate system of boiling sugar in a series of cauldrons, or coppers.

Slavery had been practiced in various forms for millennia on several continents, and has deep roots in human power relations. Slavery was encoded into labor systems of Mesopotamia as far back as 3100 BC, and is well documented for the Greek and Roman Empires (Westermann 1984). Slavery existed in Africa well before Portuguese ships of trade made their way to the shores of West and Central Africa in the fifteenth century (DeCorse 1991, Lovejoy 1989). Portuguese plantations (cotton) in Cabo Verde were dependent on enslaved African laborers from the 1460s. Hence, by the seventeenth century slavery on Portuguese plantations was nearly two centuries old (Chouin & DeCorse 2019). In the Americas, enslaved Africans were part of the early colonizing expeditions of the Spanish (Woodward 2011).

Trents Plantation and the Shift to Sugar in Barbados

Over the past several years, I have been engaged in an archaeological and historical study of the material and spatial footprint of the revolutionary shift to sugar and slavery through the examination of changes in the cultural landscape of Trents Plantation, Barbados. In 1657, Richard Ligon wrote *A True and Exact History of Barbados*, in which he described the formation of large sugar estates. Ligon observed, "when the small plantations in poor men's hands, of ten, twenty, or thirty acres, which are too small to lay to the work, be bought up by great men, and put together into plantations of five, six, or seven hundred acres, that two thirds of the island will be fit for plantation of sugar, which will make it one of the richest spots of earth under the sun."[9] In this statement, he describes two things: the shift from small-scale farms to large-scale agriculture and its related shift to large-scale agro-industrial capital enterprise.

A map of a Barbadian plantation, drawn in 1646 by John Hapcott provides an opportunity to examine this transformation (see fig. 6.1 on page 136). The map depicts a series of small, irregularly shaped, farms bounded by a newly defined 300-acre plantation indicated by a fixed rectangular boundary of making lands that have been capitalized as a sugar estate. The map was known to scholars but was simply considered an interesting early map of an unknown Barbadian plantation. Because I was looking to find examples of the presugar landscape and the later sugar plantation landscape, I recognized that this map projected spatial data for both simultaneously. Using GIS, the map was overlain on a modern topographic map (see fig. 6.2 on page 137).

The overlay showed a fit with structures that survived in the modern landscape. The map includes St. James Parish Church, constructed in 1629, which was later rebuilt on the same site. It also depicts a mansion house of what in 1627 (and 1646) was known as "Fort" Plantation. A seventeenth-century version of this house remains on the same site and is part of a plantation known today as

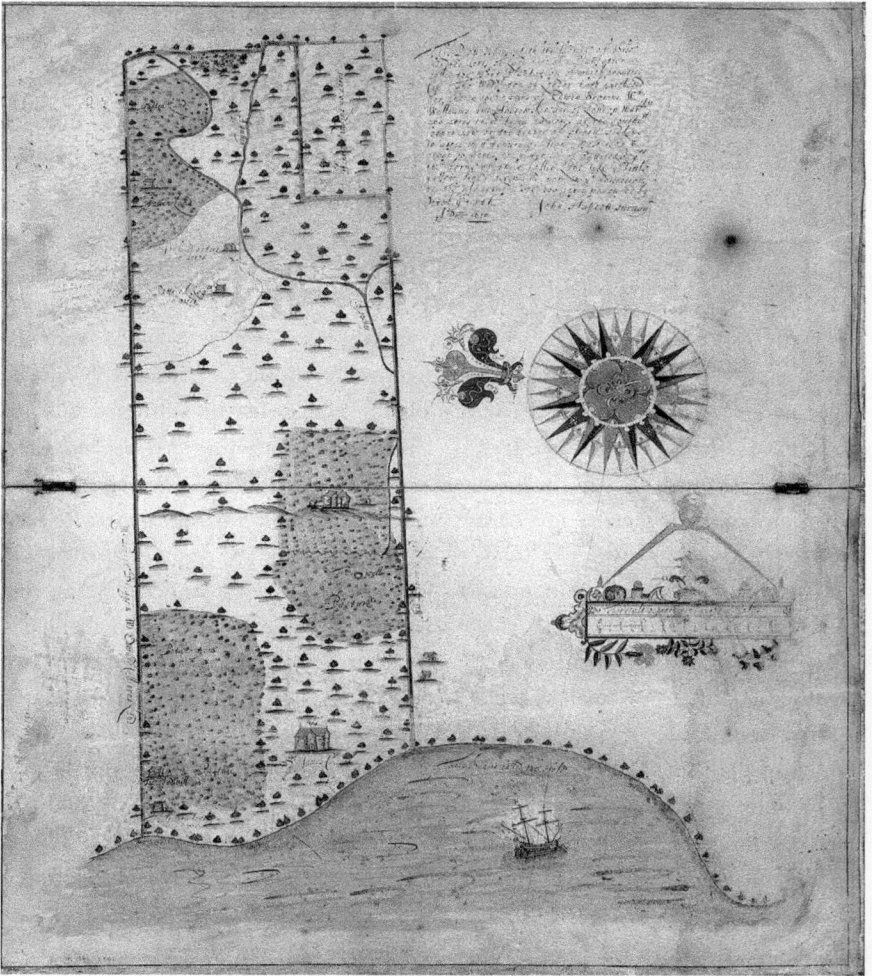

Figure 6.1. John Hapcott Map of 1646 showing "Estate plan of 300 acres of land near Holetown, Barbados." (Courtesy of the John Carter Brown Library, Brown University)

Trents Plantation (Armstrong 2015). The legend on the Hapcott map describes a mortgage, by Captain Thomas Middleton for a group of London merchant capitalists, including Owen Browne, William Williams, and Andrew Reward (Hapcott 1646). William Williams retained his interest in Fort Charles Plantation until

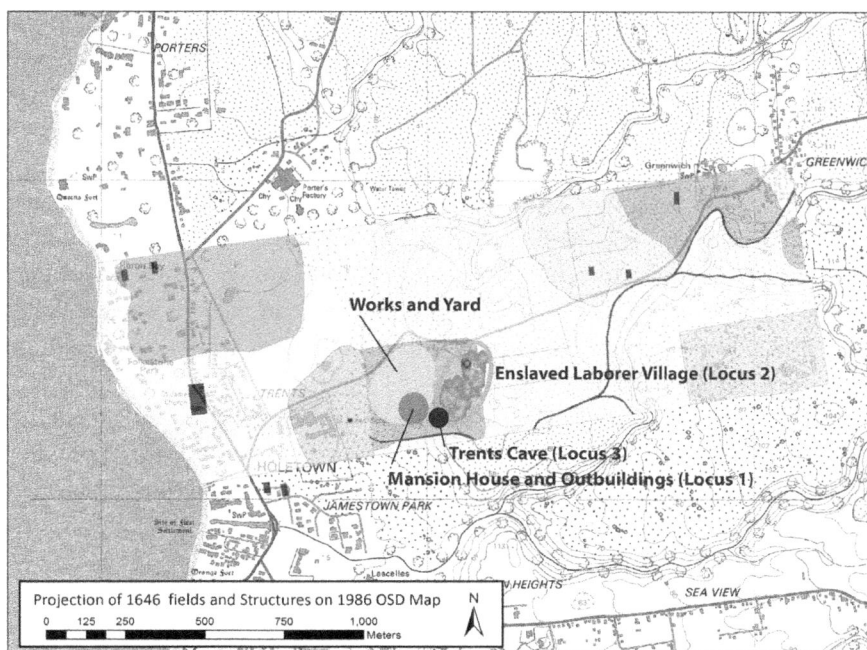

Figure 6.2. Topographic map of Barbados with an overlay of features of Trents Plantation based on the 1646 Hapcott Map and archaeological data. The locations of the early settlement, sugar-era plantation house and sugar works (Locus 1), enslaved laborer settlement (Locus 2), and Trents cave site (Locus 3) are shown. (Illustration by Douglas V. Armstrong)

1669, when he and a group of London bankers and brokers sold it to William Dyer. By then it was a sugar estate that sold for £6,990.

When first settled by English colonists in 1627, no indigenous people remained on the island, and settlers were confronted with a heavy forest. However, a group of indigenous people from Guiana contracted themselves to assist the initial settlers. This group taught slash-and-burn agriculture. In 1631, Henry Colt described the slash-and-burn farmland on the hillside below the "Fort Plantation" (Trents) mansion house: "There stands a stubb of a tree above two yards high, all ye earth covered black with cenders nothing is clear. What digged or weeded for beautye? All are bushes, and long grasse, all thinges caryinge ye face of a desolate and disorderly shew to ye beholder" (Colt 1925[1631]: 66).

Using the Hapcott map as a guide, we found midden deposits associated with the initial period of settlement at Trents Plantation. Presugar era middens near the mansion house project limited access to material goods. Artifacts from early deposits include a sparse array of items, including only a few free-blown bottle glass fragments (mostly case bottles) as well as, stoneware Bellarmine face jug fragments, a Ming-style porcelain bowl, and a variety of locally made course earthenware (see fig. 6.3a, b, e). These materials represent, the collective goods of all those who resided at the early farm during the presugar era: farmer, indentured laborers, and enslaved laborers. The number and range of types of wares is decidedly sparse, particularly in comparison with the abundant array of artifacts from the later sugar era at the site.

Fortunately, two detailed presugar era inventories were recorded. In 1641, plantation owner Captain Daniel Fletcher, secured a loan on the basis of real property (land and buildings), and the value of the contracts for fourteen indentured laborers,

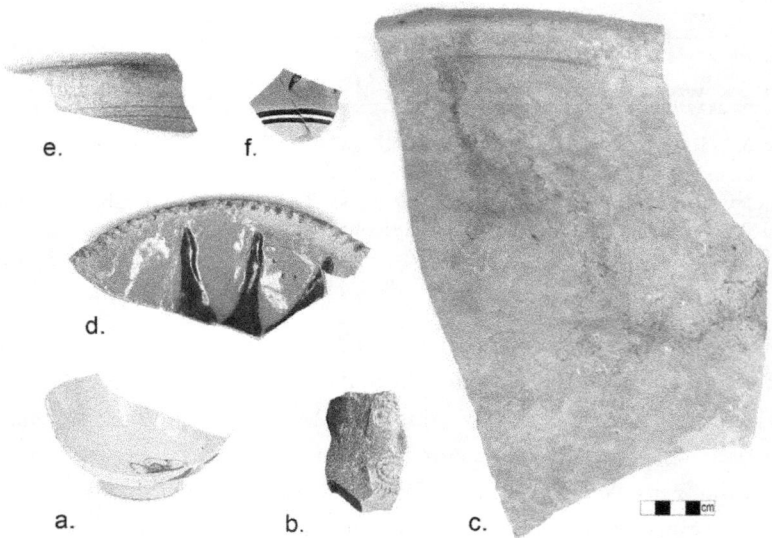

Figure 6.3. (a) Ming porcelain bowl from early-seventeenth-century planter/laborer context (Locus 1); (b) Bellarmine face jug from early- to mid-seventeenth-century planter/laborer context (Locus 1); (c) industrial earthenware sugar cone, mid-seventeenth century planter context (Locus 1); (d) slipware, late-seventeenth to early-eighteenth-century enslaved laborer settlement (Locus 2); (e) coarse earthenware decorated pot, eighteenth century, enslaved laborer settlement (Locus 2), and (f) banded creamware bowl, late-eighteenth to early-nineteenth-century enslaved laborer settlement (Locus 2).

various animal stock, and material items on the estate.[10] The mortgage, representing a half moiety (or interest), was to be repaid with a combination of 20,000 pounds of cotton and tobacco (Armstrong 2015).[11] Two years later Fletcher was involved in a second mortgage, in which repayment was to be made in a single commodity—cotton.[12] Also, there is a change, not in the size of the labor force, but in its composition. The 1643 mortgage lists five indentured laborers and eight enslaved laborers (Armstrong 2015).[13] The detailed inventory includes a sparse array of goods including: one jug (perhaps one of the Bellarmines we recovered from the site) and a few bottles.[14] Hence, both the archaeological record and the inventory indicate a paucity of possessions.

Deed books for Barbados provide a complementary set of data that are consistent with the archaeological findings. Inventories define buildings, laborers, and goods on the estates. Nearly all early deeds show considerable detail and list of items included in the transaction, for example, a mortgage made by Thomas Waller on a small tobacco- and cotton-producing plantation in parish of St. Lucy. Included were items like a gouge, one lamp, one stone jug, and one case of empty bottles.[15] This inventory projects the paucity of goods held. The listing of empty bottles, illustrates that glass bottles were valued and reused. Another example is the deed for sale of a half interest in sixteen acres of land sold by Henry Harford to William Halloway in 1641. It lists items like old bills and hoes, and includes "one iron pot, two treys, one bowl, half of all the boards, tables, benches, one new axe, one old axe, one hatchet, two old bills, two old hoes, and half of the implements on the plantation."[16] These are consistent with the majority of the dozens of deeds examined. Collectively, they project small-scale operations and a paucity of material possessions or accumulated wealth. However, a few planters accumulated considerable wealth, and when sugar production began, those who were able to hold on to their land were able to generate vast wealth and associated material possessions.

Understanding Change: Barbados's place in the Turn to Capitalism

Having introduced the presugar landscape, I will focus on the critical confluence of events that financed and empowered the sugar- and slavery-based labor regime that became ensconced in Barbados, and then throughout much of the Americas. To illustrate the complex interplay of multinational interests in the emerging capitalism in Barbados, I will focus on the role of Dutch public companies in financing the shift to sugar. As noted by Fernand Braudel (1972–1973, 545) as early as 1512, the Dutch showed an interest in Portuguese trade to the Far East. Prior to 1572, the Netherlands were under disputed control by Spain, and the Dutch were prohibited from direct contact with overseas colonies. The success of the Dutch revolt allowed its maritime merchants to engage in the lucrative spice and pepper trade with Asia. Following the practice of the Portuguese, the Dutch contracted with ports of trade in Asia to set up a regular flow of goods from which great profits were derived.

The merger of a group of Dutch trading companies in 1602 created the United Dutch East India Company (Vereenigde Oost-Indische Compagnie or VOC). The VOC was a public trading company. It was the largest and most profitable of an array of seventeenth-century joint stock companies, including English, French, and Danish companies in the East and West Indies. From 1602 to 1650, the VOC's investor-base capital grew from 6 million gilders to 37 million gilders, and its collective investors received paid distributions of 1285 percent of their investment.[17] While it can be argued that the Dutch themselves had not been organized around feudalism, much of Europe, including England, had. From a financial standpoint, the success of the VOC facilitated the shift from feudalism to modern global capitalism and the application of the capitalist model to emerging colonies in the Americas (Robertson & Fennell 2014, 1). The profits of this form of trading company generated a flow of capital in the Netherlands that allowed its shareholders, including cities and individual investors, some with ties to England, to invest in new ventures.

While trade was the objective of the VOC, when the Dutch turned toward the Caribbean, their initial interest was in inflicting damage to the colonial resources of Iberian enemies. The Dutch approach involved attaching settlements and engaging in privateering (piracy) on its shipping. The founding of the Dutch West Indies Trading Company (Westindische Companie or WIC) in 1621 was proceeded by less formally organized efforts by Dutch and English pirates and privateers (Nimako & Willemsen 2011). Collectively these efforts caused the Spanish to restrict the focus of their engagement to their larger settlements and to protect their lucrative plate fleet.[18]

The sixteenth-century Spanish and Portuguese did not formally settle islands of the Eastern Caribbean, but their presence was felt. They engaged in raiding the islands to obtain indigenous laborers, established populations of European domesticates such as hogs. When Portuguese explorer, Pedro de Campas, landed on Barbados in 1536, he declared the island to be uninhabited (Beckles 2006, 3). The disruption of the Dutch WIC and English privateers opened coastal areas of northern South America and the islands of the eastern Caribbean to possible settlement. It was on a voyage back north from a Dutch-held part of Guyana that a Dutch-backed English vessel sailed off course and landed in Barbados in 1625. The English returned and established a settlement in Barbados in 1627.

The initial settlement was a small-scale corporate venture backed by the Anglo-Dutch firm of Courteen and Co., headed by Dutch-born, Sir William Courteen, along with his brother Peter. They had ties to Zeeland, the Netherlands, and trading interests in the East, West, and Greenland. Courteen had made his way to London in 1624 (Harlow 1924, xxix) where he partnered with Peter Bourdaan, who was a member of a Committee of the Zeeland Chamber and a Director of the WIC, and V. G. Money of London, both of whom were related by marriage (Edmundson 1901, xvi; Harlow 1924, xxiv). William Courteen's company financed the pioneering settlement and he was among the pioneers who landing at Jamestown (now Holetown) February 17, 1627 (Harlow 1924, xxix). Expedition head, Captain Henry Powell, left his nephew John Powell in charge of clearing land and establishing the settlement, and almost immediately headed to a Dutch, Zeeland settlement, which was on the Essequibo River (now Disseekeeb) in Guyana from 1616–1632, for the dual purpose of supplying the Dutch settlement, for which Courteen's firm had financial connections, and collecting roots, cuttings, and seeds for the new Barbadian settlement.

While initially organized around small-scale farms, the English colonial population on Barbados grew quickly, secured in part by continued Dutch and English privateering attacks on the Spanish and Portuguese. The initial group of Courteen-backed settlers was usurped in 1629 by a group backed by William Hay (aka, Lord Carlisle), and by 1630 there were 1900 colonists. In contrast to earlier English settlements like Jamestown, Virginia, in 1607, whose initial charter targeted exploration, and gold and silver, and which by 1624 was bankrupt; the settlement in Barbados, immediately drew on the knowledge and skills of a group of thirty indigenous people from Guyana who were contracted as indentured laborers, assigned to teach the planting of American crops (Armstrong & Reilly 2014).

Hundreds of patents were let to pioneer farmers, and by the early 1630s the island population had expanded to several thousand people on 106,000 patented acres that had at least nominally been divided into between 8,000 and 11,200 properties.[19] By the early 1640s, Barbados had grown significantly, with small-scale farmers clearing land assisted primarily by indentured, or contracted, laborers from Europe, along with some African slaves (although legally slavery had not yet been fully codified by law). Prior to 1643, a range of crops were producing at least marginal profits. Tobacco grew well, but was not harvested with the same care as in Virginia, and quickly lost favor, and as production increased, prices dropped. Cotton, on the other hand, became known for its high quality and long strands, and by the mid-1630s had become the island's primary cash crop; for a time cotton "wool" became the basis of financial exchange (Beckert 2014).

Meanwhile, the Dutch captured of plantation lands at Recife in 1630, and then expanded holdings in the Pernambuco region of northeastern Brazil (Price 1998, 23; Galloway 1989, 78).[20] Dutch experience and capital, derived from the cane fields of Pernambuco become significant factors in the shift to sugar and slavery in Barbados. Barbadian planter, James Drax, traveled to Pernambuco, to examine sugar production. He brought back information on the construction of cattle-driven three-roller vertical sugar mills.[21] At the same time, he and a small group of planters, established ties with English and Dutch financiers, arranged for shipping, and negotiated contacts on future sugar crops. This group often worked together, sharing risk by taking half-interests in one another's estates, or providing access to mills and factories to process the first season's sugar prior to the completion of rapidly constructed mills and sugar factories. The construction of factories and purchase of laborers was financed by advance loans that provided the backers, who in turn were guaranteed the future crop at a set price.

Sugar grew well in Barbados. Meanwhile, the Dutch were having trouble holding control of parts of their South American settlements. Turmoil in Pernambuco restricted Dutch access to expected crops, and sugar prices went up dramatically, which in turn encouraged financial backers to invest capital in new, larger-scale plantations, with mills, sugar factories, curing houses, and much needed labor in Barbados. Based on initial successes, James Drax and others rapidly expanded sugar operations by taking on investors and business partners. Among them was entrepreneurial capitalist Thomas Middleton, who in 1646 brokered a deal with London financiers to convert "Fort Charles" Plantation, the site that would later become Trents Plantation, to sugar. Middleton had already partnered with James Drax and later bought the Mount sugar plantation from Drax (Beckles 2006; Campbell 1993, 1984a, b; Dunn 1972; Drax 1674; Gragg 2007; Harlow 1926; Ligon 1657 [2000 and 2011]; Newman 2013; Parker 2011; Smith S. 2006). The

loan, and corresponding changes in the landscape were recorded in the 1646 John Hapcott map.

At Trents, financial backers provided the up-front capital to transform forested, lands to create sugar plantations. Funds from loans and profits from the sugar crop were used to purchase enslaved African laborers to clear the land and to construct sugar mills and works. The economic success of sugar estates in the mid-1640s and 1650s, drew on the confluence of high prices, dramatically expanding markets for sugar, laissez-faire governance, and significant technological innovations; including sugar factories with rows of coppers where crushed juice was boiled to produce sugar. Mills, also shifted from sets of three vertical three-rollers powered by oxen to a wind-powered mill. Needed labor was supplied by a shift from European indentured laborers to a reliance on enslaved African labor, made available by the expanding Atlantic trade. By the late 1640s, Dutch holdings in South America were less secure and they were looking for places to reinvest their capital. Investors from England and the Netherlands provided advances (mortgages) to gain access to future crops, provided shipping, and organized further refining of the sugar in England and Holland. Ultimately, the Dutch lost their colony in Pernambuco in 1654 (Galloway 1989, 78). In the meantime, the Dutch invested in English sugar estates in Barbados, and in emerging private English corporations, and capital backers of sugar production expanded the scope and spatial range of their investments throughout the Caribbean.

The shift to sugar can be seen in significant changes to the overall cultural landscape. At Trents, enslaved laborers increased first to 50, then to 160, and finally to 176 by the time of emancipation. The deeply stratified middens associated with the planter mansion at Trents was filled with an abundance of mid- to late-seventeenth-century artifacts, as well as rubble from late-seventeenth-century remodeling of the house. Most obvious among the artifacts present are large quantities of industrial sugar-ware, including drip jars and sugar cones (see fig. 6.3c). The sheer quantity of the thousands of industrial wares indicates the scale of the sugar industry. However, this site was a domestic residence. The domestic wares include large quantities of tin enamelware, including everything from serving bowls and platters to chamber ware, along with ornate overgraze porcelain bowls and utilitarian stoneware storage vessels. Domestic coarse earthenware for cooking are present, along with relatively little slipware. The predominance of tin enamelware and Chinese porcelain are indicative of the high economic status of the planters. This is further demonstrated by the wide range of crystal stemware wineglasses and tumblers, and the presence of free-blown bottle forms, including both onion and case bottle forms. In contrast to the sparse representation of bottle glass from the presugar era context, during the sugar era, bottle glass had become expendable—bottles were unwired and uncorked, their contents consumed, and the bottles discarded.[22] New generations of owners used expendable capital to rebuild and redecorate. Diamond-shaped mullion window glass and lead came from mullion windows glass were replaced by Georgian-style counterparts still present in the house standing on the property.

By the 1650s, with the shift to sugar and a large group of enslaved labor, a new and separate laborer settlement was established. Fortunately, as part of our archaeological survey we found settlement on an adjacent hill side (see fig. 6.2). This settlement is the only unplowed enslaved laborer settlement that has been found in Barbados. In all other cases, the villages were plowed under, and in most cases the land was put into cane when free laborers moved away from the core of plantations following emancipation. Fourteen house sites were defined and four were intensively excavated. While materials project a long period of occupation, house area excavations confirmed the presence of seventeenth-century house floors with quantities of sgrafitto slipware and domestic coarse earthenware for early houses (see fig. 6.3d). The later-eighteenth and early-nineteenth-century material remains indicate a continued reliance on a wide range of course earthenware cooking pots, bowls, pans, and water bottles (see figs. 3e and 4). Imported wares include an abundance of relatively low cost creamware and pearlware with an array of complex banded, mocha, cat's eye, and machine roulette patterns, on mostly bowl forms (see fig. 6.3f). The materials point to an abrupt abandonment that coincided with emancipation. Component element characterization of earthenware using laser ablation (LA-ICP-MS) analysis shows locally produced Barbadian coarse earthenware associated with all contexts at Trents, including the early settlement, later planter contexts, and the enslaved laborer settlement (Block, Armstrong, & Galle 2017). Cluster analysis also shows distinctly different composition of local versus imported European earthenware, as well as compositional differences in locally produced domestic earthenware compared with locally produced industrial sugar cones and jars.

With respect to economic scale, by 1669, less than two decades after the shift to sugar production at Trents, the estate was sold to William Dyer for the substantial sum of £6,990 sterling.[23] The increase in the value of the property is reflected by

Figure 6.4. Barbadian made glazed coarse earthenware, early eighteenth century, enslaved laborer settlement (Locus 2, house area 1).

the absence of the type of small items defined in early deeds and the inclusion of prized items like ruby rings and pearl necklaces. By this time the scale of the sugar estate was such that transactions no longer included small items like used hoes and empty bottles. Rather, the deed included all lands and all "sugar works, negroes, Christian forths, cattle, stocks, . . . and implements of household and of other things remaining and belonging on or about said plantation."[24]

A few years later, William Dyer's will provides details related to the wealth of the planter and the economic profitability of the estate.[25] Estate inventories show a continued reliance on enslaved laborers so that by the time the estate was passed on to Lawrence Trent in 1743, there were 160 enslaved persons.[26] From that point forward the size and scale of the plantation operation remained fairly constant through the period of emancipation in 1834, with 167 enslaved laborers registered in the final return of slaves (UCL 2013). John Constant Trent, received compensation of £3,396 9S 5D as part of a total reparation of more than £10,000 for the enslaved laborers on his four plantations.[27]

Conclusion

Certainly, the roots of capitalism are much deeper than the seventeenth century and the form of capitalism that emerged in Barbados. Large-scale sugar plantations had operated successfully in places like Madeira, and even more robustly in Pernambuco in the years leading up to the English settlement of Barbados. However, there can be no doubt that the changes that were set into motion in Barbados established a new capitalistic mode of social and economic production. The change that occurred in Barbados during the 1640s was based on a shift in the scale of agro-industrial production of sugar and the use of enslaved labor. This form of capitalistic enterprise was backed by private Dutch and English financial corporations. The form of capital investments initiated in Barbados was tied to broader global change. The multinational private financing of the shift to sugar, slavery, and capitalism in Barbados had a revolutionary impact on the trajectory of what many refer to as the modern world.

Acknowledgments

This research has been carried out in partnership with the Barbados Museum and Historical Society and has benefited significantly from the assistance of Kevin Farmer (deputy director of the Barbados Museum) and Allisandra Cummins (directory, Barbados Museum). Throughout the project, Karl Watson has been of continual support and assistance. Annie Price has not only put up with archaeologists digging holes on her property, but has been a gracious host and friend to the archaeological field team, hosting parties and encouraging engagement with the community. The project has been assisted by Barbados National Trust and faculty and students from University of the West Indies, Cave Hill, as well as students from Syracuse University. This project has been funded by grants from National Science Foundation, the Wenner-Gren Foundation (two grants), the National Geographic Society (two grants), and grants from Syracuse University.

Notes

1. See also Gary Puckrein's "Little England" (1984).

2. Interestingly, in his argument against slavery Williams draws from Adam's Smith's critique of the economics of slavery: "the work done by slaves, though it appears to cost only their maintenance, is in the end the dearest of any. A person who can acquire no property can have no other interest than to eat as much, and to labor as little as possible" (Smith 1937[1777], 365). Smith defines capitalism as already well established in the mid-eighteenth century.

3. *Merriam-Webster*, 2015. Dictionary definition of "capitalism." Viewed online at http://www.merriam-webster.com/dictionary/capitalism.

4. While Marx is critical of the exploitation of laborers in pursuit of the surplus capital produced by labor, often under harsh and unregulated conditions, the focus of his argument is on exploitation of wage and contract laborers of the nineteenth century (Marx 1972, 255, 239).

5. Sugar production in Madeira began in 1433, and by about 1450 it had replaced wheat as the principal crop of the island with exports increasing significantly through the fifteenth and sixteenth centuries (Galloway 1977, 50–52; see also Mintz 1985, 51). In the Canary Islands, a Spanish mission had been established by 1352, but sugar production did not begin until cane and milling experts were brought to Grand Canary from Madeira in the 1484 (Fernandez-Armesto 1982, 14, 80). On the islands off the coast of Africa, European colonizers found a productive environment for "the cultivation of sugar that was considerably better than around the Mediterranean" (Galloway 1989, 50; 1977, 177).

6. Before, his travels across the Atlantic to the Americas, Christopher Columbus had been involved in maritime travels associated with the Madeira trade and had even married the daughter of Madeiran landowner from the island of Funchal (Morison 1942, 1:41–53). Spanish settlers grew at least some sugar cane on virtually every island that they settled. Hence, much later, when islands like St. Christopher and Martinique were settled by the English and French, they found cane growing when they arrived (Labat 1742, 3, 321–27).

7. While introduced by Columbus, sugar production on Hispaniola really began only after the exhaustion of placer gold fields in about 1515, with some form of formal production of sugar continuing until the 1630s. It was produced in combination with corn, manioc, and native cotton (Galloway 1989, 64). The rapid growth of the Portuguese sugar industry in South America probably served as a disincentive to the Spanish in the Caribbean, who quickly shifted from mining to the production of provision foods and stock, raising in support of their South American mainland and shipping enterprises.

8. By 1570 there were 60 *engenios* in Brazil, by 1580 there were over 100, by 1629 there were 346, and by 1710 there were 528 (Galloway 1989, 77).

9. Ligon 2011[1657]: 86. During the period of the shift to sugar there was a dramatic consolidation of lands and a corresponding reduction in landowners from an estimate of between "8,300 and 11,200 in the mid-1640s to 2,639 in 1679" (Handler & Lange 1978, 116).

10. 1641 BDA Deeds RB6/2, 288.

11. The names of all fourteen laborers were listed along with their term of indenture (BDA RB6, Deeds: 2/288–89, Daniell Fletcher grantor, May 3, 1641).

12. This was an era of growing financial speculation aimed at securing profits from contracts on cotton. This type of transaction shows that even before sugar swept the island into large-scale capitalistic marketing of cash crops, Barbados was already experimenting with this form of capitalism.

13. 1643 BDA RB6, Deeds: 1/92, Daniel Fletcher Grantee, September 15, 1643. Daniel Fletcher had obtained the enslaved laborers as part of a separate land transaction that included the enslaved African laborers as part of a property transaction and they were apparently then moved to what was then "Fort Plantation."

14. BDA, RB6, Deeds 1/92, Daniel Fletcher Grantee, September 15, 1643.

15. It also notes the exclusion of personal items, including "one chest, one trunk, one hammock and wearing clothes" (1643 BDA, RB3/ Deeds 1/228-2296, Thomas Waller, 6 November 1643).

16. 1641 BDA, RB3/ Deeds 1/105–6, Henry Harford to William Halloway ½ moiety, January 10, 1641.

17. Over nearly the 200 years of operation, the company (until 1798) distributed 230 million guilders to its holders, which is an average of 18½ percent (NL-HaNA: VOC,1.04.02, file 14549, folio 1 2/3).

18. Much of WIC capital came from cities with little experience in trade outside of Europe: Utrecht, Deventer, Haarlem, and Leiden; with significant investment from Johnannes de Laet of Leiden.

19. Although only small tracts of land had been cleared and many of the parcels that were defined as patented were not actually settled until the success of sugar.

20. The Dutch attempted to seize the Brazilian city of Salvador in Bahia in 1624–1625. In 1630 they returned and captured Recife, and then expanded their holdings along the coast, holding some until 1654 (Galloway 1989, 78).

21. James Drax was reported to have been among the initial group of settlers backed by William Courteen and a group of London- and Dutch-based financiers. Father Beit, a visitor to the island in 1654, suggests that Drax and others lived in modest housing, including a cave, near Holetown upon their initial arrival in 1627 (Handler 1967, 69). Beit, as translated by Jerome Handler, reported that "One day old Captain Oldiph (one must note that all plantation masters carry the title of Captain or Colonel) related to me how this island had been settled, and said that he had been one of the first settlers. It was certainly some thirty years ago, he told me, when seven or eight Englishmen, among them Colonel Drax, entered this island having been carried there by one of their ships. They sheltered in a cave in the rocks. They lived by hunting, which was good enough, and from provisions which had been left them by the ship. They cleared a piece of land which they

planted in tobacco, and this grew so well that they produced an abundance which obliged the head of the band to carry it to England-in-the first vessel they met" (Handler 1967, 69). Formal records of estate ownership begin in 1637, with additional details provided in individual wills and deeds designed to confirm ownership for sale or transfers through inheritance (Armstrong 2013b).

22. This change may be tied to overall changes in consumption and discard practice, but it is in sharp contrast with the continued paucity of and evidence of repeated reuse of bottle glass from the adjacent enslaved laborer contexts (Locus 2, ISB3-2).

23. 1669 BDA RB7/2/156, William Dyer grantee, October 8, 1669. At the time of William Dyer's acquisition of the property in 1669, it was owned by the group of London investors and operated by Edward Body and Charles Bolam.

24. 1669 BDA RB7/2/156 William Dyer grantee, October 8, 1669.

25. 1674 BDA RB6/ 212–14, William Dyer, July 30, 1674.

26. 1743 BDA RB 6/33, 300.

27. The other three plantations were: Spring, Over Hill, and Ashton Hall.

Works Cited

Armstrong, Douglas V. 2015. "Archaeology of the Enslaved Laborer Settlement at Trents Plantation: 2014–2015." *Journal of the Barbados Historical Society* 61, 146–77.

———. Forthcoming "Capitalism and the Shift to Sugar and Slavery in Mid-Seventeenth Century Barbados." *Historical Archaeology* 53 (3).

Armstrong, Douglas V., and Matthew C. Reilly. 2014. "The Archaeology of Settler Farms and Early Plantation Life in Seventeenth-Century Barbados." *Slavery & Abolition: A Journal of Slave and Post Slave Studies* 35(3): 399–417.

Beckert, Sven. 2014. *Empire of Cotton: A Global History*. New York: Alfred A. Knopf.

Beckles, Hilary. 2006. *A History of Barbados: From Amerindian Settlement to Caribbean Single Market*. New York: Cambridge University Press.

Block, Lindsay, Douglas V. Armstrong, and Jillian Galle. 2017. "Unraveling Global and Local Ceramic Production Network: An LA-ICP-MS Analysis of Ceramics from Barbados, Jamaica, and Great Britain." Paper presented at the Society for American Archaeology Conference, Vancouver, April 15, 2017.

Bridenbaugh Carl, and Roberta Bridenbaugh. 1972. *No Peace Beyond the Line: The English in the Caribbean, 1624–90: The Beginnings of the American People*. Oxford: Oxford University Press.

Chayanov, A. V. 1968. *The Theory of Peasant Economy*. Madison: University of Wisconsin Press.

Campbell, Peter F. 1984a. "Aspects of Barbados Land Tenure 1627–1663." *Journal of the Barbados Museum and Historical Society* 37(2): 112–53.

————. 1984b. "The Barbados Vestries 1627–1700—Part II." *Journal of the Barbados Museum and Historical Society* 37(2): 174–97.

————. 1993. *Some Early Barbadian History: As Well as the Text of a Book Published Anonymously in 1741 Entitled Memoirs of the First Settlement of the Island of Barbados (ca. 1677) by Major John Scott*. St. Michael, Barbados: Caribbean Graphics & Letchworth.

Chouin, Gérard, and Christopher DeCorse. Forthcoming. Atlantic Intersections: African-European Emporia in Early Modern West Africa. In *Trade and Colonization in the Ancient Mediterranean: The Emporion, from the Archaic to the Hellenistic Period*. Edited by Eric Gailledrat, Rosa Plana-Mallart, and Michael Dietler, 253–265. Montpellier, France: Presses Universitaires de la Méditerranée.

Colt, H. 1925[1631]. "The Voyages of Sir Henry Cold Knight to ye Ialands of ye Antileas in ye Shipp called ye Alexander, 1631." In *Colonizing Expeditions to the West Indies and Guiana, 1623–1667*. Edited by V. T. Harlow, 54–102. London: Hakluyt Society.

DeCorse, Christopher. 1991. "West African Archaeology and the Atlantic Slave Trade." *Slavery and Abolition* 12(2): 92–96.

Dunn, Richard. 1972. *Sugar and Slaves: The Rise of the Planter Class in the English West Indies, 1624–1713*. Chapel Hill: University of North Carolina Press.

Drax, Henry. ca. 1674. *Instructions on the Management of a Barbadian Sugar Plantation*. Oxford, UH: Bodleian Library Manuscript.

Fernandez-Armesto, Felipe. 1982. *The Canary Islands after the Conquest: The Making of a Colonial Society in the Early Sixteenth Century*. Oxford, UK: Clarendon Press.

Galloway, John T. 1977. "The Mediterranean Sugar Industry." *Geographical Review* 67(2): 177–94.

————. 1989. *The Sugar Cane Industry: An Historical Geography of Its Origins to 1914*. Cambridge, UK: Cambridge University Press.

Gragg, Larry. 2003. *Englishmen Transplanted: The English Colonization of Barbados, 1627–1660*. Oxford, UK: Oxford University Press.

Handler, Jerome. 1967. "Father Antoine Biet's Visit to Barbados in 1654." *Journal of the Barbados Museum and Historical Society* 32(2): 56–76.

Handler, Jerome S., and Frederick W. Lange. 1978. *Plantation Slavery in Barbados: An Archaeological Investigation*. Cambridge, MA: Harvard University Press.

Hapcott, John. 1646. "Estate Plan of 300 Acres of Land Near Holetown, Barbados," original housed in the John Carter Brown Library at Brown University. http://www.brown.edu/Facilities/John_Carter_Brown_Library/mapexhib/describe.html).

Harlow, Vincent T., ed. 1924. *Colonizing Expeditions to the West Indies and Guiana 1623–1667*. London: Hakluyt Society.

————. 1926. *A History of Barbados: 1625–1685*. New York: Negro Universities Press.

Higman, Barry W. 2011. A Concise History of the Caribbean. Cambridge, UK: Cambridge University Press.

Labat, Jean-Baptiste. 1742. *Nouveau vouage aux isles de L'Amérique, contentent l'histore naturelle de ces pays, l'origine, les noeurs, la religion et la gouvernement de habitants anciens et modernes.* Paris: J. B. Delespine.

Ligon, Richard. 2011[1657]. *A True and Exact History of the Island of Barbados.* Edited by Karen Kupperman. Indianapolis, IN: Hackett Press,

Lovejoy, Paul E. 1989. "The Impact of the Atlantic Slave Trade on Africa: A Review of the Literature." *Journal of African History* 30: 365.

Marx, Karl. 1972[1867]. *Capital [Das Kapital]: Selections, Karl Marx.* In *Marx-Engels Reader.* Edited by Robert C. Tucker, 191–318. New York: W. W. Norton and Company.

Marx, Karl, and Frederick Engels. 2004[1848 and 1888]. *Manifesto of the Communist Party.* Translated by Samuel Moore in cooperation with Frederick Engels, 1888. Edited by Andy Blunden. Marxists Internet Archive (marxists.org).https://www.marxists.org/archive/marx/works/1848/communist-manifesto/.

Morison, Samuel Eliot. 1942. *Admiral of the Ocean Sea: A Life of Christopher Columbus*, 2 vols. Boston: Little Brown.

Newman, Simon P. 2013. *A New World of Labor: The Development of Plantation Society in the British Atlantic.* Philadelphia: University of Pennsylvania Press.

Nimako, Kwame, and Glenn Willemsen, 2011. *The Dutch Atlantic.* London: Pluto Press.

Puckrein, G. A. 1984. *Little England: Plantation Society and Ango-Barbadian Politics 1627–1700.* New York: New York University Press.

Robertson, Jeffrey, and Warwick Funnell. 2014. *Accounting by the First Public Company: The Pursuit of Supremacy.* New York: Routledge.

Smith, Adam, 1937[1777]. *The Wealth of Nations.* New York: Random House.

Smith, Simon, D. 2006. *Slavery, Family, and Gentry Capitalism in the British Atlantic: The World of the Lascelles, 1648–1834.* Cambridge, UK: Cambridge University Press.

Trouillot. Michel-Rolph. 1995. *Silencing the Past: Power and the Production of History.* Boston: Beacon Press.

University College London (UCL). 2013. "Legacies of British Slave-Ownership." website: http://www.ucl.ac.uk/lbs). London: UCL History Department. Accessed February 28, 2013.

Watts, David. 1987. *The West Indies: Patterns of Development, Culture and Environmental Change Since 1492.* Cambridge, UK: Cambridge University Press.

Westermann, William Lynn. 1984[1955. "The Slave Systems of Greek and Roman Antiquity." *Memoirs of the American Philosophical Society* 40.

Williams, Eric. 2005[1944]. *Capitalism and Slavery,* Chapel Hill: University of North Carolina Press.

Woodward, Robyn P. 2011. "Feudalism or Agrarian Capitalism? The Archaeology of the Early Sixteenth Century Spanish Sugar Industry." In *Out of Many, One People: Historical Archaeology in Jamaica*. Edited by J. Delle, M. Hauser, and D. V. Armstrong, pp. 23–40. Tuscaloosa: University of Alabama Press.

Manuscripts

BDA: Deeds and Administrations; Barbados Department of Archives, Black Rock, St. James, Barbados.

1641 BDA Deeds and Administrations RB 6 2/288–89. Deed [mortgage]: Daniell Fletcher grantor, Edeard Seede, grantee, May 3, 1641.

1641 BDA Deeds and Administrations RB 3/1/105–6. Deed: Henry Harford to William Halloway one half moiety, January 10, 1641.

1643 BDA Deeds and Administrations RB 3/1/98. Deed of Sale between Daniel Fletcher and John Dyer, June 2, 1642.

1643 BDA Deeds and Administrations RB 3/1/228–2296. Deed: Thomas Waller, November 6, 1643.

1647 BDA Deeds and Administrations RB 3/2/:53, 55–57, Deeds of Sale between James Drax, William Drax, and Thomas Middleton.

1669 BDA Deeds and Administrations RB7/2/156. Deed: William Dyer grantee, October 8, 1669.

1674 BDA Wills RB 6/ 212–14. Will of William Dyer, July 30, 1674.

1743 BDA Wills RB 6/33: 300 Will of Lawrence Trent. RB 6/33:300.

NL-HaNA: National Archive of the Netherlands. http://en.nationaalarchief.nl/Netherlands National Archives.

NL-HaNA-VOC (Vereenigde Oost-Indische Compagnie), Company Records, 1.04.02, file 14549, folio 1 2/3.

Chapter 7

Indefensible Landscapes

Power Dynamics, Social Relations, and Antigua's Eighteenth-Century Fortifications

Christopher Kurt Waters

In this chapter I examine the incongruities in Antigua's eighteenth-century defensive landscape, and how they reflect the social, political, and economic structuring of the sugar-based plantation economy in which they were created (see fig. 7.1). While supposedly constructed to protect the island from foreign attack, many of the fortifications were poorly designed, ill-managed and maintained, and inadequately garrisoned.[1] A great deal of research on the Caribbean past has focused on the economics of sugar in galvanizing the industrial revolution, or on the social and material conditions of enslavement and the hardening of racial categories that the enslavement of millions of Africans brought about (e.g., Dunn 1972; Mintz 1985; Williams 1994). More recently, the focus shifted somewhat to incorporate social relations and the conditions of the settler societies which formed on these islands (e.g., Armstrong 2008, 2015; Armstrong & Kelly 2000; Bates, Chenowith, & Delle 2015; Delle 1998, 2014; Hauser 2008, 2011; Hicks 2007; Zacek 2012). The enduring unit of analysis throughout most of these studies is the plantation: whether as the basic unit of production within a world system, or as the space in which racial chattel slavery was practiced and resisted. Regardless of which scale researchers operate in, the plantation is always foregrounded, producing analogies then extrapolated to incorporate the wider social landscape, giving the plantation a privileged position in studying the colonial Caribbean. In this chapter, I argue that when studying the colonial landscape, the usefulness of the plantation as the

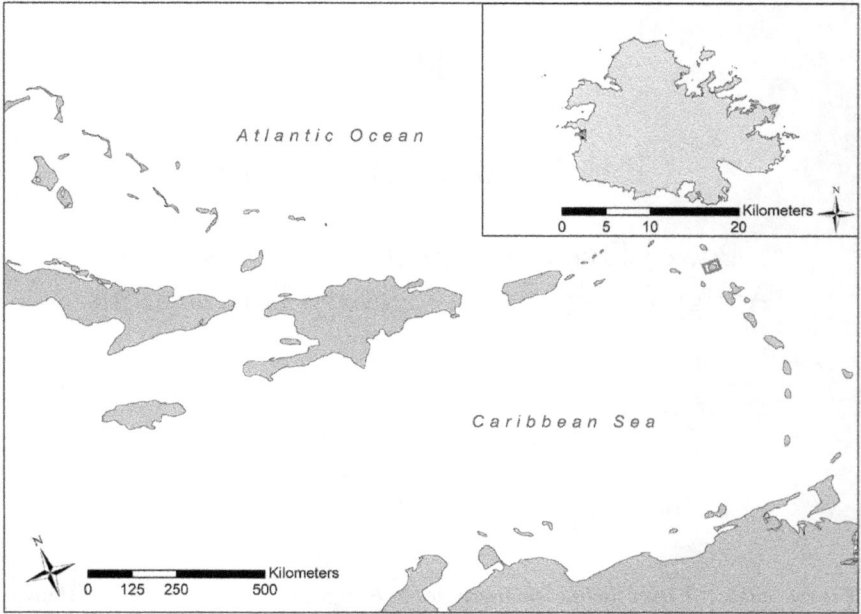

Figure 7.1. Antigua in the Caribbean. (Illustration by Christopher Kurt Waters)

dominant institution for analysis is limiting, reifying plantation boundaries as the principle vantage point, and thereby fossilizing the landscape and entrapping people within artificial spaces. Instead, I suggest that examining other colonial institutions, in this case Antigua's eighteenth-century fortification network, provides stronger loci for extrapolating social relationships and power dynamics on an island-wide scale.

Plantations in Context

The plantation has been the prevailing unit of empirical analysis for the eighteenth-century Caribbean landscape. These sites were central to the plantation economies of the Atlantic World. They were focal points of personal and coercive power imbalances related to European-indigenous relationships, colonialism, and imperialism. As such, the plantation encompasses a whole host of societal ills: a proto-industrial endeavor and the loci of extreme wealth production, enslavement, rise of modern racism, and their materiality's (Delle 1999, 2014; Hicks 2007; Higman 2001, 2005; Meniketti 2016). Nowhere is this truer than in the rise, growth, and collapse of the sugar industry in the Caribbean. As the primary analytical unit through which the colonial Caribbean is interpreted, and the strings of contemporary social issues are drawn through, the Caribbean (sugar) plantation is a multivalent unit of considerable interdisciplinary interest and investigable at myriad scales. The last forty years of scholarship, starting with the likes of Mintz (1985), Sheridan (1961, 1974), and Dunn (1972) bears witness to the power and attraction that these sites have, reflected in the thoroughness with which these landscapes are studied (for a critique see Cromwell 2014). The centrality of sugar and the plantation in the Caribbean is most evident in the regularly used visuals accompanying articles, monographs and heritage interpretations, with images from William Clark's 1824 *Ten Views in the Islands of Antigua* appearing in myriad presentations, popular literature, museum displays, and scholarly works. The attractive research potential of these sites for study is furthered by their high degree of accessibility and visibility on the landscape, and the ability to engage with subaltern populations, and investigating exploitation, enslavement, and resistance. This is fostered by rich historical and material records, and the cultural imaginary allowing contemporary populations to grapple with their plantation pasts. The abundance of records, facilitates examination of everything from household scale studies of enslaved life (Armstrong 1990, 1991, 1998, 2003; Armstrong & Kelly 2000; Ellis & Ginsburg 2010; Singleton 1999; Wilkie & Farnsworth 2005), diachronic examination landscape organization and plantation production (Bates 2015; Delle 1998, 2014; Hicks 2007; Higman 2001; 2005; Meniketti 2015; Singleton 2015), and racial and class relationship studies within the plantation (Burnard 2015; Hauser 2007; Lenik 2011), to global production chains and intercontinental trade (Curet & Hauser 2011; Mulcahy 2014).

The social, political, and economic dominance of the plantation historically is not questioned. However, it is also precisely the availability of these records and intense use of the plantation as the unit of analysis that limits our understanding of the lived experiences on the landscape, of which these plantations were only a part of. Cultural landscapes require continuity: the conceptual understanding that boundaries are artificial, often invisible, and not hindrances to movement nor proscriptions on relationships (Meniketti 2009; Johnson 2007). The plantation analytical unit has, subconsciously, become a *naturalized* and bounded space, circumscribed by the data sets on which we rely. Plantation ledgers, attorney letters, slave rolls, export records, laborer villages, great houses, and industrial complexes deal almost exclusively with the internal dynamics of plantations. Through the inner workings of plantations we see hints of cultural and economic shifts in a microcosm, phenomena that can be scaled up to the wider plantation-scape, the entire colony, and even into the wider Atlantic World. Yet, in practice, this advantage creates a situation whereby the plantation becomes a limiting unit of analysis with fixed boundaries, beyond which lies a transgressive landscape (see González-Ruibal 2014, 6–16). The landscape is marked by plantation "islands" checker-boarding the landscape, with few "betwixt and between," spaces (Turner 1964; see also Delle 2016; Hauser 2008, 28, 37–38; Singleton 2015, 210–12). In a situation where the majority of the population is violently coerced and enslaved, striding over these invisible boundaries automatically constitutes a transgression and an act of resistance, compounded by the secondary transgression of penetrating the next plantation island.[2]

Conceptually, this creates an epistemological conundrum. First, this constricts our understanding of movement and landscape. By erecting modern mental barriers based on a cultural conception of property, we constrain our understanding of the landscape as a whole: plantations never existed in isolation from their neighbors, and separated from regional and world economies. Second, by maintaining these boundaries, there is a tendency to homogenize the plantation as a replicable and reproducible unit. That is not to say that there are not analogous structures across plantations. Rather, this is a commentary on the diversity of humanity and the relationships they form. We are willing to accept that commodities like sugar, rum, and molasses can travel thousands of miles, spawn a number of primary, secondary, and even tertiary industries in Europe, North America, and Africa, but we are unwilling to consider local mobility as something other than transgressive (e.g., Lightfoot 2015, 21–24). Indeed, maintaining the plantation as an uncritical unit of analysis reduces enslaved Africans to a homogenous, bounded group locked within "the plantation." This not only creates the untenable position that reduces individuals to specific, plantation-oriented labor, but it also refuses to recognize the dynamic processes of sugar production locally, including the movement of produce and provisions overland, along the coasts, and between islands, and furthermore ignores those people—free and enslaved—who are not bound to a plantation at all.

These barriers require destabilizing. As Natasha Lightfoot, commenting on the marketplaces in Antigua, states,

Slaves around the Caribbean travelled frequently between towns and country. For huckstering, mingling, or a host of other reasons, Afro-Caribbean slaves regularly sidestepped the legal prohibitions and patrols that policed their mobility . . . in the end, white elites, cognizant of their own inability to regulate slaves' activities beyond work, tacitly accepted the everyday transgressions slaves regularly committed in their socializing about the town and frequent movement between town and countryside. (2015, 22)

W. E. Beastal's *A Negro Market in the West Indies* offers a view of the early nineteenth century, legally recognized Sunday market in Antigua, held for more than a century in the same location at Otto's Pasture.[3] Looking closely at this image, people flow into the market from the country: soldiers, white colonists, enslaved persons, and, what could be free blacks, mingle in a cacophony of color and a bustle of individual transactions. Sidney Mintz described enslaved persons engaging in the internal economies in the Caribbean as "a symbol of freedom," allowing for individuals to express themselves away from the plantations (1983, 116; see also Gaspar 1985, 145–47; Hauser 2008; Higman 2001). While these movements were technically illegal, especially in the beginning of the eighteenth century, demographic imbalances, the complete clearing of the interior, and a shift among some of the plantation elites, fostered the tacit understanding that absolute control was not attainable, and this was rapidly recognized in law.[4] The marketplace was an open space in which class, race, and gender are comingled, with individuals congregating from all parts of the island, as a quotidian part of life which, due to epistemological barriers, have been dismissed as analytical noise.

In order to break some of these conceptual walls, I propose a reconceptualizing the plantation landscape through proximal structures to reexamine movement, landscapes, and social complexity. A strict reading of Antigua's legal history indicates a brutal, coercive, strict regime of maintaining control over the enslaved population: a restrictive landscape with limited movement between plantations, let alone across the island. As an illustrative example, I will demonstrate how, by focusing on Antigua's fortification network, I can provide a new vantage from which to study the organization of the landscape as a whole, and the movements of people—free and enslaved, white and black, poor and elite—across it. This new perspective serves to destabilize the plantation as the *naturalized* unit of analysis for understanding the eighteenth-century Caribbean by moving away from property as the defining social structure.

Antigua's Fortifications

Despite calls by archaeologists to undertake more nuanced studies of Caribbean military sites (Watters 2001, 97), they have generally been conceptualized within the framework of "monumental architecture" (Armstrong 2013, 529), "renowned fortresses" (Watters 2001, 89), and "impressive batteries" (Buckley 1998, 71–72). Study of Antigua's fortifications belies this perspective. Given the local governments control and involvement in crafting Antigua's defense policy, instead of taking a monochromatic view of fortifications as defensive military sites, fortification sites can serve as a proxy for understanding the priorities and landscape ideologies of the island's elites, thereby reinvestigating social relations and the organization of and movement across the colonial landscape. As multivalent structures, there are two major circumstances that speak in favor applying Antigua's fortifications individually and defenses holistically this way. First, each fortification was the result of local initiatives legislated and paid for by the Antiguan colonial government with little imperial oversight. As local public works projects, the spatial distribution and political debates about defense policy speak to the priorities of the island's elites, namely, the protection of trade: protecting the valuable, but vulnerable, merchant vessels, from privateers or other enemies (see fig. 7.2). Second, to provide the

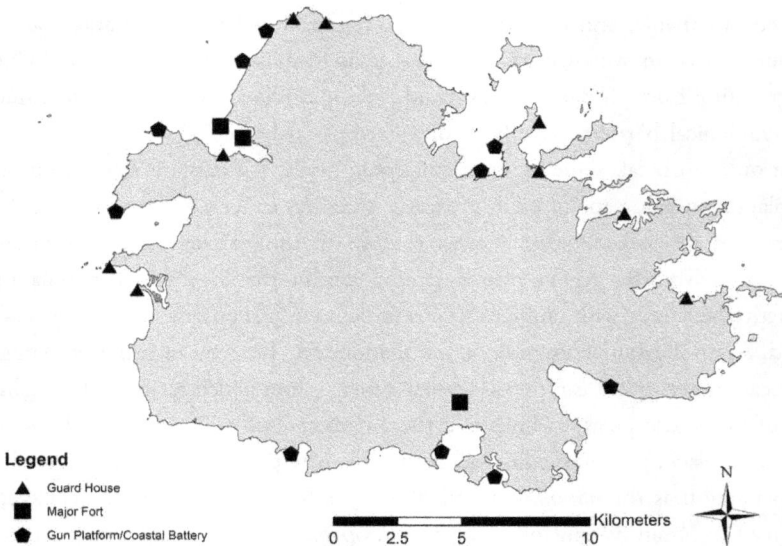

Figure 7.2. State of Antigua's fortifications in 1704. (Colonial Office Papers, Sessional Papers of Antigua, September 5, 1704). (Illustration by Christopher Kurt Waters)

labor necessary to build, and later garrison these fortifications, the government contracted and conscripted labor from a variety of different sources, not the least of which was pulling enslaved laborers off plantations for months, and sometimes years at a time. Not only did this create a new taxed on large plantations, it facilitated the movement of enslaved Africans and poor whites to move about the island in new ways.

Eighteenth-century military sites are discussed as just that: military sites, where the primary, and often singular goal is the defense of a territory. Indeed, the historical and archaeological records are littered with this symptomatic view (Babits 2011; Buckley 1998, Hart 2011; Klingelhoffer 2010; Scarmento 2011; Starbuck 2011; Webb 1979, 2013) for an alternate view see DeCorse and Beier, 2018; Johnson 2002, 4–6). Emboldened by the sheer monumentality of some of the largest, well-known military sites, and buoyed by a powerful historic literature debating the geometrical beauty in creating the perfect bulwark to protect against the enemies of the state, research into military sites tends to distill the theoretical discourse around violence and power (for a critique of this view see Ingram 2012). Drawing on insights from a resurgence in studying European castles (i.e., Johnson 2002), I posit that colonial fortification sites are more than just part of a military landscape dominated by violence and surveillance, but rather an outgrowth of local politics, pragmatic considerations and sites of interaction and agency among subaltern populations in ways that are traditionally unrecognized in military studies. In reconceptualizing the martial landscape, we recognize fortification as part of a complex landscape tied intimately into larger cultural frameworks where the seemingly military function of the fortifications may not have even been the primary goal in their construction (see fig. 7.3 on page 160).

Studying fortification offers a unique archaeological opportunity to examine a cross section of social interaction and relationships that cannot be found on plantations. Each plantation was the sole property of an individual, one who may not have been physically present, and the plantation was run through a series of managers and attorneys (e.g., Higman 2005; Sheridan 1967). The sanctity of property enshrined in the English cultural fabric extends into the Caribbean, with relatively few proscriptions on the management or day-to-day operations on the plantation. This can subconsciously create a fixed entity within the landscape, naturalizing the property boundaries as impermeable. This impermeability works both to keep persons in—enslaved laborers, managers, indentured servants—while simultaneously reducing or restricting outside interaction from the wider island population. Every island in the Caribbean possessed significant nonplantation

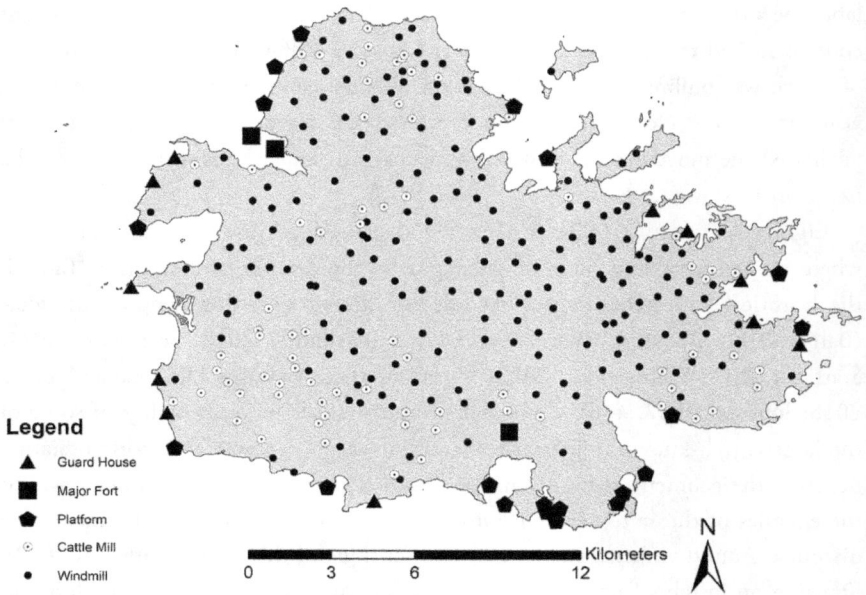

Figure 7.3. State of Antigua's fortifications, circa 1748, based on information provided by Baker (1749) and Horneck (1752). (Illustration by Christopher Kurt Waters)

populations—enslaved laborers and craftspeople, poor white farming families, free blacks, merchants and townspeople, soldiers, sailors, and others. Within the planta-tion analysis, these individuals are necessarily removed from the landscape. As loci of analysis, Antigua's defenses incorporated enslaved plantation laborers; enslaved, free, and white craftspeople; poor white mercenaries; soldiers; elite white officers; women; and children. In cases where archaeological excavation in urban settings is difficult, these fortifications offer remote, generally intact, and spatially diverse alternative areas for study.[5] Analysis of the fortifications allows us to repopulate the island with individuals who were not directly attached to a plantation. We begin to grapple with the social and demographic complexities that these islands proffer: disproportionate enslaved populations surrounded by water with nowhere to go and who negotiated their daily lives within the island.

Situated in the middle of the Lesser Antilles, Antigua historically was in a precarious position, with French Guadeloupe forty miles to the south, Dutch St. Maarten ninety miles north, and situated where the first island Spanish ships would pass on their way to the Spanish Main: all perennial British enemies. Antigua is a small island—279 square kilometers (108 square miles) of rolling hills, small mountains, and endless stretches of white sand beaches; 22.5 kilometers (14 miles) at its widest, the farthest you can get from the ocean is 6 kilometers (3.75 miles). Settled by English colonists from St. Kitts in 1632, Antigua grew slowly throughout the seventeenth century, relying on small farms and cash crops like tobacco, ginger, cotton, and indigo.[6] The turn toward large-scale sugar cultivation, though already established in the 1660s, suffered from a small population and labor shortages that hindered land clearing. Despite Antigua and the Leeward Islands surpassing Barbados in sugar exports in the early eighteenth century and a rapid growth in the number of enslaved laborers, it was not until 1750 that all of the island's arable land was cleared and cultivated (Engerman 1996, 160–61; Dyde 2000, 51). Plantations dominated the landscape with some 264 individual properties in the hands of about 139 families expanding across the island, leaving only small areas for poor white farmers, known as ten-acre men. Demographically, the eighteenth century saw a slow decline in the white population and a massive increase in the enslaved population, with enslaved Africans making up almost 91 percent of the entire population of the island by 1774 (Southey 1827, 419).

Britain was at war with other European powers for more than half of the eighteenth century, and possessions in the Americas were considered legitimate military targets. Consequently, Caribbean islands in the Lesser Antilles were constantly threatened by raids, commerce raiding, and invasion (Bridenbaugh & Bridenbaugh 1972). While Antigua only suffered a single invasion in 1666, the economic and social depredation from that French attack, continued invasion threats, and occasional raids spurred the local government to invest in a series of coastal fortifications to protect the island.

Throughout the eighteenth century there were two major driving principles forming Antigua's defense policy. The first was a general lack of tactical consideration of Antigua's coastline resulting in neglecting vulnerable areas and subsequent realization that significant parts of the island were constantly under threat. For instance, in 1704, Antigua's elites worried about "The Frontiers, and other parts of the Island Lying naked" (CO 9/1, 8)—the east coast which was sparsely settled, but easily approachable from the water in small sailing vessels or canoes. By 1712, the Antigua Assembly identified, "the Places that are generally Feared the Enemy may land are at Willoughby bay, Memorah, Proctors Bay, Bermudian Valley bay, Five Islands and Dickensons Bay, the three former being to Windward and more lyable to a surprise" (CO 9/2: August 19, 1712). By 1745, the south coast became more of an interest to the Antiguan government, especially with the construction of the Naval Dockyard at English Harbour, an enticement for the Royal Navy to keep warships stationed around Antigua permanently in order to make up for the "Defenseless Condition of the Island, and the Danger we shall be Exposed to" (NAAB 324 December 13, 1745). The proliferation of defense construction during the War of Jenkins Ear (1739–1748), and again during the Seven Years War (1756–1763) and American Revolution (1776–1783), was largely driven by the rapid identification of weaknesses, followed by conscripting enslaved labor to build fortifications without proper thinking, layout, or even armament, all in reaction to "the French our near & powerful Enemy Have put us under a necessity of Erecting at a very great Expense many additional Forts & Fortifications which remain in a great measure useless for want of proper Cannon" (NAAB 324, July 11, 1745). Even St. John's Roads, protected by no fewer than five coastal batteries and a major fort, could not protect shipping, with privateers cutting merchant vessels out from underneath the guns of Fort James (CO 9/1: 25–26, September 5, 1704; NAAB 324, July 10, 1746).

Despite the fortifications, Antigua remained vulnerable, a fact repeatedly acknowledged by the colonial government. At the root of the problem was the poor planning and no cohesive conceptualization in the development of a holistic island defense. Rather than a concerted vision, sociopolitical factors dictated their placement on the landscape. By focusing defenses on what were considered locations that were more valued socially and economically by the island's elite, the government demonstrated that plantations were not equally valued, and delineated those areas of the island considered less valuable, thereby opening those areas, including sugar growing areas, to potential attack. Thus, the location of fortifications expressed a plantation's positionality within the sociopolitical landscape that, when looking strictly within a plantation boundary, are likely not considered.

The second malpractice the Antiguan government indulged in was the willful placement of fortifications in positions, which when reflected on, were acknowledged in contemporary reports to be poor choices, or were just improperly built. For instance, in the rash of fortification building in the 1740s, two fortifications were built around Five Islands Harbour, where the committee, with consulting pilots, concluded that "a Battery upon either of the said Points will be of but very little Service to the Trade of this Island for no Ship of any Burthen can come within Gun Shot of either of them" (NAAB 324, July 11, 1744). A general reassessment of the islands defenses in 1733 realized that the entire windward coast were "much out of order," with several guard houses "useless & not well situated" (NAAB 322, February 21, 1733). The fort at the Cripplegate,[7] which overlooks St. John's Roads, the busiest shipping area, suffered two attacks in the seventeenth century. It was periodically reported to be in disrepair in the eighteenth century, including dismounted guns half submerged in the surf (e.g., CO 9/2, March 27, 1711). The platform was vastly expanded in 1778, "to be an Everlasting protection to allow Shipping which may lay over the Barr at the Mouth of the Harbour of Saint John, which from their distance from Fort James are under little or no protection, and are very liable to be Put out by the Enemy" (NAAB 329, September 24, 1778)—a recognition that came after more than a century of wars and attacks. The expansion of this battery along with other defense expenditures during the American Revolutionary War bankrupted the island. The results were that

> several forts, on the coasts of the island, were sold . . . and produced to the public about a twentieth of the sum they cost in erecting. Some of these buildings have been demolished by the purchasers for the useful materials they were composed of, while others remain in their original state, probably to be sold to the public on a future rupture, at any price their proprietors shall think proper to demand for them. (Luffman 1789, 33–34)

This pattern of construction and neglect by the local government, repeats itself in Antigua's defense history. An example from the War of Austrian Succession further reveals the uneven approach to how defenses were executed, and highlights how the politically driven decision-making process affected the island's landscape across plantation boundaries. The windward coast along the eastern side of the island was readily acknowledged as a strategic and tactical weakness in the defense of the island. As the farthest point from St. John's town and the core of the economic and population center of the island, the coast was considered a "frontier" on multiple occasions (CO 9/1, July 27, 1704). Early attempts to protect this coast include a regiment of soldiers raised and sent to Antigua during the Nine Years War (1688–1697), to augment the defenses of the Leeward Islands. The regiment was raised with the with the purpose of disbanding the regiment in Antigua at the end of the war. These men were given plots of land along the windward coast, establishing a model whereby veteran communities could subsist and provide a pool of soldiers should the island be attacked (CO 9/1, July 27, 1704). Long term, this plan failed because attracting poor white farmers to replace the veterans proved difficult with little opportunity for social and economic mobility. Robert Baker's 1749 map of Antigua labels much of this coastline as "Ten Acre Land," with fewer windmills and a larger proportion of the cheaper cattle mills and numerous farmhouses, rather than the large sugar plantations that dominated the majority of the island's landscape. Poor whites abandoned the island faster than new replacements could be found. The result of this original defense policy, however, created a marginalized landscape within the sugar economy, with small farms surrounded by a few small plantations. Despite this vulnerability, the coast's first fortification, Fort Harmon, was only built in 1745, and only armed with cannon in 1747, at the conclusion of the war (see fig. 7.4). This is despite the fact that cannon "might have been of Considerable Service," there as, "Two Vessels have been forced ashoar by the French Privateers near this Battery both which might have been Save had there been Two or Three Great Guns there" (NAAB 324: 27 January 1746/47).

The ill-preparedness of the eastern coast can be dramatically contrasted with the defenses on the west coast of the island, especially around the capitol St. John's (see fig. 7.5 on page 166). Fortifications stretched on average every 1,400 meters up this western coastline, protecting the Atlantic trade, warehouses, and the plantations of the wealthy of Antigua. At the same time that the windward coast suffered from political neglect, resources flowed into defending this coastline, even when unwarranted. And at the same time as construction started at Fort Harmon, a committee inspected the area just to the south of St. John's, evaluating the need to build fortifications at Pearne's Point and Fullerton's Point (see fig. 7.6 on page 166). They concluded that, "a Battery on either Place of the Size & for the purposes their proposed is needless, as the Channels aforesaid are out of Gun Shot from both Points." Yet, plans still went ahead and, "two Guns at each Point," were ordered anyway (NAAB 324, July 11, 1744). The three committee members, John Tomlinson, John Murray and John Watkins, owned property in St. John's and St. Mary's Parishes along the west coast, as well as in St. John's town, obviously influencing their decision.

The fortifications, as public works, offer a new way of approaching a small island landscape. By tracking the fortifications on Antigua, we start to see a heterogeneous use and valuation of the landscape by the island's political drivers. The lack of tactical consideration and the poor construction and placement of fortified sites creates an important foil to the plantation centric model of understanding the Caribbean. Specifically, whereas plantations are considered spatially organized to maximize surveillance and profits, construction and maintenance of the island's

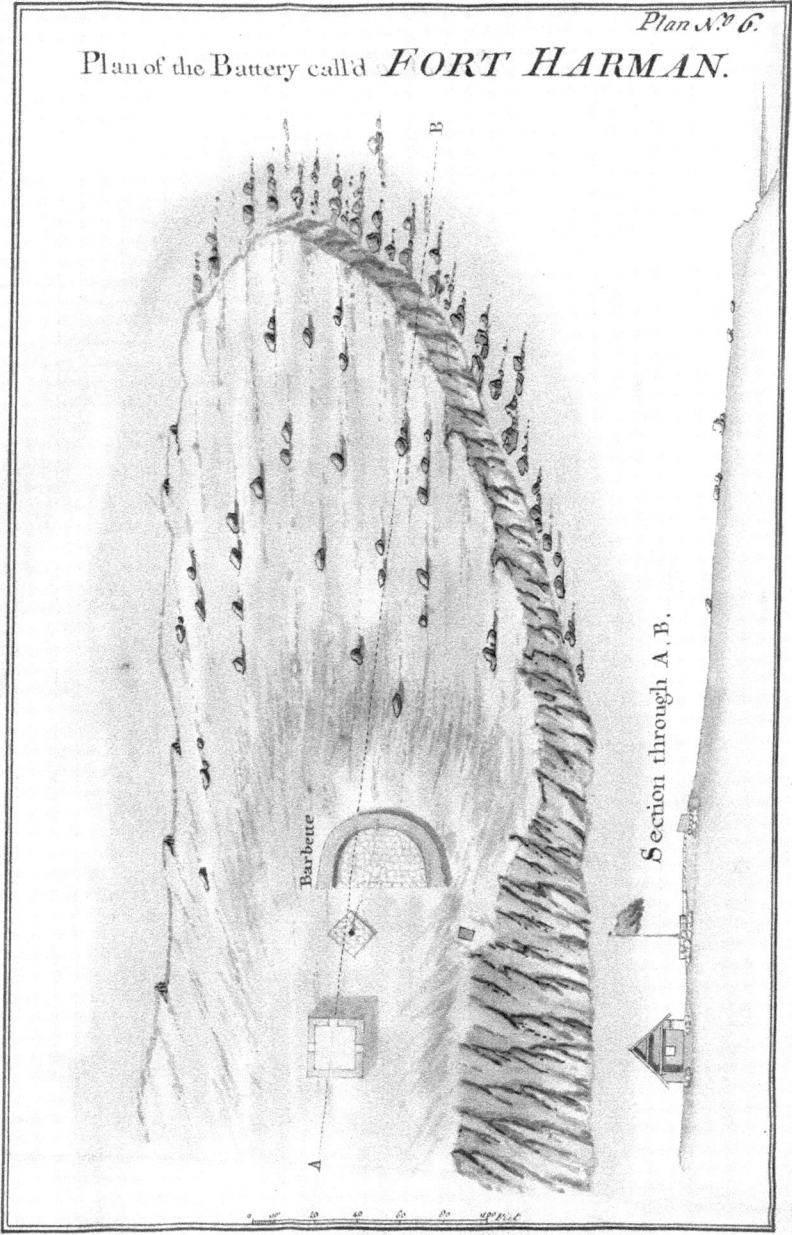

Figure 7.4. *Plan of the Battery Call'd Fort Harmon*, Kane William Horneck, 1752. (Courtesy of the John Carter Brown Library at Brown University)

Figure 7.5. Inset, *Plan of St. Johns Harbour and Parts Adjacent, Shewing the Situation of Rat Island, James Fort, Fort Hamilton and Corbinsons Point*, Kane William Horneck, 1752. Note, the Cripplegate Battery is not indicated on this map, not rating as a proper fortification in Horneck's eyes. (Courtesy of the John Carter Brown Library at Brown University)

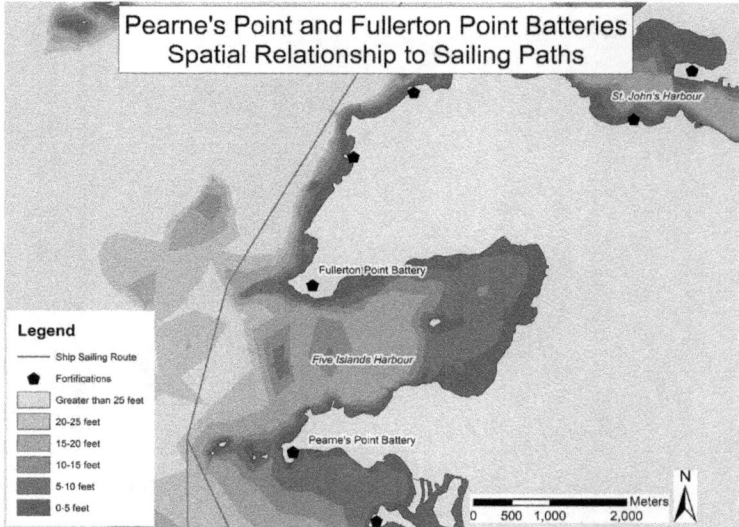

Figure 7.6. Location of Pearne's Point Battery and Fullerton Point Battery at Five Islands Harbour. The shipping lane for ship rigged vessels, based on water depth and sailing in winds directly from the east while still allowing for northerly course toward St. John's Harbour. The results are that vessels passed over one thousand meters away from the two batteries, well outside of effective cannon range (Willis 2015). Given the prevailing easterly winds and barrier reefs, only small, fore- and aft-rigged craft can sail into the harbor. Despite acknowledging the tactical situation, the Antiguan government built these batteries anyway. (Illustration by Christopher Kurt Waters)

defense appear chaotic and unplanned. Yet, this chaos is a reflection of the same plantation elite organized into a governmental body, coming to decisions with financial and social repercussions that transcend the plantation landscape, and as public works projects, reflect the broader colonial setting, impacting individual's lives from all social strata.[8]

Landscape and Movement

The social lives of people are bounded by the spaces which they occupy, rather than the spaces imposed upon them. Plantations as analytical units not only circumscribe the movement of people associated with the property, they also leave out entire swaths of society—effectively silencing anyone who is not actively inside the boundaries. Positioned outside of the plantation, the archaeology of fortifications in the Caribbean restores those people who were not integrated into a specific plantation, as well as those that people who moved on and off the plantations, both willingly and unwillingly.

As public projects, fortifications attracted a variety of individuals, ranging from visits by government committees and the elites tasked with oversight, to poor men and their families contracted to garrison these sites, and conscripted enslaved labor tasked by law to build and maintain the fortification sites. While the placement of fortifications represents the priorities of the island's elites, the archaeology at these fortifications reflects the lives and mobility of a broad spectrum of the remainder of the island's population. A series of emergency acts passed by the Antiguan government conscripted enslaved male laborers, pulling between 1 and 3 percent of the entire enslaved labor force from each parish, and sending them to various portions of island to undertake a variety of public works tasks, including building and maintaining fortifications, often for months at a time.[9] Additional enslaved men were stationed at fortifications, serving as matrosses and trained to protect the island from outside attack (e.g., CO 9/2, May 3, 1711; NAAB 323, November 15, 1736; NAAB 324, April 11, 1776; for enslaved persons serving in military capacities in the Americas generally see Voelz 1993). The Antiguan government, facing demographic pressures, brought these enslaved men to these fortifications throughout the eighteenth century, justifying this expense and action, claiming "White men to serve as Montrosses, cannot be procured" (NAAB 336, 281, August 21, 1806).[10] These movements were coerced: the enslaved did not have any say in where they were being sent to fulfill these labor commitments. Yet, just as with the Sunday markets, movements of enslaved Africans to maintain and staff fortifications serves to further complication understandings of the islands sociocultural landscape in a way that solely focusing on plantations does not. Not everyone lived and worked on a plantation—coerced or otherwise; rather, there was considerable movement across, between, and around these plantations. Including island-wide features reduces the primacy of the plantation as the dominant landscape feature of the eighteenth-century Caribbean, and returns a more complex, dynamic landscape image, within which plantations, fortifications, markets, and so forth, are analytically restored, returning movement to an otherwise cloistered, stagnant picture dominated by fixed spaces and reductive lives.

Conclusion

Studies of the eighteenth-century Caribbean generally revolve around the economic importance of the region to the world economy and incubator for proto-industrial developments as well developments of racialized policies and social inequalities, all of which reverberate today. This sugar-centric view inadvertently constrains the interpretation of the past, specifically in how we view the social complexity of a landscape in which enslaved Africans and Europeans lived, interacted, and moved across boundaries. While a central aspect of Caribbean economies and the landscapes in which they operated, the preponderance of historical, archaeological, geographical, and economic data on plantations created a situation where the plantation is a naturalized unit of spatial analysis, accidentally reifying plantation boundaries as fixed and absolute. This situation works well for considering questions on a multitude of scales, and indeed has successfully been demonstrated. However, this vantage concurrently restricts understanding of the wider island landscapes of which the plantations were a part, and the social, political, and economic organization of the island as a historically contingent and lived-in space becomes a patchwork pattern of immutable spaces, defining crossing boundaries between plantations as transgressive acts. Indeed, the local landscape is thereby ignored, and the relationships and lives lived within the island space are completely eradicated, and instead constrained to a series of 300-acre "islands."

I am not suggesting that new plantation scholarship should be abandoned. Rather, I am calling for a new series of studies where local institutions and lives off or between the plantations are investigated to restore movement on the landscape. Using Antigua's fortification network in the eighteenth century, I demonstrate that the landscape was neither a homogenous patchwork of plantations, nor was it equally valued across the island. By reducing the plantation to *an* analytical unit, rather than *the* dominant analytical unit, I privilege multiple scales and sites related to isolated stretches on the coastline, to the island as a whole, in order to reframe complex social relationships steeped in gender, race, ethnicity, and class in which these colonial settings operated.

Notes

1. The Caribbean fortification and military literature heavily focused on the history of battles, architecture, and colonial and imperial expansion policies through military force (e.g., Dawdy 2010; DeSilvey & Edensor 2012; Kingelhoffer 2010; Machling 2012; O'Shaughnessy 2000; Sarmento 2011; Stoler 2008). More recent military literature has opened up this narrative to include narratives about the individuals at these military sites, and the complicated colonial relationships between the military and nonmilitary organizations within the wider Atlantic World (DeCorse & Beier, 2018; Schroedl & Ahlman 2002).

2. This is not to suggest that resistance was not a part of daily life within the enslaved community in Antigua, or that there was no transgressive act in crossing a plantation boundary. Rather, I am raising a scalar issue, suggesting that by focusing only on the transgressive or resistive aspects reduces our ability to view the landscape as continuous and consider the island-scape more holistically (Rainbird 2007; see also Boomert & Bright 2007; Van de Noort 2011; Westerdahl 1992).

3. Natasha Lightfoot (2015, 57–59), argues that no legal protections for the markets were written into Antiguan law, but rather that the Sunday markets constituted an established custom that was tacitly recognized. Gaspar (1985, 1988), while noting that the Sunday Market was closed by act during the 1736–1737 Conspiracy, draws a distinct line between the legality of the market and the flouting of certain rules, especially the sale of alcohol, which was strictly forbidden in 1702, but was never consistently enforced until attempts in 1824. Dyde (2000, 96; 126–27), citing eighteenth-century accounts, suggests that the market system carried with it legal protections. In Act no. 202, enacted in 1757 "for the further Prevention of Damages to the Harbours, and Abuses in carrying on the Inland Trade of this Island; regulating the Hire and Manumission of Slaves; and for advertising Run-aways committed to the Goal," explicitly states in Article VI that "hawking and pedling [*sic*] (except salted Beef and Pork, salt Fish, Bread, and Biscuit, as shall be sold in the Negro-Market on the usual and customary Days)," creates a legal precedent enshrined in the Acts of Antigua that protects the Sunday slave markets (CO 8/12, 73). A further act reinforces the legality of the markets in 1784, Act no. 425—"An Act to alter and amend an Act,

entitled, An Act for the better regulating of Buildings, and to prevent Mischiefs that may happen from Fire within the Town of Saint John, dated the first Day of June, in the Year of our Lord one thousand seven hundred and seventy-one," which explicitly prohibits selling goods "at Night, by Candle-light or Lamp-light" (CO 8/21, 33). By limiting the hours of trade, the law tacitly supports the legal transactions by enslaved persons during the day. By recognizing the markets and place in the Antiguan landscape for these markets explicitly, it creates a legal recognition and offers a modicum of legal protection for the markets. With its attempted abolition in 1831, the Antiguan government recognized its legal standing, thereby lending further legitimacy to the markets than merely a tacitly acknowledged but illegal custom. Otto's Pasture was also where enslaved persons were executed in the first half of the eighteenth century, including the mass executions of seventy-seven individuals after the Antigua Slave Conspiracy in 1736. The gallows were moved in 1747, because nearby inhabitants complained of the offensive smell. The new gallows were placed "Just to Leeward of the Negro Burying Ground at the Point where it can be offensive to no One" (NAAB 324, January 27, 1747). This curious move suggests that the potency as a symbol of fear was no longer deemed sufficient, and perhaps mirrors a shift seen in plantation layouts starting at the same time, organizing around profit rather than surveillance (Armstrong 1990, 87–100; Delle 1999, 119–167; Higman 2001).

4. "The Act for the Better Government of Slaves and Free Negroes," of 1702 explicitly forbids enslaved persons from leaving the plantation on Sundays, and states that they "can only move about the island with a ticket" (CO 8/3, 143). These requirements are dropped in the next iteration of the law in 1723, which also enshrines the rights of enslaved persons to sell "logs of wood, Firewood, Crabbs, Fresh fish, Dunhill fowls, kids, Hogs and Ground Provisions" (CO 8/5, 26). This law likewise offers some other legal protections, including making the killing of an enslaved person by a white person illegal, reserving capital punishment to the state. Gaspar (1988, 15) estimates, citing a 1831 letter from Governor Ross, that *only* 1,454, or about one-twentieth of Antigua's enslaved population, attended the St. John's market on a weekly basis. Gaspar assumes that these individuals had permission to attend the market, however, this is likely an overstatement, since the estimated number of white men (eligible for the militia and tasked with patrol duties) numbered only 1,140 in 1823, making enforcement of passes and effective patrolling virtually impossible (Oliver 1899, cli).

5. For urban Caribbean archaeology see Armstrong and Williamson 2011; Hamilton 2006.

6. At the time of settlement, Europeans claimed that Antigua no longer supported a permanent indigenous population. Current archaeological evidence suggests that Antigua was abandoned by the Native population by 1300 (Muddy Bay Antigua has radiocarbon dates from the mid-thirteenth century, Murphy 1999, 224–26), and subsequently likely visited, but does not exhibit the same dense settlement patterns to the north and south of the island. (For a regional summary, see Hofman 2013.)

7. Today Fort Barrington. Between 1711 and 1778, this fortification was left off of every return, despite its strategic location, including Kane William Horneck's inventory of Antigua's defenses in 1752, and does not appear on any maps of Antigua at all until the nineteenth century. Despite protecting shipping, there are few plantations directly protected by that battery, further demonstrating the political designs in fortification placement in Antigua.

8. Menard (2006, 127–36), collated several historic sources estimating the capital investment necessary to start a plantation on different islands in the Caribbean (and the Carolinas). The capital the Antiguan government spent on building and maintaining the fortification network across the eighteenth century is roughly equivalent to purchasing and building an entire plantation every decade across the eighteenth century, making for an apt comparison.

9. A similar conscription system was used to build and maintain roads and dig and clean public ponds, engendering more movement off and between plantations by individuals (e.g., CO 8/1, 21–22, An Act for Enlarging and Keeping Clean the Highways). Additionally, between 1743 and 1749, and occasionally thereafter until the 1780s, the Antiguan government likewise conscripted enslaved labor for the Naval Dockyard at English Harbour, continuously forcing the movement of people around the landscape (respectively, NAAB 324, June 6, 1743; CO 9/20, January 2, 1748/49).

10. The first recorded instance of enslaved men living at a fortification as matrosses is in 1711, where three enslaved men had already been garrisoning Corbinson's Point Fort for three years, and the slave owner was demanding compensation for their lost labor (CO 9/2, May 3, 1711).

Works Cited

Armstrong, Douglas V. 1990. *The Old Village and the Great House*. Urbana: University of Illinois Press.

———. "The Afro-Jamaican House-Yard: An Archaeological and Ethnohistorical Perspective." *Florida Journal of Anthropology: Special Publication* 7(16): 51–63.

———. 1998. "Cultural Transformation among Caribbean Slave Communities." In *Studies in Culture Contact: Interaction, Culture Change, and Archaeology*. Edited by James Cusick, 378–401. Carbondale: University of Illinois Center for Archaeological Investigations.

———. 2003. *Creole Transformation from Slavery to Freedom: Historical Archaeology of the East End Community, St. John, Virgin Islands*. Gainesville: University Press of Florida.

———. 2008. "Excavating African American Heritage: Towards a More Nuanced Understanding of the African Diaspora." *Historical Archaeology* 42(2): 123–37.

———. 2013. "New Directions in Caribbean Historical Archaeology." In *The Oxford Companion to Caribbean Archaeology*. Edited by William F. Keegan, Corinne L. Hofman, and Reniel Rodriguez Ramos. New York: Oxford University Press, 525–41.

————. 2015. "Archaeology of the Enslaved Laborer Settlement at Trents Plantation: 2014–2015. *Journal of the Barbados Historical Society* 61: 146–77.

Armstrong, Douglas V., and Kenneth Kelly. 2000. "Settlement Patters and the Origins of African Jamaica Society: Seville Plantation, St. Ann's Bay, Jamaica." *Ethnohistory* 47(2): 369–97.

Armstrong, Douglas V., and Christian Williamson. 2011. "The Mangens House, Charlotte Amalie, St. Thomas, Danish West Indies: Archaeology of an Urban House Compound and Its Relationship to Local Interactions and Global Trade." In *Islands at the Crossroads: Migration, Seafaring, and Interaction in the Caribbean*. Edited by L. Antonio Curet and Mark W. Hauser, 137–63. Tuscaloosa: University of Alabama Press.

Babits, Lawrence E. 2011. "Introduction." In *The Archaeology of French and Indian War Frontier Forts*. Edited by Lawrence E. Babits and Stephanie Gandulla. Gainesville: University Press of Florida. 1–8.

Bates, Lynsey A. 2015. " 'The Landscape Cannot Be Said to Be Really Perfect': A Comparative Investigation of Plantation Spatial Organization on Two British Sugar Estates." In *The Archaeology of Slavery: A Comparative Approach to Captivity and Coercion*. Edited by Lydia Wilson. Carbondale: Southern Illinois University Press.

Bates, Lynsey A., John A. Chenoweth, and James A. Delle. 2015. *Archaeologies of Slavery and Freedom in the Caribbean*. Gainesville: University Press of Florida.

Boomert, Arie, and Alistair J. Bright. 2007. "Island Archaeology: In Search of a New Horizon." *Island Studies Journal* 2(1): 3–26.

Bridenbaugh, C., and R. Bridenbaugh. 1972. *No Peace Beyond the Line: The English in the Caribbean 1624–1690*. New York: Oxford University Press.

Buckley, Roger Norman, 1998. *The British Army in the West Indies: Society and the Military in the Revolutionary Age*. Gainesville: University Press of Florida.

Burnard, Trevor. 2015. *Planters, Merchants, and Slaves: Plantation Societies in British America, 1650–1820*. Chicago: University Chicago Press.

Cromwell, Jesse. 2014. "More than Slaves and Sugar: Recent Historiography of the Transimperial Caribbean and Its Sinew Populations." *History Compass* 12(10): 770–83.

Curet, L. Antonio, and Hauser, Mark W. 2011. *Islands at the Crossroads: Migration, Seafaring, and Interaction in the Caribbean*. Tuscaloosa: University of Alabama Press.

Dawdy, Shannon Lee. 2010. Clockpunk Anthropology and the Ruins of Modernity. *Current Anthropology* 51(6): 761–93.

DeCorse, Christopher R., and Zachary J. Beier, eds. N.d. *British Fort Communities: Archaeological and Historical Perspectives*. Gainesville: University Press of Florida.

Delle, James A. 1998. *An Archaeology of Social Space: Analyzing Coffee Plantations in Jamaica's Blue Mountains*. New York: Plenum Press.

————. 2014. *The Colonial Caribbean: Landscapes of Power in the Plantation System*. New York: Cambridge University Press.

DeSilvey, Caitlin, and Tim Edensor. 2012. "Reckoning with Ruins." *Progress in Human Geography* 37(4): 465–85.

Dunn, Richard S. 1972. *Sugar and Slaves: The Rise of the Planter Class in the English West Indies, 1624–1713*. Chapel Hill: University of North Carolina Press.

Dyde, Brian. 2000. *A History of Antigua: The Unsuspected Isle*. London: Macmillan Education.

Ellis, Clifton, and Rebecca Ginsburg, eds. 2010. *Cabin, Quarter, Plantation: Architecture and Landscapes of North America*. New Haven, CT: Yale University Press.

Engerman, Stanley L. 1996. "Europe, the Lesser Antilles, and Economic Expansion 1600–1800." In *The Lesser Antilles in the Age of European Expansion* Edited by Robert L. Paquette and Stanley L. Engerman, 147–65. Gainesville: University Press of Florida.

Gaspar, David Barry. 1985. *Bondmen and Rebels: A Study of Master-Slave Relations in Antigua*. Durham, NC: Duke University Press.

———. 1988. "Slavery, Amelioration, and Sunday Markets in Antigua, 1823–1831." *Slavery and Abolition* 9(1): 1–28.

González-Ruibal, Alfredo. 2014. *An Archaeology of Resistance: Materiality and Time in an African Borderland*. Lanham, MD: Rowen and Littlefield.

Hamilton, Donald. 2006. "Pirates and Merchants: Port Royal Jamaica." In *X Marks the Spot: The Archaeology of Piracy*. Edited by C. R. Ewen, 13–30. Gainesville: University Press of Florida.

Hart, James L. 2011. "Forts on the Frontier: Adapting European Military Engineering to North America." In *The Archaeology of French and Indian War Frontier Forts*. Edited by Lawrence E. Babits and Stephanie Gandulla. Gainesville: University Press of Florida, 17–51.

Hauser, Mark W. 2008. *An Archaeology of Black Markets: Local Ceramics and Economies in Eighteenth-Century Jamaica*. Gainesville: University Press of Florida.

———. 2011. "Uneven Topographies: Archaeology of Plantations and Caribbean Slave Economies." In *The Archaeology of Capitalism in Colonial Contexts*. Edited by Lindsay Weiss and Sarah K. Croucher, 121–42. New York: Springer.

Hicks, Dan. 2007. *Garden of the World: An Historical Archaeology of Sugar Landscapes in the Eastern Caribbean*. Oxford, UK: Archaeopress.

Higman, Barry W. 2001[1988]. *Jamaica Surveyed: Plantation Maps and Plans of the Eighteenth and Nineteenth Centuries*. Barbados, West Indies: University of the West Indies Press.

———. 2005. *Plantation Jamaica: Capital and Control in a Colonial Economy*. Jamaica, West Indies: University of West Indies Press.

Hofman, Corine. 2013. "Post-Salidoid in the Lesser Antilles." *The Oxford Handbook of Caribbean Archaeology*, 205–20. Oxford, UK: Oxford University Press.

Ingram, Daniel. 2012. *Indians and British Outposts in Eighteenth-Century America*. Gainesville: University Press of Florida.

Johnson, Matthew. 2002. *Behind the Castle Gate: From Medieval to Renaissance*. London: Routledge.

————. 2007. *Ideas of Landscape.* Malden, MA: Blackwell Publishing.

Klingelhofer, E., ed. 2010. *First Forts: Essays on the Archaeology of Proto-colonial Fortification.* Leiden, the Netherlands: Brill.

Lenik, Stephen. 2012. "Mission Plantations, Space, and Social Control: Jesuits as Planters in French Caribbean Colonies and Frontiers." *Journal of Social Archaeology* 12(1): 51–71.

Lightfoot, Natasha. 2015. *Troubling Freedom: Antigua and the Aftermath of British Emancipation.* Durham, NC: Duke University Press.

Luffman, John. 1789[2010]. *A Brief Account of the Island of Antigua, Together with the Customs and Manners of its Inhabitants, White as well as Black . . . in Letters to a Friend.* London: Eighteenth Century Collections Online Print Editions.

Machling, T. C. S. 2012. *The Fortifications of Nevis, West Indies, from the 17th Century to the Present Day: Protected Interests?* Oxford, UK: Archaeopress.

Menard, Russell R. 2006. *Sweet Negotiations: Sugar, Slavery, and Plantation Agriculture in Early Barbados.* Charlottesville: University of Virginia Press.

Meniketti, Marco G. 2009. "Boundaries, Borders, and Reference Points: the Caribbean Defined as a Geographic Region and Social Reality." *International Journal of Historical Archaeology* 13(1): 45–62.

————. 2015. *Sugar Cane Capitalism and Environmental Transformation.* Tuscaloosa: University of Alabama Press.

Mintz, Sidney W. 1983. "Caribbean Market Places and Caribbean History." *Radical History Review* 27: 110–20.

————. 1985. *Sweetness and Power: The Place of Sugar in Modern History.* New York: Viking.

Mulcahy, Matthew. 2014. *Hubs of Empire: The Southeastern Lowcountry and British Caribbean.* Baltimore, MD: Johns Hopkins University Press.

Murphy, A. Reginald. 1999. *The Prehistory of Antigua, Ceramic Age: Subsistence, Settlement, Culture and Adaptation within an Insular Environment.* PhD Dissertation. Calgary, AB: University of Calgary.

O'Shannessey, Andrew Jackson. 2000. *An Empire Divided: The American Revolution and the British Caribbean.* Philadelphia: University of Pennsylvania Press.

Rainbird Paul, 2007. *The Archaeology of Islands.* Cambridge, UK: University of Cambridge Press.

Sarmento, João Carlos Vicente. 2011. *Fortifications, Post-colonialism and Power: Ruins and Imperial Legacies,* Farnham, UK: Ashgate.

Schroedl, G. F., and Ahlman T. M. 2002. "The Maintenance of Cultural and Personal Identities of Enslaved Africans and British Soldiers at Brimstone Hill Fortress, St. Kitts, West Indies." *Historical Archaeology* 36(4): 38–49.

Sheridan, Richard B. 1961. The Rise of a Colonial Gentry: A Case Study of Antigua, 1730–1775. *The Economic History Review* 13(3): 342–57.

————. 1974. *Sugar and Slavery: an Economic History of the British West Indies, 1623–1775.* Baltimore, MD: Johns Hopkins University Press.

Singleton, Theresa A. editor. 1999. *"I, Too, Am America": Archaeological Studies of African-American Life*. Charlottesville: University of Virginia Press.

Singleton, Theresa A. 2015. *Slavery behind the wall: An Archaeology of a Cuban Coffee Plantation*. Gainesville: University Press of Florida.

Southey, Thomas. 1827. *Chronological History of the West Indies*, 3 vols. London: Longman, Rees, Orme, Brown, and Green.

Starbuck, David R. 2011. *The Archaeology of Forts and Battlefields*. Gainesville: University Press of Florida.

Stoler, Ann Laura. 2008. Imperial Debris: Reflections on Ruins and Ruination, *Cultural Anthropology* 23(2): 191–219.

Turner, Victor. 1964. "Betwixt and Between: The Liminal Period in *Rites de Passage*." *The Proceedings of the American Ethnological Society*: 4–20.

Van de Noort, Robert. 2011. *North Sea Archaeologies: A Maritime Biography, 10,000 BC to AD 1500*. Oxford, UK: Oxford University Press.

Voelz, Peter Michael. 1993. *Slave and Soldier: The Military Impacts of Blacks in the Colonial Americas*. New York: Garland Publishing.

Watters, David. 2001. "Historical Archaeology in the British Caribbean." In *Island Lives: Historical Archaeologies of the Caribbean*. Edited by Paul Farnsworth, 82–99. Tuscaloosa: University of Alabama Press.

Webb, Stephen Saunders. 1979. *The Governors-General: The English Army and the Definition of Empire, 1569–1681*. Chapel Hill: University of North Carolina Press.

———. 2013. *Marlborough's America*. New Haven, CT: Yale University Press.

Westerdahl, Christer. 1992. "The Maritime Cultural Landscape." *International Journal of Nautical Archaeology* 21(1): 5–14.

Wilkie, Laurie A., and Paul Farnsworth. 2005. *Sampling Many Pots: An Archaeology of Memory and Tradition at a Bahamian Plantation*. Leiden, the Netherlands: Brill.

Williams, Eric. 1994[1944]. *Capitalism and Slavery*. Chapel Hill: University of North Carolina Press.

Willis, Sam. 2015. *Fighting At Sea in the Eighteenth Century: The Art of Sailing Warfare*. Suffolk, UK: Boydell Press.

Zacek, Nathalie A. 2010. *Settler Society in the English Leeward Islands, 1670–1776*. Cambridge, UK: Cambridge University Press.

Archival Materials

Baker, Robert. 1749. *A New and Exact Map of the Island of Antigua in America according to an Actual and Accurate Survey Made in the Years 1746, 1747 and 1748*. T. Bowles, St. Paul's Churchyard. Original held at the John Carter Brown Library.

Beastal, W. E. 1806. *A Negro Market in the West Indies*. Color Lithograph on Wove Paper. Print held within the Yale University Library.

Horneck, Kane Williams. 1752. *A Report of the State of the Fortifications In the Island of Antigua and Particularly Those of English Harbour In the Said Island in the Year 1752.* Manuscript, hand colored, 19 plans. Originals held at the John Carter Brown Library.

The National Archives (Kew, UK). Colonial Office (CO) Papers. 8 Acts of Antigua and 9 Sessional Papers of Antigua.

The National Archives of Antigua and Barbuda (St. John's, Antigua). Antigua Assembly Minutes no. 314–46.

Chapter 8

Graveyards as Landscapes of Power in the Early Modern Atlantic World

Erik R. Seeman

Burial grounds represent power. A cemetery's location, dimensions, markers (or lack thereof), and residents all are diagnostic of a society's power relations. This is true both for power relations among the living and between the living and the dead. Far from quiescent "resting places," graveyards quiver with the energy of mourners, the activity of spirits, and the immanent presence of deities. As a result, to understand the complex legacy of European overseas expansion and the slave trade in the Americas, graveyards offer an unrivaled physical space for scholarly investigations, literally grounding our efforts to comprehend the past.

This chapter builds on the last decade of Atlantic world scholarship, work that employs a "bottom-up" or cultural history approach, in Lynn Hunt's recent formulation. In the last two decades of the twentieth century, Atlantic histories were typically "top-down" or macroeconomic in methodology (Hunt 2014, 54–60). This is the work of Immanuel Wallerstein and others who pioneered world-systems theory, in which the expansion of capitalism is the driving force of globalization in the early modern world (Wallerstein 1974). More recent Atlantic scholarship supplements those large economic forces with attention to religion, consumer taste, and the multiple influences on any one group's cultural practices (e.g., see Lane 2010; Norton 2008; Sweet 2011). This newer historical work, however, sometimes falls short in neglecting to root cultural practices in specific landscapes.

To address this deficiency and thereby trace the relationship between landscape and power, this chapter uses written and material sources to examine two sites in the early modern Atlantic world: a Jewish cemetery in Curaçao and the African

Burial Ground in New York City. As Jews in Curaçao confronted an unfamiliar environment, they worked to preserve their deathways as a strategy to mark the boundaries between themselves and outsiders, and between observant and non-observant Jews. Among New York City's African Americans, by contrast, little evidence exists of intragroup conflict over burial rites. Instead, the African Burial Ground, a marginal space neglected by Euro-Americans, helped free and enslaved blacks forge an African American identity.

In both locations, and by extension elsewhere around the Atlantic, burial grounds contain material expressions of religious and economic power. Overall, Jewish "deathways"—practices that include deathbed scenes, corpse preparation, burial practices, funerals, and commemoration—changed less in the Americas than did African deathways. Jews were less frequent targets of Christian missionary activity, and they also arrived in the Americas with conservative, written traditions regarding death practices. Perhaps most importantly, Africans were more highly exploited and vulnerable than were Jews. African Americans were nonetheless able to create meaningful new deathways as they negotiated power dynamics in the Americas.

Jews in the Early Modern Caribbean

Historians of religion in the early modern Atlantic world have mostly framed their analyses within a single nation-based Atlantic: the English Atlantic, French Atlantic, Dutch Atlantic, and so on (e.g., see Pestana 2009; Leavelle 2012; Haefeli 2012). These books make important contributions to our understanding of the relationship between religion and empire, but they inadvertently leave the impression that religious developments in the early modern Atlantic took place within national "silos." Bringing Jews into the discussion is a helpful antidote to such nation-based blinders (Williams 2001). Jews established communities around the Atlantic, from West Africa to Brazil, from Barbados to Montreal, and from Newport to Amsterdam. Jews did not migrate and then lose touch with their coreligionists in other lands. Instead, they maintained their economic and kinship ties across thousands of miles of ocean (Studnicki-Gizbert 2007; Stiefel 2014). Indeed, economics and kinship were intertwined: a Curaçaoan merchant whose daughter married into a Jewish family in Newport, Rhode Island, made a shrewd economic decision even as he followed his religion's call for endogamous (in-group) marriage. Thus, a focus on Jews necessarily shifts our attention away from the European nation-state as a category of analysis, and allows us to focus on the religious culture as it was expressed in specific landscapes. In the case of Jewish burial grounds, they reveal a religious culture with both a multiplicity of influences from around the Atlantic world, and one with conservative tendencies toward deathways (Ben-Ur & Frankel 2009).

Sephardic Jews arrived in the Americas as part of the remarkable expansion of the Dutch overseas empire in the seventeenth century. Dutch interest in the Americas began in the 1590s, as they were fighting for their independence against Spain. A century of colonization efforts in the Americas and East Indies had made Spain the richest country in Europe, and the Dutch sought to make inroads of their own. They hoped both to gain wealth to finance their war effort and to put a crimp in Spain's economic fortunes (Klooster 2009). The first Dutch stronghold in the Americas was in Recife, the capital of the short-lived Dutch colony in Brazil. When the Portuguese retook Recife in 1654, the city's Jews fled, most for the Dutch colony of Suriname on the north coast of South America, and many others for the Dutch Caribbean island of Curaçao. The island soon supported the largest Jewish community in the Americas, with some 1,100 residents. Even though it dwarfed the communities in mainland North America, where New York had 300 Jews and Newport only 100, Curaçao's Jewish community developed deathways that mirrored those elsewhere (Seeman 2010a: 232–62; Loker 1991).

Because of their desire to retain familiar customs, once Jews took up permanent residence in a community, one of their first goals was to establish a cemetery. For this space Jews used the Hebrew phrase *beth haim*, literally "home of the living," a pious euphemism for a cemetery. The *beth haim* at Curaçao's Mikve Israel was likely founded in 1659, and as the community grew, the original small space had to be expanded several times: in 1726, 1750, 1800, and 1822. Ultimately the cemetery would hold an estimated 5,200 to 5,500 burials, of which just under half (2,574) are marked by gravestones (Emmanuel 1957, 138). Because most of the Jews who migrated to Curaçao through the eighteenth century had spent some time in Amsterdam, and in light of Jewish conservatism regarding deathways, the Curaçao *beth haim* resembles Amsterdam's Jewish cemetery at Ouderkerk, both in its layout and in its tombstones (Vega 1975).

Like Jews around the Atlantic, those in Curaçao had to interact with the Christian residents where they lived. Had Jews in the Americas been locked into ghettos or otherwise persecuted, their interactions with Christians would have been necessarily limited. But Jews encountered little overt discrimination, though there were some exceptions to this rule: the Puritan colonies of Massachusetts and Connecticut were notoriously hostile to outsiders of all stripes in the seventeenth century, and until 1740 Jamaican Jews were taxed at a higher, discriminatory rate (Faber 1992, 17). New Netherland (later New York) bore the stamp of its anti-Semitic leader, Peter Stuyvesant. The man who led New Netherland from 1646 until its handover to the English in 1664 called Jews a "deceitful race," and worried that religious diversity would undermine social harmony (Williams 2001, 378–79). In Curaçao, however, Jews were not subject to any discriminatory taxes and they worshiped openly. Because of this tolerant climate, Jews flocked to the island and eventually formed one-third of the white population (Klooster 2001, 361).

Though a sizable percentage of the island's residents, Jews were still a minority and acutely aware of the precarity of their situation. They therefore continued the tactics they had used in Europe and tried not to antagonize their Christian neighbors. Among the early bylaws of Curaçao's Mikve Israel, passed in 1688, was the injunction that "no one of this Holy Congregation, whether man or woman, shall in any way dare discuss the subject of another religion or scandalize it by curse words or disparagement of their gods." In similarly self-conscious fashion, the executive committee of this same congregation urged Curaçao's Jews to avoid "scandal" and "private hatreds" when a series of recriminations shook the community in 1721. "We well know," the committee observed, "that those who do not care much for us will take note and with this pretext will withhold the little affection they have for us by saying that we are as hateful as pagans" (Emmanuel & Emmanuel 1970, 545, 561).

But overall, Jews in the Americas encountered greater religious and social toleration than they did in most parts of Europe, which—combined with the small size of the community—heightened the possibility for intermarriage and other centrifugal tendencies. As one historian asserts, the central dynamic of these early Jewish communities was the tension between the preservation of group distinctiveness and assimilation (Faber 1992, 2). Rituals and beliefs surrounding death are an especially sensitive barometer for gauging this tension between distinctiveness and assimilation, as deathways were central for defining Jewish identity. When Jews brought their deathways from Europe to the Americas, they strongly desired to retain familiar customs.

Elsewhere in the Americas, Jewish cemeteries were occasionally the focus of Christian resentment. In both 1746 and 1751, Jews placed ads in the New York *Weekly Post-Boy* offering a reward for information about the "malicious and evil-minded persons" who had done "very considerable damage both to the walls and tombs of the Jewish burying-place." Also in 1751 Philadelphia's *beth haim* was damaged, but in this case Nathan Levy, the author of the notice in the *Pennsylvania Gazette*, blamed "unthinking" individuals who had been "setting up marks, and firing several shots against the fence of the Jews' burying ground," which damaged the fence and a gravestone (Pool 1952, 58).[1] Whether the errant marksmen were merely "unthinking" or closer to the "malicious and evil-minded" New Yorkers is unclear. No evidence exists, however, of similar acts of desecration in Curaçao's Jewish cemetery, perhaps because of the larger size and financial clout of the Jewish community there (Emmanuel 1957, 52).

But while isolated acts of hate surely troubled Jews in the Americas, even more threatening to the community's continued viability was, ironically, tolerance, or specifically the possibility for intermarriage with the much larger Christian population. Given the small size of the New World's Jewish communities, it was always at least a theoretical possibility that individuals would assimilate and intermarry to such an extent that a distinctive Jewish identity in the Americas might be lost. For the large majority of Jews who wished to prevent such a situation, burial proved an ideal way of policing religious boundaries. To prevent their members from being swallowed by the surrounding Gentile population, many congregations tried to use the desire for proper Jewish burial that still resided in the hearts of many assimilated Jews as a lure to keep people within the fold of the Jewish community.

Congregations therefore used deathways as both an inducement for straying members to return, and as a punishment for those who strayed too far. For example, in 1753 the Curaçao congregation passed regulations stating that nonattendance of services at the synagogue would result in the "denial" of "burial to him [the non-attendee] or any near relative" (Emmanuel & Emmanuel 1970, 233). And it was not just the congregation's leaders who policed the boundaries of Jewish identity; ordinary people did so, sometimes from the grave. When Joseph Henriquez Medina died in 1716, his family learned that his sizable bequest to his nephew, Jacob, would not be paid unless young Jacob "married a Jewess" (Emmanuel & Emmanuel 1970, 750). Vigilance was required, many community members believed, to prevent Curaçao's Jewish presence from fading away.

But not all burial conflicts among Jews pitted observant individuals against their more lax coreligionists. In Curaçao between 1744 and 1750, a dispute within the observant community that originally had nothing to do with burial practices eventually played itself out most dramatically within the walls of the *beth haim*, demonstrating that deathways are among the most potent symbols of group unity and disunity. The late 1740s were turbulent throughout the island. Protestants and Jews had become accustomed to calm prosperity, but this complacency was shaken by a series of disturbing events: several high-profile murders, a terrible drought, war between France and Holland, and a slave uprising that led to the execution of thirty-six alleged participants (Emmanuel & Emmanuel 1970, 203). But for the Curaçaoan Jewish community the troubles may be dated to the 1744 arrival from Amsterdam of Samuel Mendes De Sola to serve as *Hakham* (sage or rabbi). Almost immediately De Sola alienated a portion of Curaçao's Jews with his abrasive style and his meddling in secular affairs. For several years tensions built between De Sola and several leading families.

The conflict reached a new level of animosity when the cemetery became a battleground. De Sola had excommunicated several members of the opposition for a variety of indiscretions. When one of these individuals died in April 1749, De Sola ordered that his corpse be treated with certain discriminations. Unfortunately, the records do not specify precisely what was done to the corpse, but historians suggest that the coffin may have been dragged rather than carried in the cemetery, or stones may have been cast onto the coffin in a symbolic stoning of the deceased (Emmanuel 1957, 309).

Mordechay Alvares Correa had seen enough. This highly respected merchant and antagonist of De Sola resigned as leader of the gravediggers' society. But Correa's protest had little effect. In October 1749 two members of the opposition died and at each funeral the corpses were treated with disrespect. To the horror of many, these burial discriminations led to fistfights in the cemetery between the two factions. The sad scene of Jew pummeling Jew, however, was not nearly as dramatic as the fireworks that followed Correa's death. Perhaps worn down by so much infighting, the sixty-five-year-old Correa contracted what turned out to be his final illness in 1750. Near death, Correa drew up his will and specified that only his friends were to wash and bury him: he did not want De Sola's faction to have the opportunity to treat his corpse with disrespect (Emmanuel 1957, 309).

De Sola refused to accommodate this request, so several of Correa's supporters took matters into their own hands. Under cover of darkness, they broke down the walls of the *beth haim* and removed the gates so De Sola could not lock them out of the cemetery. In response, De Sola begged the island's Protestant governor for military support. The governor dispatched twenty-two soldiers to protect the cemetery. But Correa's supporters "pushed through the guards who had orders not to defend themselves, as this would have started a revolution on the island." De Sola had hoped that the soldiers would keep Correa's supporters away from the cemetery, but the show of force had the opposite effect. According to the governor, from "500 to 600 Christians and Jews, whites as well as coloreds and mulattos" attended the funeral (Emmanuel & Emmanuel 1970, 200, 201). Correa's dying wish was fulfilled: his corpse received no indignities. Soon, with the intervention of Prince William of the Netherlands, the two sides managed to put aside their differences and reach a reconciliation. Perhaps De Sola had learned that it was one thing to harass a dissident faction with fines and sharply worded sermons, but it was quite another to interfere with their mortuary rituals.

Jewish deathways generally followed the broad patterns established in Europe, likewise reflecting a wide range of cultural influences. In Jewish cemeteries throughout the Americas, one finds gravestones with inscriptions in Hebrew, English, Spanish, Portuguese, Judeo-Portuguese, even Latin. Moreover the iconography combines Jewish and Christian images, often on the same stone. Common images unique to Jewish cemeteries include hands raised in blessing as a symbol of the *Cohanim* or the priestly caste, a synagogue scene portraying three Levites performing their ritual service, and carvings incorporating the biblical figure whose name the deceased bore. This latter group includes numerous stones of individuals named Abigail, David, Esther, Mordecai, Moses, and others. But Jews in the Americas were also comfortable using Christian symbols of the transience of life, such as winged hourglasses and death's heads. In the second half of the eighteenth century, Jews followed the Anglo-American shift away from glowering death's heads and toward chubby cherubim (Benes 1977; Blachowicz 2006).

In this multiplicity of influences, Jewish cemeteries in the Americas differed little from those in London and Amsterdam (Vega 1975; de Castro 1999). Indeed, due to a dearth of local carvers with the facility to render Hebrew letters accurately, American Jews often ordered their stones from Europe. Jews in Jamaica, New York, and Newport imported their stones from London, while Curaçao's Jews sent out to Amsterdam (Pool 1952, 166; Shilstone 1956, xxviii; Emmanuel 1957, 129). Despite these similarities in origins, the gravestones in New World cemeteries reflected, to an extent, local circumstances. The stones in Newport and New York were relatively restrained in terms of stone carving; they appear downright dowdy when compared with the exuberant carving present on Curaçaoan stones. This may reflect the relative wealth and size of the different communities, as mainland Jews were decidedly less prosperous on the whole than their Caribbean counterparts.

But other factors may have been at work. In particular, New York's Jews may have been less comfortable with human images on their gravestones, which perhaps seemed to transgress the Second Commandment's stricture against "graven images."

Such concerns apparently did not trouble Caribbean Jews. As relatively recent returnees to rabbinic Judaism (after more than a century in the Iberian Peninsula when the open practice of Judaism was prohibited), they embraced the linguistic and iconographic traditions of the lands in which they lived (see fig. 8.1). Curaçaoan stones, like their counterparts in Amsterdam's *beth haim* at Ouderkerk, frequently depict human figures. Abraham Henriques's monument, made in Amsterdam from

Figure 8.1. David Senior gravestone, Curaçao. Unlike many Curaçaoan stones, Senior's is carved only in Portuguese. His year of death is reckoned both by the Jewish calendar (5492) and the Christian one (1731). The image of God chopping down the tree of life usually represents a life cut short. This is a horizontal slab, lying flat over the tomb it covers, as were all the markers in Curaçao's Jewish Cemetery. (Courtesy of the Jacob Rader Marcus Center of the American Jewish Archives)

expensive Carrara marble in 1726, shows him confidently piloting his ship through a light chop (Anon. 2001, 3). Other stones represent the deathbed scene of the deceased. In some of these cases, the deathbed scene is allegorized, represented as a biblical story to distance it from the actual deathbed. Sara Hana's stone of 1761, for example, shows a woman dying while giving birth in a tent under a tree. Hana surely did not die in a tent; the reference is to the biblical Rachel, who in Genesis 35:18 died giving birth to Benjamin while traveling through the desert (Anon. 2001, 1). The 1726 monument to Ishac Haim Senior, by contrast, depicts the deathbed scene more realistically, with observers sitting in period chairs and weeping into handkerchiefs as Senior points toward heaven (see fig. 8.2).

Figure 8.2. Ishac Haim Senior gravestone, Curaçao. Senior died in 1726, and his stone (on the left) contains several human figures. At the top, Senior is represented by Isaac Aboab da Fonseca, an Amsterdam Rabbi. At the bottom is a deathbed scene, presumably Senior's, with several weeping observers. The stone on the right contains several images of the transience of life usually associated with Christian gravestones, including a winged hourglass and two skulls. (Courtesy of the Jacob Rader Marcus Center of the American Jewish Archives)

Ishac Senior included another depiction of a recognizable human character: he is represented by Isaac Aboab da Fonseca, an Amsterdam rabbi, as copied from a 1686 mezzotint by the artist Aernout Naghtegael. If a Christian's engraving of a rabbi seems an unlikely source for a Jewish Curaçaoan stone, consider the source for the human figures on Esther Senior's 1714 marker. The representation of the biblical Esther pleading her case before King Ahasuerus is "almost a line-for-line copy" of a woodcut from a Christian Latin Bible published in Lyon in 1581 (Weinstein 1993, 118, 124).

Jews today are often surprised by the profusion of images that would now be considered by many to be transgressions of the Second Commandment. But eighteenth-century Caribbean Jews, remembering the dark decades when Sephardim were forced to convert or keep their beliefs secret, seem to have rejoiced in their ability to proclaim to the world their faith and their varied cultural inheritances. Using deathways, they did their best to maintain the traditions they brought with them from Europe (Seeman 2018).

The African Burial Ground, Manhattan

There were enormous differences, of course, between the circumstances of Jews and Africans in the Americas. Not only were Africans forced across the Atlantic, but they also found themselves on plantations with individuals from numerous West African regions, whereas Jews shared a more unified Sephardic culture. Despite this bewildering situation, slaves were able to import many African deathways in the first century of plantation slavery. Archaeologists have unearthed grave goods and burial practices ca. 1700 that demonstrate close ties with West African practices. In Barbados, the prone burial of a suspected witch and the mortuary assemblage of a presumed healer demonstrate that the Middle Passage did not sever Africans from the deathways of their homelands (Handler 1996; Handler 1997). Other practices with presumed African antecedents that archaeologists have found in mortuary contexts in the Americas include subfloor burial or burial within the house-yard compound; burial with pipes; grave-vaulting (putting planks above the coffin before soil was thrown into the grave); and the placement of burials near silk-cotton trees and other plants that mediated between this world and the afterlife (Armstrong & Fleischman 2003; Brown 2016; Davidson 2012; Saunders 2015).

However, not all West African mortuary customs were transplanted to the Americas. Some material and ritual components of African deathways did not make it across the Atlantic. Mortuary terra-cottas, which formed an important part of the material culture of death along the Gold Coast after 1600, do not seem to have played much of a role in slave deathways. In this case one imagines that the local materials and expert craftspeople required for terra-cotta manufacture were generally not available on slave plantations. It also seems likely that certain African rituals were impossible to reproduce in the Americas, without the requisite ritual specialists and cosmologically significant plants, animals, and minerals (Seeman 2010a, 192–93; Blouet 2013, 732). As one archaeologist has recently reminded us, the objects that slaves could obtain "were frequently surveilled and severely limited" (Brown 2016, 251). Still, slave deathways through the first half of the eighteenth century drew extensively on African practices.

As time passed, however, free and enslaved blacks adopted more aspects of Euro-American material culture. This can be seen in a negative source: colonial laws that tried to ban threatening aspects of African American funerals. The first law of this sort in Anglo-America was passed by the Virginia House of Burgesses in 1680. The act explicitly drew the connection between slave funerals and the potential for violence against whites: "Whereas the frequent meetings of consider-able numbers of Negro slaves under pretense of feasts and burials is judged of dangerous consequence, it is enacted that no Negro may carry arms . . . nor go from his owner's plantation without a certificate" (Guild 1969, 45–46).

With this same fear in mind, numerous jurisdictions tried to ban slave funerals from taking place during the evening hours, when slaves could more easily mount a rebellion. Such laws were passed in Westmoreland County, Virginia in 1687; New York City in 1722; South Carolina in 1745; Antigua in 1757; and Jamaica in 1816 (Frey & Wood 1998, 55; Osgood 1905, 3:296; Morgan 1998, 641; Gaspar 1985, 145; Barclay 1828, 158). There is some evidence, however, that these statutes were difficult to enforce (*Georgia Gazette*, December 24, 1766). Ironically, laws requiring daytime funerals may have encountered resistance from slave owners, who probably could not decide which they hated more: the fear of violence threatened by night funerals, or the loss of productivity to daytime funerals.

Government officials in the Americas also attempted to legislate a variety of other African American mortuary practices. Colonists in the Danish West Indies seem to have been especially sensitive to the dangers presented by slave deathways.

In 1733 they banned African instruments at slave funerals, in 1765 they forbade slave wakes, and in 1778 they limited the number of mourners at a funeral to twelve. In 1731 New York City likewise tried to limit to twelve the number of slaves who could attend a funeral, because at such gatherings slaves "have great opportunities of plotting and confederating together to do mischief" (Hall 1992, 57, 63, 64; Osgood 1905, 4:88–89). All of these laws were aimed at preventing slaves from using funerals to gather and plot violence against their white oppressors.

But, paradoxically, there was another category of funeral regulations that aimed to prevent people of African descent from appropriating the deathways of Euro-Americans. These laws were not as common as those intended to prevent rebellion, but they were widespread enough to indicate white concerns about the symbolic appropriation of their deathways. In Manhattan, for example, it became a crime in 1731 for slaves to show respect for the dead by placing a pall over the deceased's coffin. South Carolina in 1750 declared that no "negro" could wear a funeral scarf, the distinctive Anglo-American article of mourning apparel that was worn over the shoulder like a sash. Antigua went beyond New York and South Carolina in 1757 by outlawing *both* palls and scarves (Osgood 1905, 4:89; Beasley 2009, 21; Gaspar 1985, 145).

These laws demonstrate that by the middle of the eighteenth century, people of African descent began to adopt some of the material trappings of Euro-American deathways. Because these objects were "multivalent," with multiple meanings to various observers, Euro-American material culture could be incorporated in a variety of meaningful ways into African American burials (Brown 2016, 249). The African American adoption of Euro-American material culture can also be seen in Manhattan's eighteenth-century African Burial Ground. In the middle of the eighteenth century, people of African descent made up between 16 percent and 20 percent of New York City's total population (Medford 2004, 82). Despite this large pool of potential converts, missionary activities were desultory, with an Anglican schoolmaster here and an itinerant preacher there seeking to bring the word of Christ to the city's black residents. If Christianization occurred only fitfully among black New Yorkers, Anglicization proceeded more rapidly. People of African descent learned the English language, wore English clothes, and, as most of them were bound laborers, took up the artisanal trades of their owners. Their immersion in English material culture was reflected in their deathways.

Like slaves throughout the Americas, enslaved New Yorkers were largely free to attend to their dying and dead without a great deal of interference from their masters or from the local clergy. In 1713 Anglican minister John Sharpe was upset by the lack of ministerial presence at slave deathbeds. People of African descent were, Sharpe grumbled, "buried in the Common by those of their country and complexion without the office [i.e., the Anglican burial liturgy], on the contrary the heathenish rites are performed at the grave by their countrymen" (Sharpe 1880, 355). Apparently there were enough Africans of a variety of ethnic backgrounds that members of each nation could attend to their own dead.

Sharpe's brief reference to burial "in the Common" glossed over the exclusionary Anglican burial policy in the city. In the seventeenth century some whites and blacks—primarily those not members of churches or too poor to afford church burial—had been buried in one of two public cemeteries in Manhattan. The public cemetery that was located just north of the town's wall was incorporated into the burial ground of New York's impressive new Anglican church, Trinity. One of the first orders of business for Trinity's vestrymen was to ban the burials of people of African descent (Perry et al. 2006, 1:42). Unlike evangelical missionaries in the Caribbean, who understood that providing a burial ground was one of the best ways to attract new African converts, New York's Anglicans did not care about appealing to the city's black residents. They certainly did not want to share their burial ground with them. Other denominations were equally committed to segregated burials. As a result, black New Yorkers began to bury their dead "in the Common," a rocky ravine of little use to the city's white residents, a place that would eventually be called the "Negros Burial Ground" on eighteenth-century maps (Seeman 2010b; Frohne 2015).

This would represent the sum total of our knowledge about African American deathways in colonial New York, but for the U.S. government's desire to build a gleaming new federal office building at 290 Broadway in lower Manhattan. With construction just about to start in the summer of 1991, the federal government hired a consulting firm to see if any salvage archaeology needed to be done before the project could get under way. The archaeologists found bones, and then more bones, and soon it became clear that this was the "Negros Burial Ground" that colonial-era maps suggested would be there. Under increasing pressure from black New Yorkers and others, construction was finally halted in 1992, so a full archaeological excavation could be mounted (Cantwell & Wall 2001, 277–88). By the time the work was completed, archaeologists had unearthed 419 individuals from what they now dubbed New York's African Burial Ground.

The burial ground was in use from at least 1712, and perhaps from as early as 1697, until 1795. Archaeologists estimate that the cemetery holds between 10,000 and 15,000 bodies (Perry et al. 2006, 1:87). This means that the families and friends of 10,000–15,000 black New Yorkers considered this marginal patch of land to be sacred space. It also means that many of the million or so black New Yorkers who lived in the city when the burial ground was unearthed were eager to ensure that African Americans took a leading role in handling and analyzing the human remains. Mayor David Dinkins appointed Michael Blakey of Howard University to lead the excavation (Cantwell & Wall 2001, 285).

For fifteen years, Blakey and his team published very few of their findings. Those that did appear emphasized the African origins of the material culture unearthed in lower Manhattan: beads, shells, rings, and more. Historians have eagerly followed this lead, seeing in the African Burial Ground artifacts glimpses of a long-hidden African worldview in New York (Lepore 2005, 231–32; Wilder 2001, 33; Cantwell & Wall 2001, 290–91; Foote 2004, 141–43). But it seems to me that some of the strongest claims about African influence need to be revised.

The vast majority of the 419 individuals removed from the African Burial Ground were buried in ways identical to those of their white neighbors. Or, to be more precise, the *material remains* of the vast majority of the African Burial Ground interments are identical to those of white New Yorkers. Religious rituals rarely leave a trace in the material record, and thus archaeology is unable to shed light on most of the rites that meant a great deal to those who performed and observed them. Still, it is striking that so few of the burials contain African elements.[2]

Of the individuals whose remains were sufficiently well preserved to allow for analysis, 92 percent (352/384) were buried in coffins, 94 percent (393/419) were single interments, 98 percent (367/375) were buried with the head facing west, and 100 percent (269/269) were supine, that is, lying face-up. This is precisely how white New Yorkers were buried in the eighteenth century: coffined (with perhaps a few exceptions for indigents), west-headed, supine, single interments (except for a few mothers with infant children and children who died at the same time). Likewise, 93 percent (351/376) had no personal adornment such as rings, buttons, or cufflinks, and 93 percent (350/376) were not buried with coins, shells, pipes, and other durable objects (Perry, Howson, & Bianco 2006, 1:134–44, 382, 419).

Other aspects of the material record demonstrate fewer connections with Africa than the first reports from the site suggested. In 1995 *Update* published an article by Kwaku Ofori-Ansa, an expert in African art, analyzing the heart-shaped symbol found on the coffin lid of Burial 101, a young man between the ages of twenty-six

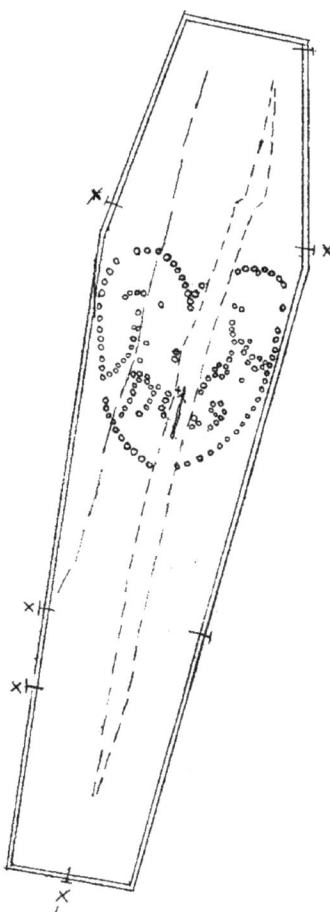

Figure 8.3. Coffin lid with heart, Burial 101. This coffin was made of larch, a wood similar to pine. The dashed lines represent cracks in the coffin, which make the date (1769?) and deceased's initials difficult to read. Original sketch of in-situ burial, African Burial Ground Collection, Howard University, Montague Cobb Laboratory Record Group. (Courtesy of U.S. General Services Administration, New York City)

and thirty-five (see fig. 8.3). The design, about eighteen inches wide and nineteen inches high, was made out of fifty-one iron tacks with heads about three-eighths of an inch in diameter, hammered into the center of the coffin lid. Ofori-Ansa wrote that "it could be safely concluded that the image was meant to be" a Sankofa symbol used by the Akan people of Ghana (Ofori-Ansa 1995, 3) (see fig. 8.4). The Sankofa symbol is connected with modern-day Akan mortuary practices; the word *Sankofa* translates as "go back to fetch it." This refers to a proverb, "It is not a taboo to return and fetch it when you forget," that describes the connections between the spirit world and this world (Willis 1998, 188). For this reason, the Sankofa is one of the hundreds of symbols that are today stamped onto *adinkra* cloth—meaning "a message one gives to another when departing"—out of which Akan mourning garments are made. Scholars rapidly incorporated this example from the African Burial Ground into their narratives as evidence of African cultural survivals in the Americas (Foote 2004, 143; Bond 2007, 92; Singleton 2004, 331).

Figure 8.4. The first documented appearance of the Sankofa. Symbols 13 and 14 in the lower left are different Sankofa variations. (R. S. Rattray, *Religion and Art in Ashanti* [1927])

There are three problems with this interpretation. First, there is no evidence that the Sankofa symbol was a part of eighteenth-century Akan mortuary practices. It is, of course, impossible to disprove the existence of a cultural form in the past. But there is no way to place *adinkra* cloth definitively in the eighteenth century, and there is evidence that the Sankofa symbol in particular may have emerged as late as the early twentieth century (Rattray 1927, 265). Second, even though slaves had a great deal of autonomy in burying their dead, masters were customarily responsible for providing coffins for their slaves.

The third problem with seeing the heart as a Sankofa symbol is that hearts made out of tacks were not uncommon on Anglo-American coffin lids. Nathaniel Harrison, for example, who died in 1727 in Surry County, Virginia, was buried in a pine coffin elaborately decorated with brass tacks in the shape of a heart (and a skull and crossbones) (Tharp 2003, 124). When nineteenth-century local historian Arthur W. Dowe entered the Wainwright family tomb in Ipswich, Massachusetts, he found ten coffins in various states of disintegration. On five coffin lids "were hearts formed with iron nails; and initials and dates with brass nails"; the dates ranged from 1731 to 1798 (Dowe 1881, 2). More recently, when archaeologists removed thirty-four coffins from the Bulkeley family tomb in Colchester, Connecticut, twenty of them (covering the period 1775 to 1826) had lids with heart-shaped designs made out of tacks (Bastis 2006, 46, 48–51) (see fig. 8.5). Also relevant is evidence from a New York coffin maker, who included in his account book an order for a fancy coffin of expensive "bilsted" or sweet gum wood, almost certainly for a wealthy white individual. The coffin maker had a heart with the deceased's name, age, and date of death "struck" on the lid, presumably with tacks.[3] This description sounds uncannily like the design on the lid of Burial 101's coffin, which included not only a heart but what appear to be the deceased's initials and year of death (1769?) (Perry et al. 2006, 1:253).

It is possible that the family and friends of the young man now known only as Burial 101 ascribed meanings to the heart-shaped symbol on his coffin different from, or in addition to, the meanings the same symbol evoked for their Euro-American neighbors. If the Sankofa existed 175 years before its first appearance in the historical record, the symbol on Burial 101's coffin may even have recalled the Akan proverb about crossing from the spirit world to this world. But in the absence of any literary or archaeological evidence supporting the eighteenth-century appearance of the Sankofa, and in the absence of any grave goods in Burial 101's coffin to indicate that this was an African-style burial, and in light of the numerous ways that black New Yorkers incorporated aspects of Anglo-American deathways

Figure 8.5. Coffin lid of Asa Bulkeley. Archaeologists found thirty-four well-preserved coffins in the Bulkeley family tomb in Colchester, Connecticut, twenty of which had heart-shaped designs made out of brass tacks on the lid. As the design indicates, Asa Bulkeley died at age thirty in 1804. His pine coffin was marked with this heart, as well as tacks around the edges of the coffin. (Courtesy of John J. Spaulding, Friends of the Office of State Archaeology)

such as coffins into their own mortuary rituals, that interpretation must remain highly speculative.

By contrast, there are indisputable material links with African practices for a small minority of the African Burial Ground interments. One of the most evocative of these is the adult woman known as Burial 340. Despite her anonymity, this woman has left behind a material record that personalizes some of the ways black New Yorkers used their mortuary practices to keep alive their memories of Africa. This woman was between the ages of thirty-nine and sixty-four when she died, evidently before 1735. This woman was almost certainly forced from her homeland: her incisors had been filed, one into the shape of an hourglass, another into the shape of a peg, a practice that is usually diagnostic of African birth (Perry et al. 2006, 1:154).

Her grave goods show how objects of European, American, and African origin could be combined to create distinctively African American mortuary practices. Into her grave, near her pelvis, had been placed an unused, white kaolin clay pipe of British or American manufacture. Both white and black New Yorkers enjoyed smoking tobacco, but only people of African descent placed goods into coffins to be used by the deceased in the afterlife. Even more uniquely African were the beads with which the woman was buried. She wore a bracelet around her right wrist made up of forty-one glass beads, and around her hips she wore a string of waist beads consisting of seventy glass beads, one amber bead, and seven cowrie shells. The amber bead, translucent red with fourteen facets, might have been made in Africa, the cowries came from the Indian Ocean coast of Africa, and the glass beads were manufactured in Europe, likely Venice, though at least one fired glass bead was probably produced in southern Ghana (DeCorse 2000). It is not the origin of the beads that makes them characteristically African, but their use as waist beads. West African women wore waist beads under their garments, as a way to tuck in and hold up their skirts or aprons, and thus they were visible only to a woman's spouse or lover or her female bathing partners (Perry et al. 2006, 1:387, 403, 410, 393). Whoever prepared this woman for burial must have known how important the waist beads were to her, and therefore made sure that she was buried with them.

Whereas waist beads were African objects of daily use, conjuring bundles were reserved for spiritual and supernatural purposes. Called *minkisi* (singular *nkisi*) by Kongolese but used elsewhere in Africa and throughout the African diaspora, where they were known by different names, conjuring bundles were small cloth or fiber bags containing objects with magical or ritual significance (Samford 1996, 107–9). Burial 147 was an old man for his time, fifty-five to sixty-five years old, probably buried in the last decades that the African Burial Ground was in use, sometime after 1776. He was found with four straight pins and fourteen tiny copper-alloy rings—at eleven millimeters in diameter too small to fit on an adult's fingers—between his upper-right arm and his chest. It seems likely that the rings had been contained in some kind of small cloth sack pinned to his burial garment. It is impossible to know for what purposes the man carried his tiny rings in a small sack, or whether he carried them in daily life as in death attached to his arm, although there is evidence of African men in the eighteenth and nineteenth centuries wearing amulets and protective bracelets on their upper arms (Perry et al. 2006, 1:432–33). But he likely kept his bag of precious, possibly magical rings hidden from the white New Yorkers he interacted with—including, if he was a slave, his master—just as the bag remained hidden from view in his coffin for over two centuries.

Overall the evidence from New York's African Burial Ground paints a more complicated portrait of black life in eighteenth-century New York than is sometimes seen in the historical works that have used evidence from the cemetery. Some of the graves show connections with African material culture or African cosmology, including Burial 147 with his mysterious bundle of rings; Burial 340 with her prized waist beads; and several others not discussed here, such as Burial 328 with a broken pot placed atop the coffin lid, and Burial 397 with oyster shells left on top of the coffin (Perry et al. 2006, 1:420). But the large majority included nothing to distinguish them from contemporary white burials. Indeed, many included aspects of Anglo-American material culture—linen shrouds held together by straight pins, pine coffins secured with iron nails—that were not part of contemporary West African deathways.

Conclusion: Graveyards as Intersections

Graveyards are outstanding vantage points from which to view the complex interplay between the local and the global that forms a central theme of this volume. Like cacao plantations in colonial Guatemala, military fortifications in eighteenth-century Antigua, and illegal trading posts in nineteenth-century Guinea, burial grounds in the Americas provide evidence of the interaction between expanding European maritime empires and local cultural practices. In general, historians have not adequately followed the lead of archaeologists in taking seriously the materiality of landscapes for understanding the past. The comparison presented in this chapter between Curaçaoan and Manhattan burial grounds demonstrates that much can be gained by examining the physical remains—both above- and belowground—that survive in cemeteries.

From this comparison we learn that as Europeans and Africans migrated across the Atlantic—some voluntarily, most not—they brought with them ideas about what constituted proper deathbed behavior, burial practices, and memorialization customs. Those ideas interacted with the New World environment in ways shaped by the particular circumstances of the migration stream and the local conditions where newcomers and their offspring set down roots. Although Africans and Jewish Europeans brought different deathways with them to the Americas, and those deathways changed to varying degrees, both groups employed deathways that were marked by multiple influences from a variety of cultures. Both groups also expressed powerful, distinctive beliefs through their deathways. Evidence for those beliefs—and for the change (or lack thereof) they underwent—persists in the materiality of the New World's countless burial grounds.

Notes

1. The gates of Savannah's Jewish cemetery were damaged in 1800 and 1812 (Pencak 2005, 170).

2. This is also recognized by the authors of the final historical report on the African Burial Ground: "the deceased were laid to rest in a manner not unlike that of white New Yorkers" (Medford 2004, 184).

3. On the importance of heart imagery in early American Protestantism, see Promey 2007, 109–16.

Works Cited

Anon. 2001. *They That Are Born Are Destined to Die and the Dead Brought to Life Again: The Jewish Cemetery Beth Haim Curaçao*. Willemstad, Curaçao: Mikvé Israel-Emanuel.

Armstrong, Douglas V., and Mark L. Fleischman. 2003. "House-Yard Burials of Enslaved Laborers in Eighteenth-Century Jamaica." *International Journal of Historical Archaeology* (7)1: 33–65.

Barclay, Alexander. 1828. *A Practical View of the Present State of Slavery in the West Indies*. London: Smith, Elder, & Co.

Bastis, Kristen. 2006. "Health, Wealth, and Available Material: The Bioarchaeology of the Bulkeley Tomb in Colchester, Connecticut." MA Thesis, University of Connecticut.

Beasley, Nicholas M. 2009. *Christian Ritual and the Creation of British Slave Societies, 1650–1780*. Athens: University of Georgia Press.

Benes, Peter. 1977. *The Masks of Orthodoxy: Folk Gravestone Carving in Plymouth County, Massachusetts, 1689–1805*. Amherst: University of Massachusetts Press.

Ben-Ur, Aviva, and Rachel Frankel. 2009. *Remnant Stones: The Jewish Cemeteries of Suriname.* Jerusalem, Israel: Hebrew Union College Press.

Blachowicz, James. 2006. *From Slate to Marble: Gravestone Carving Traditions in Eastern Massachusetts, 1770–1870.* Evanston, IL: Graver Press.

Blouet, Helen C. 2013. "Interpretations of Burial and Commemoration in Moravian and African Diasporas on St. John, Virgin Islands." *International Journal of Historical Archaeology* 17(4): 731–81.

Bond, Richard E. 2007. "Shaping a Conspiracy: Black Testimony in the 1741 New York Plot." *Early American Studies* 5(1): 63–94.

Brown, Brittany. 2016. "Reexamining English Clay Pipes in Captive African Burials on the Island of Barbados." *Journal of African Diaspora Archaeology and Heritage* 5(3): 245–62.

Cantwell, Anne-Marie, and Diana diZerega Wall. 2001. *Unearthing Gotham: The Archaeology of New York City.* New Haven, CT: Yale University Press.

Davidson, James M. 2012. "'They Laid Planks 'Crost the Coffins': The African Origin of Grave Vaulting in the United States." *International Journal of Historical Archaeology* 16(1): 86–134.

de Castro, D. Henriques. 1999. *Keur van grafstenen op de Portugees-Israëlische begraafplaats te Ouderkerk aan de Amstel.* Ouderkerk aan de Amstel, Netherlands: Stichting tot Instandhouding en Onderhoud van Historische Joodse Begraafplaatsen.

DeCorse, Christopher R. 2000. "An African Bead in New York City." *Update: Newsletter of the African Burial Ground and Five Points Archaeological Projects* 3(1): 6–7.

Dowe, Arthur W. 1881. "Col. John Wainwright's Tomb." *Ipswich Antiquarian Papers* 2:2.

Emmanuel, Isaac S. 1957. *Precious Stones of the Jews of Curaçao: Curaçaon Jewry, 1656–1957.* New York: Bloch Publishing.

Emmanuel, Isaac S., and Suzanne A. Emmanuel. 1970. *History of the Jews of the Netherlands Antilles.* 2 vols. Cincinnati, OH: American Jewish Archives.

Faber, Eli. 1992. *A Time for Planting: The First Migration, 1654–1820.* Baltimore, MD: Johns Hopkins University Press.

Foote, Thelma Wills. 2004. *Black and White Manhattan: The History of Racial Formation in Colonial New York City.* New York: Oxford University Press.

Frey, Sylvia R., and Betty Wood. 1998. *Come Shouting to Zion: African American Protestantism in the American South and British Caribbean to 1830.* Chapel Hill: University of North Carolina Press.

Frohne, Andrea E. 2015. *The African Burial Ground in New York City: Memory, Spirituality, and Space.* Syracuse, NY: Syracuse University Press.

Gaspar, David Barry. 1985. *Bondmen and Rebels: A Study of Master-Slave Relations in Antigua.* Baltimore, MD: Johns Hopkins University Press.

Guild, June Purcell, ed. 1969. *Black Laws of Virginia: A Summary of the Legislative Acts of Virginia Concerning Negroes from Earliest Times to the Present.* New York: Negro Universities Press.

Haefeli, Evan. 2012. *New Netherland and the Dutch Origins of American Religious Liberty*. Philadelphia: University of Pennsylvania Press.

Hall, Neville A. T. 1992. *Slave Society in the Danish West Indies: St. Thomas, St. John, and St. Croix*. Kingston, Jamaica: University of the West Indies Press.

Handler, Jerome S. 1996. "A Prone Burial from a Plantation Slave Cemetery in Barbados, West Indies: Possible Evidence for an African-type Witch or Other Negatively Viewed Person." *Historical Archaeology* 30(3): 76–86.

———. 1997. "An African-Type Healer/Diviner and His Grave Goods: A Burial from a Plantation Slave Cemetery in Barbados, West Indies." *International Journal of Historical Archaeology* 1(2): 91–130.

Hunt, Lynn. 2014. *Writing History in the Global Era*. New York: W. W. Norton.

Klooster, Wim. 2001. "The Jews in Suriname and Curaçao." In *The Jews and the Expansion of Europe to the West, 1450–1800*. Edited by Paolo Bernardini and Norman Fiering, 350–68. New York: Berghahn Books.

———. 2009. "Networks of Colonial Entrepreneurs: The Founders of the Jewish Settlements in Dutch America, 1650s and 1660s." In *Atlantic Diasporas: Jews, Conversos, and Crypto-Jews in the Age of Mercantilism, 1500–1800*. Edited by Richard L. Kagan and Philip D. Morgan, 33–49. Baltimore, MD: Johns Hopkins University Press.

Lane, Kris. 2010. *Colour of Paradise: The Emerald in the Age of Gunpowder Empires*. New Haven, CT: Yale University Press.

Leavelle, Tracy Neal. 2012. *The Catholic Calumet: Colonial Conversions in French and Indian North America*. Philadelphia: University of Pennsylvania Press.

Lepore, Jill. 2005. *New York Burning: Liberty, Slavery, and Conspiracy in Eighteenth-Century Manhattan*. New York: Alfred A. Knopf.

Loker, Zvi. 1991. *Jews in the Caribbean: Evidence on the History of the Jews in the Caribbean Zone in Colonial Times*. Jerusalem, Israel: Institute for Research on the Sephardi and Oriental Jewish Heritage.

Medford, Edna Greene, ed. 2004. *The New York African Burial Ground: History Final Report*. Washington, DC: U.S. General Services Administration.

Morgan, Philip D. 1998. *Slave Counterpoint: Black Culture in the Eighteenth-Century Chesapeake and Low Country*. Chapel Hill: University of North Carolina Press.

Norton, Marcy. 2008. *Sacred Gifts, Profane Pleasures: A History of Tobacco and Chocolate in the Atlantic World*. Ithaca, NY: Cornell University Press.

Ofori-Ansa, Kwaku. 1995. "Identification and Validation of the Sankofa Symbol." *Update: Newsletter of the African Burial Ground and Five Points Archaeological Projects* 1(8): 3.

Osgood, Herbert L., ed. 1905. *Minutes of the Common Council of the City of New York, 1675–1776*. 8 vols. New York: Dodd, Mead and Company.

Pencak, William. 2005. *Jews and Gentiles in Early America, 1654–1800*. Ann Arbor: University of Michigan Press.

Perry, Warren R., Jean Howson, and Barbara A. Bianco, eds. 2006. *New York African Burial Ground: Archaeology Final Report.* 2 vols. Washington, DC: U.S. General Services Administration.

Pestana, Carla Gardina. 2009. *Protestant Empire: Religion and the Making of the British Atlantic World.* Philadelphia: University of Pennsylvania Press.

Pool, David de Sola. 1952. *Portraits Etched in Stone: Early Jewish Settlers, 1682–1831.* New York: Columbia University Press.

Promey, Sally M. 2007. "Mirror Images: Framing the Self in Early New England Material Piety." In *Figures in the Carpet: Finding the Human Person in the American Past*, edited by Wilfred M. McClay, 71–128. Grand Rapids, MI: William B. Eerdmans.

Rattray, R. S. 1927. *Religion and Art in Ashanti.* London: Oxford University Press.

Samford, Patricia. 1996. "The Archaeology of African-American Slavery and Material Culture." *William and Mary Quarterly* 52(1): 87–114.

Saunders, Paula. 2015. "Analysis of an African Burial Ground in Nineteenth-Century Jamaica." *Journal of African Diaspora Archaeology and Heritage* 4(2): 143–71.

Seeman, Erik R. 2010a. *Death in the New World: Cross-Cultural Encounters, 1492–1800.* Philadelphia: University of Pennsylvania Press.

———. 2010b. "Reassessing the '*Sankofa* Symbol' in New York's African Burial Ground." *William and Mary Quarterly* 67(1): 101–22.

———. 2018. "Jews in the Early Modern Atlantic: Crossing Boundaries, Keeping Faith." In *The Atlantic in Global History, 1500–2000*, 2d ed. Edited by Jorge Cañizares-Esguerra and Erik R. Seeman, 41–62. New York: Routledge.

Sharpe, John. 1880. " 'Proposals for Erecting a School, Library and Chapel at New York,' 1712–13." *New-York Historical Society Collections* 13: 341–63.

Shilstone, E. M. 1956. *Jewish Monumental Inscriptions in the Burial Ground of the Jewish Synagogue at Bridgetown, Barbados.* New York: American Jewish Historical Society.

Singleton, Theresa A. 2004. "Before the Revolution: Archaeology and the African Diaspora on the Atlantic Seaboard." In *North American Archaeology.* Edited by Timothy R. Pauketat and Diana DiPaolo Loren, 319–36. Oxford, UK: Oxford University Press.

Stiefel, Barry L. 2014. *Jewish Sanctuary in the Atlantic World: A Social and Architectural History.* Columbia: University of South Carolina Press.

Studnicki-Gizbert, Daviken. 2007. *A Nation upon the Ocean Sea: Portugal's Atlantic Diaspora and the Crisis of the Spanish Empire, 1492–1640.* New York: Oxford University Press.

Sweet, James H. 2011. *Domingos Álvares, African Healing, and the Intellectual History of the Atlantic World.* Chapel Hill: University of North Carolina Press.

Tharp, Brent W. 2003. " 'Preserving Their Form and Features': The Commodification of Coffins in the American Understanding of Death." In *Commodifying Everything: Relationships of the Market.* Edited by Susan Strasser, 119–40. New York: Routledge.

Vega, L. Alvares. 1975. *Het Beth Haim van Ouderkerk: Beelden van een Portugees-Joodse begraafplaats*. Amsterdam, the Netherlands: Van Gorcum.

Wallerstein, Immanuel. 1974. *The Modern World-System*. New York: Academic Press.

Weinstein, Rochelle. 1993. "Stones of Memory: Revelations from a Cemetery in Curaçao." In *Sephardim in the Americas: Studies in Culture and History*. Edited by Martin A. Cohen and Abraham J. Peck, 81–140. Tuscaloosa: University of Alabama Press.

Williams, James Homer. 2001. "An Atlantic Perspective on the Jewish Struggle for Rights and Opportunities in Brazil, New Netherland, and New York." In *The Jews and the Expansion of Europe to the West, 1450–1800*. Edited by Paolo Bernardini and Norman Fiering, 369–93. New York: Berghahn Books.

Willis, W. Bruce. 1998. *The Adinkra Dictionary: A Visual Primer on the Language of Adinkra*. Washington, DC: Pyramid Complex.

Chapter 9

Life beyond the City

Historical and Archaeological Perspectives on Colonial Andean Mobility

Noa Corcoran-Tadd

The great silver-mining centers of Potosí, Porco, and Oruro in the Bolivian altiplano have long formed an important focus for understanding the Spanish Americas, both for the colonial imagination and for the contemporary historian. In comparison with the contexts of production and exchange at these mining centers, however, their wider landscapes of mobility and logistics within the altiplano and the valleys leading west to the Pacific Coast have been comparatively underinvestigated by historians and archaeologists alike. The following chapter considers these peripheral and "interstitial" landscapes and the communities they constituted (particularly as they articulated with pre-Hispanic legacies of mobility and infrastructure), while also synthesizing some of the recent research on the archaeology of the colonial south-central Andes. The resulting discussion highlights some of the ongoing interpretive tensions between focuses on urban and rural environments, between different scales of analysis, and between textual and archaeological approaches to the region's past.

The Emergence of the Colonial Andean Landscape

The late pre-Hispanic settlement pattern in the Andean highlands was one of relatively low nucleation, with much of the population living in small communities connected to wider worlds through ties of political allegiance and economic interdependency. Even in the case of Cuzco, the capital center of the Inka Empire (c. 1400–1532), the permanent population was comparatively small (with estimates suggesting a population of 15,000 to 20,000 in the urban core; Hyslop 1990, 64). Archaeological surveys of the Titicaca Basin to the south of Cuzco have revealed a high overall population density by the late pre-Hispanic period yet also show a settlement pattern with considerable distribution across the landscape with about 20 percent of the occupation located in high-altitude pastoralist zones (Stanish 2003).

This pattern was to change dramatically with the arrival of Spanish colonists in the central Andes in 1532. The early colonial urban form that was imposed across the region had a complex genesis influenced by a Mediterranean urban culture as well as the emerging economic and sociopolitical forces shaping life in the Americas. Considerable focus was placed on the establishment of the urban grid (*traza*) both as an imposed built form and as an idealized matrix seeking to render legible the new colonial urban social order (Morse 1982; Kinsbruner 2005). Similar attention was also placed on projects during the sixteenth and seventeenth centuries that aimed toward a top-down restructuring of the rural landscape in both the Andes and Mesoamerica through the resettlement of indigenous communities into new gridded towns, usually referred to as *reducciones* and *congregaciones* in the Andes and Mesoamerica, respectively (Cummins 2002; Mumford 2012). From this perspective, "colonization, then, was largely a labor of 'urbanization,' that is, a strategy of settlement nucleation for appropriating resources and implanting jurisdiction" (Morse 1982, 78).

At the same time, the rapid growth of mining cities like Potosí and Oruro during the early colonial period also led to the appearance of emergent, unplanned urban forms. Driven by a mixture of forced labor obligations and market opportunities, the city of Potosí in the Bolivian highlands, for instance, would grow to 160,000 by the first decade of the seventeenth century (Mangan 2005, 43) in a process paralleled in other Spanish colonial mining cities such as Zacatecas (modern-day north-central Mexico, Velasco Murillo 2009). Beyond the central *trazas* of these cities, halos of indigenous barrios soon were built to house the rapid influx of indigenous workers and marketers. Through this combination of top-down planning and bottom-up aggregation processes, a regionally unprecedented urban order had largely been established in the Andes by the end of the sixteenth century and would endure throughout the colonial period.

Urban Perspectives

Understandably, these new urban centers have dominated much of the historiography of the colonial Andes. Mid-twentieth century work tended to emphasize a strongly dual model of opposed indigenous and Spanish economies, with market participation and regimes of forced labor in the mining of precious metals (gold, silver, and mercury) driving a trend toward the "destructuration" of native communities (Wachtel 1977). The spectacular case of Potosí (Hanke 1956; Assadourian 1982) has formed the focus for much of this discussion. Discovered in 1545 (although see Platt and Quisbert 2008 for an alternative account), the Cerro Rico silver deposits at Potosí in particular would come to be seen by both contemporaries and historians as a salient location for understanding the colonial Andes as a whole. Following the late-sixteenth-century reforms that formalized the *mita* system of forced tributary labor, the city of Potosí and its indigenous *mita* workers frequently came to stand in for wider debates over wealth, labor, and "Black Legend" violence in the Spanish colonies (Bakewell 1984).

Beyond its status as economic center where history was made, the colonial city also long retained its status as the primary position from which history was written. In this sense, the Spanish colonial city has an additional layer of significance as the domain of the man of letters or *letrado* (Rama 1996) and the hegemonic production of a colonial archive with its persistent urban bias (a bias extending even to the corpus of humble notarial records; Lockhart 1994, 303). Beyond the *letrado* himself, the lettered city was also home to a broader cultural logic that privileged the urban perspective. The primary beneficiaries of the initial conquests of the sixteenth century—the *encomenderos*—notably resided in the new cities and interacted with the newly emerging rural economy of their indigenous labor grants (*encomiendas*) primarily via intermediaries (Lockhart 1994, 257). Relatively few Spanish colonists lived outside the limits of the city and Mills has noted the challenges this posed to the task of evangelization, suggesting that "the seventeenth-century *diligencia* (anti-idolatry campaign) was a rearguard action, an imperfect, late advance by churchmen into an unconquered countryside, with the expectation of a retreat to the safety and order of their urban bases" (Mills 1997, 272).

Drawing on new archival sources and the rising influence of sociocultural anthropology, the "ethnohistory" boom of the 1970s and 1980s (Abercrombie 2012) brought a wave of revisionist readings to key themes in colonial Andes historiography and underlined the active roles played by indigenous actors both within and beyond the city. New research into labor organization at Potosí, for instance, revealed the parallel presence of wage labor (*minga*) and informal labor (*kajcheo*) in the mines (Tandeter 1981; Bakewell 1984; Cole 1985). The reception of these studies that complicated standard accounts focusing solely on *mita* labor at Potosí was uneasy, as highlighted in a now-classic 1988 exchange between Steve Stern and Immanuel Wallerstein on questions of economic structure and analytical scale in the history of colonial economies (Stern 1988; Stern 1988; Wallerstein 1988). More recent work has also highlighted the work of women both as mining laborers and in the massive markets supplying Potosí's burgeoning population (Mangan 2005; compare Velasco Murillo 2013 for parallel work on the women of Zacatecas in New Spain).

Careful biographical research on the economic activities of the indigenous elite (particularly the emergent figure of the indigenous leader as "mercantile cacique") has raised wider questions about the traditional model of two separated ethnic "republics" shaping the colonial Andean economy. Beginning with prescient accounts of seventeenth-century Aymara caciques in the Bolivian highlands (Choque Canqui 1978; Rivera Cusicanqui 1978), several scholars began to develop a much more complex picture of early indigenous participation in market-oriented production and exchange (e.g., Pease 1988; Stern 1995).

Previous visions of the colonial lettered city also came under reexamination. A number of studies have pointed to a greater degree of literate production among some sectors of indigenous society (Burns 2011), while others have pushed for a reconsideration of the nature of writing within wider colonial practices of reading and recording (Salomon & Niño-Murcia 2011; Rappaport & Cummins 2012). In light of this continuing wave of historical research extending beyond the central *traza* to consider a diverse cast of Spanish, African, and indigenous actors, the colonial city has since become a much more complex location from which to understand colonial Andean history. And yet, particularly given the richness of their archives, the urban centers of Lima, Cuzco, and Potosí continue to have a determinative impact on the writing of colonial histories in a region that continued to have a rural majority through and beyond the wars of independence of the early nineteenth century.

Historical Perspectives on the Andean Countryside

This is not to suggest that historians of the period have failed to grapple with rural life in the Andes. Indeed, the previously mentioned ethnohistoric turn involved an important spatial shift toward the history of provincial life and the tapping of previously ignored local civic and ecclesiastical archives that might shed light on the nonurban, the subaltern, and the indigenous. In exploring both the potentials and limitations of this important body of historiography, I would like to focus particularly on research exploring the theme of rural connectivity and the region of the south-central Andes. This research forms a particularly rich vein of ethno-historical investigation but also provides an important foil to the archaeological case studies that follow.

Loosely defined, the south-central Andes comprises the Lake Titicaca basin and the altiplano stretching south toward Potosí and the great salt flat of Uyuni (as well as the western valleys leading down to the Pacific and the humid *yungas* valleys leading to the eastern lowlands). This spatial unit is as much a human geographi-cal as a topographical one, with several archaeologists and historians outlining the emergence of a distinct ethno-linguistic (Aymara, Puquina, and Uru) and ecologi-cal (agro-pastoralist and focused on tubers, pseudocereals, and camelids) landscape rooted in several millennia of human occupation in the region (Bouysse-Cassagne 1978; Stanish 2003).

In understanding the emergence and persistence of the diverse, fractured south-central Andes as an integrated human landscape, questions of mobility and connectivity are salient. Of the many analytical scales available for the study of the region, the scale of the long term has had a particularly enduring influence, particularly in the wake of John Murra's influential vertical archipelago model. Developed to explain some of the commonalities in human ecology, economy and ethnicity across the central Andes, the vertical archipelago model has had especial resonance in the south-central Andes given that one of the key case stud-ies involved the Aymara-speaking Lupaqa confederation based on the southern shores of Lake Titicaca.

In an analysis that drew on the 1567 survey made by Garci Diez de San Miguel of the province of Chucuito (previously the territory of the Lupaqas), Murra (1972) described a pattern of altiplano communities expanding a patchwork "archipelago" of discontinuous colonies out from the Lake Titicaca basin and down into the Pacific and eastern *yungas* valleys as part of a long-term strategy aimed at the exploitation of ecologically complementary resources. Following Murra's lead, subsequent scholars have argued that the region's vertically stratified ecology shaped a long-term pattern of highland-lowland connectivity with its origins in the Late Intermediate Period (1100–1400), a previous period of Tiwanaku colonization (Goldstein 2000), or even earlier.

The emphasis on continuities in regional patterns of mobility and connectivity has been reinforced by a tradition of French scholarship in Bolivia that has developed a synthesis of altiplano history over the long term (Wachtel 1978; Saignes 1985; Platt, Bouysse-Cassagne, & Harris 2006). Writing in a special issue of the *Annales* journal edited by Murra and Wachtel, Bouysse-Cassagne (1978) pushed scholars to consider a classification of the south-central Andean landscape that was neither Inka nor Spanish but rooted instead in the enduring Aymara political and cultural dominance in the region.

This emphasis on longer-term continuities has been contested by other scholars who have questioned longevity and extant of the pattern of "vertical" ecological control and intracommunity exchange described by Murra. Van Buren (1996) has pointed toward the politically charged context in which the survey of Chucuito, the archival source at the heart of Murra's initial argument, was compiled in 1567. Rather than seeing descriptions of an archipelago of Lupaqa possessions stretching from Lake Titicaca down to the Pacific coastal valleys as indicative of a deep tradition, she suggests that the documents represent, at least partly, a series of new political claims being made in the wake of Inka collapse and the uncertainties of the new early colonial order.

Others have questioned the applicability of the vertical model across the space of the south-central Andes. Nuñez and Dillehay (1978) for instance, argue that the vertical model often presumes the presence of central Andean features (e.g., greater emphasis on sedentism, urbanism, and agriculture) in other areas where rather different conditions prevailed. Emphasizing the particularities of the south-central Andean environment, they proposed an alternative model of circulating mobility (*movilidad giratoria*) that foregrounded the roles of intergroup exchange and long-distance caravanning in driving social complexity and connectivity both within the altiplano and into adjacent ecological zones. Nuñez and Dillehay also drew attention to patterns of historical change, noting fluctuations in network connectivity and questioning particularly the tendency to take as baselines the Tiwanaku (400–1100) and Inka (1400–1532) periods of state-driven centralization.

A second scale of analysis—the ethnographic study of mobility and caravanning in the present and recent past—has also come to the fore over the last several decades. Partly driven by concern over disappearing patterns of "traditional" mobility, several scholars have documented communities that continue or recently abandoned practices of caravanning. Romero's (2015) recent work on the oral histories of mule and camelid caravanning in Arica has highlighted the multiple scales of connectivity in the region from local intercommunity barter to long-distance travel to the cities of Bolivian altiplano. Other scholars have focused on still-existing traditions of long-distance camelid caravans in southern Bolivia (Nielsen 1997; Nielsen 2000) and southern Peru (Tripcevich 2016), with an emphasis on documenting the material signatures and social contexts of caravanning to better understand the pre-Hispanic archaeological record.

While these studies highlight the enduring importance of caravanning in the south-central Andes, they also face the classic challenge of ethnoarchaeological research that aims to use observations of the ethnographic present to understand the deeper archaeological past (Stahl 1993; Sillar & Ramón Joffré 2016). Like ethnohistorians seeking to move upstream from the colonial archives into the pre-Hispanic period, the ethnoarchaeologists who have studied Andean caravanning traditions in the twentieth and twenty-first centuries have had to carefully consider the relationships between their observations in the present and the shifting patterns of mobility over the past six centuries of colonial and postcolonial history.

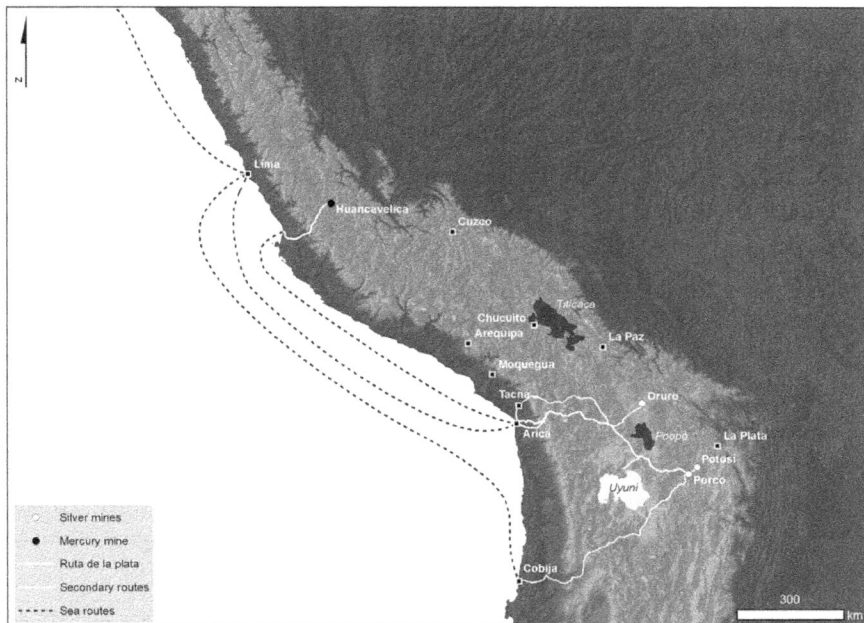

Figure 9.1. Map of the central Andes showing major colonial cities and routes (including the *ruta de la plata*). (Illustration by Noa Corcoran-Tadd)

The third scale of analysis—between the sixteenth and nineteenth centuries—examines the important "middle term" between deep traditions of mobility and observations of the ethnographic present. In the south-central Andes, this analytical scale has often taken an explicitly spatial turn as well, aiming to connect our understandings of the emergent mining cities of Potosí, Porco, and Oruro with the much wider, interconnected landscape of mobility and logistics that was essential for their flourishing (see fig 9.1). The mining cities of the altiplano were connected to the rest of the Spanish colonial world via a network of shifting routes known collectively as "the silver road" (*ruta de la plata*).

Beyond articulating Potosí with new global networks of mercantile circulation, the *ruta de la plata* also formed part of an new regional space of production and consumption, a spatial scale that historian Carlos Assadourian (1982) identified as an emergent *espacio peruano* ("Peruvian space"). While a primary axis of this new space was the Potosí—Arica—Huancavelica route formed by the movement of processed mercury and silver, the space also included key zones of production and transit within the fractured landscape of the altiplano and its neighboring valleys. As in the late pre-Hispanic period, the vertical stratification of ecological zones in the region shaped the new patterns of provisioning, with key products—maize, coca, wine, brandy, salt, firewood—being brought from across the south-central Andes to the cities of the altiplano.

The bases for this new space of circulation were the caravans of camelids and mules and a network of preexisting roads and roadside installations. This body of labor and infrastructure was partly a legacy of Inka imperial organization and local traditions of mobility, while also reshaped by the new demands of the Spanish colonial order. Archival research has highlighted the central (and contested) roles played by indigenous and Spanish caravanners (*trajinantes*) in maintaining the flows of precious metal and subsistence items (notably in the pioneering work of Glave 1989). The *trajinantes* in turn relied in the support of local indigenous communities who supplied the way stations (*tambos*) that dotted the roads and routes of the south-central Andes. While the Spanish crown sought to regulate the *trajinantes* and the *tambos*, this new system of provisioning the high-altitude mining centers appears to have emerged largely from the bottom-up, drawing as it did on older traditions of mobility and logistics.

The effects of this new sphere of circulation were wide-ranging. Most importantly, the provision and support of transport labor (human and animal) fostered an enduring relationship between the mining economy and the indigenous agro-pastoralist world, linking otherwise isolated communities throughout the south-central Andes with the wider networks of the colonial market. In some cases, indigenous herders could negotiate their own way as llama caravanners (e.g., among the Quillaca to the south of Oruro), while in other instances, the new articulations between communities and the market were mediated by traditional indigenous hierarchies (most notably in the Lupaqa case). Indeed, almost all of the documented cases of the "mercantile caciques" emerged in these contexts of pastoralist communities reorganizing around the new mining economy (Medinaceli 2010, 136). In these new landscapes of specialized mobility, such individuals could amass considerable wealth through their control over human labor and long-distance camelid and mule caravans.

The increased connectivity and trade moving through Arica and the *ruta de la plata* also had an impact on the region's religious geography, forming a focus for early missions, the formation of indigenous confraternities, and the construction of new churches built within an emergent "Andean baroque" style. Art historical studies of these churches and chapels that were built along the route primarily in the seventeenth and eighteenth centuries have highlighted their paradoxical roles as both indices of early evangelization efforts and arenas for the continued negotiations over orthodox and local readings of the Catholic faith (e.g., Moreno & Pereira 2011).

And while the *ruta de la plata* as a term is suggestive of a relatively fixed route connecting Potosí with Lima and the Pacific, careful exploration of the archival record reveals a dynamic set of routes reacting to local and global forces. Clara Lopez Beltran (2016), in particular, has traced the shifting cultural geography of the *ruta de la plata* (Potosí-Arica) and the *ruta del pescado* (Potosí-Cobija) as the changing fortunes of Potosí, the emergence of Buenos Aires as a major port, and the impacts of piracy on the Pacific coast transformed patterns of mobility in the region.

These ethnohistorical approaches to rural mobility in the south-central Andes illustrate important moves against the previously discussed urban-centric bias in the historiography of the period, as well as the wider tendency toward abstraction in some of the world systems-inspired approaches. By highlighting the importance of what might otherwise be ignored as "interstitial" spaces, this research underlines the agency of rural communities in making and remaking the colonial landscape and raises questions about overly simplistic models of rural isolation and stagnation (compare the debate on rural early modern Europe in Le Roy Ladurie 1977; de Vries 1994; Prak 2005). The previously mentioned interventions of Glave, Medinaceli, and others move beyond a focus on production (whether agricultural or extractive) to consider the particular roles of mobility and logistics in the articulation of the colonial economy. Just as Mangan (2005) and Velasco Murillo (2013) shifted from the silver mine to the colonial city as sites of analysis, so a focus to mobility encourages us to move our attention even farther out into the wider hinterlands.

In addition to developing these important insights, ethnohistorical research in the Andes has repeatedly run into the limits of the written record. Moving beyond the urban archives of Seville, Lima, and La Plata, ethnohistorians have sought alternative sources of historical information, often locating local archives and bringing them into dialogue with oral historical accounts (e.g., Abercrombie 1998; Salomon 2002). At the same time, there is recognition of the limits of a purely textual approach, with one historian noting that "Peru's [colonial] landscapes, and the meanings that emerged around them, were not simply determined by particular discursive systems or ways of seeing, but instead were variously mediated by corporeal encounters with the physical environment and by the indigenous peoples who both inhabited and played a part in shaping it" (Scott 2006, 482). It is here that the spatial and the material emerge as particularly salient domains for an exploration of colonial life that moves beyond the archives to incorporate methods from archaeology, anthropology, and historical geography. If, as historian Miguel Glave suggests, "llamas, ropes, ceramic jars, and rafts were fundamental factors in the creation of new social relationships" (2000, 160 [author's translation]) in the emerging city of Potosí and its hinterlands, then a turn to an archaeological analysis of the heterogeneous, circulating materials that constituted life on the move during the colonial period is vital.

Landscapes of Production

The archaeological investigation of the colonial Andes has expanded dramatically over the past two decades. As a full survey of this rapidly changing subfield is beyond the scope of this chapter (see van Buren 2010; Traslaviña et al. 2017), the following focuses on the archaeology of production and mobility in the region of the south-central Andes. In particular, the aim is to put these archaeological results into dialogue with the preceding discussion of ethnohistorical research and its limits in the region.

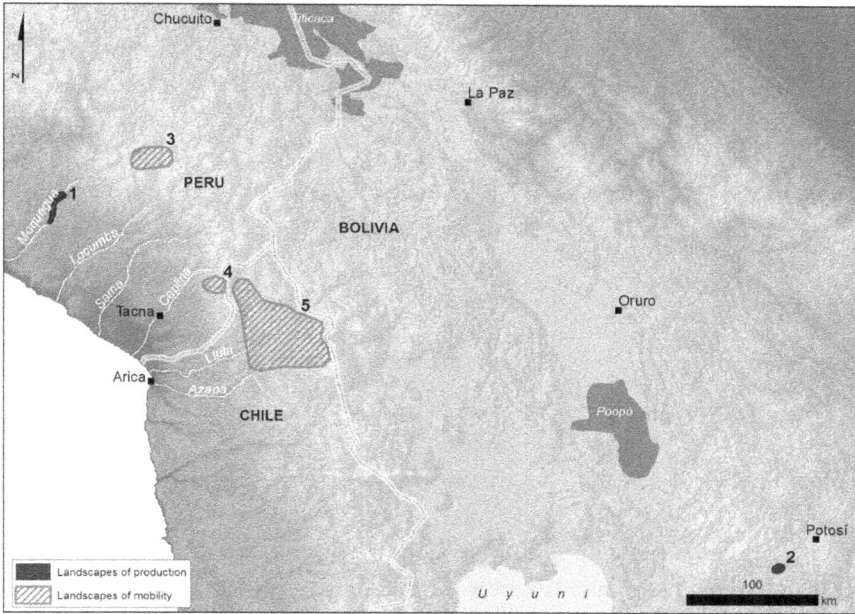

Figure 9.2. Map of the south-central Andes showing the landscapes of production ([1] middle Moquegua valley, [2] Porco and mobility [3] Lake Suches, [4] Palca, [5] Parinacota) mentioned in the chapter. (Illustration by Noa Corcoran-Tadd)

Two productive landscapes with sustained programs of archaeological investigation stand out in the south-central Andes—the vineyards of Moquegua and the silver mines and refineries of Porco (see fig. 9.2). Beginning in the early 1980s, the Programa Contisuyo in the Moquegua drainage on the south coast of Peru represented an important turning point in archaeological approaches to the Andean past. While largely focused on the ecology and political economy of the late pre-Hispanic period, a substantial effort was made to explore the rich colonial-period landscape of haciendas, resettled indigenous communities, and ceramic production sites in the valley (Smith 1991; Bürgi 1993; deFrance 1993; van Buren 1993). Drawing on the seminal work of Kathleen Deagan (1983), Charles Ewen (1987), and others, the Moquegua projects brought Andean archaeology into contact with ongoing debates in US and Caribbean historical archaeology, including questions of political economy and cultural mixture (*mestizaje*).

Rice's archaeological survey in the middle Moquegua valley (Rice & Smith 1989; Rice 2011; Rice 2014) revealed the emergence of a transformed agrarian landscape during the sixteenth and seventeenth centuries as the existing indigenous agricultural infrastructure was gradually appropriated by Spanish colonists and turned to new ends. During this period, the series of Pacific coastal valleys from the Moquegua south to the Azapa and beyond were converted into important centers for the production of comestibles such as wine, brandy, fish, and chili peppers oriented toward the new markets of the altiplano. Excavations at several of the *bodegas* revealed seventeenth- and eighteenth-century occupations focused on the industrial production of wine and brandy, as well as ancillary products including pitch and ceramic jars (*botijas*; see fig. 9.3).

More recently, several projects have investigated the colonial mining landscapes of Porco and Potosí in southern Bolivia. While the epicenter of the mining boom that shaped the colonial Andean order, archaeologists have only recently joined the long tradition of historical research on Potosí and its surrounds. This work has already begun to deepen and even question previous understandings of the region's history. Contrary to Spanish accounts, archaeological survey has revealed significant occupation around Potosí prior to the Spanish conquest (Cruz & Absi 2008), as well as an emphasis on silver extraction and refinement in Porco during the Inka Empire (van Buren & Presta 2010).

Figure 9.3. *Botija* jar fragments from a colonial caravan campsite in Palca, far-southern Peru. (Photograph by Noa Corcoran-Tadd)

The Porco landscape was gradually reshaped during the sixteenth century as labor organization was reorganized under the new Spanish colonial regime, with van Buren and Weaver (2012) identifying a possible settlement of *yanacona* (mining specialists) at Ferro Ingenio suggestive of the persistence and local remaking of precolonial labor regimes during the mid- to late sixteenth century. At the same time, the presence of *botijas* and Panamanian glazed ceramics are suggestive of participation in the emerging market economy centered in Potosí. Research in the Porco landscape has also highlighted the contribution of local technologies to the initial silver-mining boom in the sixteenth century, most notably with the persistence of the indigenous smelting technique using small, wind-driven furnaces (*huayrachinas*) (van Buren & Mills 2005).

Landscapes of Mobility

While these two case studies of agricultural (Moquegua) and mining (Porco-Potosí) landscapes highlight the transformations of production under Spanish colonial rule and the impact of burgeoning interregional markets, research in several adjacent areas highlights the importance of exploring the "interstitial" landscapes of the south-central Andes. Such landscapes include the altiplano areas and high-altitude passes that otherwise tend to remain blank spaces in historical mappings of the colonial period.

Archaeological survey in the Lake Suches basin in the highlands of Moquegua revealed the traces of colonial caravan routes connecting the vineyards of Moquegua with the altiplano markets of Chucuito and Potosí (Vining 2012). Located at an altitude of over 4,400 meters above sea level, the area forms a corridor connecting the upper drainage of the Moquegua with the Titicaca Basin and the Bolivian altiplano to the east via a series of lakes and wetlands. These aquatic resources both supported local communities of camelid pastoralists and formed an important node for movement through the otherwise arid, high-altitude landscape. Colonial use of this route by caravans originating in the bodegas of Moquegua is suggested by the linear scatters of *botija* fragments along east-west alignments across the Suches basin, with ceramic and documentary evidence suggesting a peak in traffic during the eighteenth century (Vining 2012, 399).

A second high-altitude corridor to the south of Suches—centered around the passes of Palca in the highlands of Tacna—reveals a parallel pattern of colonial caravanning (Corcoran-Tadd 2017). Here intensive pedestrian survey recorded multiple caravan camps (*jaranas*) consisting of ephemeral artifact scatters, fire rings, and small windbreaks, and resembling the ethnographic *jaranas* described by Nielsen (1997) in his study of contemporary camelid caravans in southern Bolivia. Located on one of the later branches of the *ruta de la plata* connecting Potosí and Oruro with the Pacific cities of Arica and Tacna, these sites show a mixture of ceramics (*botijas, mayolicas,* and persistent altiplano traditions) suggestive of the multiple actors (long-distance merchants, indigenous caravanners, local pastoralists) moving along this route.

The primary routes forming the *ruta de la plata* passed farther to the south through the Lluta and Azapa valleys in the modern-day Chilean region of Arica y Parinacota. Here there is particularly strong evidence for the reuse of Inka roads and roadside structures as infrastructure for the new silver route (Muñoz, Chacama, & Santos 1997; Santoro et al. 2010). Several Inka *tambos* along what came to be the colonial routes to Potosí, Oruro, and La Paz show levels of reoccupation with colonial ceramics and glass, including at Chungará, Zapahuira and Tacora (see fig. 9.4). While some of these occupations may represent the expedient reuse of convenient structures, in other cases (as at Chungará) there is suggestive evidence

Figure 9.4. Inka way station of Tambo Tacora with evidence of colonial reuse, Parinacota, far northern Chile. (Photograph by Noa Corcoran-Tadd)

for the more formal persistence of these sites as colonial way stations maintained by local indigenous communities.

These landscapes in the south-central Andes have never had any claim to major historical importance in a traditional sense. From the perspective of colonial Lima, the overriding focus of attention was on the "pillars" of Potosí and Huancavelica and the defense of strategic Pacific ports such as Valdivia and Arica. In this sense, these regions were politically and economically marginal areas. And yet the transport corridors through Suches, Palca, and Parinacota provide useful case-studies in understanding the paradoxically influential role played by those interstitial spaces in structuring the extensive economic and administrative network of the colonial Andes.

Following in this vein, there is the possibility to use these marginal spaces to test the outer limits of political and economic networks (both pre-Hispanic and historical). As noted earlier, the urban Spanish perception of the Andean highlands as a landscape both in need of order and resisting the imposition of this order was an enduring one. Indeed, there are important possibilities for the archaeological exploration of particularly remote, mountainous landscapes in the Andes as regions of refuge and resilience during the colonial period (cf. Beltran 1979; Given 2004). At the same, I have argued that it would be mistake to simply recenter the rural and the peripheral as pivotal regions of resistance to be valorized by the archaeologist. Rather it is important to carefully explore the *multiple* kinds of marginal spaces (e.g., transport corridors, regions of refuge, and abandoned landscapes) that emerged in relation to the colonial metropole (cf. Déry, Leimgruber, & Zsilincsar 2012).

In the cases of the transport corridors outlined here, an archaeological attention to the material qualities of these marginal landscapes highlights several topics that deserve further consideration in the study of the colonial Andes and perhaps beyond. First, much remains to be understood about the impacts of previous moments of infrastructural investment—for instance, the roads and *tambos* of the Inka state—on the daily task-scape of movement through treacherous highland environments and on the rise of new market networks. In the case of Arica, the levels of reoccupation at the Inka *tambos* are particularly suggestive of an enduring infrastructural legacy although they remain little investigated.

Second, archaeologists are well situated to explore the ways in which colonial life was shaped as much by persistent indigenous technologies as by foreign innovations (Montón-Subías 2015, 154). Just as the early mining operations in Porco relied on the *huayrachina* furnace, so the technologies and knowledge networks of camelid caravanning enabled trade through the "interstitial" landscapes of the altiplano. While some economic historians have suggested that mules soon dominated the *ruta de la plata* and other colonial routes in the Andes (Assadourian 1982), both the archaeological documentation of high-altitude *jaranas* and fragmentary archival references suggest a long-term persistence of camelid caravanning. Indeed, archival sources are likely to overrepresent the role of mules given the Spanish/urban biases in documentary production (Sanhueza 2011, 294).

Third, it is worth considering the possibilities for both leverage and exploitation that these spaces of mobility offered to highland communities. The aforementioned phenomenon of the "mercantile caciques" that emerged in the sixteenth and seventeenth centuries points to the advantageous position afforded to particular communities and individuals on the transport corridors. Indeed, the frictions of difficult topographies and contracted caravans were fundamental to the profit-making of these new middlemen. At the same time, a careful attention to the material conditions of mobility through the analysis of campsites and the osteoarchaeological record also highlights the violence of logistics as the labor of *trajinantes*, *tambo* workers, and camelids was captured and commoditized under precarious conditions (deFrance 2010; Cowen 2014; Corcoran-Tadd and Pezzarossi 2018).

Conclusions

This chapter has taken a historiographical perspective to outline some of the complementarities and tensions between the multiple approaches using textual and material evidence to explore colonial Andean history, with an especial emphasis on the resulting, often uneven spatial understandings of the region. Following some of the pioneering researchers in Andean ethnohistory (the peculiar hybrid approach to indigenous history that emerged across the Americas during the 1970s and 1980s) and archaeology, the discussion has highlighted some of the possibilities and difficulties in understanding the landscapes of production and mobility that emerged between the sixteenth and nineteenth centuries around the silver mines of highland Bolivia.

A note of humility is perhaps in order in concluding this discussion. As exciting as the new wave of archaeological investigations into the colonial Andes is in pushing against the limits of what is knowable using traditional archival methods, archaeologists will also need to acknowledge the limits of their own methods (see, e.g., Montón-Subías 2015). Historical archaeology has often been advanced as key in unearthing the histories of subaltern subjects otherwise excluded from the metropolitan archive (Beaudry, Cook, & Mrozowski 1991; Orser & Funari 2001; Liebmann & Murphy 2012). And yet marginalized communities often leave little trace in the archaeological record as well, a fact highlighted in this chapter by the ephemerality of caravanning sites and the consequent near-invisibility of indigenous caravanners.

More optimistically, an archaeological turn in the investigation of colonial mobility in the central Andes also brings into relief the necessity of connecting multiple analytical scales. Archaeology has long formed the background for constructing timescales—the ethnographic, the ethnohistoric, the long term—in the Andean region. Now, with the rapid growth of new data sets from the colonial period, archaeologists are increasingly able to move beyond a focus on single sites and landscapes and to grapple with what some have termed a "multi-sited" approach (Ryzewski 2012), that traces processes and products across multiple, wider spatial scales. As I have suggested with the conjunction of landscapes of production (e.g., the vineyards of Moquegua), landscapes of mobility (e.g., the passes of Palca), and circulating materials (e.g., *botijas*), there are new possibilities for reconnecting the cities and rural landscapes that have otherwise tended to be separated in our analyses.

Such a focus on scales and mobility also raises further questions about the position of the south-central Andean case study within a much wider context of connectivity along the Pacific Rim. With its desert ports, connections to Mexico and the Philippines, and vulnerability to piracy, the *ruta de la plata* was as much a seascape as a landscape. While much remains to be done in exploring this seascape, an integrated archaeological and historical understanding of connectivity at this scale is crucial as scholars begin to both integrate the histories of the Pacific (Padrón 2009; Skowronek 2009; Carr et al. 2015) and question the hegemonic models (Flynn and Giráldez 1995; Elliott 2012; Osorio 2016) that continue to place the Atlantic at the center of early modern history.

Works Cited

Abercrombie, Thomas A. 1998. *Pathways of Memory and Power: Ethnography and History among an Andean People*. Madison: University of Wisconsin Press.

———. 2012. "The Ethnos, Histories, and Cultures of Ethnohistory: A View from the US Academy." *Memoria americana* 20(1): 137–45.

Assadourian, Carlos Sempat. 1982. *El sistema de la economía colonial: Mercado interno, regiones y espacio económico*. Lima, Peru: Instituto de Estudios Peruanos.

Bakewell, Peter John. 1984. *Miners of the Red Mountain: Indian Labor in Potosí, 1545–1650.* Albuquerque: University of New Mexico Press.

Beaudry, Mary, Lauren Cook, and Stephen A. Mrozowski. 1991. "Artifacts and Active Voices: Material Culture as Social Discourse." In *The Archaeology of Inequality.* Edited by R. H. McGuire and R. Paynter. Oxford, UK: Blackwell.

Beltran, Gonzalo Aguirre. 1979. *Regions of Refuge.* Washington, DC: Society for Applied Anthropology.

Bouysse-Cassagne, Thérèse. 1978. "L'espace aymara: Urco et uma." *Annales* 33(5–6): 1057–80.

Bürgi, Peter T. 1993. "The Inka Empire's Expansion into the Coastal Sierra Region West of Lake Titicaca." PhD dissertation, Department of Anthropology, University of Chicago.

Burns, Kathryn. 2011. "Making Indigenous Archives: The Quilcaycamayoc of Colonial Cuzco." *Hispanic American Historical Review* 91(4): 665–89.

Carr, Dennis, Gauvin A. Bailey, Timothy Brook, Mitchell Codding, Karina Corrigan, and Donna Pierce. 2015. *Made in the Americas: The New World discovers Asia.* Boston, MA: Museum of Fine Arts Publications.

Choque Canqui, Roberto. 1978. "Pedro Chipana: Cacique comerciante de Calamarca." *Avances* 1: 28–32.

Cole, Jeffrey A. 1985. *The Potosí Mita, 1573–1700: Compulsory Indian Labor in the Andes.* Palo Alto, CA: Stanford University Press.

Corcoran-Tadd, Noa. 2017. "Tambos and the Andean Longue Durée: Landscapes of Mobility in Far Southern Peru." PhD dissertation, Department of Anthropology, Harvard University.

Corcoran-Tadd, Noa, and Guido Pezzarossi. 2018. "Between the South Sea and the Mountainous Ridges: Biopolitical Assemblages in the Spanish Colonial Americas." *Post-Medieval Archaeology* 52(1): 84–101.

Cowen, Deborah. 2014. *The Deadly Life of Logistics.* Minneapolis, MN: University of Minnesota Press.

Cruz, Pablo, and Pascale Absi. 2008. "Cerros ardientes y huayras calladas: Potosí antes y durante el contacto." In *Mina y metalurgia en los Andes del Sur sede la época prehispánica hasta el siglo XVII.* Edited by P. Cruz and J.-J. Vacher. Sucre, Bolivia: Tupac Katari.

Cummins, Thomas B. F. 2002. "Forms of Andean Colonial Towns, Free Will, and Marriage." In *The Archaeology of Colonialism.* Edited by C. L. Lyons and J. K. Papadopoulos. Los Angeles, CA: The Getty Research Institute.

de Vries, Jan. 1994. "The Industrial Revolution and the Industrious Revolution." *Journal of Economic History* 54(2): 249–70.

Deagan, Kathleen A. 1983. *Spanish St. Augustine: The Archaeology of a Colonial Creole Community.* New York: Academic Press.

deFrance, Susan D. 1993. *Ecological Imperialism in the South-Central Andes: Faunal Data from Spanish Colonial Settlements in the Moquegua and Torata Valleys.* PhD dissertation, Department of Anthropology, University of Florida.

———. 2010. "Paleopathology and Health of Native and Introduced Animals on Southern Peruvian and Bolivian Spanish Colonial Sites." *International Journal of Osteoarchaeology* 20: 508–24.

Déry, Steve, Walter Leimgruber, and Walter Zsilincsar. 2012. "Understanding Marginality: Recent Insights from a Geographical Perspective." *Hrvatski geografski glasnik* 74(1): 5–18.

Elliott, John. 2012. *History in the Making*. New Haven, CT: Yale University Press.

Ewen, Charles Robin. 1987. "From Spaniard to Creole: The Archaeology of Cultural Formation at Puerto Real, Haiti." PhD dissertation, Department of Anthropology, University of Florida.

Flynn, Dennis O., and Arturo Giráldez. 1995. "Born with a "Silver Spoon": The Origin of World Trade in 1571." *Journal of World History* 6(2): 201–21.

Given, Michael. 2004. *The Archaeology of the Colonized*. New York: Routledge.

Glave, Luis Miguel. 1989. *Trajinantes: Caminos indígenas en la sociedad colonial: Siglos XVI–XVII*. Lima, Peru: Instituto de Apoyo Agrario.

———. 2000. "Trajines, abastecimiento y mercado: Potosí, siglos XVI–XVII." In *Potosí: plata para Europa*. Edited by J. Marchena Fernández and J. Villa Rodríguez. Seville, Spain: Universidad de Sevilla.

Goldstein, Paul S. 2000. "The Vertical Archipelago and Diaspora Communities in the Southern Andes." In *The Archaeology of Communities: A New World Perspective*. Edited by M. A. Canuto and J. Yaeger. New York: Routledge.

Hanke, Lewis. 1956. *The Imperial City of Potosi*. The Hague, the Netherlands: Martinus Nijhoff.

Hyslop, John. 1990. *Inka Settlement Planning*. Austin: University of Texas Press.

Kinsbruner, Jay. 2005. *The Colonial Spanish-American City: Urban Life in the Age of Atlantic Capitalism*. Austin: University of Texas Press.

Le Roy Ladurie, Emmanuel. 1977. "Motionless History." *Social Science History* 1(2): 115–36.

Liebmann, Matthew, and Melissa Murphy, eds. 2012. *Enduring Conquests. Rethinking the Archaeology of Resistance to Spanish Colonialism in the Americas*. Sante Fe, New Mexico: SAR Press.

Lockhart, James. 1994. *Spanish Peru, 1532–1560: A Social History*. Madison: University of Wisconsin Press.

López Beltrán, Clara. 2016. *La Ruta de la Plata de Potosí al Pacífico: Caminos, comercio y caravanas en el os siglos XVI y XIX*. La Paz, Bolivia: Plural de Ediciones.

Mangan, Jane E. 2005. *Trading Roles: Gender, Ethnicity, and the Urban Economy in Colonial Potosí*. Durham, NC: Duke University Press.

Medinaceli, Ximena. 2010. *Sariri: Los llameros y la construcción de la sociedad colonial*. Lima, Peru: Instituto Francés de Estudios Andino.

Mills, Kenneth R. 1997. *Idolatry and Its Enemies: Colonial Andean Religion and Extirpation, 1640–1750*. Princeton, NJ: Princeton University Press.

Montón-Subías, Sandra. 2015. "Colonialismo, Monarquía Hispánica y cultura material: algunas contribuciones desde la Arqueología." *Índice Histórico Español* 128: 137–74.

Moreno, Rodrigo and Magdalena Pereira. 2011. *Arica y Parinacota: La Iglesia en la Ruta de la Plata*. Viña del Mar, Chile: Ediciones Altazor.

Morse, Richard M. 1982. "The Urban Development of Colonial Spanish America." In *The Cambridge History of Latin America*. Edited by L. Bethell. Cambridge, UK: Cambridge University Press.

Mumford, Jeremy Ravi. 2012. *Vertical Empire: The General Resettlement of Indians in the Colonial Andes*. Durham, NC: Duke University Press.

Muñoz, Iván R, Juan M. Chacama, and Mariela Santos. 1997. "Tambos, Pukaras y Aldeas, evidencias del poblamiento humano prehispánico tardío y de contacto indígena-europeo en el extremo norte de Chile: análisis de los patrones habitacionales y nuevas dataciones radiométricas." *Dialogo Andino* 16: 123–91.

Murra, John V. 1972. El *"control vertical" de un máximo de pisos ecológicos en la economia de las sociedades andinas*. Huánuco, Peru: Universidad Hermilo Valdizan.

Nielsen, Axel E. 1997. "El tráfico caravanero visto desde La Jara." *Estudios Atacameños* 14: 339–71.

———. 2000. "Andean Caravans: An Ethnoarchaeology." PhD dissertation, Department of Anthropology, University of Arizona.

Núñez, Lautaro, and Tom D Dillehay. 1978. *Movilidad giratoria, armonía social y desarrollo en los Andes meridionales: patrones de tráfico e interacción económica (ensayo)*. Antofagasta, Chile: Universidad Católica del Norte.

Orser, Charles E., and Pedro PA Funari. 2001. "Archaeology and Slave Resistance and Rebellion." *World Archaeology* 33(1): 61–72.

Osorio, Alejandra. 2016. "El Imperio de los Austrias españoles y el Atlántico: propuesta para una nueva historia." In *Fronteras: Procesos y prácticas de integración y conflictos entre Europa y América (siglos XVI–XX)*. Edited by V. Favarò, Manfredi Merluzzi, and Gaetano Sabatini. Mexico City: Fondo de Cultura Ecónomica.

Padrón, Ricardo. 2009. "A Sea of Denial: The Early Modern Spanish Invention of the Pacific Rim." *Hispanic Review* 77(1): 1–27.

Pease, Franklin. 1988. "Curacas coloniales: riqueza y actitudes." *Revista de Indias* 48(182): 87–107.

Platt, Tristan, Thérèse Bouysse-Cassagne, and Olivia Harris. 2006. *Qaraqara-Charka: Mallku, Inka y Rey en la provincia de Charcas (siglos XV–XVII). Historia antropológica de una confederación aymara*. La Paz, Bolivia: Plural editores.

Platt, Tristan, and Pablo Quisbert. 2008. "Tras las huellas del silencio. Potosí, los inkas y el virrey Toledo." In *Mina y metalurgia en los Andes del Sur, desde la época prehispánica hasta el siglo XVII*. Edited by P. Cruz and J. Vacher. Sucre, Bolivia: Instituto Francés de Estudios Andinos.

Prak, Maarten, ed. 2005. *Early Modern Capitalism: Economic and Social Change in Europe 1400–1800.* New York: Routledge.

Rama, Angel. 1996. *The Lettered City.* Durham, NC: Duke University Press.

Rappaport, Joanne, and Thomas B. F. Cummins. 2012. *Beyond the Lettered City: Indigenous Literacies in the Andes.* Durham, NC: Duke University Press.

Rice, Prudence M. 2011. *Vintage Moquegua: History, Wine, and Archaeology on a Colonial Peruvian Periphery.* Austin: University of Texas Press.

———. 2014. *Space-Time Perspectives on Early Colonial Moquegua.* Boulder: University Press of Colorado.

Rice, Prudence M., and Greg C. Smith. 1989. "The Spanish Colonial Wineries of Moquegua, Peru." *Historical Archaeology* 23(2): 41–49.

Rivera Cusicanqui, Silvia. 1978. "El mallku y la sociedad colonial en el siglo XVII: El caso de Jesús de Machaca." *Avances: Revista boliviana de estudios históricos y sociales* 1: 7–27.

Romero Guevara, Álvaro. 2015. *Arrieraje en la Región de Arica y Parinacota.* Antofagasta, Chile: Consejo Nacional de la Cultura y las Artes.

Ryzewski, Krysta. 2012. "Multiply Situated Strategies? Multi-sited Ethnography and Archeology." *Journal of Archaeological Method and Theory* 19(2): 241–68.

Saignes, Thierry. 1985. "Caciques, Tribute and Migration in the Southern Andes: Indian Society and the 17th Century Colonial Order (Audencias de Charcas)." *ISA Occasional Papers*: 1–43.

Salomon, Frank. 2002. "Unethnic Ethnohistory: On Peruvian Peasant Historiography and Ideas of Autochthony." *Ethnohistory* 49(3): 475–506.

Salomon, Frank, and Mercedes Niño-Murcia. 2011. *The Lettered Mountain: A Peruvian Village's Way with Writing.* Durham, NC: Duke University Press.

Sanhueza, Cecilia. 2011. "Tráfico Caravanero, Arriería y Trajines en Atacama Colonial: síntesis y discusiones sobre un proceso de adaptación andina." In *Temporalidad, interacción y dinamismo cultural: La búsqueda del hombre: Homenaje al Dr. Lautaro Núñez Atencio.* Edited by A. Hubert, J. A. González and M. Pereira. Antofagasta, Chile: Universidad Católica del Norte.

Santoro, Calógero M., Verónica Williams, Daniela Valenzuela, Álvaro Romero, and Vivien G. Standen. 2010. "An Archaeological Perspective on the Inka Provincial Administration from the South-Central Andes." In *Distant Provinces in the Inka Empire: Toward a Deeper Understanding of Inka Imperialism.* Edited by M. A. Malpass and S. Alconini. Iowa City: University of Iowa Press.

Scott, Heidi V. 2006. "Rethinking Landscape and Colonialism in the Context of Early Spanish Peru." *Environment and Planning D: Society and Space* 24(4): 481–96.

Sillar, Bill, and Gabriel Ramón Joffré. 2016. "Using the Present to Interpret the Past: The Role of Ethnographic Studies in Andean Archaeology." *World Archaeology* 48(5): 656–73.

Skowronek, Russell K. 2009. "On the Fringes of New Spain: The Northern Borderlands and the Pacific." In *International Handbook of Historical Archaeology*. Edited by D. R. Gaimster and T. Majewski. New York: Springer.

Smith, Greg Charles. 1991. "Heard It through the Grapevine: Andean and European Contributions to Spanish Colonial Culture and Viticulture in Moquegua, Peru." PhD dissertation, Department of Anthropology, University of Florida.

Stahl, Ann B. 1993. "Concepts of Time and Approaches to analogical Reasoning in Historical Perspective." *American Antiquity* 58(2): 235–60.

Stanish, Charles. 2003. *Ancient Titicaca: The Evolution of Complex Society in Southern Peru and Northern Bolivia*. Los Angeles: University of California Press.

Stern, Steve J. 1988. "Feudalism, Capitalism, and the World-System in the Perspective of Latin America and the Caribbean." *American Historical Review* 93(4): 829–72.

———. 1988. "Feudalism, Capitalism, and the World-System in the Perspective of Latin America and the Caribbean: Ever More Solitary." *American Historical Review* 93(4): 886–97.

———. 1995. "The Variety and Ambiguity of Native Andean Intervention in European Colonial Markets." In *Ethnicity, Markets, and Migration in the Andes: At the Crossroads of History and Anthropology*. Edited by B. Larson and O. Harris. Durham, NC: Duke University Press.

Tandeter, Enrique. 1981. "Forced and Free Labour in Late Colonial Potosi." *Past & Present* 93: 98–136.

Traslaviña, Abel, Zachary Chase, Parker VanValkenburgh, and Brendan J. M. Weaver, eds. 2017. *Arqueología Histórica en el Perú. Primera Parte (Boletín de Arqueología 20)*. Lima, Peru: Fondo Editorial PUCP.

Tripcevich, Nicholas. 2016. "The Ethnoarchaeology of a Cotahuasi Salt Caravan: Exploring Andean Pastoralist Movement." In *The Archaeology of Andean Pastoralism*. Edited by J. M. Capriles and N. Tripcevich. Albuquerque: University of New Mexico Press.

van Buren, Mary. 1993. "Community and Empire in Southern Peru: The Site of Torata Alta under Spanish Rule." PhD dissertation, Department of Anthropology, University of Arizona.

———. 1996. "Rethinking the Vertical Archipelago: Ethnicity, Exchange, and History in the South Central Andes." *American Anthropologist* 98(2): 338–51.

———. 2010. "The Archaeological Study of Spanish Colonialism in the Americas." *Journal of Archaeological Research* 18(2): 151–201.

van Buren, Mary, and Barbara H. Mills. 2005. "Huayrachinas and Tocochimbos: Traditional Smelting Technology of the Southern Andes." *Latin American Antiquity* 16(1): 3–25.

van Buren, Mary, and Ana Maria Presta. 2010. "The Organization of Inka Silver Production in Porco, Bolivia." In *Distant Provinces in the Inka Empire: Toward a Deeper Understanding of Inka Imperialism*. Edited by M. A. Malpass and S. Alconini. Iowa City: University of Iowa Press.

van Buren, Mary, and Brendan J. M. Weaver. 2012. "Contours of Labor and History: A Diachronic Perspective on Andean Mineral Production and the Making of Landscapes in Porco, Bolivia." *Historical Archaeology* 46(3): 79–101.

Velasco Murillo, Dana. 2009. "Urban Indians in a Silver City: Zacatecas, Mexico, 1546–1806." PhD dissertation, Department of History, UCLA.

———. 2013. "Laboring above Ground: Indigenous Women in New Spain's Silver Mining District, Zacatecas, Mexico, 1620–1770." *Hispanic American Historical Review* 93(1): 3–32.

Vining, Benjamin R. 2012. "Ruralism, Land Use History, and Holocene Climate in the Suches Highlands, Southern Peru." PhD dissertation, Department of Archaeology, Boston University.

Wachtel, Nathan. 1977. *The Vision of the Vanquished*. Hassocks, UK: Harvester Press.

———. 1978. "Hommes d'eau: le problème uru (XVIe–XVIIe siècle)." *Annales*: 1126–59.

Wallerstein, Immanuel. 1988. "Feudalism, Capitalism, and the World-System in the Perspective of Latin America and the Caribbean: Comments on Stern's Critical Tests." *American Historical Review* 93(4): 873–85.

Chapter 10

Landscapes of Emergent Frontier Economies at Mission San Buenaventura

Thomas E. Tolley

In this chapter, I consider the economies and landscapes of the missions of Alta California, founded by the Catholic Church and the regal government of New Spain between 1769 and 1823.[1] Earlier studies of these missions have a tradition of being nested in Eurocentric frameworks of commerce, protocols, and engagement.[2] Many of these analytical lenses are world-systems theory-based models that often assume a similitude of experiences and impose a hierarchy of socioeconomic interactions that privilege ". . . European subjects and leaving Native people in the background, despite the fact . . . they constituted a resident majority over the handful of European missionaries and mestizo soldiers stationed at the mission sites" (Schneider & Panich 2014, 19). The lived experiences and economies at the mission level in Alta California, however, were anything but homogeneous. These assumptions of similarity do not survive the scrutiny of the archaeological and historical data from each mission (Costello 1992, 67–68). While global in their interconnections and consequences, the missions and their economic hinterlands were shaped locally and uniquely formed. The economic significance of the missions did not just occur after Mexican independence in 1821. Rather, the missions began developing small-scale but robust economies not long after each site was founded.

This chapter examines the economic landscapes of Mission San Buenaventura. I consider the local, Native context in which the missions were established and their distinctive articulations with global economies. Missions in Alta California were founded where Native people had already settled. In the case of Mission San Buenaventura, established in 1782, the mission was located near over a dozen existing Native settlements (King 1975). I use a transidiomatic approach to explore how the experience of Mission San Buenaventura represents a unique example of concurrent landscape engagements within a broader frontier zone. Part of what makes these engagements unique is the economic variables contained within these frontier landscapes. The priests who administered the foundation and development of Mission San Buenaventura utilized Native culture and traditions to better understand components of the landscapes, and to ensure mission survival from its early formative years until secularization in 1834. San Buenaventura also supported New Spain by helping to sustain the presidio at Santa Barbara and further the goals of expanding the number of missions in Alta California. Another significant factor was the degree to which San Buenaventura participated in surreptitious trade with nonsanctioned merchants on the coast, independently extending the sphere of influence of the mission into larger global economies at a slow but increasingly noteworthy volume.

Mission Landscapes

For this chapter, I consider landscapes[3] to be the individual aegises of influence surrounding each mission, nebulous vessels accommodating vestiges of human activity, interaction, influence, and environment that have taken in and produced with other landscapes. This chaotic interplay is precisely why the missions were successful. In Alta California, under the umbrella of unique forms of colonialism came a collision of landscape formation processes, imbued meaning, and methods of melding that fabricated diaphanous parameters, more webs than linear systems. This lens captures the varied elements of the past, allowing the possibility of unexpected or unpredictable outcomes.

Kent Lightfoot (2015) engaged a similar comparative overview of pluralistic colonial communities, describing missions as "settlements where missionaries, colonial soldiers, and managers, and hundreds of native peoples resided" (Lightfoot 2015, 9217). Considering pluralistic communities within landscapes reveals how landscapes occupied by multiple cultural expressions define and structure their perceptions, and how these perspectives can merge or morph into new definitions. Lee Panich and Tsim Schneider utilized studies from Mission Santa Clara de Asis, the San Francisco Bay, and the central valley of California to examine "how indigenous people organized and used space at mission establishments, along the shifting frontiers between native homelands and colonial hinterlands, and in areas outside of direct colonial control" (Panich & Schneider 2015, 48). Panich and Schneider posit the indigenous populations that were part of mission landscapes expressed their autonomy across multiple zones and within multiple locations (Panich & Schneider 2015, 55–56).

Here I engage a similarly nuanced approach, considering the missions as primarily Native sites with mixed European/Mexican components that experienced a type of colonialism unique to Alta California.[4] A landscape-based perspective brings to the fore palimpsests of these Native-lived experiences. Participants—in this case, Native peoples of varied ethnicities, Europeans, and their descendants—were brought together for a variety of reasons (Comaroff & Comaroff 1991, 10–11; DeCorse 2012, 1–3; Lightfoot & Martinez 1995, 483–86; Loren 2008, 7–9), including colonial expansionist agendas. What actually occurred within these contact zones was often something far different than what was intended or expected by the groups involved. That is, New Spain may have anticipated the missions becoming large, economically productive population centers that attracted Spanish settlers with the promise of land and inexpensive Native labor, but this was not what occurred in Alta California. Large population centers did not gain velocity until after Mexican Independence in 1821.

It is important to recognize that the European or non-Native occupants of the missions were always a minority. The Native population of Alta California at the time of the founding of the missions is not clear. Albert Kroeber estimated the Native population of Alta California at 133,000 (Kroeber 1925, 880–91). Sherburne Cook put the total population at 135,000 (Cook 1976a), but by 1970 he had increased his estimate to 310,000 (Cook 1976b, 36–43). Rawls also puts the total population closer to 300,000, with over 100 nations or tribes (Rawls 1984, 6). In contrast, an estimate of the entire non-Native population in Alta California in 1775 was less than 170 (Mason 1998, 20). There was to be no watershed moment when the Europeans occupying the missions would have had the volume of force of numbers or technology to overcome every point of conflict with Native populations. Other means would need to be developed for the missions to first survive, and then ultimately become economically stable.

Although the original intent for the missions included providing materials to settlements and presidios and creating surplus for commerce, what eventually emerged was something that went beyond those projections. Missions were largely left on their own to develop the means necessary for their survival. Paul Farnsworth observed that the missions were of a purpose similar to slave plantations in the eastern United States, in that both productive landscapes were ". . . developed to efficiently and cheaply produce raw materials, on a large scale, in peripheral areas, using cheap labor. These products could then be shipped to the core state in return for manufactured goods produced by skilled labor in the core state" (Farnsworth 1987, 598). Natives, however, were not simply reactionary regarding the Spanish (Farnsworth 1998, 48). By retaining control of their labor, Native groups engaged in complex negotiations that allowed them to retain significant amounts of their culture and traditions. The nature of negotiations and manifestations were unique to each mission. As such, the economic landscapes of each mission were also different.

San Buenaventura had to evaluate all potential resources for the goods needed to ensure the mission's ability to first survive, then to develop economically. New Spain poorly supplied the missions and presidios until 1810, when the supply virtually ceased.[5] The ecclesiastics of San Buenaventura utilized Chumash knowledge of available resources, trade routes, and transport to sustain the mission until European agricultural crops and livestock could be developed to support the mission and its increasing economic output. Because the demand from other missions on the limited resources provided by New Spain continued to grow, the mission had to look for other providers. Whether it was iron for tipping plows, hardware, coopering, and making horseshoes, ceramics, or cloth preferable to the coarse wool woven at the mission, San Buenaventura found potential suppliers in multinational merchants active along the west coast of North America. In order to barter effectively, the mission had to alter its output to include items that held particular trade value. This included furs, pelts, foods, tallow, cowhides, and wine.

In examining Alta California and the Pacific world, it is critically important that markets and products from Asia, particularly China, be considered. Claiming and colonizing the land as a means to secure and expand the territory Spain held in the Americas was of lesser concern; the Crown may have wanted a protective buffer from Russia and England (who both had massive debts in Asian markets), but due to the extreme amount of debt also being held by Spain both in the Americas and in Europe, the priority was the exploitation of rapidly available resources. Also important to consider are Franciscan economic philosophies (Todeschini 2009). These concepts shaped social definitions and identity, created bonds to strengthen markets, increased profits for individuals and the group, and increased the trust people had in social organization (Todeschini 2009, 192–93). Economic control was structured as a form of common morality; endeavors that benefited the community as a whole were venerated. Because of their basis in Franciscan economic philosophy, the missions were already prepared to participate in market economies, even if these were local in focus and locally articulated.

Mission locations represent unique and intersecting landscapes that shaped the ways in which each mission operated and interacted with the rest of the world. These landscapes represent the resource bases, economic activities undertaken, local agencies, and cultures of which each was part. Due in part to San Buenaventura not being located in direct proximity to a governmental center or presidio,[6] the mission had more opportunities to conduct itself with less regulatory interference. This point is crucial in developing an accurate analysis of how missions operated within an environment where government interests or authority may not have been strongly represented or enforced.

The Alta California Missions

In July 1769, the first of what was to be a chain of twenty-one Catholic missions in Alta California was founded at the Kumeyaay site of *Kosoi* (Engelhardt 1920, 4–7; Leffingwell 2005, 17–18), and was christened Mission San Diego de Alcalá. The final mission, San Francisco Solano, was founded in 1823, near the Miwok settlement of *Huchi* (James 1911; Ruscin 1999). Mission San Buenaventura (located near the Chumash settlement of *Shisholop*) was initially planned as the third mission (Engelhardt 1930). However, political infighting and the limited availability of resources delayed its founding until 1782, making it the ninth mission (see fig. 10.1 on page 232). The missions were intended to occupy positions of strategic value based on geography, proximate population availability (from where labor could be extracted, and colonial and religious indoctrination could occur), and suitability for the development and exploitation of agricultural resources. Each mission was founded at or near preexisting Native settlements; many of these villages were given Spanish place-names and were labeled as *rancherías*. New Spain also planned for the establishment and development of settlements (pueblos) in association with the missions that would augment Spain's ability to retain possession of the land and control of its coasts and resources. Considering the relatively small number of non-Natives at each mission, in order to survive, the padres had no option but to forge relationships with the local populations who vastly outnumbered them.

New Spain had been trading in the Philippines, and indirectly with China, for over 200 years by the time the first mission was founded in 1769. This trade, facilitated by the Manila galleons, supplied items such as altar stones, censors,

Figure 10.1. Map of the coast of Alta California. The shaded area indicates the approximate sphere of influence of Mission San Buenaventura. (Drawing by Thomas Edward Tolley)

processional items, crucifixes, iron goods, and textiles to the missions early in their histories (Galvin 1964). The coast of Alta California was also of economic interest to foreign navigators. The missions had begun a small trade in otter pelts with Native populations by 1780 (Ogden 1941, 2). The volume at this stage of trade was not great, however, the economic potential of the prized otter pelts had been noted (Gibson 1992; Melillo 2015; Ogden 1941). In 1784, Vicente Vasadre y Vega fabricated a plan to ship otter skins to China in exchange for mercury that was needed in New Spain for smelting silver. The plan received final approval from Viceroy Bernardo de Gálvez in 1786 (Archibald 1978, 116), and Vasadre was granted exclusive trading rights *as a representative of the government*. The missions became de facto agents of Vasadre, handing pelts directly to him for prices determined largely by Vasadre, who then supervised their shipment to Manila, where he worked to further his own mercantile interests. Ultimately, the fur trade as envisioned by Vasadre failed. The *Audiencia* in New Spain felt the agreed on prices were too high, and suspended Vasadre's exclusive rights in 1790. Nonetheless, this focus on trade is indicative of the economic trajectory Alta California had set upon.

With the end of Vasadre's monopoly, Father Fermín Lasuén[7] saw the missions as exclusive vendors to any and all potential buyers (Kenneally 1965, 155–58), and continued the collection and trade in otter pelts with foreign vessels. New Spain's ongoing pursuit of the fur trade led to conflict with the British over the island of Nootka—adjacent to Vancouver, in what is now British Columbia—which nearly precipitated war in Europe (Pethick 1980; Tovell 2008). Although the conflict was settled with the Nootka Conventions by 1794, the events ended Spanish control of sea commerce in the Pacific, and left the coast of Alta California open for increased international trade (see fig. 10.2 on page 234). Each mission developed its own mercantile economy, producing products, and surreptitiously trading in hides, tallow, wine, and foodstuffs in order to obtain desired goods, including iron, silk, cloth, tea, church materials, and ceramics. Trade partners included merchants from England, Russia, the United States, other parts of the Spanish Empire, and indirectly, China.

Many authors have noted a large shift in economic production at the missions after 1821 due to Mexican independence and the opening of Alta California to global free trade (e.g., Archibald 1978; Costello 1989; Costello 1992; Duggan 2000; Hornbeck 1989). However, much earlier in their existence, each mission was forced by necessity to engage in surreptitious means to obtain resources not provided by the government of New Spain, and the missions were consequently active in international trade well before 1821, albeit at a smaller scale. These global connections were locally articulated. Missions may have fed indirectly into capitalist

Figure 10.2. North and Central America, with emphasis on the Pacific Coast. (Drawing by Thomas Edward Tolley)

economies in Europe as Mintz suggests regarding Spain and England (Mintz 1985, 38), but the immediacy of their economies were anything but capitalist. While European and Asian empires were busy feeding off each other, the missions were etching out markets and product-centered exchange systems on their own, with minimal controlling influence from New Spain. Where systems of free labor that sold their labor to those who had access to means of production were emerging in Europe (Mintz 1985, 43–44), labor in Alta California became a negotiated entity that varied mission to mission, was dependent on need and availability of resources, and moved throughout the landscapes.

Mission San Buenaventura

The future location of Mission San Buenaventura was known to New Spain in the late eighteenth century. However, the area had been largely unvisited by officials from New Spain since first explored by Juan Rodríguez Cabrillo in 1542 (Engelhardt 1930, 3), and by Sebastian Vizcáino in 1602 (Mathes 1973, 65–66). At the time of Vizcáino's arrival, the coastline of the Santa Barbara Channel was densely populated by the Chumash, a well-defined and well-established group[8] of linguistically and culturally connected peoples (Shipley 1978, 86). By some estimates the Chumash population before the establishment of the missions was approximately 18,000–20,000 (Arnold 2000, 12; Cook 1976a, 34–41; Johnson 2001).

Mission San Buenaventura was founded within a fabric of landscapes that included several Chumash settlements near the floodplain and mouth of what is now called the Ventura River (see fig. 10.3). One settlement, Shisholop, located

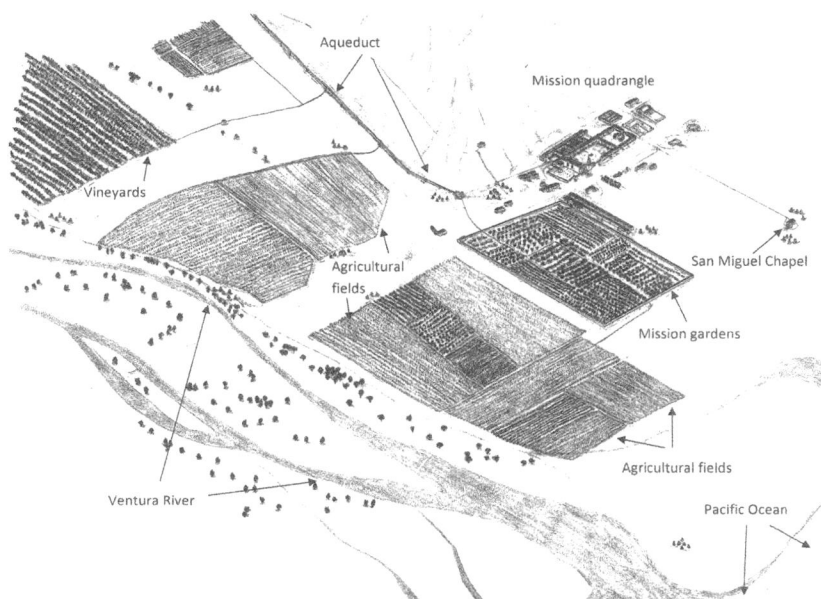

Figure 10.3. Mission San Buenaventura and the lower Ventura River valley. (Drawing by Thomas Edward Tolley)

approximately 0.4 kilometer south of the mission, has been archaeologically identified as a possible trade/exchange site for multiple bands of Chumash (Greenwood 1975; Greenwood 1976). A smaller settlement, Mishkanakan, was located west of the current mission church. The Chumash living in the sphere of influence of San Buenaventura had access to multiple sources of marine life, small and medium-sized fauna, seed grasses, nuts, and squashes (Tolley 2002). The Chumash managed the growth cycles of some of their plant resources via clearing and burning, but no large-scale archaeological evidence of formal cultivation has been recorded. Traditional means of exploiting and utilizing resources contained within Chumash landscapes involved trade, including foodstuffs and other desired goods such as baskets, lithic tools and bowls, and shell goods. Ties between inland, coastal, and island Chumash and their neighbors were resources that the mission would capitalize on. Trade between mainland and island Chumash utilized wood plank and asphalt canoes called *tomols*—fast, highly seaworthy vessels that could perhaps carry cargos of up to 4,000 pounds (Arnold 1995, 737–38, Hudson, Timbrook & Rempe 1978, 23; McCawley 1996, 46). Ethnographic data suggests that the owners of canoes were of higher social status and economic power, and banded together in guilds, or brotherhoods, that controlled access to technical knowledge and regulated trade between the Channel Islands and the mainland Chumash (Hudson et al. 1978, 143–67; Johnson 2001, 54–55; McCawley 1996, 46–47).

Sustained contact between the Chumash and Europeans began in the second half of the eighteenth century. As trade between China and the Americas accelerated after 1760, the Spanish commander of Baja California, Don Joseph de Gálvez, issued orders for an expedition to relocate Vizcáino's Monterey Bay. During the August 1769 journey north, the expedition encountered the Chumash near the present bay mouth of the Santa Clara River, approximately four miles southeast of modern Ventura. The expedition, led by Gaspár de Portolá and Father Juan Crespi, noted several substantial Native villages along the coast (Engelhardt 1930, 7). Mission San Buenaventura was subsequently established on March 31, 1782. Padre Serra, along with Padre Pedro Cambón, oversaw the initial *jacal* (mud-and-timber) construction (with Chumash assistance) of a chapel and quarters for priests and guards.[9] *El Camino Real*, a route connecting all of Alta California's missions, veered away from the ocean near San Buenaventura, followed the Ventura River north, then veered west through the hills beyond *Saptutu/Sulukukiy*,[10] and above a Chumash settlement known as *Somis* or *Casitas*.[11] This route was indicative of the challenges of traveling along this stretch of the coastline and the need for a reliable overland route between Santa Barbara and San Buenaventura. The coast was subject to variable tides, unstable soils only seasonally conducive to travel by loaded carts, and rapid changes in weather. Also significant to note, El Camino Real connected multiple Native settlements to each other.

According to Mission documentation, the population of the mission in 1782 stood at twenty-two, although the actual number of people living in proximity to the mission was much higher.[12] Five years after its founding, Governor Fages reported San Buenaventura as having well-developed crops in grains and fruits, burgeoning herds of livestock, and an advanced population of Native peoples (Fages 1787, 44). After a stop in Santa Barbara in November 1793, English Captain George Vancouver sailed his ship *Discovery* back to San Buenaventura with Father Vicente de Santa Maria in company (Vancouver 1798, 455, 460–61). Santa Maria had traveled to Santa Barbara with several sheep and twenty mule pack-loads of fruits and vegetables for Vancouver and his crew as an enticement to bring him to his mission. Upon arrival, Father Dumetz received the men in a manner that impressed Vancouver.

> . . . entertained in a manner that proved the great respectability of the Franciscan order, at least of that part of their numerous community with whom we had become acquainted.
>
> The morning, which was most decidedly pleasant, was employed in viewing the buildings of the mission, the arrangement of the gardens and cultivated land in its immediate vicinity. These all appeared to be in a very superior style to any of the new settlements I had yet seen . . .
>
> . . . we directed our course the next morning to the southeastward, gratefully thankful for the hospitable reception and benevolent donations of our religious friends at Buena Ventura. (Vancouver 1798, 264)

At the time of Vancouver's visit, the internal rectangle of room walls[13] (south, east, and north) were well over five *varas*[14] in height (Hastings 1975, 101). The original *ladrillo* (adobe brick) and mortar church had collapsed due to faulty construction in autumn 1791. A new church building was started in its present location by the end of 1791, and was approximately half completed by March 1795 (Engelhardt 1930, 24–25, quoting Lasuén, March 11, 1795). This new location radically altered the way the mission's quadrangle had been originally conceptualized (Tolley 2002). Because of the relocation of the church, new wings of room walls were added to the east and north room walls of the quadrangle (see fig. 10.4), along with connecting hallways on the north. The current church was completed in 1809. San Miguel Chapel was constructed about half a kilometer south of the mission, near the village of Shisholop. A second brick-and-mortar chapel named for Santa Gertrudis was located about nine kilometers north of the mission to serve Chumash villages farther north along the Ventura River, and a smaller *asistencia*[15] called La Purisima was built near the modern town of Santa Paula in order to serve villages along the Santa Clara River, as well as the Chumash ranch hands tending to the mission's cattle herds. Chumash villages often had small gardens that supplemented daily dietary needs; residents continued to hunt, fish, and utilize traditional sources of food throughout the Mission era. By 1800, the span of influence of Mission San Buenaventura extended over 500,000 acres, or roughly 2,100 square kilometers.

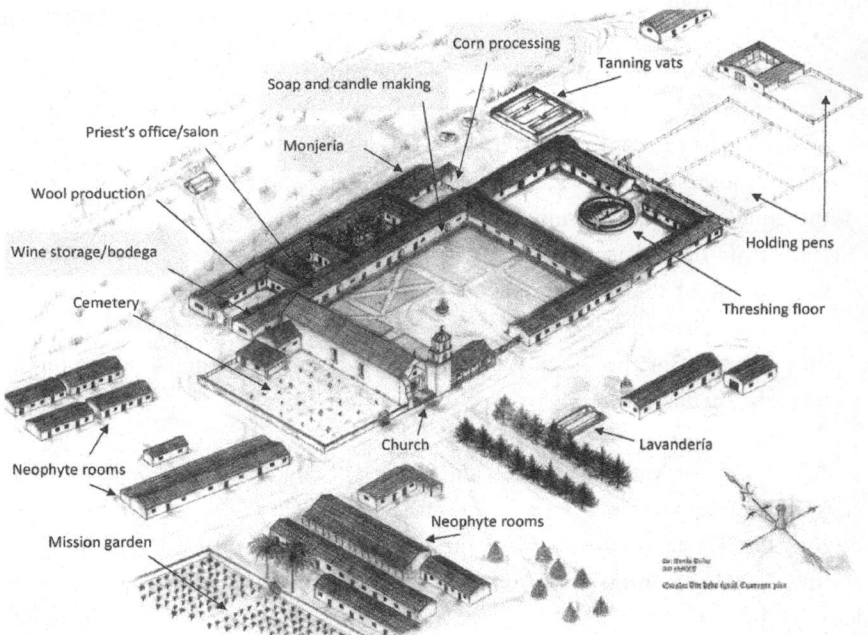

Figure 10.4. The quadrangle and immediately surrounding landscapes of Mission San Buenaventura. (Illustration by Thomas Edward Tolley 2012; quadrangle features translation and identifications by Tolley 1998)

A part of each mission's retinue were small garrisons (*escoltas*) of soldiers referred to as *soldados de cuera* (leatherjackets) stationed at each mission to assist the priests in supervision of Native populations, as well as to assist with labor as needed. Their usual numbers were five to seven, with one lieutenant or sublieutenant (Moorhead 1975; Perissinotto 1998; Whitehead 1996). At San Buenaventura, one to two priests would have served with five to ten *soldados*, but numbers could vary slightly based on seasonal need or call to duty at other locations such as Santa Barbara. These small military groups were an effective presence at the missions, yet several hundred Native people who were highly knowledgeable about their surroundings with effective familiarity of the tools and technology available to them could also be a significant force, one not readily intimidated, and one the priests and soldiers were quite aware of.

Upon establishment, Mission San Buenaventura began the process of securing a source of less brackish water for consumption, agricultural, and industrial purposes through the construction of a system of aqueduct and ancillary channels. Wells were dug, along with the first system of earthen conduits (*zanjas*) bringing water away from the lower Ventura River. By the 1790s, a Vitruvian-influenced aqueduct system 11.5 kilometers in length was under construction from collection pools at the confluence of the Ventura River and San Antonio Creek south to a settling tank/castellum 0.13 kilometers west of the quadrangle. Several zanjas carried water from the aqueduct to agricultural fields and settlements along the river. Zanjas lined with mortar and stone supporting ceramic pipes ran east to the quadrangle. One zanja fed an indoor settling tank that provided drinking water, and then continued to a fountain in the main quadrangle courtyard. The indoor settling tank also acted as a climate control for the bodega (wine/aguardiente storage and fermentation room). Zanjas also fed other parts of the mission, including grain-processing areas, threshing floors, tanning vats, a *lavandería*, the mission's garden area, and San Miguel Chapel. By 1809, a total of sixty-five neophyte and married couple's quarters had been constructed to the west and south of the quadrangle (Engelhardt 1930, 26). Industries around the main quadrangle included tallow production, specialized agriculture (the mission garden), olive processing, wine making, soap and candle production, wool processing, and tanning hides. Additional buildings included a mayordomo's quarters, corrals, blacksmith shops, and mills (Berger 1948, 181; Engelhardt 1930, 24–25; Weber 1977; Tolley 2002).

Moving east from the quadrangle, land was utilized mainly for grazing livestock, including cattle, horses, sheep, and mules. The mission's cattle herds, numbering in the thousands, were quartered in the vicinity of Santa Paula Creek along the Santa Clara River and grazed from this area south beyond the location of modern Oxnard. Although little is known archaeologically about this area, it is probable that the Chumash who managed the herds also lived in traditional structures and engaged many of the same cultural and dietary traditions as they had before 1782. There were no priests or soldados permanently assigned to this part of San Buenaventura's territory. The mission maintained an authoritative presence across the valley via trusted supervisory Chumash *alcaldes* and *vaqueros* and an *asistencia*, but the distance between the mission and the herds was significant. Round-trip travel would have involved multiple days, supplies, and means of shelter, at minimum. As with many of the Chumash living in the Ventura River valley, it is likely the Chumash living in the easternmost region of the mission's zone of influence continued to engage elements of their cultural traditions with limited challenges by the priests and soldados.

Conclusion

The relationships between Native peoples and the missions have often been measured in terms of labor, nested in the imagery of the main quadrangle of each mission. Mission landscapes extended well beyond the immediacy of their quadrangles. Labor was an enormous part of the reality of the Chumash experience at San Buenaventura, but these Native experiences were not detached monochromatic encounters. The Chumash were adept at adapting Spanish technologies and strategies (Hackel 2005)—adaptations that required the investment of personal and group beliefs. The Chumash were laborers in the fields, but their lives were more than ghosts of labor. They were masons, bricklayers, blacksmiths, artisans, weavers, supervisors; they were parents, children, and spiritual leaders who contributed their own views and customs to every aspect of life at the mission.

Each element of the evaluation of the landscapes of San Buenaventura needs to be considered a possible palimpsest of Chumash experiences. As Schneider and Panich (2014) note, the missions were not the endpoint of Native culture. Unique Chumash adaptations reflected both continued and modified cultural traditions and were key to the economic viability of each mission.[16] It bears noting the missions were founded at, or adjacent to, Native sites that may have been in existence for hundreds of years. In part, this is why I believe a solipsistic Eurocentric perspective ultimately devalues the potential realities of Native experiences at the missions, as well as misrepresenting or debasing Native peoples' lives and agencies. The Chumash formed the vast majority of residents in and around San Buenaventura. Much of the mission's population, however, did not live at the main quadrangle. The immediate space around the quadrangle was organized to promote the mission's economic goals; residences were constructed to organize Native residents closer to the industries they were participating in. Many preexisting traditional Chumash villages did remain. This may have been due in part to the need for labor to be mobile to respond to shifting priorities. For example, part of the mission's population could be involved in planting one day, processing hides another, and harvesting yet another.

I submit (as an analytical perspective) consideration of the founding of the Alta California missions as a Spanish endeavor that prioritized an assertive, perhaps desperate, exploitation of the area's available resources for the purpose of expanding the more lucrative trade with Asia. New Spain established only four moderately sized presidios in the region, and maintained no appreciable naval presence. Fiscally, New Spain was never fully committed to supporting the missions, and the missions were left to their own devices to secure their subsistence. Material and documentary records bring to further light how the missions based many decisions on use of space and significant portions of their total economic output for the purposes of trading with non-Spanish merchants for materials and goods they were not able to produce themselves.

Fernand Braudel hypothesized the state in capitalist countries more comfortably served monopolists, not free competitive markets (Braudel 1982). The missions may have fed into New Spain's participation in a capitalist world, but the everyday existence-level economies were more exchange or free trade-based, as monopolies were not possible. Cash and credit were not significant commodities in Alta California; goods were predominant. Merchants and traders returning from Asia could bring iron and iron goods, ceramics, desired cloths, altar stones, and materials for the missions, in exchange for furs, hides, food, wine, fresh water, tallow, and repair materials. The missions chose to produce unique goods (along with those products mandated by New Spain) to trade with non-Spanish and Spanish merchants with the goal of procuring the items they wanted. Without exclusive dependency on any one source, each could act as a force majeure that could drop out and return as climate, availability, and need arose.

Surreptitious trade involved either producing undocumented surpluses of materials already being manufactured at the missions, or the production of materials that were not necessarily (if at all) required to be well-documented by the missions. Records of this trade, by their nature, would be few and far between, rendering much of the activity as invisible. Evidence of trade may include the growth of specialized crops such citrus, olives, bananas, and other produce; viniculture; and processing of dried meats. Other sources of evidence can include the introduction of floral species from other parts of the globe (wheats, cabbages, legumes, fruits, etc.) that did not come through New Spain or Southern Europe. Recent research has begun to shed light on how the Alta California missions developed and expanded unique economic processes that New Spain could not hope to interrupt nor had the strength to control. The missions simply were not just colonial extensions of the government of New Spain. While the intent in part may have been to extend Spanish presence northward and to generate some measure of revenue based on surpluses for the cash-starved government in New Spain, the missions were left largely on their own to survive, to become self-sufficient, and to develop their economies and landscapes in their own ways.

Notes

1. The examination of mission landscapes, economies, and the developing relationships occurring within broader frontier zones are part of my wider research focusing on the entire Alta California mission system.

2. For example, Bancroft 1885–1886, Berger 1948, Bolton 1917, Chapman 1916, Deetz 1978, Engelhardt 1897–1932, Erlichman 2010, Geiger 1969, Hittel 1885, Weber 1990, and Weber 1992.

3. For varying perspectives of landscape in archaeology see Ashmore 2004, Aston 1997, Ingold 1993, Rockman 2003, Schneider and Panich 2014, and Tilley 1994; for cultural constructs and economic production, see Anschuetz, Wilshusen, and Scheik 2001, Barrett and Ko 2009, Bowser and Zedeño 2009, and Sahlins 1976.

4. This is not simply an inversion of perspective. Each mission in Alta California was founded proximate to Native settlements, and was built, operated, and maintained by Native peoples who, although their populations were dramatically affected, never fully surrendered their cultural traditions.

5. This stoppage was due to political unrest in New Spain beginning with the Hidalgan Revolution (Hamnett 1986, 2006) continuing until the collapse of New Spain in 1821.

6. Presidios were originally intended to be defensive military garrisons (Moorhead 1975, 4–5, 165), but were modified into extensions of governmental and fiscal regulation by the Marqués de Rubí's survey, which led to Carlos III's *Reglamento* of 1772. The presidio, coupled with a proximate mission, was meant to instill confidence and encourage more

settlement from New Spain, extend the crown's commercial interests, and to facilitate the control of indigenous peoples.

7. Father Fermín Lasuén was the second Father President of the Alta California missions after the death of Junípero Serra in 1784, serving until his own death in 1803.

8. The nomenclature for many Chumash groups has often been associated with proximate missions (e.g., Ventureño and Mission San Buenaventura, Barbareño and Mission Santa Barbara). These labels do not reflect Chumash cultural identities.

9. According to Engelhardt (1930), a stockade or wooden fence encircled the structures. However, material evidence of the stockade has not been documented.

10. Saptutu/Sulukukiy was a Chumash village, also the location of Chapel Santa Gertrudis, about five miles north of the main quadrangle.

11. *Casitas*: little houses.

12. The mission's documentation only lists those who were baptized. San Buenaventura was founded near the location of several Chumash villages. The local population within a five-to-seven-mile radius was likely several hundred, at minimum.

13. I define a *room wall* as a linear series of conjoined rooms that serve both as functional spaces and as a structural partition or barrier.

14. One *vara* = eighty-six centimeters.

15. An *asistencia* is a smaller satellite extension of a mission, meant to serve remote locations within a mission's territory. In many instances, these *asistencias* were not occupied year-round.

16. Lightfoot (2006) suggests a four-tiered plan to better understand how Native peoples negotiated their lives and navigated colonial entanglements. This involves removing the artificial boundaries created by our own research methods and engaging a more comparative approach to looking at indigenous cultures. Native groups out of necessity relocated themselves at different locations within landscapes and moved openly between them (Hurtado 1988; Moss and Wasson 1998). This sort of movement is difficult to trace, which is why the examination of fringe or frontier sites are key to understanding how Native peoples created their identities.

Works Cited

Anschuetz, Karl F., Richard H. Wilshusen, and Cherie L. Scheik. 2001. "An Archaeology of Landscapes: Perspectives and Directions." *Journal of Archaeological Research* 9(2): 157–211.

Archibald, Robert. 1978. *The Economic Aspects of the California Missions*. Washington, DC: Academy of American Franciscan History.

Arnold, Jeanne E. 1995. "Transportation Innovation and Social Complexity among Maritime Hunter-Gatherer Societies." *American Anthropologist* 97: 733–47.

————, ed. 2000. *The Origins of a Pacific Coast Chiefdom: The Chumash of the Channel Islands*. Salt Lake City: University of Utah Press.

Ashmore, Wendy. 2004. "Social Archaeologies of Landscape." In *A Companion to Social Archaeology*. Edited by Lynn Meskell and Robert W. Preucell. Malden, MA: Blackwell Publishing, 255–71.

Aston, Michael. 1997. *Interpreting the Landscape: Landscape Archaeology and Local History*. London: Routledge.

Bancroft, Hubert Howe. 1885. *History of Mexico, Vol. IV*. San Francisco: The History Company.

————. 1886. *History of California*, vols. I–IV. San Francisco: The History Company.

Barrett, John C., and Ilhong Ko. 2009. "A Phenomenology of Landscape: A Crisis in British Landscape Archaeology?" *Journal of Social Archaeology* 9(3): 275–94.

Berger, John A. 1948. *The Franciscan Missions of California*. Garden City, New York: Doubleday & Company.

Bolton, Herbert E. 1917. "The Mission as a Frontier Institution in the Spanish American Colonies." *American Historical Review* 22: 42–61.

Bowser, Brenda J., and Maria Nieves Zedeño. 2009. "The Archeology of Meaningful Places." In *The Archeology of Meaningful Places*. Edited by Brenda J. Bowser and Maria Nieves Zedeño. Salt Lake City: University of Utah Press.

Braudel, Fernand. 1982. *Civilization and Capitalism, 15th–18th Century, Vol. 1: The Structures of Everyday Life*. Translated by Siân Reynolds. Berkeley: University of California Press.

Chapman, Charles Edward. 1916. *The Founding of Spanish California*. New York: MacMillan Company.

Comaroff, Jean, and John Comaroff. 1991. *Of Revelation and Revolution, Volume 1: Christianity, Colonialism, and Consciousness in South Africa*. Chicago: University of Chicago Press.

Cook, Sherburne F. 1976a. *The Conflict between the California Indian and White Civilization*. Berkeley and Los Angeles: University of California Press.

————. 1976b. *The Population of the California Indians 1769–1970*. Berkeley and Los Angeles: University of California Press.

Costello, Julia G. 1989. "Variability among the California Missions: The Economics of Agricultural Production." In *Columbian Consequences, Vol. 1: Archaeological and Historical Perspectives on the Spanish Borderlands West*. Edited by David Hurst Thomas. Washington, DC: Smithsonian Institution, 345–50.

————. 1990. *Variability and Economic Change in the California Missions: An Historical and Archaeological Study*. PhD Dissertation, University of California-Santa Barbara.

————. 1992. "Not Peas in a Pod: Documenting Diversity among the California Missions." In *Text-Aided Archaeology* Edited by Barbara J. Little. Boca Raton, Florida: CRC Press, 67–81.

DeCorse, Christopher R. 2012. *Postcolonial or Not? West Africa in the Pre-Atlantic and Atlantic Worlds*. Ibadan, Nigeria: African Studies Center.

Deetz, James J. 1978. "Archaeological Investigations at La Purisima Mission." In *Historical Archaeology: A Guide to Substantive and Theoretical Contributions.* Edited by Robert L. Schuyler. Farmingdale, NY: Baywood, 160–90.

Duggan, Marie Christine. 2000. *Market and Church on the Mexican Frontier: Alta California, 1769–1832.* PhD Dissertation, New School University, New York.

———. 2015. "Bourbon Imperialism: Fiscal Transfers and Contraband Trade in Alta California, 1769–1809." *Terceras Jornadas de Historia Económica, Asociación Mexicana de Historia Económica*: 272–96.

———. 2016. "With and Without an Empire: Financing for California Missions Before and After 1810." *Pacific Historical Review* 85(1): 23–71.

Engelhardt, Father Zephryn, 1897. *The Franciscans in California.* Harbor Springs, MI: Holy Childhood Indian School.

———. 1908. The *Missions and Missionaries of California, Volume I.* San Francisco, CA: James H. Barry Company.

———. 1912. The *Missions and Missionaries of California, Volume II.* San Francisco, CA: James H. Barry Company.

———. 1913. The *Missions and Missionaries of California, Volume III.* San Francisco, CA: James H. Barry Company.

———. 1915. The *Missions and Missionaries of California, Volume IV.* San Francisco, CA: James H. Barry Company.

———. 1920. *Mission San Diego.* San Francisco, CA: James H. Barry Company.

———. 1929. *Mission Nuestra Senora de la Soledad.* Santa Barbara, CA: Mission Santa Barbara.

———. 1930. *San Buenaventura: Mission by the Sea.* Santa Barbara, CA: Mission Santa Barbara.

———. 1932. *Mission La Concepcion Purisima de Maria Santisima.* Santa Barbara, CA: McNally and Loftin.

Erlichman, Howard J. 2010. *Conquest, Tribute, and Trade: The Quest for Precious Metals and the Birth of Globalization.* Amherst, NY: Prometheus.

Fages, Gov. Pedro. 1787. Report on the Missions of Alta California. Santa Barbara Mission Archives and Library CMD 44.

Farnsworth, Paul. 1986. "Spanish California: The Final Frontier." *Journal of New World Archaeology* 6(4): 35–46.

———. 1987. *Economics of Acculturation in the California Missions: A Historical and Archaeological Study of Mission Nuestra Señora de la Soledad.* PhD thesis, University of California, Los Angeles.

———. 1989. "The Economics of Acculturation in the Spanish Missions of Alta California." *Research in Economic Anthropology* 11: 217–49. London: JAI Press.

———. 1992. "Missions, Indians, and Cultural Continuity." *Historical Archaeology* 26(1): 22–36.

————. 1998. "Native American Cultural Negotiation at Mission Soledad." *Proceedings of the Society for California Archaeology* 11: 44–49.

Farnsworth, Paul and Robert H. Jackson. 1995. "Cultural, Economic, and Demographic Change in the Missions of Alta California: The Case of Nuestra Señora de la Soledad." In *The New Latin American Mission History*. Edited by Erick Langer and Robert H. Jackson. Lincoln: University of Nebraska Press.

Galvin, John. 1964. "Supplies from Manila for the California Missions, 1781–1783." *Philippine Studies* 12(3): 494–510.

Geiger, Maynard. 1969. *Franciscan Missionaries in Hispanic California 1769–1848: A Biographical Dictionary*. San Marino, CA: Huntington Library.

Gibson, James R. 1992. *Otter Skins, Boston Ships, and China Goods: The Maritime Fur Trade of the Northwest Coast, 1785–1841*. Seattle: University of Washington Press.

Greenwood, Roberta S., ed. 1975. *3500 Years on One City Block: Ventura Mission Plaza Archaeological Project*. San Buenaventura, CA: Redevelopment Agency.

————, ed. 1976. *The Changing Faces of Main Street: Ventura Mission Plaza Archaeological Project*. San Buenaventura, CA: Redevelopment Agency.

Hackel, Steven W. 2005. *Children of Coyote, Missionaries of Saint Francis: Indian-Spanish Relations in Colonial California, 1769–1850*. Chapel Hill: University of North Carolina Press.

Hamnett, Brian R. 1986. *Roots of Insurgency: Mexican Regions, 1750–1824*. Cambridge, UK: Cambridge University Press.

————. 2006. *A Concise History of Mexico*. Cambridge, UK: Cambridge University Press.

Hastings, Richard. 1975. "San Buenaventura Mission: An Architectural View." In *3500 Years on One City Block: Ventura Mission Plaza Archaeological Project*. Edited by Roberta Greenwood. City of San Buenaventura, CA: Redevelopment Agency.

Hittel, Theodore H. 1885. *History of California Vols. 1–4*. San Francisco, CA: Pacific Press Publishing House and Occidental Press Co.

Hoover, Robert L. 1985. "The Archaeology of Spanish Colonial Sites in California." *Comparative Studies in the Archaeology of Colonialism*. Oxford, UK: BAR International Series.

————. 1987. *Spanish Colonial Research within the Framework of World Systems Theory*. California Mission Studies Association Newsletter 4(1).

————. 1992. "Some Models for Spanish Colonial Archaeology in California." *Historical Archaeology* 26(1): 37–44.

Hoover, Robert L., and Julia G. Costello, eds. 1985. *Excavations at Mission San Antonio 1976–1978*. Monograph 26, Institute of Archaeology, University of California, Los Angeles.

Hornbeck, David. 1989. "Economic Growth and Change at the Missions of Alta California, 1769–1846." In *Columbian Consequences, Vol. 1: Archaeological and Historical Perspec-*

tives on the Spanish Borderlands West. Edited by David Hurst Thomas. Washington, DC: Smithsonian Institution, 423–33.

Hudson, Travis, Janice Timbrook, and Melissa Rempe, eds. 1978. *Tomol: Chumash Watercraft as Described in the Ethnographic Notes of John P. Harrington.* Banning, CA: Ballena Press.

Hurtado, Albert L. 1988. *Indian Survival on the California Frontier.* New Haven, CT: Yale University Press.

Hylkema, Mark G., and Rebecca Allen. 2009. "Archaeological Investigations at the Third Mission Site, Santa Clara University, and a Comparison of Shell Bead Assemblages with Recent Mission-Era Findings." *Proceedings of the Society for California Archaeology* 21: 28–35.

Ingold, Tim. 1993. "The Temporality of the Landscape." In *World Archaeology* 25(2): 152–74.

Jackson, Robert H., and Edward Castillo. 1995. *Indians, Franciscans, and Spanish Colonization: The Impact of the Mission System on California Indians.* Albuquerque: University of New Mexico Press.

James, George Wharton. 1911. *In and Out of the Old Missions of California.* Boston: Little, Brown, and Company.

Johnson, John R. 2001. "Ethnohistoric Reflections of Cruzeño Chumash Society." In *The Origins of a Pacific Coast Chiefdom: The Chumash of the Channel Islands.* Edited by Jeanne E. Arnold. Salt Lake City: University of Utah Press, 53–70.

Kenneally, Finbar, trans. 1965. *The Writings of Fermín Francisco de Lasuén, Vols. 1–2.* Washington, DC: Academy of American Franciscan History.

King, Chester. 1975. "The Names and Locations of Historic Chumash Villages (assembled by Thomas Blackburn)." *The Journal of California Anthropology* 2(2): 171–79.

Kroeber, Alfred Louis. 1925. *Handbook of the Indians of California.* Washington, DC: Government Printing Office.

Leffingwell, Randy. 2005. *California Missions and Presidios.* New York: Voyageur Press.

Lightfoot, Kent G. 2003. "Russian Colonization: The Implications of Mercantile Colonial Practices in the North Pacific." *Historical Archaeology* 37(4): 14–28.

———. 2005. *Indians, Missionaries, and Merchants: The Legacy of Colonial Encounters on the California Frontiers.* Berkeley: University of California Press.

———. 2006. "Missions, Furs, Gold, and Manifest Destiny: Rethinking an Archaeology of Colonialism for Western North America." In *Historical Archaeology.* Edited by Martin Hall and Stephen W. Silliman, 272–92. Malden, MA: Blackwell Press.

———. 2015. "Dynamics of Change in Multiethnic Societies: An Archaeological Perspective from Colonial North America." *Proceedings of the National Academy of Sciences* 112(30): 9216–23.

Lightfoot, K. G., and A. Martinez. 1995. "Frontiers and Boundaries in Archaeological Perspective." *Annual Review of Anthropology* 24: 471–92.

Loren, Diana diPaulo. 2008. *In Contact: Bodies and Spaces in the Sixteenth- and Seventeenth Century Eastern Woodlands*. New York: Altamira Press.

Mason, William Marvin. 1998. *The Census of 1790: A Demographic History of Colonial California*. Menlo Park, CA: Ballena Press.

Mathes, W. Michael. 1973. *Sebastián Vizcaíno y la Expansión Española en el Océano Pacífico: 1520–1630*. Mexico City: Universidad Nacional Autónoma de México Ciudad Universitaria.

McCawley, William. 1996. *The First Angelinos: The Gabrieliño Indians of Los Angeles*. Banning, CA: Malki Museum Press.

Melillo, Edward Dallam. 2015. *Strangers on Familiar Soil: Rediscovering the Chile-California Connection*. New Haven, CT: Yale University Press.

Mintz, Sidney W. 1985. *Sweetness and Power: The Place of Sugar in Modern History*. New York: Penguin Books.

Moorhead, Max L. 1975. *The Presidio: Bastion of the Spanish Borderlands*. Norman: University of Oklahoma Press.

Moss, M. L. and G. B. Wasson Jr. 1998. "Intimate Relations with the Past: the Story of an Athapaskan Village on the Southern Northwest Coast of North America." *World Archaeology* 29(3): 317–32.

Ogden, Adele. 1932. *McCulloch, Hartnell, and Company*. Master's thesis, Berkeley: University of California.

———. 1941. *The California Sea Otter Trade 1784–1848*. Berkeley: University of California Press.

Panich, Lee M., and Tsim Schneider. 2015. "Expanding Mission Archaeology: A Landscape Approach to Indigenous Autonomy in Colonial California." *Journal of Anthropological Archaeology* 40: 48–58.

Perissinotto, Giorgio, ed. 1998. *Documenting Everyday Life in Early Spanish California: The Santa Barbara Presidio Memorias y Facturas, 1779–1810*. Santa Barbara, CA: Santa Barbara Trust for Historic Preservation.

Pethick, Derek. 1980. *The Nootka Connection: Europe and the Northwest Coast 1790–1795*. Vancouver, BC: Douglas and McIntyre.

Rawls, James J. 1984. *Indians of California: The Changing Image*. Norman: University of Oklahoma Press.

Rockman, Marcy. 2003. "Knowledge and Learning in the Archaeology of Colonization." In *Colonization of Unfamiliar Landscapes: The Archaeology of Adaptation*. Edited by Marcy Rockman and James Steele. London: Routledge, 3–24.

Ruscin, Terry. 1999. *Mission Memoirs*. San Diego, CA: Sunbelt Publications.

Sahlins, Marshall. 1976. *Culture and Practical Reason*. Chicago: University of Chicago Press.

Schnieder, Tsim D., and Lee M. Panich. 2014. "Native Agency at the Margins of Empire: Indigenous Landscapes, Spanish Missions, and Contested Histories." In *Indigenous Land-*

scapes and Spanish Missions: New Perspectives from Archaeology and Ethnohistory. Edited by Lee M. Panich and Tsim D. Schneider. Tucson: University of Arizona Press, 5–22.

Shipley, William F. 1978. "Native Languages of California." In *Handbook of North American Indians*, Vol. 8 (California). Edited by William C. Sturtevant and Robert F. Heizer. Washington, DC: Smithsonian Institution.

Silliman, Stephen W. 2004. *Lost Laborers in Colonial California: Native Americans and the Archaeology of Rancho Petaluma*. Tucson: University of Arizona Press.

Skowronek, Russell K., and Julie C. Wizorek. 1997. "Archaeology at Santa Clara de Asís: The Slow Rediscovery of a Moveable Mission." *Pacific Coast Archaeological Society Quarterly* 33(3): 54–92.

Skowronek, Russell K., M. James Blackman, and Ronald L. Bishop. 2014. *Ceramic Production in Early Hispanic California: Craft, Economy, and Trade on the Frontier of New Spain*. Gainesville: University Press of Florida.

Tilley, Christopher. 1994. *A Phenomenology of Landscape: Places, Paths and Monuments*. Oxford, UK: Berg Publishers.

Todeschini, Giacomo. 2009. *Franciscan Wealth: From Voluntary Poverty to Market Society*. Translated by Donatella Melucci. Saint Bonaventure, NY: The Franciscan Institute, Saint Bonaventure University.

Tolley, Thomas E. 1998. "Reproduction and Translation of the Fernando Librado (Kitsepawit) Figures of Mission San Buenaventura, from J.P. Harrington's Ethnographic Notes." Syracuse University.

———. 2002. "Excavando Los Espiritus: The Holy Cross School Archaeological Project." Master's thesis, Syracuse University.

Tovell, Freeman M. 2008. *At the Far Reaches of Empire: The Life of Juan Francisco de la Bodega y Quadra*. Vancouver: University of British Columbia Press.

Vancouver, Captain George. 1798. *A Voyage of Discovery to the North Pacific Ocean, and Round the World: In Which the Coast of North-West America has been Carefully Examined and Accurately Surveyed, Vol. II*. London: G. G. and J. Robinson.

Voss, Barbara L. 2006. "Engendered Archaeology: Men, Women, and Others." In *Historical Archaeology*. Edited by Martin Hall and Stephen W. Silliman. Malden, MA: Blackwell Publishing.

———. 2008. *The Archaeology of Ethnogenesis: Race and Sexuality in Colonial San Francisco*. Berkeley: University of California Press.

———. 2015. "What's New? Rethinking Ethnogenesis in the Archaeology of Colonialism." *American Antiquity* 80(4): 655–70.

Voss, Barbara L., and Eleanor Conlin Casella. 2012. *The Archaeology of Colonialism: Intimate Encounters and Sexual Effects*. New York: Cambridge University Press.

Weber, David J. 1990. "Blood of Martyrs, Blood of Indians: Toward a More Balanced View of Spanish Missions in Seventeenth Century North America." In *Columbian*

Consequences, vol. 2. Edited by David Hurst Thomas. Washington, DC: Smithsonian Institution, 429–48.

———. 1992. *The Spanish Frontier in North America*. New Haven, CT: Yale University Press.

Weber, Msgr. Francis J. 1977. *A History of San Buenaventura Mission*. Hong Kong: Libra Press Limited.

Whitehead, Richard S. 1996. *Citadel on the Channel: The Royal Presidio of Santa Barbara, Its Founding and Construction, 1782–1798*. Santa Barbara, CA and Spokane, WA: The Santa Barbara Trust for Historic Preservation and the Arthur H. Clark Co.

Chapter 11

Bending but Unbroken

The Nine Tribes of the Northern Tsimshian through the Colonial Era

Andrew Martindale, George MacDonald, and Sage Vanier

> When I say that we have no history of love, no history of joy, you must realize
> that I am not asking for a study of love or of joy throughout all periods, ages,
> and civilizations, I am indicating lines of research. And I am not doing so
> with isolated individuals in mind. Or pure physiologists. Or pure moralists. Or
> pure psychologists in the usually accepted sense of the word. Far from that. I
> am asking for a vast collective investigation to be opened on the fundamental
> sentiments of man and the forms they take.
>
> —Lucien Febvre, 1973

When Europeans first appeared on the shores of Tsimshian territory near Prince Rupert, British Columbia, on the Northwest Coast of North America (see fig. 11.1) they entered a complex political landscape that had emerged from thousands of years of history. Any analysis of the nature and effect of colonization needs to consider the organizational structure of Tsimshian society at the time of contact, in or about AD 1787, through today. Our thesis is that colonization impacted both Tsimshian people and their societal relationships, causing them to flex and change, but not wholly transform. Rather we see considerable evidence of resilience and continuity in which Tsimshian people accommodated new ideas, things, and relationships while maintaining traditional principles. We associate this resilience, in part, with a long tradition of political flexibility. Here we explore one facet of Tsimshian society—tribal organization—through material, documentary,

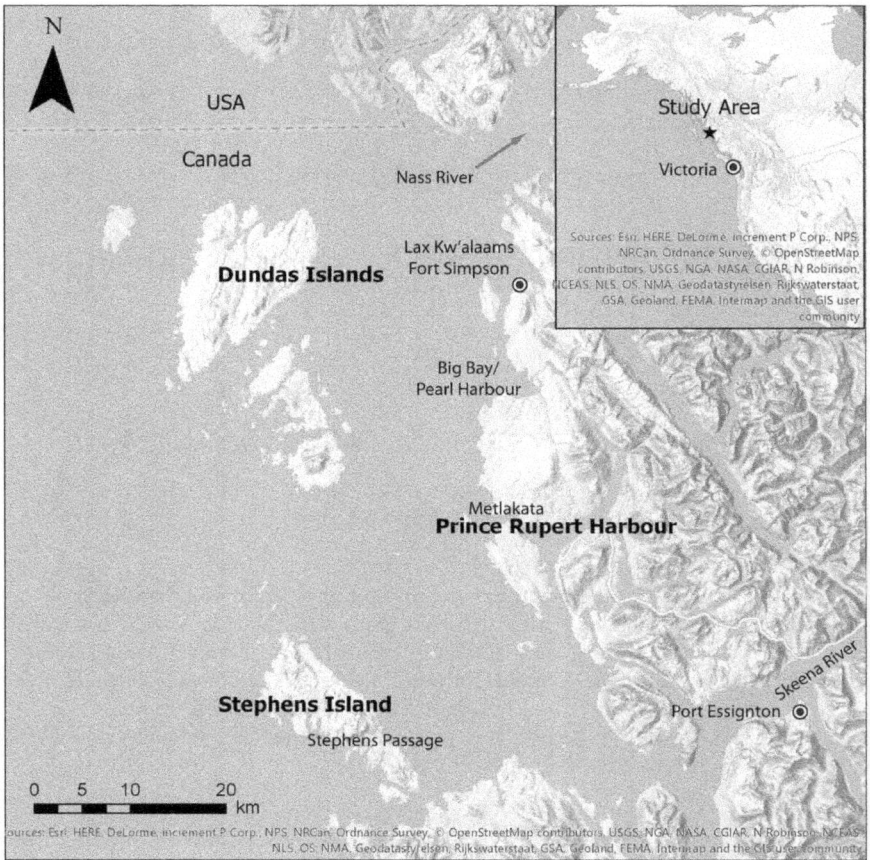

Figure 11.1. Map of the study area showing places mentioned in the text. (Illustration by A. Martindale)

and oral records to better understand change and continuity in Tsimshian society through colonization.

An archaeological study of history is a complicated endeavor, one made more so when it explores subjects across the colonial divide, such as Indigenous history through the postcontact period from an archaeological perspective. The challenges are numerous. Though material things are empirically resilient, their meanings fracture through the experiences of individual perception. Documentary records are available from colonial contexts, but often reflect the situated biases of their mostly nonnative authors. Oral records, though rarer, provide an important Indigenous view on the events of colonial encounters, but often in ways that non-Indigenous scholars struggle to appreciate and understand. Interpretation itself is freighted with disciplinary and societal ethnocentrisms that create schisms between the past and present, between the largely Western discipline of archaeology and the Indigenous history of this subject, and between the individual scholars and the individuals of history. This case study is both an attempt to capture some of the complexity of history and find meaningful patterns therein.

Setting the Stage

In order to evaluate how tribes responded to colonization, it is necessary to define them in social, legal, and historical terms. Socially, Tsimshian tribes are not synonymous with anthropological constructs, US legal definitions, or with vernacular non-Tsimshian usage. Tsimshian people and their governments use the term *tribe* as an Anglicization of the Sm'algyax word *galts'ap* (*contra* Halpin & Seguin 1990, 274), which refers to one of a series of nested and interconnected political entities in Tsimshian society. The *galts'ap* are associations of *wilnat'aał* or lineages, which are themselves associations of *wilp/walp* or house groups. House groups are thus the coresident elements of the intergenerational lineage, which have allied to form tribes. This nested arrangement is crosscut by clan identities, which are ancestral exogamous associations that link closely related lineages through connection to spiritual beings/communities. Importantly, lineages within tribes are not all from the same clan; indeed all four clans are usually represented in each tribe, at least in its contemporary manifestation. It is also significant that the territorial owning entity in Tsimshian law is the house group, not the lineage, tribe, clan or individual. This complex arrangement was managed in traditional society matrilineally and with avunculocality for men and patrilocality for women. This means that house groups are defined by their constituent female siblings and transmitted from mother to daughter, creating matrilines (see Rosman & Rubel 1971). However, since marriages are patrilocal, the women of a matriline did not traditionally live in their house groups, but in the house groups of their husbands. The house group as a residential entity that coresides in the physical houses was composed of the brothers of the matriline, their wives and children who belong to the matrilines of their wives. The house group was avunculocal, which means that when boys came of age they left the home of their father (who belongs to a different lineage) and returned to the ancestral home of their uncles, the male representatives of their matriline.

The social entity that is the tribe is thus a product of a Tsimshian legal system in which rights, including title rights, were held by house groups collectively, as the living representatives of ancestral matrilines. Rights include territory (both land and water) from which to extract resources and on which to build settlements and live. Although title rights confer access to resources, they appear to have been conceived of via a spiritual lens in which humans find or negotiate acceptance with the spiritual beings whose realms are accessible via portals in territorial spaces (Marsden 2002). Tsimshian law also includes a category of right referred to as a privilege, an agreement to allow other lineages access to one's territory (Sterritt et al. 1998). Privilege was a kind of usufructory right, often between affines, that was often perpetuated intergenerationally; but it was not an inheritable right. Both rights and privilege are important in the understanding of tribes since tribes are associations of lineages and house groups that often have conjoining territory. While tribes do not own territory, the territories of their constituent house groups represent a larger contiguous space, a tribal territory in which privilege mediates access.

The history of the concept of tribes is complex but relevant to this analysis, for it is in the development of this sociopolitical construct that we see patterns that recur in response to the intrusion of colonial settlers. Oral records indicate that at some point in the mid-Holocene, larger aggregations of lineages formed in response to emerging networks of trade and ceremonialism (Martindale et al. 2017a). These are associated with the emergence of larger village forms, although the spatial data of this period is modest in part because these components are often buried under later settlements. What is clear is that population and settlement frequencies increase dramatically from around 4,000 to 2,000 years ago, likely due in part to the arrival of waves of newcomers from the north (Martindale & Marsden 2003). By 2000 BP, the settlement pattern had expanded with villages across the coastal territory and concentrations of settlement in the Prince Rupert Harbour, Dundas, and Stephens Passage areas. This pattern of small villages associated with land ownership and large villages in clustered regions came to a dramatic end after 1500 BP, when war broke out between the Tsimshian and northern invaders, who are referred to as the Tlingit in the oral record (Marsden 2000, 2001). The conflict spread across Tsimshian territory and resulted in a wholesale retreat from the coastal region by Tsimshian house groups into the Skeena Valley (Martindale et al., 2017b).

The war transformed the spatial and political landscape (Marsden 2000). This trend is visible in settlement patterns (Martindale et al., 2017b). The oral record describes how both the southern and the northern Tsimshian formed local alliances and launched counterattacks against the invaders, eventually driving them out of their territory. The northern communities had borne the brunt of the invasion, and upon reclaiming their lands these Tsimshian groups did not rebuild their settlements throughout their territories. Rather, they relocated to the more defensible Metlakatla Pass region of the Prince Rupert Harbour, where they constructed permanent villages from which they traveled to their lands for resources, establishing the seasonal logistical pattern identified in the ethnohistoric records (Halpin & Seguin 1990).

The northern communities who had retreated into the Skeena Valley formed an alliance that was distinct from their southern neighbors and included ten tribes (Gitwilgyoots, Ginax'angiik, Gitnadoiks, Gitzaxłaał, Giluts'aaw, Git'iis, Gispaxlo'ots, Gitlaan, Gitando, and Gitwilkseba). The latter was comprised largely of earlier northern migrants who had become integrated into Tsimshian territory via gifts of land from extant house groups. It did not remain viable and these lands and people were reabsorbed, leaving nine tribes. Thus, by 1100 BP, the northern Tsimshian had formed a military alliance that had transformed into a parliamentary association of ten, later nine, tribes. The Nine Tribes alliance was in place when Europeans first appeared in the northern territories, and remains the traditional leadership of the northern Tsimshian, represented by the Lax Kw'alaams and Metlakatla First Nations.

The Nine Tribes through the Nineteenth Century

The concept of a tribe is clearly foundational to Tsimshian social and legal history. Tribes present a coherence of lineages and their house groups that take on a collective aspect for shared purpose over their history. Tribal chiefs, who are the leaders of the leading lineages within the tribe, are supported by a cadre of advisers made up of the leaders of other tribal lineages. As Marsden and Galois (1995, 170) argue, the tribe is the outward face of its house groups, strategizing on matters of economic and political well-being on behalf of its member houses.

At the same time, at contact, the tribe was a mosaic of disparate house groups from different clans. This created a countervailing tension against the unifying forces of tribal identity. Individuals, including leaders of house groups and tribes had connections with, obligations to, and identities within social and political enterprises that cross-cut tribes, giving them a networked and flexible structure. It is this flexibility that comes into play during the most recent major upheaval in Tsimshian society, the arrival of Europeans.

Analyses of the impact of colonial encounters on the Nine Tribes alliance have focused on seven kinds of data: oral traditions (Marsden & Galois 1995), historic documents (Bolt 1983; Beynon 1941; Clayton 1992; Dean 1994; Fiske 1991; Galois 1997; Neylan 2003; Rettig 1980; Usher 1974; Wellcome 1887), ethnographic analysis (Boas 1916; Garfield 1939, 1951) settlement patterns (Martindale 2003, 2006b), material changes (Martindale & Jurakic 2004; 2006), political changes (Martindale 2009), and symbolic patterns. These approaches generally identify, formally or informally, a series of distinct temporal stanzas. The division of history into periods of time is a useful heuristic as it identifies broad patterns that can illustrate key trends. Such an approach usually focuses on specific themes such as shifts in economic (Martindale 2003) or political (Martindale 2009) structures and relations. Table 11.1 lists a series of moments in time visible to us today largely because scholars have identified them as significant or they were sufficiently momentous to have been recorded at the time in historic records, often a combination of both.

Spatial Patterns of Tribes

The spatial organization of communities conveys data about social organization, although the relationship between the two is complex. In addition, like much of the data regarding Indigenous postcontact history, it is incompletely sampled, giving us only snapshots of specific moments. The precontact pattern is understood in general terms, but lacking specifics. We know that more than 1,100 years ago, the Nine Tribes alliance formed in response to the war with the Tlingits (Marsden 2000) that shifted settlement into the Prince Rupert Harbour region (Martindale et al. 2017a). While house groups continued to own their territory, the tribes reorganized to accommodate the change. Recent data has expanded the inventory of sites that date after 1100 BP (Eldridge 2014; Letham et al. 2015; Martindale et al. 2017b), and while the pattern is not fully resolved, it does not contradict the ethnohistoric record of a series of tribal villages located across the Metlakatla Pass area. The key issue here is not the specific locations, but that tribes had spatial independence. Martindale et al. (2017b) use regional spatial metrics in hundred-year intervals to argue that while this represented a strong clustering pattern, it

Table 11.1. Events in Nine Tribes History through the Colonial Era from Published Sources

Dates (AD)	Events	Source
650–850	War with Tlingit results in hiatus in Tsimshian coastal territories. Nine Tribes alliance consolidates and established permanent settlements of all Tribes in the Metlakatla Pass area of Prince Rupert Harbour (PRH)	Marsden (2000); Martindale et al. (2017a; 2017b); Edinborough et al. (2017).
1787, 1792	Arrival of first Europeans (Colnett, Caamano) in Tsimshian territory.	Bolt (1983); Galois 2003; Menzies (2016); Martindale (2003).
1790's to 1800's	Initiation and expansion of the coastal (sea otter) fur trade.	Dean 1994; Marsden and Galois 1995; Martindale 2003.
1810's to 1820's	Decline in sea otter populations, shift to land-based furs from interior valleys. Trade entrepôts expand to include Nass River estuary. All interior fur-shipping is conducted up the Skeena River, primarily by Nine Tribes people using traditional freighting canoes. This supply line would remain the only bulk shipping option to the interior until steamships began regularly running the Skeena in the 1870s.	Dean 1994; Marsden and Galois 1995; Martindale 2003.
Sometime in the 1820's	Attempted murder of Ligeex resulting in challenge to his authority. Ligeex consolidates the Nine Tribes under his leadership. Pictographs at Tyee and Red Bluff are commissioned to signal the unification.	Beynon 1939; Marsden and Galois 1995; Martindale 2003; 2009.
1821	The Hudson's Bay Company (HBC) and Northwest Company merge, creating a fur-trading monopoly in Western Canada.	Dean 1994; Marsden and Galois 1995; Martindale 2003.
1825	The ship *William and Anne* begins regular runs between the Nass River and Fort Vancouver in the south, regularizing access to markets for Tsimshian fur traders and providing a supply line for bulk imports.	Dean 1994.

continued on next page

Table 11.1. *Continued.*

Dates (AD)	Events	Source
1831	HBC established Fort Nass (1831) on the Nass River as its base of operations in Nine Tribes territory. Chief factor at Fort Nass is John McLoughlin.	Bolt 1983; Dean 1994; Marsden and Galois 1995.
1832	HBC chief factor (Peter Skene Ogden) meets Nine Tribes chiefs Neishot and Tsa-qaks on the Skeena River, and they invite him to trade with their tribes. There are three main trading factions within the Nine Tribes lead by these chiefs and Ligeex. Thomas Sinclair, an employee of the HBC, makes a map of the area between Lax Kw'alaams and Metlakatla.	Dean 1994; Hudson's Bay Co. Map # G.1/170.
1833	Wilson Duff's map reconstructing Tribal settlement at Lax Kw'alaams prior to the construction of Fort Simpson.	
1834	HBC moves Fort Nass to Fort Simpson at Lax Kw'alaams, creating a new economic organization to the fur trade. Oral records indicate that this was at the urging of Nine Tribes leaders. Trade with neighboring nations (Haida, Tongass, Nisga'a and Tlingit).	Bolt 1983; Dean 1994; Marsden and Galois 1995.
1836	The *Lagrange*, an American trading vessel begins trading with the Nine Tribes causing HBC's Ogden to threaten revocation of trade. Tsa-qaks calls his bluff and tells HBC to leave his land. Smallpox epidemic in Nine Tribes territory, decimating up to one-third of the Indigenous population, including Neishot and Tsa-qaks, but Ligeex is vaccinated at Fort Simpson. Lax Kw'alaams become a refuge for people fleeing the epidemic.	Dean 1994.
1837	More Tsimshian people arrive at the already crowded Fort and take up residence in the woodpile on the Island. The HBC orders their eviction and a small skirmish ensues. Eventually a few are allowed to stay in their makeshift "lodges." One of the first commemorative mortuary feasts for a dead chief was performed at Fort Simpson.	Dean 1994; Marsden and Galois 1995.

Year	Event	References
1839	Russians cede Northwest seaboard to the HBC for an annual rent of 2,000 sea otters, giving HBC control of the area. Conflict between the Haida and the Nine Tribes escalates into a gun battle. HBC Fort Taku established on the northern coast.	
1840	Death of "old" Ligeex, replaced by Paul Legaic. Beginning of wage labor economics at HBC post.	Bolt 1983; Clayton 1992; Marsden and Galois 1995.
1843	Decline in fish attributed to improper disposal of fish bodies by HBC, in violation of tradition. HBC was being supplied in fish by Nine Tribes.	Bolt 1983.
1850	Nine Tribes winter villages move to Lax Kw'alaams/Fort Simpson.	Bolt 1983; Clayton 1992; Dean 1994; Marsden and Galois 1995; Martindale 2003; 2009.
1853	British Admiralty surveys Lax Kw'alaams creating the *Virago Map*. The map illustrators (Officers Inskip, Gordon and Knox) also composed twelve scenes of daily and ceremonial life. Frederick Alexcee (1853–1940), a Tsimshian painter, created a series of illustrations of Lax Kw'alaams from memory that date to about this time. Barbeau and Beynon, working in the twentieth century, create a map of houses at Lax Kw'alaams from these sources and others, noting chiefs and tribal affiliations.	Clayton 1992.
1857	Arrival of fist missionary, William Duncan (Anglican) in Lax Kw'alaams. By 1859, Duncan estimates that a quarter of the Nine Tribes community travels to Victoria for trade during the summers.	Bolt 1983; Clayton 1992; Fiske 1991; Galois 1997; Martindale 2003; Rettig 1980.
1862	The Nine Tribes become fragmented as a result of missionization. Duncan establishes a new settlement at a traditional village site in Meltkatla Pass, where he leads a splinter group of Tsimshians (mostly Gitlaan Tribe) who have converted to Christianity and, at least in Duncan's mind, rejected traditionalism.	Bolt 1983; Clayton 1992; Fiske 1991; Galois 1997; MacDonald 1990; Martindale 2003; Neylan 2003; Rettig 1980.

continued on next page

Table 11.1. *Continued.*

Dates (AD)	Events	Source
1863	Duncan appointed Justice of the Peace at Metlakatla, increasing his authority.	Rettig 1980.
1866	The overland telegraph line to Kispiox used the first steamships on the Skeena River, opening a route to the interior for non-Tsimshian traders.	Galois 1997.
1867	Paul Legaic converts to Christianity and moves to Metlakatla, abandoning his traditional role as chief of the Gispaklo'ots.	Dean 1994; Murray 1981.
1869	Non-Tsimshian exploration and trade along the Skeena increases with the Omineca Gold Rush. Paul Legaic dies while in Lax Kw'alaams.	Galois 1997.
1870	Port Essington established on the south bank near the mouth of the Skeena River to serve as the coastal terminus of a steamship line that would eventually run to Hazelton in the interior. The land was preempted (thus removed without permission from the Gitwigyot's tribe) and became home to interior Tsimshian who staffed the shipping line.	Bolt 1983; Clayton 1992; Fiske 1991; Galois 1997; MacDonald 1990; Martindale 2003; Neylan 2003; Rettig 1980.
1873	Alfred and Kate Dudoward convert to Methodism in 1873 and petition for a missionary; Charles Horetzky visits Lax Kw'alaams and creates a large series of photographs of the town.	Bolt 1983; MacDonald 1990.
1874	Thomas Crosby arrives at Lax Kw'alaams in 1874.	Bolt 1983; MacDonald 1990.
1876	The first salmon cannery (Inverness) opened near the mouth of the Skeena River.	Galois 1997.
1877	The Metlakatla mission is transferred from Duncan to A. J. Hall, whose revivalist approach generates a return to more traditional forms of ceremony; Duncan's return in 1878 quells this movement.	Rettig 1990.
1878	George Dawson visits Lax Kw'alaams and creates a sketch map of the town site and the land owners.	Beynon 1939, 120n1; Martindale 2009.

1879	An ascension potlatch is held in 1879 for a new Legaic (Paul Legaic II).	
1880	Fort Simpson becomes Port Simpson.	Bolt 1983.
1881	The Canadian secular state arrives in force in Nine Tribes territory with the Indian Agent (Powell) and the Indian Reserves Commissioner (O'Reilly) in 1881. The reserve allocations are defined without input from tribal chiefs (who are away fishing) and thus the list of reserve lands is incomplete. Tribal chiefs petition for revision but are turned down.	Bolt 1983; Clayton 1992; MacDonald 1990; Neylan 2003; Rettig 1980.
1883	Nonnatives begin preempting land not allocated to reserves in anticipation of expanded settlement and the arrival of the western terminus of the Grand Truck Railway.	Bolt 1983.
1884	Amendment to the Indian Act creates (1) required attendance at school by all Indigenous children, creating the Residential School system, and (2) a ban on all ceremonies (potlatches) and dances. Government inquiry into reserve allocations concludes that the Nine Tribes were given bad advice by missionaries rather than the Indian Agent, hence, the government is not liable.	Bolt 1983.
1886	Tsimshian chiefs and Crosby visit Victoria to make their case regarding reserve allocation, Crosby reluctant to assist. Their appeal is not heard.	Bolt 1983.
1887	Duncan, facing conflict with the Anglican Church Mission Society for his authoritarian rule and differences of doctrine and the extending Canadian state, negotiates with the US Government for a Tsimshian reserve on Annette Island, Alaska, where he relocates with 800 Tsimshian followers. The Joint Commission on Indian Reserves visit Lax Kw'alaams to review reserve allocations. Traditional leaders are again away fishing. No change to reserves.	Bolt 1983; Fiske 1991.
1888	Department of Indian Affairs creates the "Northwest Coast Agency," signaling the expansion of governmental control in the region and introducing new modes of demarcation between natives and nonnatives.	Clayton 1992.

continued on next page

Table 11.1. *Continued.*

Dates (AD)	Events	Source
1889	Crosby visits Ottawa to advocate for Nine Tribes reserve allocation. Visit unsuccessful.	Bolt 1983.
1890	Paul Legaic II dies, succeeded by his sister, Martha Legaic.	
1891	Petitions to the federal government in 1891 to secure land rights are unsuccessful. Notable return to traditional practices. Tribal chiefs send letter to MPP Robert Hall complaining of lack of resolution to title rights. Hall requests federal government (DIA) to extend rights, rejected by Deputy Superintenent Vankoughnet as the policy was that Indigenous people had been granted too much and rights should be curtailed not increased.	Bolt 1983; Rettig 1980.
1894	Lax Kw'alaams invokes the Indian Act to create a band council, an alternative to traditional leadership, in an effort to advance their title interests. The leader of such elected councils could not be Indigenous and Lax Kw'alaams chose the Indian Agent over the missionary Crosby.	Bolt 1983.
1896	Council requests the removal of the Indian Agent from the council after failure to advance rights claims.	Bolt 1983.
1902	Martha Legaic dies, the last of the matriline. Chief of House of Ligeex transferred to George Kelly of the House of Sgagweet.	Garfield 1939.

was not the most clustered settlement pattern in Tsimshian history. This occurred prior to the war, peaking around 2,000 years ago. Thus, the late precontact pattern can be interpreted in part as the maintenance of tribal spatial independence against a trend of consolidation.

With the establishment of Fort Simpson at Lax Kw'alaams in 1834, the Nine Tribes began relocating to the area. Initially, this may have been a seasonal occupation Dean (1994, 52). In 1837, the first mortuary feast was held at Fort Simpson (Dean 1994, 60), and by 1849, the tribal villages had relocated permanently such that all the winter ceremonial season events were being held at Lax Kw'alaams. Clayton (1992, 31) argues that the Nine Tribes moved permanently to Lax Kw'alaams by 1840, where a permanent population of 2,000 developed. The movement of all the Nine Tribes to permanent residence at Lax Kw'alaams is a process that probably took many years, perhaps the entire decade to complete.

We have three sources for the settlement pattern at the emergent center at Lax Kw'alaams, all of which indicate that the tribal identities were being preserved in spatial form: each tribe had its own district where it constructed an analogue of their autonomous village and large chief's houses were constructed to host ceremonial events. The only direct cartographic data from this period comes from the British vessel the *Virago*, whose cartographers produced a map in 1853 of the anchorage that included the buildings around the Fort (see fig. 11.2 on page 264), although there is no information on how the community was organized.

The Tsimshian artist Fredee Alexcee, who was born at Lax Kw'alaams in 1853, drew a series of perspective paintings of the town in the late nineteenth century that captured his memories, probably from around the 1860s. In 1944 William Beynon developed a map of the tribal and house group locations that has similarities to the *Virago* map and was based on Alexcee's paintings (see fig. 11.3 on page 265). Beynon, who was both Tsimshian and a scholar of Tsimshian history and oral records, is specific about areas that are "tribal locations" around the fort. In a separate map, he identifies individual houses by their lineages, a level of detail that warrants further study. From these sources we can see that by the mid-nineteenth century, Fort Simpson had become a hybrid space in which tribes were both spatially associated and yet maintained their independence. In some ways this was the precontact pattern at Metlakatla, though at Lax Kw'alaams it is more spatially compressed. Thus, the interpretation is that spatial independence between tribes remained strong at this time, indicative of the durability of tribal organization and identity.

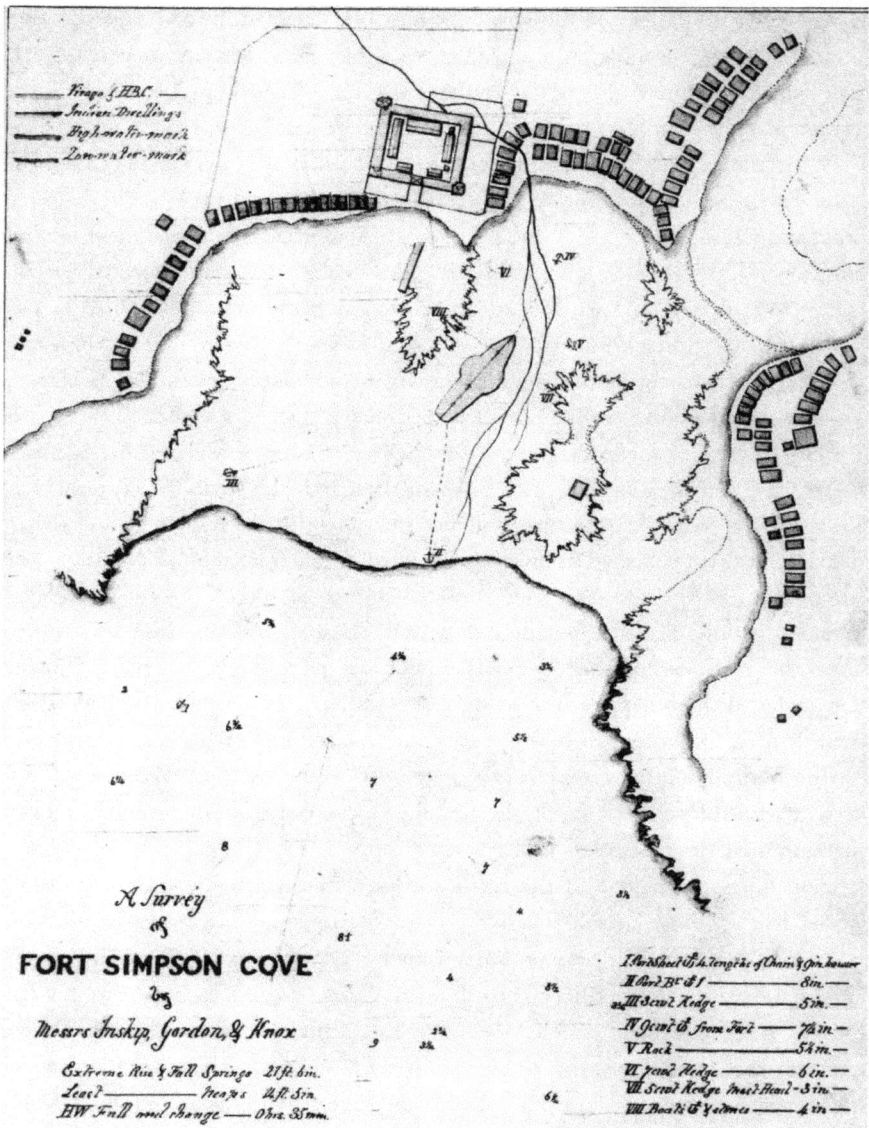

Figure 11.2. The Virago Map from 1853 showing the earliest known image of Lax Kw'alaams. (Courtesy of the Library and Archives Canada)

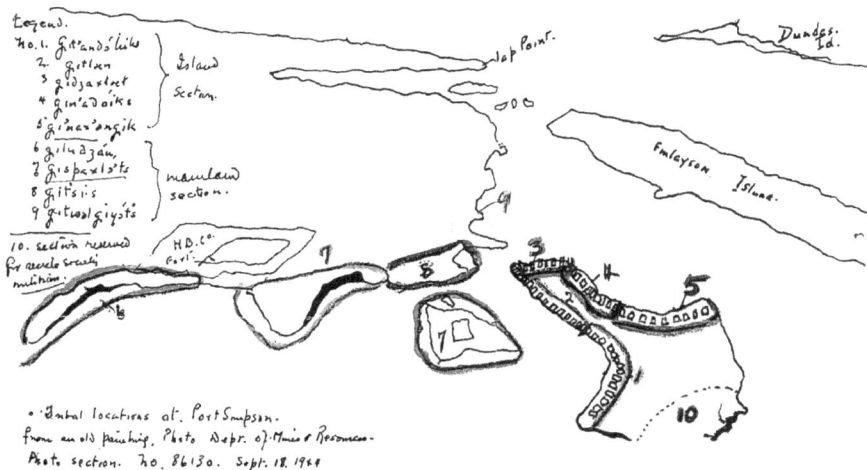

Figure 11.3. Beynon map showing tribal divisions at Lax Kw'alaams. Beynon, William (n.d.) *The Beynon Manuscript: Tsimshian Texts*. Manuscripts from the Columbia University Library. (Unpublished manuscript held on file at the Lax Kw'alaams and Metlakatla Indian Bands. Photograph by Andrew Martindale)

The next suite of spatial data is a series of photographs by Charles Horetzky taken in 1873, as he traveled up the Pacific Coast (Horetzky 1874). These show the town in perspective similar to that recorded by Alexcee, with traditional houses located in rows facing the coastlines. Some houses extend out into the intertidal zone on stilts, much as recorded in the Alexcee paintings. Clayton (1992, 44) estimates that in 1870, the population of Lax Kw'alaams had increased to over 10,000, yet the traditional tribal structure remained intact (see also Rettig 1980, 1). The only significant change up to this point is the replacement of traditional architecture with professionally constructed Victorian-inspired designs, a trend that indicates that the Nine Tribes remained economically powerful.

However, when George Dawson takes similar photos in 1878, the town is wholly different (see fig. 11.4 on page 266). By this time many of the traditional houses have been replaced with European-style constructions arranged in a Western-style town plan. This rapid change is attributable to the arrival of the Methodist missionary Thomas Crosby in 1874 who, as Bolt (1983, 39) notes, "is remarkably successful in transforming the village from an Indian settlement into a model Canadian town." This is clearly visible in the next suite of hydrological surveys

Figure 11.4. Photograph of Lax Kw'alaams taken in the 1878 by George Dawson, showing the transition toward Western-style houses. (Courtesy of the Library and Archives Canada)

and maps from the 1880s (see fig. 11.5), which show a grid of roads subdividing the community and a shift in house locations from the beaches to the interior roadways. This pattern, with some modernization, remains the spatial organization of Lax Kw'alaams today, and it signals the 1860s as a time of considerable reorganization in the community. Indeed, the latter half of this decade is an inflection point in a number of lines of evidence that suggests that tribal structures were shifting away from spatial and economic arenas and consolidating around cultural and political identity.

Economic Transitions

Between the 1790s and the 1800s trade between the Europeans and Tsimshian increased significantly, with as many as 300 vessels visiting the region (Martindale 2003). Europeans were drawn by sea otter furs, which they could purchase from the

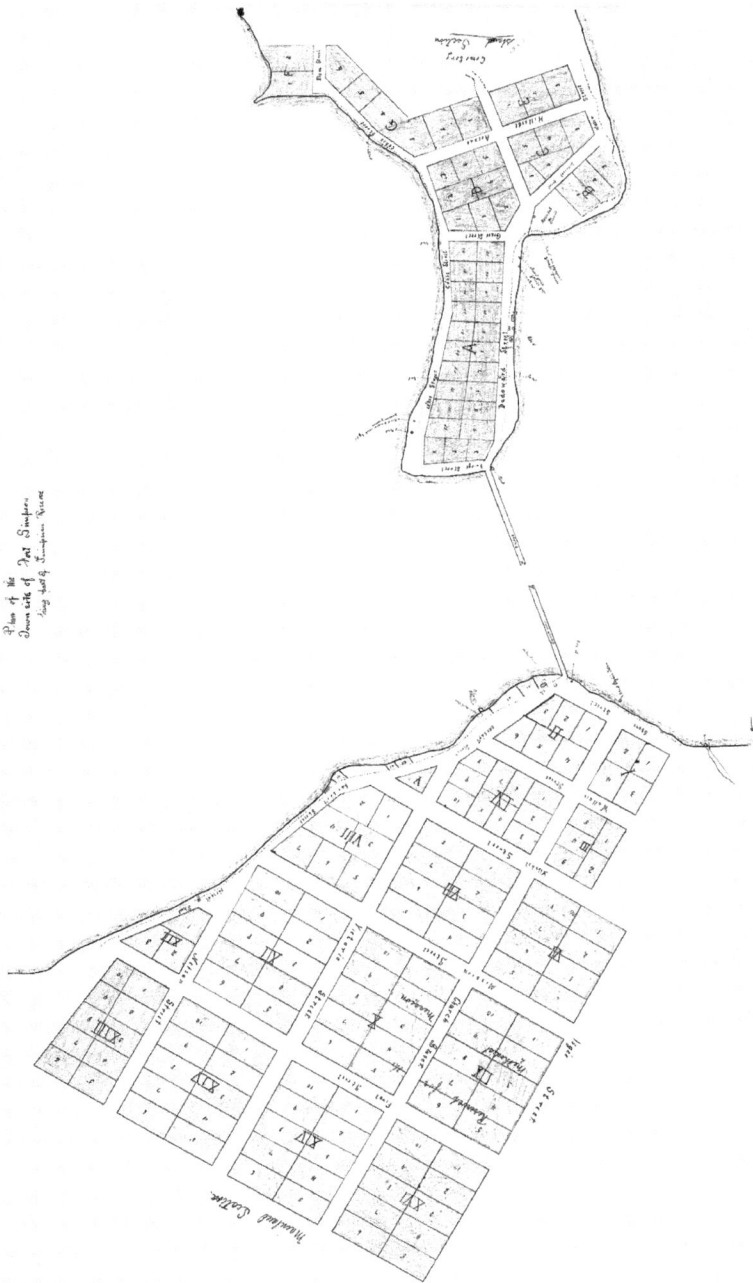

Figure 11.5. An early plan of the town site of Port Simpson (later Lax Kw'alaams), dating from after 1880 and showing the early street grid constructed after 1878 that is still in place today. (Used with permission of the Canadian Museum of History, Map B-8, IMG2014-0085-0007-Dm)

Tsimshian for a few dollars and sell in Asia for over one hundred dollars. The main entrepôt in Nine Tribes territory was Big Bay on the Tsimpsean Peninsula, possibly known to the Europeans as Pearl Harbour. The coastal fur trade created considerable demand with two effects. First, demand was lopsided with Europeans seeking furs and Tsimshian suppliers expressing eclectic tastes that ranged from metal, guns, china, clothing, tobacco, alcohol, umbrellas, and musical instruments (Martindale 2006b). This created an inflationary market for furs focused on nonessential goods. Second, tribes without house group territories that included sea otter hunting grounds worked to gain access to these resources via marriage alliances (Marsden & Galois 1995). Both created stresses on the traditional Tsimshian system with demand for imported objects shifting economic attention toward sea otter hunting and away from the traditional use of surplus food products as trade wealth (Martindale 2003). Tribes with sea otter resource territories rose in influence and economic power, but the Nine Tribes alliance of peers persisted. The coastal fur trade caused the tribal system to stretch toward new economic opportunities, but without major structural change.

Sea otter populations began declining in the early nineteenth century due to overhunting, perhaps as early as 1805. Tsimshian traders were able to shift supply toward beaver pelts from the interior, thereby perpetuating the fur trade economy. In 1821, the Hudson's Bay Company (HBC) and Northwest Company merged, creating a fur-trading monopoly in Western Canada. Most interior to coast fur shipping was conducted along the Skeena River, primarily by Nine Tribes people using traditional freighting canoes. This supply line would remain the only bulk shipping option to the interior until steamships began regularly running the Skeena in the 1860s. The reorienting of trade to interior fur sources shifted the economic benefits toward tribes that held preexisting prerogatives to the interior fur trade (for groundhog and moose hides) (Marsden & Galois 1995). Prominent among these was the Gispaklo'ots tribe lead by the chief Ligeex (Dean 1994). In the early decades of the nineteenth century, Ligeex consolidated power using his Eagle clan relatives and eventually controlled three of the four main interior-to-coast trade routes (Marsden & Galois 1995). However, in 1832 the HBC chief factor at Fort Simpson, Peter Skene Ogden, visited the tribal chiefs "Nieshot" and "Tsa-qaks" at their villages on the Skeena River, indicating that other tribes remained powerful independent economic entities (Dean 1994, 50). The HBC gifted suits of clothing to all three chiefs in 1836, suggesting that this symmetry continued. Thus, the shift to interior furs created preferential benefits for some of the Nine Tribes, but the alliance remained intact.

In 1831, the HBC established Fort Nass on the Nass River as the base of its northern coastal trading operations. Marsden and Galois (1995) argue that through the machinations of Ligeex, the HBC was persuaded to relocate their base to Fort Simpson, more solidly within Nine Tribes territory. Construction of European trading forts marks a new phase in colonial relations with the first permanent European settlements in Nine Tribe territory. These become focal points for regional trade with Indigenous peoples beyond the Nine Tribes, including the Haida, Nisga'a, Tsongass, and other Tsimshian groups (Dean 1994, 32). There is some evidence that the Tsimshian were exacting a tariff for access to the HBC; tensions over trade access resulted in a pitched battle between the Haida and Nine Tribes at Fort Simpson in 1839 (Dean 1994, 68–71). In 1836, a smallpox epidemic ravaged the Nine Tribes killing about a third of the population, including both Nieshot and Tsa-qaks. Ligeex survived, having secured an inoculation from the HBC (Marsden & Galois 1995).

In the late 1830s and 1840s the economics of life at Lax Kw'alaams changed considerably. In 1839, the Russian government ceded the northern coast to the HBC in exchange for an annual rent of 2,000 otter pelts, giving the trading cartel control over the entire area (Dean 1994, 51). The HBC built Fort Taku on the coast north of Fort Simpson and Fort Stikine in the northern interior as a result; both drew furs away from the Nine Tribes. A decline in fish catch in 1846 is attributed among the Tsimshian to be a result of the improper disposal of fish bodies by the staff at the HBC fort (fish remains are to be returned to the ocean so that they may be reunited with souls and return again as fish), suggesting that the Nine Tribes were supplying food to the fort. This changed with increased farming at the fort and increased shipping traffic that allowed for more bulk goods to be supplied north (Dean 1994, 73). At the same time the HBC began employing Nine Tribes people as laborers, signaling the beginning of a cash economy. Increased shipping also allowed the Nine Tribes to expand their trading relations and seek better prices for furs as far south as Victoria (Galois 1997). This movement of goods and people increases such that by 1859 the missionary William Duncan estimates that a quarter of the Nine Tribes population has moved south, some lured by the Fraser Canyon Gold Rush of 1857 (Bolt 1983,42). At the same time, Garfield (1939) notes that the Tsimshian continued to have a high percentage of slaves in the 1860s, perhaps as high as 3 percent to 4 percent of the population (Fiske 1991, 533–34). Thus, while economic changes are considerable in the nineteenth century, facets of traditional economic practice remain intact.

In 1862, Duncan's missionization attempts fission the Nine Tribes, as he recruited one tribe (Gitlaan) and other lineages to build a utopian Christian community at Metlakatla in the traditional, precontact settlement area. Metlakatla became a rival economic and cultural center to Lax Kw'alaams, further dissipating Nine Tribes traditional economic organization. These trends only increase in the latter half of the nineteenth century. The construction of the overland telegraph line to Kispiox in the interior was followed by the first steamships on the Skeena River in 1866, opening a route to the interior for non-Tsimshian traders (Galois 1997, 139). Non-Tsimshian exploration and trade along the Skeena increased with the Omineca Gold Rush of 1869 that expanded the overland trail network (Galois 1997, 123). In 1876, Port Essington was established on the south bank of the Skeena River near its mouth to serve as the coastal terminus of a steamship line that would eventually run to Hazelton in the interior. The land was preempted (thus removed without permission) and became home to interior Tsimshian who staffed the shipping line, bringing Tsimshian outsiders to settle in Nine Tribes territory. In 1876, the first salmon cannery (Inverness) opened north of the mouth of the Skeena River. Eventually fishing and canning would become the major employers of Tsimshian people in the late nineteenth century (Galois 1997, 128).

The establishment of the steamship line and the salmon canneries accelerated the conversion of the Tsimshian economic structure from corporate groups to individuals engaged in wage labor. These economic structures also dislocated people from their traditional homes and lands as workers and their families moved to the canneries and shipping terminals. This pattern became exacerbated with the plans for an overland rail terminus on Kaien Island in Prince Rupert Harbour in the 1880s (Bolt 1983, 49). Preemption of these lands was made possible by the imposition of Indian Reserves in 1881. Peter O'Reilly, the Indian Reserve Commissioner arrived in Lax Kw'alaams to allocate reserves, but appeared without notice at a time when chiefs were away, likely fishing. Nine Tribes people have since this date argued that his list of reserves was incorrect and inadequate, a position that has consistently been rebuffed by the government of Canada. The reserve system was itself an asymmetrical and inappropriate process from the Tsimshian point of view. It provided an average of twenty acres per family, thereby imposing a rights system (ownership by family) that contradicted Tsimshian law (ownership by house group). These lands are held in trust by the Canadian government and often administered by bands, a kind of governance that was not part of traditional Tsimshian law. It also reduced traditional territories considerably, and communities faced the difficult choice of picking tiny allotments from their vast lands to define as reserves. Reserves represent a range of such choices and were chosen as traditional village locations, fishing stations, resource collection lands, or access points to traditional territory. Some tribes responded to the inequity of this system by not signing on for any reserves in protest. Lands not on reserve, the vast majority of Nine Tribes territory, was open for preemption by nonnative settlers who could claim it by request from the provincial government.

The pattern of challenges to traditional Tsimshian economic principles through imposed systems of land ownership, patrilineal inheritance, and wage labor mark an increasing transition away from traditional economic patterns of corporate ownership and collective wealth within house groups. Tsimshian people responded in part through economic means. When James Woodworth, the Superintendent of Methodist Missions visited Lax Kw'alaams in 1896, he noted that the Tsimshian were eager to own their own businesses and control their own government and society (Bolt 1983, 52). Increasingly in the late nineteenth century, this effort shifted toward the political arena.

Political Events

A subset of politically important events—which we define as those that generate organizational change in Tsimshian society and its power dynamics—is visible in this history, although there are likely others that are not as clearly recorded. These provide a sequence of key moments that give us some evidence on how Tsimshian tribes were responding to colonial intrusions.

The first recorded encounter between the Tsimshian and Europeans occurred in 1787 between the British explorer James Colnett and Hale of the Gitkxaała (Martindale 2003). This was violent (Menzies 2016, 34) and set the tone for later interactions in which Tsimshian people were wary of Europeans. Shortly thereafter the mercantile vessels began visiting Tsimshian communities including the American captain Robert Haswell who traded for furs in the Duncan Bay area west of Metlakatla in 1789 (Howay 1990). The Spanish explorer Jacinto Caamaño met the Gitkxaała in the south and passed near Metlakatla in July of 1792, but he records no encounter with the Nine Tribes (Wagner & Newcome 1938a, 1938b). The events of initial contact lead to the coastal fur trade period in which Tsimshian tribal organization shifted to take advantage of new economic opportunities.

The shift to land based furs realigned the economic benefits toward tribes with interior trade relations, such as the Gispaklo'ots. This generated two political events in the early nineteenth century. First, when interior Tsimshian groups attempted to bypass Nine Tribes authority via the Nisga'a through the Nass River, Ligeex lead an army to burn five villages to the ground, thereby enforcing Tsimshian law (Marsden & Galois 1995). This act signals both the collective power of the Nine Tribes at this time and also the ascendency of Ligeex and the Gispaklo'ots. At some time in the early nineteenth century, Ligeex's rise in power caused sufficient concern from the other tribal chiefs that a plot to murder him was proposed (Martindale 2009). Ligeex discovered this through a niece living in another tribal village and preemptively invited the eight other chiefs to a feast where he confronted them. Arguing that his wealth was greater than all of theirs combined, he challenged them to pool theirs and compare. The eight other chiefs declined the challenge, effectively electing Ligeex as a paramount. Ligeex memorialized this transition by commissioning two pictographs be painted at Red Bluff and Tyee noting his wealth and claims. The Red Bluff pictograph was erased in 1915, but the Tyee image is still visible (see fig. 11.6). These events suggest that the economic developments of

Figure 11.6. The Tyee pictograph showing Ligeex's face and crests representing the Nine Tribes at the entrance to the Skeena River. (Credit: A. Martindale)

the fur trade were creating disparity between the Nine Tribes. At the same time, the tensions with European colonization pressed the Nine Tribes to consolidate. The result was a bit of both: a more hierarchical internal organization that created a more unified alliance. The relocation to Fort Simpson marks a similar trend of consolidation around the main trading post and the assertion of Nine Tribes economic and political authority over their trade and territorial rights.

At the same time, a series of events in the 1830s and '40s worked against the coherence of the tribal alliance. The smallpox epidemic and the death of the three most powerful chiefs between 1836 and 1840 caused political disarray, potentially unraveling the emergent hierarchy under Ligeex. Martindale (2003) refers to this paramountcy as incipient, that is, not fully formed. At the same time the centripetal effects of the collective resettlement of the Nine Tribes at Lax Kw'alaams continued, reinforcing the alliance as a collective enterprise, greater than the sum of its parts. By the 1850s, the expansion of trade and wage labor economics beyond Nine Tribes territory was both a symptom and a cause of the shifting of economic power from corporate groups (such as house groups) to individuals. Despite these tensions, tribal identity remained a powerful force at Lax Kw'alaams. Duncan's initial efforts at missionization focused on powerful tribal leaders such as Paul Legaic (the successor to old Ligeex). That Duncan's fissioning of the alliance was along tribal lines and able to recruit only one of the tribal chiefs suggests that tribal principles remained powerful.

Paul Legaic's conversion to Christianity, and his subsequent relocation to Metlakatla in 1867, created political turbulence. By abandoning his traditional role as chief of the Gispaklo'ots, Paul Legaic sent a powerful political signal that his fortunes and that of his formerly powerful tribe were waning. This period was dominated by changing fortunes for traditional tribal principles. New economic opportunities across the region diluted the role of Lax Kw'alaams and drew individuals into a wider network of economic relations. Wage labor and market forces eroded the importance of the collective corporate house group. These centrifugal forces become visible with the reorganization of Lax Kw'alaams from a collection of tribal villages into a western town-site through the work of the missionary Thomas Crosby. Whereas Duncan arrived of his own accord, Crosby was invited by Alfred and Kate Dudoward in 1873, partly as an effort to find an avenue of influence against colonial forces. At Metlakatla, Duncan is temporarily replaced by A. J. Hall, whose revivalism created opportunities for greater synthesis between Christianity and traditional Tsimshian spirituality (Rettig 1980, 28). Neylan (2003) argues that Tsimshian conversion to Christianity was less of a loss of traditionalism and more of its transition into a new synthetic frame comprised of similar spiritual and social principles.

As a result of these events, the 1870s appears as a decade of some turmoil. It is punctuated in 1879 by the ascension feast for a new Ligeex (Paul Legaic II) (Martindale 2009). The ascension triggered a debate about traditional practice in the wake of missionization. According to Beynon, the Gispaklo'ots had lost all rank due to the lack of ceremonial obligations after Paul Legaic's conversion. The Gispaklo'ots argued that they had been so generous over the past century, that they still held preeminent rank. This ascension resolved the debate by returning the Nine Tribes to an alliance of equals, a political decision that effectively undid the early nineteenth-century consolidation of the Nine Tribes under Ligeex. The negotiations over the ascension of a new Ligeex indicate that the Nine Tribes were increasingly rejecting the influences of colonization and returning to traditional political principles, a trend seen in economic and material patterns (Martindale & Jurakic 2004; 2006). The rise of wage labor economics, and the erosion of traditional corporate oversight of resource collection, processing, and shipping, undermined Tsimshian authority across the Nine Tribes. At the same time, movements in less-economic arenas of power, such as missionization and politics, indicates that the Tsimshian were continually seeking avenues of defending their collective interests.

The Canadian secular state arrived in force in Nine Tribes territory with the Indian Agent (Powell) and the Indian Reserves Commissioner (O'Reilly) in 1881 (Bolt 1983, 48). Indian agents were assigned by Canada to facilitate negotiations between Indigenous communities and the state, ostensibly to act on behalf of First Nations. Powell assured Nine Tribes leaders that their rights would be respected. Meanwhile there was considerable Nine Tribes opposition to the allocation of reserve lands by O'Reilly, who visited Lax Kw'alaams and Metlakatla when house leaders were away fishing and thus was not able to properly represent rights owners.

The imposition of the Indian Agent and reserve system on the Nine Tribes generated the modern, confrontational system. Agents were legally responsible for Indigenous rights, but often acted in the interests of the state. The reserve system shifted title rights from house groups to families and deprived house groups of the vast majority of their traditional territory and thus economic foundations. Reserve allocation opened up Nine Tribes lands to preemption. Tsimshian frustration with this result and with their previous efforts at negotiation through missionary intermediaries triggered a greater focus on direct political action. The Indian Residential

School system, which emerged in this decade, made clear to Indigenous people that Canada did not have their interests at heart and treated them as noncitizens with limited rights. This accentuated the conflict that was already fomenting.

Petitions to the federal government in 1891 to secure land rights were unsuccessful (Clayton 1992, 51). Lax Kw'alaams invoked the Indian Act in 1894 to create a band council, an alternative to traditional leadership, in an effort to advance their title interests (Bolt 1983, 51). By the late nineteenth century, the Canadian state was restricting rather than accommodating Indigenous claims to land and rights. Government policy was that Indigenous people had received too much already and that rights and title should be curtailed (Bolt 1983, 53). In British Columbia, this resulted in the arbitrary reduction of reserve lands. With the emergence of band governance, the Nine Tribes had a new avenue through which to advance their interests with Canada. However, band authority existed outside of traditional tribal leadership, creating tension that resonates today.

Discussion: Evidence of Resilience in Tsimshian-ness through Tribal Identity

In 2009, Martindale noted that by most measures the nineteenth century tracked significant transitions in the lives of Tsimshian people. He also reported the response of Tsimshian elder Wayne Ryan of the Gispaxlo'ots to this observation. Ryan explained that the idea that Tsimshian people were somehow fundamentally different from their ancestors was both amusing and absurd. He went on to say that these things did not matter; all that was important was what was in your heart.

Ryan's thesis is in many ways an invocation of the Braudelian *longue dureé*, that cultural tradition perpetuates on an intergenerational time cycle, beyond the lives of individuals. Archaeologists, who see evidence of this durability in material records, have embraced Braudel's (1973) observation, but like Braudel himself, have struggled to explain why. Ryan believed that all of the social, economic, material, and political changes in Tsimshian history are immaterial to the nature of Tsimshian-ness, that what it means to be cultural must reside far below what Geertz (1973) called its hard surfaces. Recent theoretical explorations of the power of practices and the affectations of living find a measure of cultural knowledge embodied within the philosophical realms of epistemology and expectation that is, if not independent of the circumstances of life, at least resilient to its vagaries

(Ortner 2016). Oliver (2014) has appropriately challenged the idea of something inherently Tsimshian withstanding tumultuous colonial change as invoking a form of "creeping essentialism." Yet there is something here. Oliver argues that the construct of tradition is in danger of recapitulating the subaltern marginalization by denying Indigenous actors the agency to respond to colonial incursion. His attention to the constraints of agency shifts scale from individual acts to the "life projects" within the biographies of people. Thus, he draws our attention to the improvisational and emergent facets of Native-lived colonialism. Martindale (2009) has explored this through constructs of entanglement and tinkering: the continuous remodeling of identity triangulated from experience in the trial and error of living. Oliver also returns us to the provocative idea that colonialism to some degree acculturated indigenous peoples.

Wayne Ryan, we think, would disagree, though he seemed on the outside to be more European than Tsimshian. Was he, as Oliver (2014) suggests, strategically mobilized to draw on an amalgam of tropes that was transforming his cultural identity? Or was he, as Martindale (2009) proposed, embarking on a long biographical exploration of what Ricoeur (1966) would call his "logos"—his identity? There is a third, more likely explanation. Wayne was able to juxtapose the apparent contradiction of practicing the tropes of one culture while living the reality of another because as he put it, he was Tsimshian in his heart. Ryan was perhaps invoking a way of knowing the world that emerged from a belief in the reality, which was confirmed by the emotional fidelity of his experiences. In other words, the content of Tsimshian constructs could change, but their forms would retain their shape, even as they flexed and distorted under the pressures of change.

Tsimshian tribes are, we propose, one such form. They have existed for thousands of years in a range of iterations and a variety of associations. The tribal entities that existed when Europeans arrived in the late eighteenth century had already reshaped at least once to form the Nine Tribes alliance over 1,000 years ago. Through the colonial era, tribal identities realigned into a more coherent and hierarchical form to contain the economic geyser that was the fur trade, forestalling its more deleterious effects. When these effects became manifest, the Nine Tribes realigned again, both returning to its less hierarchical organization and shifting from economic to political and cultural domains. Tribes were always all of these things, and their resilience derives in part from their flexibility in defining what it is that connects individuals, house groups, and lineages together. This stability within dynamism is possible in part because of the complex interlocking of Tsimshian social and political entities.

Table 11.2 outlines our view of the key trends in spatial, economic, and political events in recent Nine Tribes history and identifies the points of inflection (where change seems most evident) and trends (the longer-term consequences of change to create new arrangements). Here we follow Stahl's (2002) cartographic model of aligning different historical themes over time and identifying moments of coordinated event and effect. Table 11.1 presents the detail of events, and Table 11.2 (on page 278) presents the larger trends, which we can further distil as a narration of tribal response to colonization. The Nine Tribes alliance existed prior to contact as an integrated economic, social, cultural, and political (including military) entity. It persisted largely in this form with the arrival of Europeans and the coastal and then interior fur trades. However, the smallpox epidemic of 1836, the death of key chiefs, and the rise of wage labor economics and missionization at the mid-century resulted in an unsettled period for tribal structures. As their economic foundations were diluted through market economics, depopulation, and regional competition, they experienced a period of declining significance. This was reversed in 1879 as the Nine Tribes sought a return to traditional organizational principles. With the advent of the reserve system and widespread encroachment shortly thereafter, tribal identity reasserted itself focusing on its political role as the outward-facing defender of house group interests. This trend resulted in the formation of band councils, which have continued this effort, although somewhat independently of traditional tribal leadership.

Since tribes have never been rights owning polities, they have always existed in part because Tsimshian people wanted them to exist. This is a second facet to the resilience of tribes. They persist because Tsimshian people believe in them. The social factualness of tribes is perpetuated by ongoing collective and individual confirmations of their importance, an emotional belief in their truth that resides along with other facets of Tsimshian identity, as Wayne Ryan argued, in the heart. We know from many sources that cultural truths are not judged by their logical rigor, but by what Lucien Febvre (1973), the original annalist, saw as their emotional fidelity. Martindale and Nicholas (2014) use the construct of race, an imaginary taxonomy that is historically real and long-lasting, to illustrate the operation of this principle in the modern world. We propose then, that the *longue dureé* is characterized by perpetuations of conversance in collectively maintained systems of expectation about

Table 11.2. Patterns, Trends, and Points of Inflection in Recent Nine Tribes History

Dates	Spatial Patterns	Economic Patterns	Political Patterns	Trend and Points of Inflection
Prior to Contact	Tribal settlement focused on independent villages in Metlakatla Pass and Prince Rupert Harbour.	Wealth and necessities consequent to food production and surplus, coordinated by house groups.	Alliance of Nine Tribes as a legacy of the War with the Tlingits.	Inflection: War with the Tlingit results in the Nine Tribes alliance. Trend: the Nine Tribes alliance stabilizes after 1100 BP as a political partnership of equals based on the economic productivity of house group resource territories.
1790s	Possible construction of villages in Big Bay, north of Prince Rupert Harbour, the main anchorage for fur trading vessels.	Coastal fur trade shifts surplus production to trade with Europeans, favoring tribes with coastal sea otter territories.	Europeans appear in the late eighteenth century. Possible smallpox epidemic.	Inflection: European arrival and coastal fur trade. Trend: Tribal alliance flexes to accommodate new resource and demand in trade network.
1800–1830	Expansion of village locations along the Skeena River to participate in and monitor inland fur trade.	Overhunting of sea otters causes extirpation, Tsimshian shift supply to land-based furs, favoring tribes with trade prerogatives. HBC merges with Northwest Company to create a major trading cartel. Regular shipping begins to the fort.	Infringements on Nine Tribes interior-to-coast trade prerogatives by interior suppliers results in an invasion and war initiated by Ligeex, chief of the Gispaklo'ots. Foiled plot to murder Ligeex by other eight tribal chiefs results in incipient paramountcy. Painting of the Tyee pictograph.	Inflection: HBC forts established, decline in sea otter populations. Trend: Tribes respond to shift to interior furs via traditional principles and law, resulting in increased consolidation of the alliance.

1830–1850	Fort Nass established by Hudson's Bay Company in 1831, relocated to Fort Simpson at Lax Kw'alaams in 1834. Tribal villages relocate to Lax Kw'alaams surrounding the Fort. Each maintains spatial independence along a stretch of coastline.	Wage labor economics initiated at the Fort Simpson. HBC extends control up the northern coast. Shipping in bulk permits allows for trade in food, undermining traditional house group economic cooperative structure.	Death of the three major chiefs, two from a smallpox epidemic.	Inflection: HBC encroachment on Nine Tribes land. Trend: Nine Tribes negotiates a relocation of the Fort and consolidates around Fort Simpson to mediate access, thereby maintaining the strength of the alliance.
1850–1870	Lax Kw'alaams fissions in two with the Gitlaan tribe and others returning to Metlakatla under the leadership of missionary William Duncan.	Tsimshian people move south for trade and employment. European construction and mining expand inland.	Arrival of William Duncan and establishment of Metlakatla. Conversion of Paul Legaic to Christianity and relocation to Metlakatla removes Gispaklo'ots Tribe from traditional practices.	Inflection: Missionization and fissioning. Trend: Centrifugal economic forces undermine traditional structures of authority. Relocation of chiefs leads to erosion of traditional practices.
1870–1880	Modern town site plan implemented under the guidance the missionary Thomas Crosby. Canneries and sawmills appear along the coast and the Skeena River, often on existing village sites.	Steamship line up the Skeena circumvents traditional Nine Tribes shipping and brings Interior Tsimshians to settle at Port Essington. Canneries create large demand for wage laborers.	Methodist missionary Thomas Crosby arrives at Lax Kwalaams at the request of Alfred and Kate Dudoward. 1879 ascension feast for Paul Legaic II realigns the Nine Tribes to an alliance.	Inflection: Reorganization of Lax Kw'alaams, resetting of the parameters of the alliance. Trend: The Nine Tribes asserts its identity as an alliance in the face of economic, political, and spatial intrusion, shifting toward a more political focus.

continued on next page

Table 11.2. *Continued*.

Dates	Spatial Patterns	Economic Patterns	Political Patterns	Trend and Points of Inflection
1880–1890	Metlatkala fissions to create New Metlakatla under the leadership of Duncan.	Imposition of the reserves system disenfranchises Nine Tribes house groups from their traditional lands and resource rights.	Indian Agent appointed, Reserve system and residential school system imposed on Nine Tribes. Reserve allocations argued by Nine Tribes to be inadequate and unfair.	Inflection: European removal of traditional lands in exchange for minute reserves. Trend: Efforts to advocate for rights using European intermediaries proves unsuccessful.
1890 and Beyond	Increasing urban development at Melatkatla and Lax Kw'alaams. Prince Rupert established in 1910 as the terminus of the Grand Truck Rail line.	Industrialization increases focused on resource extraction of fish, lumber and mineral resources.	Petition to Federal government regarding reserve allocation dismissed, Lax Kw'alaams forms a Band Council. Metlakatla Band Council follows.	Inflection: Dismissal of appeal to reconsider reserve allocation. Trend: Tribes reform as Band governments, starting a new era of self-directed advocacy.

reality that are informed by reality but exist independently of it, all of which is manifest in feeling as much as in thought. As important as tribal identity is in this context, it is only one of many such frameworks of expectation. As Martindale et al. (2017a) illustrate, the lineage has an even longer and more complex history.

Conclusions

The history of Indigenous communities in the face of colonial encroachments is complex and entangled (Martindale 2009), at least on a proximal level. Since 1787, Nine Tribes people have accommodated novel structures in economic, social, material, ideological, and political worlds. At the same time, Tsimshian principles such as the importance of tribes and tribal identity have been resilient, and are traceable as recurring institutions throughout this history and into today. Shifts of emphasis in their economic and political roles are part of their resilience. At the same time as the idea of tribal identity was emerging in new forms, much of its philosophical and emotional content remained unchanged. Thus, the experimentation of the paramountcy in the early nineteenth century could be set aside in favor of a more traditional arrangement in 1879 by people who had not been alive when the initial transformation had occurred. This reversal was partly aspirational—a return to a state of affairs that people believed to have existed. It was also partly scholarly, a return to an arrangement that people understood from their analysis and records of history. But it was also authentic, and as Jackson (2005) argues, sincere. Where authenticity is assessed by the external judgment of others, sincerity is an internalized understanding that emerges less discursively from the shared experiences of collective practice and resides in part in the emotional register of belief. Since it is undisclosable because it forms the epistemological foundations to reality rather than the observation of reality, it is inaccessible to those who have not shared similar experiences. Tribal identity thus perpetuates in Nine Tribes history in part because Tsimshian peoples' understanding of it resides in their hearts.

Works Cited

Beynon, W. 1939. *Tsimshian Texts*. Manuscripts from the Columbia University Library. Unpublished manuscript. University Microfilms International, Ann Arbor.

Beynon, William. 1941. "The Tsimshians of Metlakatla, Alaska." *American Anthropologist* 43(1): 83–88.

Boas, Franz. 1916. "Tsimshian Mythology: Based on Texts Recorded by Henry W. Tate." *31st Annual Report of the Bureau of American Ethnology for the years of 1909 to 1910*, 29–1037. Washington, DC: Bureau of American Ethnology.

Bolt, Clarence R. 1983. "The Conversion of the Port Simpson Tsimshian: Indian Control or Missionary Manipulation?" *BC Studies* 57: 38–56.

Clayton, Daniel. 1992. "Geographies of the Lower Skeena." *BC Studies* 94: 29–58.

Dean, Jonathan R. 1994. "'These Rascally Spackaloids': The Rise of Gispaxlots Hegemony at Fort Simpson, 1832–40." *BC Studies* 101: 41–78.

Edinborough, Kevan, Marko Porčić, Andrew Martindale, T. J. Brown, Kisha Supernant, and Kenneth M. Ames. 2017. "A Radiocarbon Test for Demographic Events in Written and Oral History." *Proceedings of the National Academy of Sciences* 114(47): 12436–41.

Eldridge Morley, Alyssa Parker, Christine Mueller, and Susan Crockford. 2014. *Archaeological Investigations at Ya asqalu'i/Kaien Siding, Prince Rupert Harbour*. Report for the British Columbia Archaeology Branch. Victoria, BC: Government of British Columbia.

Febvre, Lucien. 1973. *A New Kind of History: From the Writings of Lucien Febvre*. London: Routledge and Keagan Paul.

Fiske, Jo-Anne. 1991. "Colonization and the Decline of Women's Status: The Tsimshian Case." *Feminist Studies* 17(3): 509–35.

Galois, Robert M. 1997. "Colonial Encounters: The Worlds of Arthur Wellington Clah, 1855–1881." *BC Studies* 115/116: 105–48.

Garfield, Viola E. 1939. "Tsimshian Clan and Society." *University of Washington Publications in Anthropology* 7(3): 167–340.

———. 1951. "The Tsimshian and their Neighbors." In *The Tsimshian Indians and Their Arts*. Edited by Viola E. Garfield and Paul Wingert. Vancouver, BC: Douglas and McIntyre.

Geertz, Clifford. 1973. *The Interpretations of Cultures*. New York: Basic Books.

Halpin, Marjorie, and Margaret Seguin. 1990. "Tsimshian Peoples: Southern Tsimshian, Coast Tsimshian, Nishga, and Gitksan." In *Handbook of North American Indians, Vol. 7: Northwest Coast*. Edited by Wayne Suttles. Washington, DC: Smithsonian Institution Press, 267–84.

Horetzky, Charles. 1874. *Canada on the Pacific*. Montreal, QC: Dawson Brothers.

Howay, Frederic, ed. 1789[1990]. *Voyages of the Columbia to the Northwest Coast 1787–1790 and 1790–1793*. Portland: Oregon Historical Society Press in cooperation with the Massachusetts Historical Society.

Jackson, John, Jr. 2005. *Real Black: Adventures in Racial Sincerity*. Chicago: University of Chicago Press.

Letham Bryn, Andrew Martindale, Duncan McLaren, et al. 2015. "Holocene Settlement History of the Dundas Island Archipelago, Northern British Columbia." *BC Studies* 187: 51–84.

Marsden, Susan. 2000. *Defending the Mouth of the Skeena: Perspectives on Tsimshian Tlingit Relations*. Prince Rupert, BC: Tin Ear Press.

———. 2002. "Adawx, Spanaxnox, and the Geopolitics of the Tsimshian." *BC Studies* 135 (Autumn): 101–44.

Marsden, Susan, and Robert Galois. 1995. "The Tsimshian, The Hudson's Bay Company, and the Geopolitics of the Northwest Coast Fur Trade, 1787–1840." *The Canadian Geographer* 39(2): 169–83.

Martindale, Andrew 2003. "A Hunter-Gatherer Paramount Chiefdom: Tsimshian Developments Through the Contact Period." In *Emerging from the Mist: Studies in Northwest Coast Culture History*. Edited by Quentin Mackie, Gary Coupland, and R.G. Matson. Vancouver: University of British Columbia Press, 12–49.

———. 2006. "Methodological Issues in the Use of Tsimshian Oral Traditions (Adawx) in Archaeology." *Canadian Journal of Archaeology* 30(2): 158–92.

———. 2006b. "Tsimshian Houses and Households through the Contact Period." In *Household Archaeology on the Northwest Coast*. Edited by E. Sobel, A. Trieu Gahr, and K. M. Ames. Ann Arbor, MI: International Monographs in Prehistory, 140–58.

———. 2009. "Entanglement and Tinkering: Structural History in the Archaeology of the Northern Tsimshian." *Journal of Social Archaeology* 9: 59–91.

Martindale, Andrew, and Irena Jurakic. 2004. "Northern Tsimshian Plant Resource Use in the Late Pre-contact to Post-contact Era." *Canadian Journal of Archaeology* 28(2): 254–80.

———. 2006. "Identifying Expedient Glass Tools in a Post-Contact Tsimshian Village." *Journal of Archaeological Science* 33(3): 414–27.

Martindale, Andrew, Natasha Lyons, George Nicholas, Bill Angelbeck, Sean P. Connaughton, Colin Grier, James Herbert, Mike Leon, Yvonne Marshall, Angela Piccini, David M. Schaepe, Kisha Supernant, and Gary Warrick. 2016. "Archaeology as Partnerships in Practice: A Reply to La Salle and Hutchings." *Canadian Journal of Archaeology* 40(1): 191–204.

Martindale, Andrew, and Susan Marsden. 2003. "Defining the Middle Period: (3500 BP to 1500 BP) in Tsimshian History through a Comparison of Archaeological and Oral Records." *BC Studies* 138/139: 13–50.

Martindale, Andrew, Susan Marsden, Katherine Patton, Angela Ruggles, Bryn Letham, Kisha Supernant, David Archer, Duncan McLaren, and Kenneth M Ames. 2017a. "The Role of Small Villages in Northern Tsimshian Territory from Oral and Archaeological Records." *Journal of Social Archaeology* 17(3): 285–325.

Martindale, Andrew, Bryn Letham, Kisha Supernant, T. J. Brown, Jonathan Duelks, and Kenneth M. Ames. 2017b. "Monumentality and Urbanism in Northern Tsimshian Archaeology." *Hunter Gatherer Research* 3(1): 133–63.

Martindale, Andrew, and George Nicholas. 2014. "Archaeology as Federated Knowledge." *Canadian Journal of Archaeology* 38(2): 434–65.

Menzies, Charles. 2016. *People of the Saltwater: An Ethnography of Git lax m'oon*. Lincoln: Nebraska University Press.

Neylan, Susan. 2003. *The Heavans Are Changing: Nineteenth Century Missions and Tsimshian Christianity*. Montreal, QC and Kingston, ON: McGill-Queens University Press.

Oliver, Jeffrey M. 2014. "Native-Lived Colonialism and the Agency of Life Projects: A View from the Northwest Coast." In *Rethinking Colonial Pasts through Archaeology*. Edited by N. Ferris, R Harrison, and M. Wilcox. Oxford, UK: Oxford University Press, 76–102.

Ortner, Sherry B. 2016. "Dark Anthropology and Its Others: Theory since the Eighties." *Journal of Ethnographic Theory* 6(1): 47–73.

Rettig, Andrew. 1980. "A Nativist Movement at Metlakatla Mission." *BC Studies* 46: 28–39.

Ricoeur, Paul. 1966[1950]. *Freedom and Nature: The Voluntary and the Involuntary*. Translated by Erazim Kohak. Evanston, IL: Northwestern University Press.

Rosman, Abraham and Paula G. Rubel. 1971. *Feasting with Mine Enemy: Rank and Exchange among Northwest Coast Societies*. Prospect Heights, IL: Waveland Press.

Stahl, Anne B. 2002. "Colonial Entanglements and the Practices of Taste: An Alternative to Logocentric Approaches," *American Anthropologist* 104(3): 827–45.

Sterritt, Neil J., Susan Marsden, Robert Galois, Peter R. Grant, and Richard Overstall. 1998. *Tribal Boundaries in the Nass Watershed*. Vancouver: UBC Press.

Usher, Jean. 1974. *William Duncan of Metlakatla: A Victorian Missionary in British Columbia*. Ottawa, ON: National Museums of Canada.

Wagner, Henry R., and W. A. Newcome. 1938a. "The Journal of Jacinto Caamaño. Part 1" Translated by Capt. Harold Grenfell *B.C. Historical Quarterly* 2(3): 189–222, (4): 265–301.

Wagner, Henry R., and W. A. Newcome. 1938b. "The Journal of Jacinto Caamaño. Part 2" Translated by Capt. Harold Grenfell, *B.C. Historical Quarterly* 2(4): 265–302, (4): 265–301.

Wellcome, Henry S. 1887. *The Story of Metlakahtla*. New York: Saxon.

Chapter 12

Crisis and Transformation in the Bight of Benin at the Dawn of the Atlantic Trade

Gérard L. Chouin and Olanrewaju Blessing Lasisi

Eustache Delafosse stood on the bridge of La Mondadine, a small Flemish caravel that had left the port of Bruges a few months earlier. His future had never been less certain and, at that moment, he likely could not have imagined that he would live to write an account of his journey to Guinea. The day before, in the early hours of January 7, 1480, four Portuguese vessels had taken advantage of the mist to surprise the interloper. A few warning shots had sufficed to overpower the Flemish ship.[1]

Delafosse's task had been to sail along the West African coast to barter his master's trade goods for spices and gold. This was a profitable but risky business. Vessels armed by the Portuguese crown jealously watched over these recently discovered shores of Atlantic Africa, seizing non-Portuguese ships and threatening to hang the crew members of a growing number of interlopers that challenged their monopoly. The capture of Delafosse offers exceptional insight into the earliest Portuguese activities in the Gulf of Guinea. Particularly significant is Delafosse's account of the resale on the Coast of Mina of enslaved Africans purchased by the Portuguese in the Bight of Benin, the earliest evidence we know of a practice that continued well into the sixteenth century.[2] While Delafosse found himself reduced to selling his trade goods to the benefit of his Portuguese captors, he took mental note of the movements of Portuguese ships. Within a few days of his capture, he observed the departure of two caravels to the east, and their return by mid-February with a cargo of about 200 slaves each.[3] Most of them, he later wrote, were sold at "*la minne d'Or*," the name of the site where, two years later in 1482, Diogo de Azambuja would supervise the construction of the *Castelo São Jorge da Mina*.[4] This mention of a Portuguese-led interregional trade in captives from one point on the Gulf of Guinea to another, decades before the beginning of the trans-Atlantic slave trade, serves as this chapter's departure point. Why would large numbers of enslaved Africans be readily available in the Bight of Benin in the 1470s, while in great demand elsewhere? What were the long-term demographic, sociopolitical, and economic dynamics at work to generate such a regional pattern?

Unfree Labor in the Gulf of Guinea in the Late Fifteenth Century

Under the leadership of Fernão Gomes, a handful of Portuguese explorers had arrived in sight of modern Ghana in 1471, before pursuing their explorations in the Bight of Benin and Biafra in 1472. They were the first Europeans to establish contact with the populations living along the coast and beyond the seashore, up some of the rivers where the Portuguese were able to sail. They quickly understood that, to maximize profit, they could exchange not only European goods for valuable African products, but also carry high-value African goods from where they were produced or available for export to where they were in demand (see fig. 12.1).

The Portuguese were probably not the originators of such regional circuits of supply and demand; instead, they likely inserted themselves into preexisting, lagoonal networks of exchange and coastal trade that connected distant parts of West Africa. Caravels were faster and could carry much heavier cargos than even the largest West African canoes, resulting in both a rapid increase in the volume of available goods and more rapid circulation. Early Portuguese commercial activities in the Gulf of Guinea also prefigured the later Atlantic triangular trade, when slaves sent to the West Indies from West Africa would be bartered for sugar or other plantation products, which in turn were carried to Europe and transformed into financial capital. For late-fifteenth-century Portuguese agents at work in the Gulf of Guinea, the prime African commodity was not sugar or even slaves, but gold, which they principally obtained from the littoral of modern Ghana. To increase purchases of the precious metal, the Portuguese were keen to meet the local demand for both European and African goods. The Bight of Benin rapidly emerged as a secondary market where Europeans acquired African luxury items for resale on the Coast of Mina. There, they saturated the market with a large variety of goods, attempted to contain African and European competition alike,

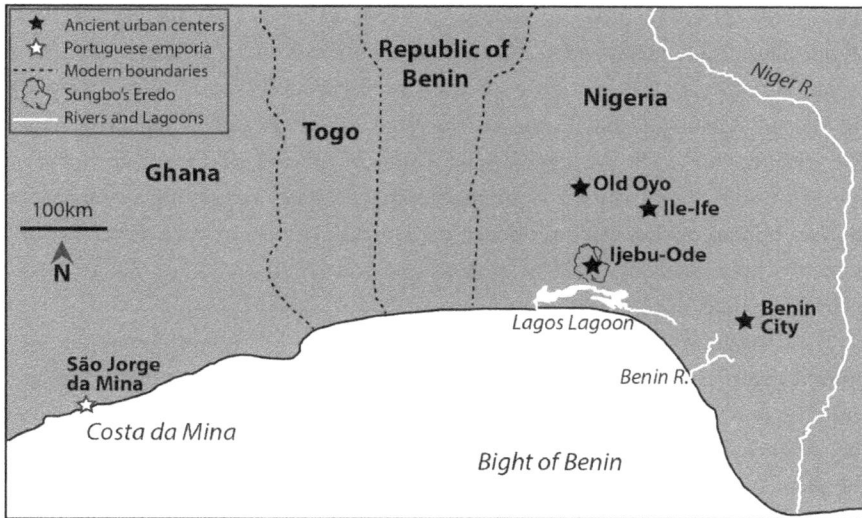

Figure 12.1. The Gulf of Guinea between the Portuguese emporium of São Jorge da Mina and the Ijebu and Benin polities, main players in the interregional slave trade between the Costa da Mina in the West and the Slave Rivers area in the East. (Illustration prepared by Gérard Chouin ©Mission Archéologique d'Ife-Sungbo)

and gradually established themselves as purveyors of luxury commodities in long-distance trade circuits.

The dearth of evidence supporting our claim that the Portuguese placed themselves in preexisting economic circuits results mainly from the compartmentalization of historical and archaeological research in the Gulf of Guinea. To date, most research efforts have focused on bounded cultural areas on different points of the coast rather than on regional perspectives and interconnectedness. The modern maritime landscape is also different from that of the fifteenth century, given that ancient lagoonal waterscapes were impacted by large-scale environmental transformations in the twentieth century and now form a series of disjointed bodies of water.

Robin Law is one of the few historians who have attempted to place this "important medium of lateral communication" along the West African coast and its environs in its larger, historical context (Law 1989, 222; also see Chouin 2017, 612–13). On the basis of eighteenth- and nineteenth-century European documentary evidence, he argued for the existence before the twentieth century of an extensive network of waterways connecting—at least seasonally—an area stretching from the Volta River, in modern Ghana, to the Niger Delta, and possibly beyond

(Law 1989, 213–17). These interlocked waterways, which later became "feeders" of the Slave Trade (Law 1989, 222–24), probably existed long before the arrival of the Portuguese. The best early evidence of the importance of such a network for the pre-Atlantic regional economy may be found on early Portuguese maps. For instance, the 1571 Portuguese map *Costa da África e da Guiné até à ilha de São Tomé* notes "*dos canalos*" [two canals] east of "*Jabu*," suggesting the existence of early human-made waterways between the Lekki Lagoon and the River Benin.[5] Some of these canals may still be visible in coastal Ondo State, Nigeria, but their archaeology and history are yet to be researched.

The Portuguese were not oblivious of the existence of inland waterways, and they utilized these to their advantage. They also discovered that while enslaved people could be procured from local polities in the Bight of Benin, on the Coast of Mina the internal demand for slaves exceeded the number offered. We do not know if the circulation of unfree people predates the arrival of the Portuguese; however, Portuguese maritime trade would have considerably facilitated such a trade. The sale of slaves from the Bight of Benin boosted the trade in gold at São Jorge da Mina and became a significant part of the new African Atlantic economy up to the 1530s, with Portuguese settlers on the island of São Tomé gradually playing an increasing role as brokers in the provision of slaves purchased from the mainland (Rodney 1969; Vogt 1973).[6] In her quantitative study of this early Portuguese slave trade, Ivana Elbl (1997) estimated that from 1475 to 1499 at least 7,500 slaves were displaced from the Bight of Benin to the Mina Coast of Mina.[7] These numbers seem to increase significantly during the first decades of the sixteenth century, although from the 1510s, a growing number of slaves shipped to the Coast of Mina may have originated from western Central Africa (Elbl 1997, 71–72).

Beyond the analysis of the quantitative data and the place occupied by these slaves in the Portuguese Atlantic economy, few studies have attempted to explain why slaves were available for sale in the Bight of Benin and why fifteenth- and sixteenth-century African merchants from the Coast of Mina's hinterlands were eager to acquire them. Walter Rodney and Ivor Wilks may be the only scholars who have attempted to make historical sense of these imports of slaves. In his article of 1969, Rodney first linked the import of slaves and the economic growth in Ghana's hinterland, stimulated by the gold trade. In an influential essay published in 1977, Wilks built on Rodney's argument to articulate his "big bang" theory, which suggested that the development of political complexity in the forests of Ghana coincided with the opening of the Atlantic trade.[8] The change from demographically weak bands of hunters-gatherers living in the forests to settled, agrarian communities was at the heart of this theory.[9]

Access to unfree labor was a key ingredient of the model, as the agricultural revolution Wilks envisaged could not have taken place before the massive, labor-intensive clearing of the pristine tropical forest. In this context, slaves sold by the Portuguese at São Jorge da Mina served the "big bang" theory well. In the words of Wilks,

> The demand for labour in those forests led Akan entrepreneurs to offer gold in exchange for slaves. That accession of labour—or such at least is the burden of my argument—was a sine qua non of the agricultural revolution in the forest lands. (1982, 239)

Wilks's theoretical framework inspired several generations of scholars, who added the production of gold to his functional interpretation of the early import of slaves.[10] However, in 2010, the publication of archaeological evidence establishing the presence of a dense network of entrenched agrarian communities in the forests of Ghana long before the opening of the Atlantic trade marked the end of the domination of the "big bang" paradigm (Chouin & DeCorse 2010). The same article suggested that the communities settled in the forests of Ghana had been radically affected by a demographic crisis in the mid-fourteenth century, possibly in the context of the Second Pandemic of Plague.[11] Within the framework of the plague hypothesis, the demand for slaves in the late fifteenth century could be understood as a strategy to cope with an acute labor crisis resulting from a demographic collapse in the mid-fourteenth century. Such a crisis would have been aggravated by the increase in mining, trading, and farming activities as well as escalated competition for exotic goods, all resulting from the newly established Atlantic connections. In the context of a generalized labor shortage, access to labor was a luxury. As such, imported slaves may need to be understood not only as sources of labor, but also as sources of wealth and prestige for their acquirers. In fact, we suggest that whereas Portuguese traders saw enslaved Africans brought to the Coast of Mina as trade items, they were more like prestige commodities to those who received them and were not traded but, rather, exchanged along channels of the regional prestige economy. Dependents eventually found their place as providers of labor, wealth, and prestige—and fecundity, since their reproductive capacity also would have contributed to the accelerated demographic recovery of their host communities.

But why were slaves readily available for the Portuguese to purchase in the Bight of Benin? In contrast to the pioneering investigations of the early demand for slaves on the Coast of Mina, researchers have yet to examine the supply side of the traffic. Curiously, the ready availability of slaves in the Bight of Benin, at the very beginning of the Atlantic trade, does not seem to have stimulated questions among scholars, as though the procurement of slaves was an organic and essential function of early modern African polities. We believe it is necessary to question such a foregone conclusion and inquire into the historical processes that allowed societies of the Gulf of Guinea to deprive themselves of the labor force, productivity, and fertility of thousands of individuals, and this possibly in the aftermath of a demographic calamity. In fact, the disproving of the "big bang" theory and the emergence of the globally relevant Black Death hypothesis complicates the narrative about the early slave-trading activities in the Gulf of Guinea. If, as we contend, a plague struck sub-Saharan Africa in ways similar to the way it did in the rest of the Old World in the second half of the fourteenth century, then populations of the Coast of Mina and the Bight of Benin would have experienced similar demographic setbacks. Yet, the same cause produced radically different strategies regarding the production, management, and consumption of unfree labor. On the Coast of Mina, documented evidence for the acquisition of unfree labor fits well with the expected response of a society recovering from a demographic crisis. In contrast, the export of slaves in the Bight of Benin emerges as an unexpected, counterintuitive phenomenon.

Here, we explore avenues to replace the early production of slaves for export in historical context. We focus our attention on Ijebu, a polity first encountered by the Portuguese on the Lagos Lagoon in the early 1470s, and one that participated in the provision of slaves for the market of the Coast of Mina. We rely primarily on archaeological work conducted in 2016 under the Ife-Sungbo Archaeological Project, to propose an exploratory narrative that reconciles the plague hypothesis with the documented traffic in slaves in the Gulf of Guinea. While open to evaluation, we believe this narrative helps explain why West African polities entered into the Atlantic world the way they did. In fact, we firmly believe the making of the Atlantic world cannot be understood when severed from its pre-Atlantic antecedents. We contend that the Atlantic world did not impose its rules on the old orders in a top-to-bottom fashion, but plugged itself into a variety of existing systems and transformed them from within.

Raising Lazarus:
Reassessing Early Ijebu's Historiography and Archaeology

The historiography of Ijebu is overwhelmingly dominated by studies of the recent periods, especially after 1892, when the polity was incorporated into the British colonial empire. Ijebu resistance against free circulation of goods and people across its territory was a constant of its foreign policy throughout the nineteenth century, and its opposition to the growing influence of the British Colony in nearby Lagos spiraled into a short but bloody conflict (Aderibigbe 1962; Law 1973; Oduwobi 2004). This conquest led to swift changes in Ijebu.

In contrast with the later periods, there are few documentary sources that provide information on Ijebu prior to the seventeenth century, and most have been conveniently discussed by Law (1986). The first and best known is an excerpt from Pacheco Pereira's *Chronicle*, written during the first decade of the sixteenth century but including information he had probably obtained in the 1490s. Pereira provides the first mention of the ditch-and-bank system of Ijebu—"*muito grande caua*"—as well as what is likely the first mention of *Awujale*—or "*Agusale*"—the royal Ijebu title (Mauny 1956, 130; Law 1986, 246). He is also the earliest author to mention the availability of slaves for purchase in Ijebu, in addition to ivory: "*ho comercio que aquy pode haver, sam escravos, que se vendem por manilhas de latam a doze e quinze manilhas a peça, e alguūn dentes de elephantes*"[12] (Mauny 1956, 130). With Pacheco Pereira, Sebastião Lopez's map of 1558 and the travel accounts of Joshua Ulsheimer (1603) and Derrik Ruiter (1623) are among the few early European documentary sources on Ijebu (Law 1986).

Oral traditions occupy a prominent place in the historiography of Ijebu, and they afford potential insight into the past. Echoes of Ijebu oral traditions were first published in 1845 by French scholar and administrator Marie-Armand d'Avezac de Castera-Macaya (Lloyd 1967; Oduwobi 2003). This fascinating dialogical document attempted a comprehensive description of the people, institutions, and geography of early nineteenth-century Ijebu but failed to provide the reader with much historical depth. D'Avezac's informant Ochi-Fêkouè Dê remembered the names of only three Ijebu rulers, including the one reigning when he was enslaved. The oral traditions he shared with d'Avezac are shallow and limited to his own lineage group. J. A. Payne's 1893 *Table of Principal Events in Yoruba History* comes next as the only other example of published information directly related to individuals of Ijebu descent before the twentieth century and is limited to a king list starting with Payne's own grandfather, Gbelegbuwa (ca. 1760–1790). This limited king list has often been reproduced in later published local histories, although variations exist.[13]

Beyond king lists, limited documented traditions exist that pertain to early Ijebu history. Narratives discussing the origins of the Ijebu people or Ijebu kingship started with controversial statements by Samuel Johnson in his *History of the Yorùbás*.[14] These contrasted with locally recorded histories derived from Ijebu—rather than Oyo—traditions, in the line of that published by Epega in 1919.[15] However, Ijebu-sourced traditions also do not agree on the details and sequencing of early Ijebu history. As noted by Tunde Oduwobi, they "present a confusing picture."[16] Most recount several waves of migrations, often originating from or at least passing through Ile-Ife. In a remarkable analysis of oral traditions collected or published before 1960, Oduwobi (2006) disentangled the main narratives in circulation and provided historical context to explain their divergences. He convincingly demonstrated that one of these strands, based on the fictitious character of Olú-Iwa, was probably a calculated response to Johnson's claim of the slave status of the founders of the Ijebu polity (Oduwobi 2006, 150–1). He further suggested that another strand postulating the existence of an earlier kingdom called Idoko deserved more critical examination. Indeed, during the first half of the twentieth century, many communities in Ijebu attempted to take advantage of the weakening of the central authority of Ijebu-Ode, to claim autonomy on the basis of reinvented traditions.[17]

Once the twentieth-century, politically motivated additions are set aside, what remains of Ijebu traditions of origin is strikingly homogenous. The core narrative includes two layers articulated through the character of *Obanta*, presented as the founder of the Kingdom of Ijebu, and related to the Ife royal house. The two layers are compressed memorial devices of Ijebu history that worked within the codes of oral traditions. They form a collective myth of unity easy to apprehend and to adhere to by the commoners, while also encapsulating higher levels of interpretation accessible only to a few initiates. First, there is a pre-Obanta period tentatively characterized by autonomous towns (*ode*) forming a confederation headed by *Osi*, an ancient title of authority comparable to the modern *Qba*, which may represent "an abstraction of political headship in pre-kingdom times" (Oduwobi 2006, 150). The arrival of *Obanta* from Ife marks the end of this early stage of Ijebu history and coincides with deep institutional reforms and a process that transforms Ijebu into a tightly centralized polity, which we will refer to here as "kingdom." There is no evidence in Ijebu oral traditions that the transfer of power from *Osi* to *Obanta* was a violent one. On the contrary, one gets the impression that the newcomer was invited to take over the destiny of the Ijebu people.[18]

Traditions are not self-explanatory about the process that led to the transition from *Osi* to *Obanta*. Following Oduwobi suggestion, however, we believe *Osi* was not an historical character but rather the embodiment of a particular phase of Ijebu history that ended with the rise of *Obanta*.[19] The memory of a shift from an old order to a new one is clearly present in Ijebu traditions and may coincide with a major crisis that might have brought a sociopolitical crisis and a dynastic reshuffle. During the *Obanta* period, Ijebu was reborn, and, as Oduwobi (2006) suggested, this era can be equated with that of the formation of the Ijebu kingdom as a centralized polity ruled by a king (*Awujale*) tracing his origins from outside Ijebu and who emerged both as a warrior and as a religious leader.[20]

Additional clues to Ijebu's past are provided by archaeology although, in comparison with many parts of the Yoruba and Edoid-speaking world, Ijebu appears as a near archaeological terra incognita. The limited number of published scholarly productions falls into two groups: on the one hand, a small number of miscellaneous publications with very limited overlap in content; on the other hand, the bulk of the work related to the monumental enclosure often referred to as Sungbo's Eredo.[21] Here, we will focus exclusively on the latter.

Sungbo's Eredo is the largest single human-made monument in sub-Saharan Africa. This formidable barrier, five to twenty meters high when measured from the bottom of the trench to the top of its bank, forms a circa 170-kilometer-long, irregular loop encompassing an area of more than 1,000 square kilometers. Ijebu-Ode is located near its center (see fig. 12.2 and 12.3 on page 294).

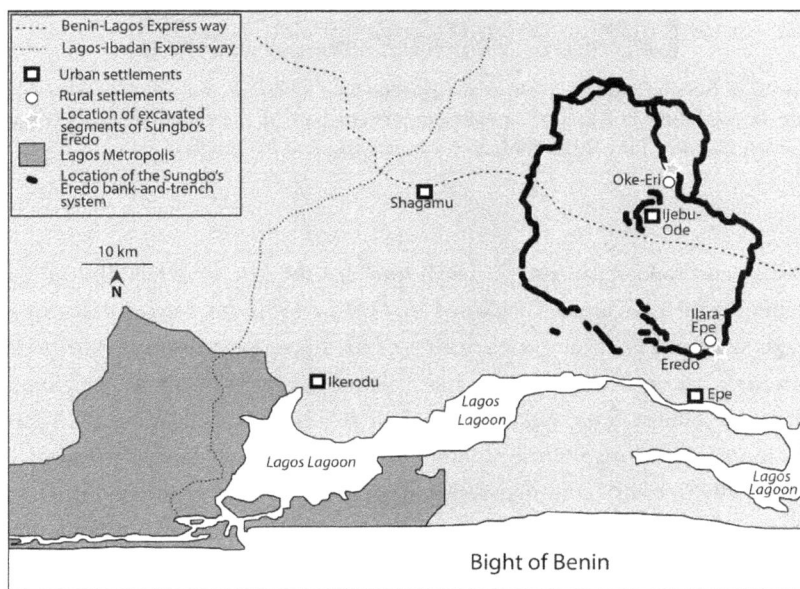

Figure 12.2. Location of excavated archaeological sites along the monumental Sungbo's Eredo enclosure, probable boundary of early-fifteenth-century Ijebu. (Illustration prepared by Gérard Chouin on a map of Sungbo's Eredo published by Patrick Darling [1998: 56] ©Mission Archéologique d'Ife-Sungbo)

Figure 12.3. Sungbo's Eredo. View of the current state of the monumental ditch-and-bank system at the locality of Eredo, on the southeastern part of the monument. (Photograph by Gérard Chouin, June 2015 ©Mission Archéologique d'Ife-Sungbo)

British anthropologist Peter C. Lloyd provided the first academic description of this monumental enclosure. Published in *Odù* in 1959, his brief article provides a rough sketch of its layout, a discussion of its topography, some attempt to synthesize its place in oral traditions, and a tentative discussion of its function and chronology. Almost forty years later, British scholar Patrick Darling published a much more detailed map of the monument, largely based on extensive field surveys (Darling 1997, 1998). The first archaeological excavations were conducted from 2011 to 2014 on the bank of Sungbo's Eredo at Oke-Eri, in Ogun State, under the supervision of David Aremu. Two five-by-five meter test units were sunk into the bank, exposing its stratigraphy and the ancient surface on which it was erected (Aremu et al. 2013; Chouin 2014; Lasisi & Aremu 2016). Radiocarbon dates obtained by Darling and Ogiogwa from uncontrolled locations in different parts of the monument, including Oke-Eri, pointed to the eleventh to thirteenth centuries CE (Chouin 2014, 43).[22] Another date obtained at Oke-Eri by Aremu's team suggested even earlier dates, a few thousand years BCE (see Aremu et al. 2013, 17). These different results fueled controversies about the chronology of Sungbo's Eredo and its place in the long-term history of sub-Saharan Africa and Ijebu.

The Ife-Sungbo Archaeological Project was launched in 2015 with a focus on clarifying the long-term chronology of Ife and Ijebu. In June 2016, we excavated a segment of the southeastern part of Sungbo's Eredo, on the campus of the Augustine University at Ilara-Epe (see fig. 12.4).

For the first time, we documented a complete profile of the earthworks and recorded the stratigraphy from the top of its internal bank (at Augustine 1 and 4 sites) to the original bottom of its ditch (at Augustine 1 site only).[23] Using samples

Figure 12.4. Sungbo's Eredo. View of the partially excavated ditch (left) and a section of the inner bank (right) of the enclosure, Augustine 1 site, Augustine University at Ilara-Epe, June 2016. Note the lower, darker layer marking the old surface onto which the bank was elevated at the turn of the fifteenth century. (Photograph by Patrice Georges ©Mission Archéologique d'Ife-Sungbo)

recorded in their stratigraphic context, we provided nine new radiocarbon dates, providing a strong chronological framework to the interpretation of the stratigraphy of the ditch-and-bank complex. Five of these dates form a very homogenous series, securely dating the construction of the monument to the turn of the fourteenth and fifteenth centuries (Chouin et al. 2016).[24] Earlier dates obtained from the old soils under the bank suggest agrarian activities beginning at least in the mid–first millennium CE.[25] Although still very limited in scale, results from the excavations of Sungbo's Eredo provide us with the first tangible chronological evidence of a process of sociopolitical change whose feeble echoes still structure Ijebu oral traditions. On the basis of this newly established, firm chronological anchor in the deep past, we believe we can extend and renew the historical narrative of early Ijebu and develop an understanding of why this polity entered into the Atlantic world as one of the early regional providers of unfree labor.

Long-Term Transformations in Ijebu: A Tentative Historical Narrative

Results from the 2016 archaeological study of Sungbo's Eredo open a series of new questions about early historical processes in the Gulf of Benin, questions that push back the historiographical horizon marking the early making of the Atlantic world. This, in turn, may enable us to reframe the opening of the Atlantic trade from being a heuristic starting point in historical knowledge to an event entangled in a much larger process of change and continuity. Why did Ijebu enter into the Atlantic trade the way it did? Why was Ijebu willing and able to provide enslaved individuals to the early Portuguese vessels in the Lagos Lagoon in the late fourteenth century? We think these questions can be answered only if placed in their proper pre-Atlantic context. However fragile and fragmented our knowledge of the latter may be, we believe this is a worthwhile historiographical frontier to investigate.

We first need to ask what had happened in the late fourteenth century that resulted in the building of such a monumental embankment and to address both the function and meaning of the enclosure. There is little doubt that the embankment marked the boundaries of the Ijebu polity at this particular time in its history. This action of marking the boundaries is remembered in oral traditions in a narrative that sees *Ajebu* marking the borders of Ijebu while *Olode* does the same for its capital (Ogunkoya 1956, 49). In fact, the stratigraphy of the bank still clearly indicates an early phase in its construction: surface soil taken out from where the trench was to be dug was packed where the bank was to be built. This points to a powerful hand that translated in concrete steps the will of a centralized authority. The necessity to mark boundaries, however, cannot explain the massive size of the monument. Elsewhere, the first author has suggested that earthworks in West Africa should be apprehended through a multifunctional interpretative framework (Chouin & DeCorse 2010, 141). In fact, the monument not only would have marked the boundaries of the redefined polity during the *Obanta* period; it also probably played a defensive role while enhancing the prestige of the central authority responsible for planning the pharaonic project and mobilizing labor to execute it. As such, Sungbo's Eredo can be interpreted as the founding statement of a new dynasty responsible for the upheaval of the Ijebu political system. Such a grand statement was about power as much as governance, about wealth in people and the readiness to protect this demographic capital. It was a message addressed both to external forces—power, wealth, and capacity to defend it—and to internal parties—unity, order, and subjection. Clearly, this message was not presented in a regional vacuum. Excavations of the city walls of Benin City provided a radiocarbon date (unfortunately unique) that fits with that of Sungbo Eredo's chronology.[26] Dates provided by Darling on the dense network of earthworks that surround Benin City also placed these in a range between the 1270s and the 1400s.[27] In spite of the absence of strong chronologies in the region, it seems probable that the construction of Sungbo's Eredo echoed similar large-scale ditch-and-bank projects emerging in the area between the late thirteenth and the early fifteenth century. Beyond the development of earthwork systems, there is much convergence between Ijebu and Benin during this period, starting with the pervasive account of the Benin origins of the founder of the new Ijebu kingdom. Particularly relevant is the fact that both polities went through a political crisis that led to the emergence of new stranger-dynasties led by warrior-kings that imposed more centralized forms of governance.[28] The passage from Ogisoship to Obaship in Benin, and from Osiship to Obantaship in Ijebu may have resulted from the same process of collapse and subsequent reformation/reconstruction of these political entities on redefined social, political, and spiritual foundations.

Echoes of a crisis between the fall of the *Ogiso* dynasty and the rise of its successor still resonate in Edo oral traditions in the form of *Osogan*, a human-eating monster that could only be killed by the red-hot hammer of a blacksmith—a possible allusion to the role played by members of the cult of *Ogun* in the transition and the establishment of the new political order (Barnes & Girshick Ben-Amos 1997). While this is not the place to revisit Edo historiography, we wonder if the evil monster *Osogan* could be understood as a personification of death that emerged in response to mass mortality and disorder—in effect, an avatar comparable to the Grim Reaper that came to prominence in Western representations of death in the wake of the second pandemic of plague?[29] In fact, we suggest that the succession crises and transformations recorded in the oral traditions of Ijebu and Benin may echo an episode of great mortality due to the spread of the plague during the Second Pandemic. A unique picture of such an event, we believe, is encapsulated in the mass burial discovered by Graham Connah in Benin City, on the Clerk's Quarters site, in the fill of a well-like cistern.[30]

In the light of this scenario, the earthworks expresses the importance of demographic wealth in these societies. What better signal could be sent to neighboring polities about one's demographic recovery that a labor-intensive monument of the scale of Sungbo's Eredo? At the same time, if the demographic recess was as catastrophic as we think it may have been, it is not surprising that regional polities and their elites became weakened and undermined to the point of being forced into political transitions. It is not surprising either to witness the emergence of military elites and warrior-kings in environments that must have been threatened by social collapse and disorder. We should also expect the new elites to take measures to control the movements of its surviving population while competing with other regional polities to attract new communities and to force others to resettle within their realms. The forced relocation of raided individuals and communities to empty lands, together with the military conquest and integration of new, adjacent territories and their settlements would have been a fundamental feature of these militaristic, centralized, postplague polities looking for ways to reconstitute a solid demographic basis. In this context, large defensive earthworks such as Sungbo's Eredo would have served the dual purpose of controlling population movement and protecting settlements, while at the same time inscribing on the landscape a demonstration of the strength, wealth, and resolve of a new leading elite.

Early Benin, as described by early European witnesses and documented in the sixteenth-century bronze plates kept in the king's palace before its sack by the British in 1897, was such a society. Unfortunately, we do not have equivalent source material for Ijebu, but the structure and functioning of this early polity was probably analogous to that of Benin: a society constantly at war with surrounding communities, dominated by its horse-mounted military elite, possibly the heir to small groups of mounted men that raided neighboring communities at the end of the fourteenth century. After all, according to oral traditions collected by Jacob U. Egharevba, it is Oranyan/Oranmiyan, the warrior from Ife and founder of the Oba dynasty in Benin, who is credited with bringing the first horse to the area (Law 1980, 21–22, esp. 21n144); and it is from Ife that Obanta is said to have originated. The wide ditches and banks of early Ijebu and of Benin would have been very effective in breaking the momentum of mobile groups of horsemen specialized in raiding and capturing dependents, and we need to wonder if the introduction of the horse—probably the smaller, pony breed that constituted the original horse population of West Africa (Law 1980, 24–27)—in warfare and raiding during this period did not play a crucial role in the development of territorial embankments as a passive yet effective anticavalry mechanism.

Examining the course of events in the Gulf of Benin in the fourteenth and fifteenth centuries leads us to situate in a deeper past the response of the Ijebus and their neighbors to the early Portuguese demand for enslaved labor intended for the regional market. The fact that the Portuguese were able to obtain relatively large numbers of individuals from polities along the "Slave Rivers" is an indication that these polities were engaged in active competition over the control of human communities in the area. Through warfare and raiding, these militaristic polities seem to have been very successful in recovering from the demographic crisis that shaped them. So successful were local elites that they accumulated considerable numbers of captives, which could be mobilized for agricultural labor, military service, sacrifices, and hyperpolygamy. Since the accumulation of dependents was a source of wealth that translated into increased power and prestige, it is probable that part of the captives—especially women—circulated as gifts along with other prestige goods such as textiles, metals, and ivories on specific channels of redistribution largely controlled by the central authority, but also on long-distance routes that crossed much larger territories. This could explain the ready availability of captives in Ijebu, Benin, and neighboring coastal areas defined loosely by the Portuguese as the "Slave Rivers."

A rapid examination of the goods brought by the Portuguese in the late fifteenth and early sixteenth centuries shows that they corresponded perfectly to the categories of prestige goods that the African elite groups they dealt with had defined long before the opening of the Atlantic trade (Herbert 1984, 125–32; Alpern 1995). Textiles, glass beads, and copper goods, especially, were rare and prestigious items that had long only been percolating in limited quantities from North Africa, besides possible other small production centers in sub-Saharan Africa. Whereas Portuguese and other early European actors of the trade thought of themselves as merchants, they actually plugged themselves into preexisting networks that, from an African perspective, did not belong to the realm of trade but to that of diplomatic relations. Such a prestige goods economy was distinct from trade in foodstuffs and other ordinary items, for it was not driven by some form of financial profit or surplus-generating process. It was a domain exclusively and closely controlled by the king and his entourage, because power belonged to whoever could control the flow of prestige goods through a particular territory and regulate their redistribution. Whereas the Portuguese thought of "purchasing" captives, they actually did not. They obtained them in return for other prestige items that were thought of as countergifts, not as commodities in the mercantile sense of this term. From the perspective of a prestige economy, the arrival of maritime foreigners was equivalent to a geostrategic reversal, the opening of a new frontier in place of a former economic dead-end, the promise of an unlimited supply in prestige goods that was likely to overturn the prevailing regional diplomatic hierarchy and propel coastal polities from the bottom of the prestige goods circulatory pyramid—as mainly consumers on the receiving end—to its top—as primary and large-scale brokers. It was not, however, without risk, as it needed to extend violence to procure captives and was exposed to a flooding of the prestige "market" with excess supply of prestige goods, leading to a deflation of their symbolic value that could in turn destabilize the elites who depended on them to secure their privileged status and to maintain social order.

Notes

Field research and writing were supported by funds from the GlobAfrica ANR Project; French Ministry of Foreign Affairs; College of William & Mary; IFRA-Nigeria; INRAP; IMAf; ITB Nigeria Ltd., and Total Nigeria Ltd.

1. Escudier 1992, 28–31.

2. Vogt 1973; Elbl 1997.

3. The Portuguese referred to the region where they purchased captives as the "Slave Rivers" (Ryder 1959, 294). This area stretched approximately from the Mahin River (Rio Primeiro) to the Ramos River, in the Gulf of Benin. Here, we use this same definition, extended slightly westward to include the parts of the Lagos Lagoon under Ijebu influence where the Portuguese also procured captives.

4. See Hair 1994.

5. A reproduction of an excerpt of this map is available in Lovejoy and Ojo (2015, 354). The authors translate *canalos* as *channels*, and suggest that they refer to the Lagos Lagoon. We believe the choice of the word *canal* rather points to artificial waterways east of the Lekki Lagoon.

6. Elbl (1997, 44) estimated 10 percent of the gold procured on the Coast of Mina was paid for in slaves. Vogt (1973, 454) arrived at a relatively similar estimate of 15 percent.

7. This figure was calculated on the basis of Elbl's estimates (1997, 70). Documentary evidence is scanty for this period, and the figure is probably on the low side.

8. Later articles built on this early framework (e.g., Wilks 1982a, 1982b, 1982c). The 1977 chapter was later republished in *Forest of Gold* (1993).

9. For critiques of Wilks's "big-bang" theory, see Chouin 2012, Pavanello 2012.

10. See for instance Kea 1982, 200–1; Shumway 2011, 26–27.

11. Chouin 2018. This emerging plague hypothesis seeks to relate the late fourteenth-century hiatus often observed across Africa with the second plague pandemic documented in Europe and in the Mediterranean world during the same period. It suggests that plague spread to Africa and impacted African societies.

12. "Trade one can do here is that of slaves, which are sold for brass manilas at the rate of 12 to 15 manilas per slave, and that of elephant teeth" (translation by first author). This differs from the translation proposed by Law (1986).

13. For a close study of published Ijebu king lists, see Oduwobi (2017). Beyond Payne's king list, he identifies three others, published by O. Odutola (1946, 5–6), J. A. Olusola (1968, 36–37), and B. Adebonojo (1990, 9–21).

14. The manuscript was originally completed in 1897, and then lost. It was later rewritten by Samuel Johnson's brother and finally published in 1921.

15. We were able to check only the second edition of Epega's work, published in 1934.

16. Oduwobi 2006, 149. Oduwobi's presentation and analysis of early Ijebu traditions is a fascinating analysis of the different narratives published and those concealed in the colonial archives.

17. See, for instance, Oduwobi 2000.

18. This needs to be taken with a grain of salt, but it perfectly fits the "phenomenon of stranger-king" regularly commented on by anthropologists in Africa, a phenomenon little understood from a historical perspective. See, for instance, Haour 2013, 33–38.

19. *Obanta* may have been a variation for *orisha Obatala*, the dying and rising spiritual entity often associated with early Ife.

20. Oduwobi remarked that the *Awujale* is addressed by the epithet *Ajogun* (warrior). On the early kings of Ijebu as warrior-kings and their possible links to Benin, see also Oduwobi, 2017. The *Awujale* tutelary deity was the object of a centralized cult (*Agemo* cult) with a hierarchy of priests located in all districts of the kingdom.

21. See Fagg 1959; Calvocoressi 1978; Momim 1989; Olukole and Aremu 2002.

22. Particularly Ketu II WSU 4819 and Oke-Eri Beta-346665. A third date of 730 ± 30 BP from Oke-Eri was also published in Aremu et al. 2013, 17.

23. We did not find evidence of the existence of an outer bank.

24. These five dates were derived from charcoal samples collected either from the bottom of the ditch (Beta-446302) or from the base of the bank (Beta-446299, Beta-446301, Beta-446303, and Beta-446304).

25. See Beta-446307, Beta-423707, and Beta-427251. Beta 446300, anchored in the first millennium BCE, was probably the result of an old wood effect. A detailed discussion is available in Chouin et al. 2016, and is currently being developed for publication.

26. See Connah 1975, 80–89, 98–106, and 182. The date is N-379, given by the author as AD 1340±105. Once processed in Calib Rev. 7.02, we obtain 1202–1488 CE at a 96 percent confidence interval and, more significantly, 1288–1411 CE at a 68 percent confidence interval.

27. See Sutton 1982, 309, 312. Here, only Birm-952a and Birm-952b were recalibrated using Calib. Rev. 7.02.

28. On such a political crisis, see Bondarenko and Roese 2004. We disagree with the chronological framework and interpretation proposed in the latter article, which appears to have been made to fit a predefined theory of social change. Curnow (2017, 5–7, 9, 28) adopts a chronological framework closer to ours; her discussion includes reference to disease, which are worth looking into. On related chronological issues with the king list of Benin, see Eisenhofer 1997.

29. On the evolution of the Grim Reaper, see for instance Magill 2013.

30. Feature 21, cutting II, contained at least forty-one individuals. See Connah 1975, 61–67, Rascovan et al. 2016, supplementary information, 2–3. Connah interpreted the mass burial as resulting from human sacrifices.

Works Cited

Adebonojo, Badejo O. 1990. *Itan Ido Ijebu* (A History of Ijebu). Lagos, Nigeria: John West.

Aderibigbe, Adeyemi B. 1962. "The Ijebu Expedition 1892: An Episode in the British Penetration of Nigeria Reconsidered." *Proceedings of the Leverhulme Inter-Collegiate History Conference, University College of Rhodesia and Nyasaland: 1960*, 267–82.

Alpern, Stanley. 1995. "What Africans Got for Their Slaves: A Master List of European Trade Goods." *History in Africa* 22, 5–43.

Aremu, David, A. Ogiogwa, Joan-Mary, Aleru, Jonathan O., Tubosun, Bolanle J., Ogunfolakan, Adisa, and Phillip, Oyelaran A. 2013. "Sungbo Eredo, Materiality, Ecology, and Society in Prehistoric Southwestern Nigeria." *West African Journal of Archaeology* 43(1): 1–21.

Barnes, Sandra T., and Paula Girshik Ben Amos. 1997. "Ogun, the Empire Builder." In *Africa's Ogun. Old World and New.* Edited by S. T. Barnes, 39–64. Bloomington and Indianapolis: Indiana University Press.

Bondarenko, Dmtri, and Peter M. Roese. 2004. "Between the Ogiso and Oba Dynasties: An Interpretation of Interregnum in the Benin Kingdom." *History in Africa* 31: 103–15.

Calvocoressi, David. 1978. *Rescue Excavation of the First Otunba Suna at Imodi, Ijebu-Ode, May 1977*, 6. Ibadan, Nigeria: Department of Archaeology, University of Ibadan.

Chouin, Gérard L. 2012. "The 'Big Bang' Theory Reconsidered: Framing Early Ghanaian History." *Transactions of the Historical Society of Ghana* 14: 13–40.

———. 2014. "Fossés, enceintes et peste noire en Afrique de l'Ouest forestière (500–1500 AD): Réflexions sous canopée." *Afrique: Archéologie & Arts* 9: 43–66.

———. 2017. "L'Afrique et la mer à l'époque moderne." In *The Sea in History—The Early Modern World.* Edited by Christian Buchet and Gérard Le Bouëdec. Woodbridge, UK and Rochester, NY: Boydell and Brewer, 609–21.

———. 2018. "Reflections on Plague in African History (14th–19th c.)." *Afriques: Débats, méthodes et terrains d'histoire* 8.

Chouin, Gérard L., and Christopher R. DeCorse. 2010. "Prelude to the Atlantic Trade: New Perspectives on Southern Ghana's Pre-Atlantic History (800–1500)." *The Journal of African History* 51(2): 123–45.

Chouin, Gérard L., Adisa Ogunfolakan, Bertrand Poissonnier, and Patrick Georges. 2016. Preliminary Report on Excavations at Ita yemoo, Ile-Ife, Osun State and Augustine University at Ilara, Ilara-Epe, Lagos State, May–June 2016. Williamsburg, VA.

Connah, Graham. 1975. *The Archaeology of Benin: Excavations and Other Researches in and around Benin City, Nigeria.* Oxford, UK: Oxford University Press.

Curnow, Kathy. 2007. "Sensemaking in Benin Kingdom Oral Traditions: Repetitive Recall of Actual and Traditional Enmity between the Ọba and the Ogiamiẹn." *Umẹwaẹn: Journal of Benin and ẹdo Studies* 2: 1–50.

Darling, Patrick. 1998. "Sungbo's Eredo, Southern Nigeria." *Nyame Akuma* 49: 55–61.

———. 1997. "Sungbo's Eredo: Africa Largest Monument." *Nigerian Field* 62: 113–129.

D'Avezac, Marie-Armand. 1845. *Notice sur le pays et le peuple des Yébous en Afrique.* Paris: Librairie Orientale de Mme Veuve Dondey-Dupré.

Eisenhofer, Stefan. 1997. "The Benin Kinglist/s: Some Questions of Chronology." *History in Africa* 24: 139–56.

Elbl, Ivana. 1997. "The Volume of the Early Atlantic Slave Trade, 1450–1521." *Journal of African History* 38(1): 31–75.

Epega, Onadele D. 1934. *Iwe itan Ijẹbu ati awọn ilu miran* (A History of Ijebu and Some Other Towns), 2d ed. Lagos, Nigeria: Ife-Olu Printing Works.

Escudier, Denis. 1992. *Voyage d'Eustache Delafosse sur la côte de Guinée, au Portugal & en Espagne (1479–1481).* Paris: Editions Chandeigne.

Fagg, William. 1959. "Grooved Rocks at Apoje Near Ijebu-Igbo, Western Nigeria." *Man* 59 (December): 205.

Hair, Paul Hedley E. 1994. *The Founding of the Castelo de São Jorge da Mina: An Analysis of Sources*. Madison: University of Wisconsin, African Studies Program.

Haour, Anne. 2013. *Outsiders & Strangers: An Archaeology of Liminality in West Africa*. Oxford, UK: Oxford University Press.

Herbert, Eugenia. W. 1984. *Red Gold of Africa: Copper in Precolonial History and Culture*. Madison: University of Wisconsin Press.

Kea, Ray. A. 1982. *Settlements, Trade and Polities in the Seventeenth-Century Gold Coast*. Baltimore, MD and London: Johns Hopkins University Press.

Lasisi, Olanrewaju B., and David A. Aremu. 2016. "New Lights on the Archaeology of Sungbo's Eredo, South-Western Nigeria." *Dig It: Flinders Journal of Australian Archaeology* 3: 54–63.

Law, Robin. 1980. *The Horse in West African History*. Oxford, UK: Oxford University Press.

———. 1984. "How Truly Traditional Is Our Traditional History? The Case of Samuel Johnson and the Recording of Yoruba Oral Tradition." *History in Africa* 11: 195–221.

———. 1986. "Early European Sources Relating to the Kingdom of Ijebu (1500–1700): A Critical Survey." *History in Africa* 13: 245–60.

———. 1989. "Between the Sea and the Lagoons: The Interaction of Maritime and Inland Navigation on the Precolonial Slave Coast" (Entre mer et lagune: les interactions de la navigation maritime et continentale sur la Côte des Esclaves avant la colonisation). *Cahiers d'études africaines* 29(167): 209–37.

Lloyd, Peter. 1959. "Sungbo's Eredo." *Odù* 7: 5–22.

———. 1967. "Osifekunde of Ijebu." In *Africa Remembered: Narratives by West Africans from the Era of the Slave Trade*. Edited by Philip Curtin. Madison, Milwaukee, and London: University of Wisconsin Press, 217–288.

Lovejoy, Henry. B., and Ojo Olatunji. 2015. "'Lucumí,' 'Terranova,' and the Origins of the Yoruba Nation." *Journal of African History* 56(3): 353–72.

Magill, Daniel. 2013. "The Evolution of the Reaper." In *Confronting Death. College Students on the Community of Mortals*. Edited by Alfred G. Killilea and Dylan D. Lynch. Bloomington, IN: iUniverse, 229–36.

Mauny, Raymond. 1956. *Esmeraldo de situ orbis: Côte occidentale d'Afrique du Sud marocain au Gabon par Duarte Pacheco Pereira (vers 1506–1508)*. Bissau: Publicações do Centro e Estudos da Guiné Portuguesa.

Momin, K. N. 1989. "Urban Ijebu Ode: An Archaeological, Topographical, Toponymical Perspective." *West African Journal of Archaeology* 19: 37–50.

Odutola, Odubanjo. 1946. *Iwe Kini Ilosiwaju Eko Itan Ijebu* (A Study of Ijebu History, Book I). Ijebu-Ode, Nigeria: Eruobodo Press.

Oduwobi, Tunde. 2000. "Oral Traditions and Political Integration in Ijebu." *History in Africa* 27: 249–59.

———. 2003. "Some Considerations Concerning d'Avezac's Notice sur le Pays et le Peuple des Yebous en Afrique." *Lagos Notes and Records* 9(1): 106–14.

Oduwobi, Tunde. 2006. "Early Ìjèbú History: An Analysis on Demographic Evolution and State Formation." In *Yorùbá Identity and Power Politics*. Edited by Toyin Falola and Ann Genova. Rochester, NY: University of Rochester Press, 145–58.

———. (2017). "The Age and Kings of the Ijebu Kingdom." In *History and Diplomacy: Essays in Honour of Ade Adefuye*, edited by Rufus T. Akinyele. Glassboro, NJ: Goldline and Jacobs, 48–70.

Ogunkoya, T. O. 1956. "The Early History of Ijebu." *Journal of the Historical Society of Nigeria* 1(1): 48–58.

Olukole, Titilayo, and David A. Aremu. 2002. "The Use of Geographical Information Systems for Documenting Archaeological and Tourism Resources of Ijebuland, Southwestern Nigeria." *West African Journal of Archaeology* 32: 35–61.

Olusola, J. A. 1968. *Ancient Ijebu-Ode*. Ibadan: Abiodun Printing Works.

Pavanello, Mariano. 2015. "Foragers or Cultivators? A Discussion of Wilks's 'Big Bang' Theory of Akan History." *Journal of West African History* 1(2): 1–26.

Payne, John Augustus. 1893. *Tables of Principal Events in Yoruba History*. Lagos, Nigeria: A. M. Thomas.

Rascovan, Nicolás, Hong Huynh, Gérard Chouin, Kolawole Adekola, Patrice Georges-Zimmermann, Michel Signoli, Yves Desfosses, Gérard Aboudharam, Michel Drancourt, and Christelle Desnues. 2016. "Tracing Back Ancient Oral Microbiomes and Oral Pathogens Using Dental Pulps from Ancient Teeth." *NPJ Biofilms and Microbiomes* 2: 6.

Rodney, Walter. 1969. "Gold and Slaves on the Gold Coast." *Transactions of the Historical Society of Ghana* 10: 13–28.

Ryder, Alan. 1959. "An Early Portuguese Trading Voyage to the Forcados River." *Journal of the Historical Society of Nigeria* 1(4): 294–321.

Shumway, Rebecca. 2011. *The Fante and the Transatlantic Slave Trade*. Rochester, NY: University of Rochester Press.

Sutton, John E. G. 1982. "Archaeology in West Africa: A Review of Recent Work and a Further List of Radiocarbon Dates." *Journal of African History* 23(3): 291–313.

Vogt, John L. 1973. "The Early São Tomé-Principe Slave Trade with Mina, 1500–1540." *International Journal of African Historical Studies* 6(3): 453–67.

Wilks, Ivor. 1977. "Land, Labour, Capital and the Forest Kingdom of Asante: A Model of Early Change." In *The Evolution of Social Systems*. Edited by Jonathan Friedman and Michael J. Rowlands. London: George Duckworth, 487–534.

Wilks, Ivor. 1982a. "Wangara, Akan and Portuguese in the Fifteenth and Sixteenth Centuries, I: The Matter of Bitu." *Journal of African History* 23(3): 333–49.

———. 1982b. "Wangara, Akan and Portuguese in the Fifteenth and Sixteenth Centuries, II: The Struggle for Trade." *The Journal of African History* 23(4): 463–72.

———. 1982c. "The State of the Akan and the Akan States: A Discursion" (L'état des Akan et les États akan: discursion). *Cahiers d'études africaines* 22 (87/88): 231–49.

———. 1993. *Forests of Gold: Essays on the Akan and the Kingdom of Asante.* Athens: Ohio University Press.

Chapter 13

Nineteenth-Century Coastal Guinea

Manifestations of the "Illegal" Slave Trade in a Local System

Kenneth G. Kelly

At the turn of the nineteenth century, political decisions by Denmark, Britain, and the United States to prohibit their nationals and ships from trading in slaves had far-reaching impacts. Principally, this led to a dramatic realignment of the now-clandestine trade away from the large-scale forts and castles, such as typified the Gold Coast of present-day Ghana and Cote d'Ivoire (so named because of the gold that was initially obtained there by Europeans), and the Slave Coast of present-day Togo, Benin, and western Nigeria (so called because of the considerable trade in captives that occurred there) (DeCorse 2001, 2010; DeCorse & Spiers 2009; DeCorse et al. 2009; Kelly 1997, 2002; Norman 2009). In their place, the commerce in captive Africans shifted toward a more dispersed, small-scale trading presence that was frequently located in less visible locations. One such location was the tidal Rio Pongo, located in present-day Guinea, about 100 kilometers north of Conakry and the trading center of the Iles de Los (see fig. 13.1 on page 308). Trade in this region was facilitated by an extensive network of personal and family ties that linked local African elites with European and American traders, forming a caste of Atlantic Creoles (Kelly 2011; Kelly & Fall 2015) whose networks spanned oceans and continents. The networks, though perhaps broader in their reach, were structured in the same ways as the long-standing "landlord-stranger" relationship that governed traditional trade agreements (see Mouser 1975; Brooks 1993). This relationship placed considerable economic and political power in the

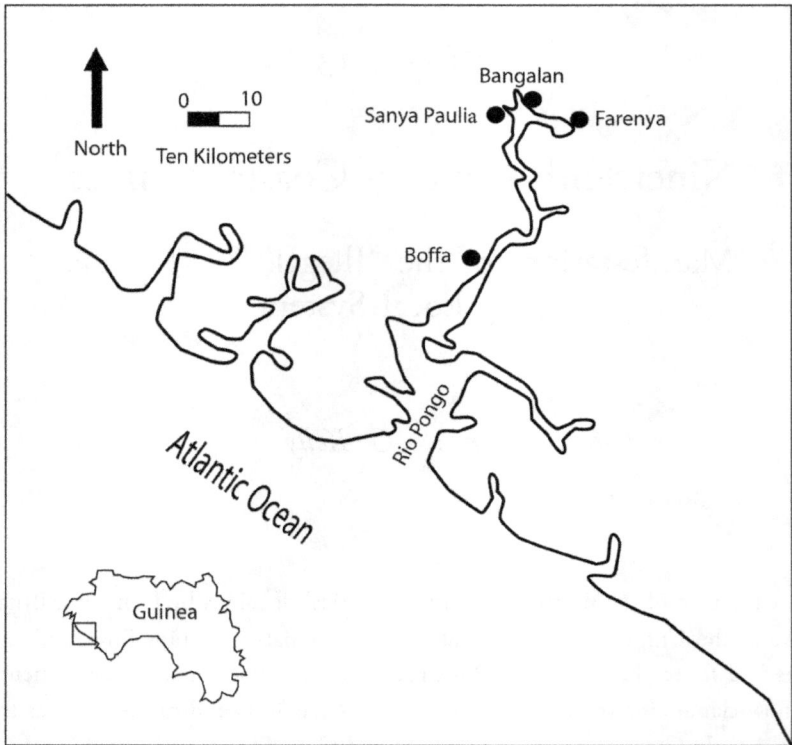

Figure 13.1. Map of the Rio Pongo with principle sites mentioned in the text. (Map by Kenneth G. Kelly)

hands of charismatic and connected private individuals. Unlike perspectives that draw on the actions of large-scale processes, such as the state-based interactions of World Systems Theory (e.g. Chase-Dunn & Hall 1991; Polanyi 1966; Wallerstein 1974; Wolf 1982), which prioritizes power relations that emanate from the global North or core, and are seen to exert impacts on the periphery, the landlord-stranger relationship sees the trade and social developments on the upper–Guinea coast as a result of the agentive actions of specific individuals in a specific cultural context. In this way, research into the interactions of foreign and local actors is closely allied with microhistorical approaches (DeCorse 2008; Tomich & Zeuske 2008; see contributions in Brooks et al. 2008). The landlord-stranger relationship recognizes the key roles individuals play in negotiating the parameters of the trade arena.

Between the late sixteenth century and the middle of the nineteenth century, one of the primary motivations for European traders to visit the West African coast was to seek captive Africans for sale into the plantation economies of the Americas, primarily Brazil and the Caribbean, and to a much lesser extent, the Indian Ocean (Blackburn 1997; Law 1991). For most of this period, the trade in slaves and other commodities was centered around large European trading establishments, such as the forts and castles that dotted the West African coast from Senegal to Nigeria (DeCorse 1991, 2010, 2016; Lawrence 1963). Traditional views of the organization of the slave trade, the European factories, their forts and interactions, has generally been framed in the idiom of merchant capital, supported by the power of the nation-state. Here joint stock companies with active and silent partners financed ships, backed companies, and facilitated the movement of goods (Pettigrew 2014). Typical trade establishments included forts such as on James Island in the Gambia River (DeCorse et al. 2010; Gijanto 2011, 2014), Bunce Island in Sierra Leone (DeCorse 2015, 2015), Cape Coast, Fort Ruychaver and Elmina in present-day Ghana (Simmonds 1973; Posnansky &Van Dantzig 1976; DeCorse 2001), and Ouidah in present-day Benin (Kelly 1997, 2002; Norman 2009). At these coastal or near coastal locations, impressive European forts arose, surrounded by the settlements of local Africans, some of whom worked in the trading posts, and others who serviced the local communities.[1] A number of these locations have been the focus of archaeological work geared toward either understanding the lives of the relatively small number of European traders and the others in their employ, or more frequently, toward understanding how the presence of the European traders impacted local society, communities, and economies (DeCorse 2001, 2015; Gijanto 2011, 2014; Kelly 1997, 2002; Norman 2009; Posnansky & Van Dantzig 1976).

Less discussed, but equally important, is the role of private trade, and specifically the way in which private trade was sensitive to alternate idioms of financial organization. While private trade was endemic to merchant companies it was not until the end of the eighteenth century that it became a far more important appendage of the Atlantic slave trade. As some of the key players in the slave trade began to prohibit their nationals from participating in the trade, with Denmark initiating this in 1803, and Great Britain and the United States following in 1807/1808, national agendas shifted from supporting the slave trade to actively opposing it (Blackburn 1988). It was in this setting that private trade, not that dissimilar to the "interloper" trade of the late seventeenth and early eighteenth century (Law 1977), grew to occupy a now-yawning gap in the supply of captives. While Britain and the United States continued to practice an internal slave trade to satisfy growing demands in new territories, the end of the Haitian Revolution and the elimination of what had been the largest producer of sugar and coffee from the marketplace, led to a resurgence of slavery in previously underexploited regions, in particular Cuba and Puerto Rico (Blackburn 1997; Landers 2008; Tomich 2004). This "second slavery" (Tomich 2004; Tomich & Zeuske 2008; Kaye 2009) was satisfied in part by a shifting organization of the slave trade to one in smaller scale, private hands. Given the greater risk to participation in the slave trade with the advent of the anti–slave trade patrols, a more flexible and rapidly responsive decentralized private trade was more advantageous.

The Rio Pongo region had been integrated in European trade early during European exploration (Blackburn 1997; Sorry 1975), but fell from favor as the larger and more extensive trading forts began to be developed elsewhere along more populated stretches of the coast. The greater population density of the Slave Coast (Law 1991, 31, 58–61) and its hinterland, and possibly that of the Gold Coast, also contributed to the shift away from the Upper Guinea Coast, as more hierarchically organized states were able to mobilize for slave acquisition in ways the smaller-scale societies could not. Following several hundred years as a backwater, the Rio Pongo rose to prominence again in the face of increasingly organized opposition, as slave traders sought captives from trade entrepôts that were less visible to the anti–slave trade patrols that sailed along the coast seeking to intercept the now illegal trade (Mouser 1973). With the expansion of the "second slavery," many of the captives from the Upper Guinea Coast were destined for plantations of Cuba, Puerto Rico, and Brazil (Landers 2008; Tomich 2004; Tomich & Zeuske 2008).

Hidden locations like the Rio Pongo provide an important lens through which to examine the different ways in which the slave trade was enacted. They proved ideal as protected anchorages where slave traders could obtain their cargo relatively unmolested by prying eyes. Importantly, the nineteenth-century trade along the Rio Pongo was organized through family and other ties of obligation. At times, as many as two dozen different private traders (mostly European and American, or mixed race) operated out of trading lodges built in or adjacent to small local villages, and conducted their business under the protections and obligations of the so-called landlord-stranger relationship (Mouser 1972, 2003; Schafer 1999). Frequently the traders were married into local elite families, as was the case with Styles Lightbourne and John Fraser, or were descendants of such unions, as obtained with John Ormond Jr., and played important roles in the local societies (Mouser 1972, 1973, 1975; Schafer 1999).

On the Rio Pongo, these families included Styles Lightbourne, from South Carolina, and his African wife, Nyara Belli, who were associated with trading at Farenya; the Fraser and Ormond families, associated with trading at Bangalan; and the Faber and Curtis families, associated with Sanya Paulia. Trader Edward Joseph and notorious slave trader Theodore Canot (Mayer 1968) were associated with the trading post of Gambia, although Canot did not apparently establish a dynasty. In spite of the impression that these trading locations were a backwoods frontier, the traders, their families, and even the settlements themselves, were remarkably cosmopolitan, playing host to a diverse array of international actors who maintained extensive networks of personal connections across the Atlantic world and beyond. Some of these families sent their children to Sierra Leone and Europe to pursue their education (Koger 1985; Mouser 2003, 774, 777; Schafer 1999, 5). John Fraser and others (Schafer 1999, 2) split their time between the Rio Pongo, Charleston, South Carolina, and, later, north Florida. Evidence associated with the move of the mixed race Holman family to South Carolina to establish a rice plantation, and several maritime trials of the 1820s and 1830s demonstrate the sophistication with which these networks operated (Koger 1985; Mouser 2011, 2015).[2]

The Archaeological Exploration of Private Trade

Instead of the large trading castles familiar from the Gold Coast or Slave Coast, on the Rio Pongo, the trading establishments were small lodges—simple one- and two-story structures where the trader lived with his family or associates, and an array of dependencies including storehouses or warehouses for goods being traded in or out. Historic accounts describe some of these establishments, though usually in a roundabout manner (Mayer 1968; Mouser 1972; Schafer 1999). Documentary and material evidence suggests that many of these structures materialized the distinctive social role of their inhabitants through their architecture, embodying the "Afro-Portuguese" style elements that were employed in the region for several hundred years (Mark 1996, 1999, 2002). These elements included second floors, balconies, and galleries, as well as decorative embellishments. Historical evidence also indicates that settlements of local people grew up around the trading posts, unless the post was established adjacent to an existing village. Residents of these villages, who lived in the housing that was traditional to their heritage, were occasional employees of the trader, and others who took advantage of economic or other opportunities presented by proximity to the trading post. This might include providing services to visiting ships, such as canoe transport, or growing foodstuffs to provision the slave ships as they departed the region. As a result of these ancillary activities, each trading establishment was linked to a considerable settlement of local Africans, and at least occasionally, traders from more distant locations in the region. Thus, each entrepôt was a collection of people of various ethnicities, origins, and perspectives, all of whom interacted with one another on the basis of new or traditional practices. These settlements were characterized by a village of traditional, single-story mud-brick houses associated with larger "Afro-Portuguese" buildings also constructed of mud brick that included two-story trader's residences and storerooms (Mark 1996, 1999, 2002). Schafer (1999, 5) describes several factories in Guinea, including that of Ormond as a "building 150 feet in front," and cites Joseph Hawkins's description of an unnamed factory as constructed of sun-dried bricks and two stories in height with associated outbuildings, demonstrating that the architectural signaling associated with the Afro-Portuguese was employed broadly.

Archaeological research has long been used to explore households and the dynamics therein (see Barile & Brandon 2004; Fogle, Nyman, & Beaudry 2015). By studying the remains associated with individual house sites, archaeologists are able to identify the range of materials used by the residents and the way in which residents arranged the space and activities within those households. Given that the range of materials used may be governed by what is available, as well as structured by consumer choice, a comprehensive and comparative study of household artifacts can tease out differences between individual households, which can then be interrogated to determine if variation is due to ways of expressing social identity, analogous to what we see in architecture. If the residents of the trading lodges saw themselves as distinct from the residents of the surrounding village (as is suggested in the historical accounts and in the work on Luso Africans [Mark 1996, etc.]), we would expect that there would be ways in which that distinction was signaled through the material culture used.

Archaeological survey and excavation in 2006, 2013, 2016, and 2017 has shed light on the materialities of these contexts through the investigation of a series of localities known to be the sites of slave-trading lodges and the various sorts of ancillary structures and components that grew up around these establishments (Kelly 2006, 2011; Kelly & Fall 2015; Goldberg 2016). Three of the site complexes, Sanya Paulia, Bangalan, and Farenya, still have active villages surrounding or nearby the nineteenth-century sites, and one, Gambia, is largely abandoned. The largest site complex is that associated with the modern village of Farenya, located at the easternmost head of the tidal Rio Pongo (see fig. 13.2). Here, there are remains of the trading lodge, known locally as the "palace" of "Queen" Nyara Belli, several cannon emplacements, a cemetery, foundations of other trading lodges, and at the outskirts of the modern village, a location claimed to be where captives were kept waiting for sale to the Atlantic trade. At a little farther remove to the south and west, there is the site of one of the earliest churches in the region, along with several still-visible stone-delimited graves. This sector, where the church site is located, has a continuous distribution of nineteenth-century imported artifacts, suggesting that it may be the original location of the village of Farenya. Farther west from the church and on the steeply sloping south bank of the Rio Pongo, are the remains of two rather imposing structures, Betia and Yenia, which local history states were the houses, and maybe lodges, of two daughters of Nyara Belli. The earthen mound at each of these house sites is associated with a paved causeway leading to a stone jetty on the upper Rio Pongo which is a pattern associated with trading establishments in the area.

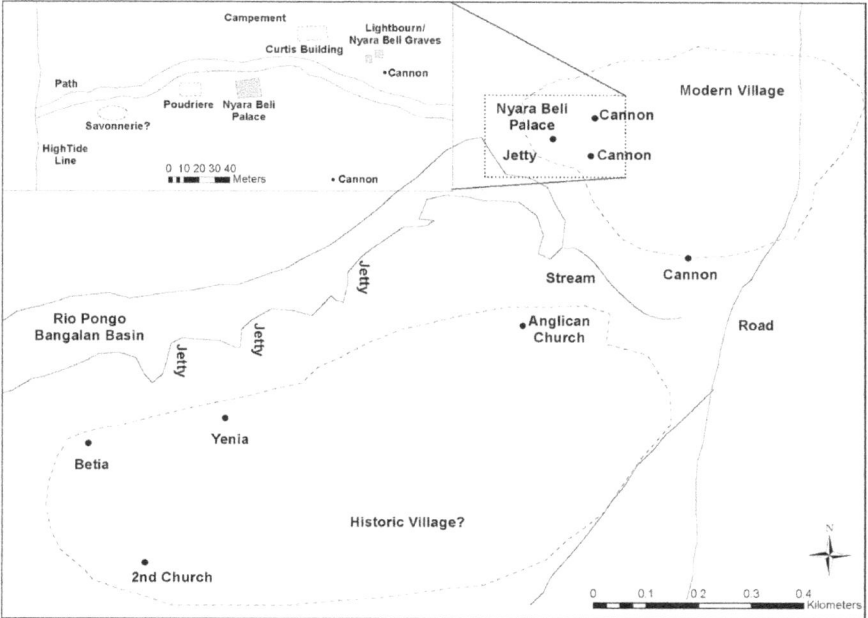

Figure 13.2. Map of the head of the Rio Pongo showing the archaeological sites and features in the Farenya area. (Map drafted by Kelly Goldberg and published in Kelly et al. 2015: 17)

The other site complexes are located on the north bank of the Rio Pongo. Bangalan is the site closest to Farenya, and is associated with several traders, including John Fraser, Canot, and John Ormond and his son, John Ormond Jr. The ruins of the lodge complex here (presumed to be that of Ormond based on local tradition) are reasonably well preserved, with several earthen mounds over one meter tall, and a series of other, smaller mounds. A cast iron, muzzle-loading cannon sits in the center of the courtyard formed by some of these mounds, and a 160-meter-long stone paved causeway leads from this courtyard, past the vestiges of several warehouses, to the waters' edge where cargos would have been loaded and unloaded (see fig. 13.3). At Bangalan, the modern village is approximately 1 kilometer away, helping to preserve the ruins from present-day impacts. The area surrounding the ruin complex exhibits an extensive scatter of local and imported nineteenth-century artifacts, suggesting that there was a significant settlement surrounding the lodge.

Continuing along the north bank of the Rio Pongo, near the present day settlement of Bakoro is the site of Gambia, the trading establishment associated with Theodore Canot and Joseph Edwards, following their departure from the employ of Ormond at Bangalan. This site complex is the subject of ongoing work directed by

Figure 13.3. Bangalan site complex. Jetty or causeway from trading lodge to port (image on left), eighteenth-century cannon in center courtyard of trading lodge (upper-right), excavations in the main building of the trading lodge, with dark bands near the base showing burning events (lower right). (Photos by Kenneth G. Kelly)

Kelly Goldberg as part of her recently completed PhD research. She has identified a series of earthen mounds, corresponding to trading lodges and other structures, a stone jetty for transshipping goods, a probable lookout post on an adjacent knoll, and the site of a now-abandoned village, dating to the nineteenth century (Goldberg 2016, 2018). As her research is ongoing, there are currently limited results to report other than the inventory of the site components.

The remaining site complex thus far investigated is that of Sanya Paulia, also on the north bank of the Rio Pongo, where it broadens out into the Bangalan Basin. This complex is associated with the Paul and Mary Faber family, although oral histories suggest that other European traders were also in residence near this village. Sanya Paulia takes its second name from Paul Faber, and at the water's edge are the remains of a stone jetty, and at least two large earthen mounds that appear to correspond to trading lodges and/or residences. Sanya also has the remains of two cannon emplacements, and local tradition states that there were two others that have now been removed. There is also an extensive grove of large mango trees, underneath which excavations identified several house structures, probably corresponding to the nineteenth-century village location. Sanya also has a large area of exposed rock and sand with fairly dense nineteenth-century artifacts that appear to have been where additional parts of the village may have been located, but have been subjected to extensive deflating erosion (see fig. 13.4). Less than

Figure 13.4. Selection of nineteenth-century artifacts typical to the sites of the Rio Pongo. (Photo by Kenneth G. Kelly)

a kilometer from Sanya lies the location of another early mission church in the region, along with several cut-stone masonry structures, and several graves, said to be those of the priests. Other trading families were present at Sanya as well. Descendants of the Curtis family who were active at a number of trading sites in the region (Schafer 1999), pointed out the location of their family's concession to me in 2013, and the vestiges of the houses still remain and could be the subject of archaeological work.

Local Impacts of the Atlantic Trade

Following a preliminary visit in 2006, and a three-month campaign of mapping and testing in 2013, it is possible to arrive at some initial thoughts regarding the nature of interactions along the Rio Pongo. These preliminary observations will be complimented by the results of research in the area and 2016–2017 excavations conducted by Kelly Goldberg (2018). Clearly the density and scale of archaeological remains in the area speak to its importance during the nineteenth century. Historical documents make clear the important role of traders in the region during the late eighteenth and early nineteenth centuries. However, artifactual material datable to the beginning of the nineteenth century is relatively limited. All of the sites explored had much denser accumulations of materials dating to the mid- to late nineteenth century, which corresponds to the illegal slave trade that continued to the 1860s, and the later trade in agricultural products, particularly peanuts. Architectural remains in the region are limited, mostly restricted to the remains of formerly imposing one- or two-story structures made of sun-dried earthen bricks. Some of these structures, particularly those of the several mounds at Sanya and possibly the lodge at Bangalan, appear to be associated with the residences of European or American traders on the coast. However, the structural remains of the "palace" at Farenya and the structures at Yenia and Betia suggest that buildings associated with elite local residents exhibited a mix of characteristics such as those associated with the Atlantic Creole or "Afro-Portuguese" residents of the coast (Kelly 2011; Mark 1996).

It is important to remember what "Afro-Portuguese" or Luso African signifies in this context. This architecture, materializing the heterogeneous and fluid nature of the cultural identity of these elites, served as visible symbols that proclaimed their unique status. However, it is important to remember how kin networks, and indeed the way that family is conceptualized, shaped these architectural forms. In the case of all of these ruins, they were located in places that were highly visible, and accompanied by other architectural or engineering features such as warehouses, wharves, jetties, or paved causeways or paths that further signaled their importance. The trading establishments at Farenya, Sanya, Gambia, and Bangalan were organized in ways that demonstrated their commitment to commerce, and the sites of Betia and Yenia may exhibit these features as well. These features include the riverside wharf for loading and unloading goods directly in front of the mounds that remain of the warehouses and traders' dwellings, the cannon emplacements in front of or adjacent to the structures, to defend the outpost, or more likely, to signal approaching vessels, and then at some distance surrounding the trading post, the artifacts that indicate the location of the local village (or villages—in some cases different ethnic groups may have occupied different quarters).

During the nineteenth century, a key aspect of the commerce on the Rio Pongo lay in captives who were brought from the Futa massif some 200 or more kilometers to the east (DeCorse 2012, this volume). In these highlands, the expansion of the Futa theocratic state resulted in conquest that led to the capture and enslavement of others (Mouser 1972, 2003). These captives were then taken in coffles along paths leading to the heads of the tidal rivers, where trading establishments were able to engage in trade for the human cargo. Canot (Mayer 1968:87) describes some of these caravans of captives in his account, and notes that the caravans consisted of much in addition to captives. One caravan, from Timbo, he describes included 700 people, most of whom were porters carrying hides, ivory, rice, and wax. This caravan also included forty captives, whose combined value was roughly the same as that of the 3,500 hides, and nineteen elephant tusks also being transported. These African commodities were purchased in this instance with firearms, gunpowder, and tobacco, most of which went back to the Futa region with the return caravan. Hence, while today we are particularly struck by the human commerce, it is well to note that other "traditional" items of trade were as, or more, important than the captives. While it is not certain, it is likely that kin networks, such as that of the Lightbourne family, with brothers based in Savannah, Bermuda, Charleston, and on a Low Country rice plantation, may well have structured the kinds of commodities provided for trade. Demonstrating the reach of the interpersonal connections forged on the Rio Pongo, other people with Rio Pongo connections include the African American Holman family who operated a plantation for a short period in South Carolina (Koger 1985: 110–18), and the

Fraser family, who maintained plantations in Florida and a slave-trading presence in the Rio Pongo region as well as close connections to the Lightbourne, Curtis, and Skelton families (Schafer 1999).

This study also serves to remind us that in spite of the importance of the clandestine slave trade in global terms, locally, there may be a much more visible impact of the other "legitimate" trade items and consequences. For example, the arrival of a caravan of 700 people, even if allowing that 40 or more are captives destined for sale abroad, is going to have a major impact on the local communities. The needs of ship provisioning were considerable, as well. In Mouser's (2015) account of the seizure and trial of the *Spitfire of New Orleans*, a slaver taken in 1845, he notes also that given the illegal nature of the commerce, and the great efforts at subterfuge the ship captains and owners engaged in, other items of cargo brought to the coast included barrel staves to be assembled for rice and water obtained locally. These staves would build thirty-five casks destined to feed the 346 slaves on board during the voyage to the Americas (2015, 25). Today, the villages on the upper Rio Pongo have populations that are considerably less than 700, and likely were relatively small in the past, so the arrival of such a number of visitors for a week, two weeks, or more would put considerable stress on the local economy, in terms of food availability or shelter.

The degree to which individual traders were in competition with one another is also hinted at by Canot's account. Certainly the desire of individual traders to have sufficient numbers of captives on hand to fit out a complete ship was a powerful motivating force, as ship's captains and crews were reluctant to stay on the coast any longer than was necessary, particularly during the periods of fever as the rainy season got underway. This was accomplished in part through the bulking centers of the Iles de Los, offshore of present-day Conakry (Mouser 2003: 763–64). This suggests that to a degree perhaps not seen with the more centralized trading establishments of the eighteenth century, these nineteenth-century traders may have been able to adjust their cargos and trade more rapidly than the larger companies. This may have implications for understanding the archaeological record, as we may be able to see a more idiosyncratic and individual response to local demand for goods. Individual traders maintained their own networks of supply and connection, based on their external links, whether through their children who had been sent abroad to Europe for education (Koger 1985; Schafer 1999), or the economic ties they had with particular supply houses in Europe or the United States. Again, Canot (Mayer 1968, 96–98) describes exactly this process as it occurred with Edward

Joseph, who, like Canot, had been in the employ of Ormond at Bangalan, but who then struck out on his own as an independent trader. In the case of Joseph, he requested that his creditors in Freetown advance him capital, and he would promptly repay them with results of his trading on the Rio Pongo.

Mouser (2011) discusses conflicts and factions among the traders of the Rio Pongo beginning in the late 1810s and continuing through the 1820s, as some of the traders, and their local connections responded to the growing presence of the British and American anti–slave trade patrols. Some of the traders chose this period to get out of the slave trade and concentrate on other goods, while other traders effectively doubled down on the trade in captives. These traders took advantage of the continued legality of slavery in what was then nominally the British colony of Sierra Leone (which was larger than the modern nation), and the legality of inter-African slave trade. These traders, of whom Ormond and Lightbourne were leaders, maintained thousands of local "attached slaves" (Mouser 2011, 158) who were by tradition not to be sold, but could be used in payment of debt, and who in addition to serving as agricultural labor, could take up arms for their master. Many abolitionists viewed this as a ruse, designed to make the stockpiling of human captives for eventual sale appear to be innocent or traditional, when in fact they could be sold at any time. In light of the increasingly belligerent relations between the anti–slave trade squadron and the traders on the Rio Pongo, in addition to using these attached slaves as combatants, the trading establishments that continued to function began to fortify their presence with mud walls, towers, and cannon batteries. While the mud walls at locations such as Bangalan (where they included over thirty cannon [Mouser 2011, 158]) and Farenya have left no visible trace, the locations of batteries for cannon have been identified at Farenya and at Sanya Paulia.

Considering the ways in which kinship and capital were linked and how these two idioms of trade intertwined at these trading establishments elucidates an important element of the functioning of the slave trade and the development of the second slavery (Tomich & Zeuske 2008). While the trade in captive Africans was structured by global economic patterns, its operation was not an external force that structured the trade in the Rio Pongo. Rather kinship networks integral to understanding "West African" societies were equally important in understanding European merchant capital. The social arrangements on the Rio Pongo were dramatically different from those Europeans would expect in the encounter. Status, power, and social capital were amassed and arbitrated by the number of dependents, slaves, and affiliations one accumulated. Labor and the knowledge possessed by dependents generated wealth that can be used to accumulate further dependents (Guyer & Bellinga 1995). Global markets or capital forms of valuation were not external to these arrangements. Often operating through idioms of kinship, they worked alongside and complemented capitalist modes of accumulation. The expansion of the role this alternative embodiment of Atlantic Creoles created new sets of identities that continue to play an important role in the coastal societies of modern-day Guinea.

Notes

The research reported in this article was supported by the Wenner Gren Foundation for Anthropological Research International Collaboration Grant, the American Philosophical Society, and the University of South Carolina. Many thanks to the people of Farenya, Bangalan, and especially Bakoro and Sanya Paulia for welcoming us in their midst. This work would not have been possible without the tireless support of my colleague Elhadj Ibrahima Fall, and the late Minister of Culture Ahmed Tidjiane Cissé.

1. DeCorse's 2001 book on Elmina provides a well-researched archaeological example of the study of the town surrounding one such fort.

2. See Landers 2008 and Schafer 1999 for a description of the entangled nature of personal connections in the Rio Pongo region and beyond, as they were manifest in Cuba and Florida.

Works Cited

Barile, Kerri S., and Jamie C. Brandon, eds. 2004. *Household Chores and Household Choices: Theorizing the Domestic Sphere in Historical Archaeology.* Tuscaloosa: University of Alabama Press.

Blackburn, Robin. 1988. *The Overthrow of Colonial Slavery, 1776–1848.* London: Verso.

———. 1997. *The Making of New World Slavery: From the Baroque to the Modern, 1492–1800.* London: Verso.

Brooks, George E. 1993. *Landlords and Strangers: Ecology, Society, and Trade in Western Africa, 1000–1630.* Boulder, CO: Westview Press.

Brooks, James F., Christopher R. DeCorse, and John Walton, eds. 2008. *Small Worlds: Method, Meaning, and Narrative in Microhistory.* Santa Fe, NM: School for Advanced Research Press.

Chase-Dunn, Christopher, and Thomas D. Hall, eds. 1991. "Conceptualizing Core/Periphery Hierarchies for Comparative Study." In *Core/Periphery Relations in Precapitalist Worlds*. Edited by Christopher Chase-Dunn and Thomas D. Hall. Boulder, CO: Westview Press, 5–44.

DeCorse, Christopher R. 1991. "West African Archaeology and the Atlantic Slave Trade." *Slavery and Abolition* 12(2): 92–96.

———. 2001. *An Archaeology of Elmina: Africans and Europeans on the Gold Coast, 1400–1900*. Washington DC: Smithsonian Institution Press.

———. 2008. "Varied Pasts: History, Oral Tradition, and Archaeology on the Mina Coast." In *Small Worlds: Method, Meaning, and Narrative in Microhistory* Edited by James F. Brooks, Christopher R. DeCorse, and John Walton. Santa Fe, NM: School for Advanced Research Press, 77–96.

———. 2010. "Early Trade Posts and Forts of West Africa." In *First Forts: Essays on the Archaeology of Proto-colonial Fortifications*. Edited by E. Klingelhofer. Leiden, the Netherlands: Brill, 209–33.

———. 2014. "Archaeological Fieldwork at Bunce Island: A Slave Trading Entrepôt in Sierra Leone." *Nyame Akuma* 82:12–22.

———. 2012. "Fortified Towns of the Koinadugu Plateau: Northern Sierra Leone in the Pre-Atlantic and Atlantic Worlds." In *Power and Landscape in Atlantic West Africa*. Edited by J. Cameron Monroe and Akinwumi Ogundiran. Cambridge, UK: Cambridge University Press, 278–308.

———. 2015. "Sierra Leone in the Atlantic World: Concepts, Contours, and Exchange." *Atlantic Studies* 12(3): 296–316.

———. 2016. "Tools of Empire: Trade, Slaves, and the British Forts of West Africa." In *Building the British Atlantic World*. Edited by Daniel Maudlin and Bernard L. Herman, 165–87. Chapel Hill: University of North Carolina Press.

DeCorse, Christopher R., Greg Cook, Rachel Horlings, Andrew Pietruszka, and Samuel Spiers. 2009. "Transformation in the Era of the Atlantic World: The Central Region Project, Coastal Ghana 2007–2008." *Nyame Akuma* 72: 85–94.

DeCorse, Christopher R., Liza Gijanto, Bakary Sanyang, and William Roberts. 2010. "An Archaeological Appraisal of Early European Settlement in the Gambia." *Nyame Akuma* 73: 55–64.

DeCorse, Christopher R., and Samuel Spiers. 2009. "A Tale of Two Polities: Socio-Political Transformation on the Gold Coast in the Atlantic World." *Australian Journal of Historical Archaeology* 27: 29–42.

Fogle, Kevin R., James A. Nyman, and Mary C. Beaudry, eds. 2015. *Beyond the Walls: New Perspectives on the Archaeology of Historical Households*. Gainesville: University of Florida Press.

Gijanto, Liza. 2011. "Exchange, Interaction, and Change in Local Ceramic Production in Niumi Commercial Center on the Gambia River." *Journal of Social Archaeology* 11(1): 21–48.

———. 2014. "Events and Happenings: Uncommon Meals and the Atlantic Trade at Eighteenth Century Juffure (the Gambia)." *Afriques* 05. Accessed October 10, 2017. http://afriques.revues.org/1618; 10.4000/afriques.1618.

Goldberg, Kelly. 2016. "Preliminary Results from Excavations at Bakoro, an 'Illicit' Slave Trade Site on the Rio Pongo, Guinea." *Nyame Akuma* 86: 43–50.

———. 2018. That Diabolical Traffic: Archaeological Explorations of the Nineteenth Century Slave Trade in Coastal Guinea. PhD dissertation, Department of Anthropology, University of South Carolina.

Guyer, Jane I., and Samuel M. Eno Berlinga. 1995. "Wealth in People as Wealth in Knowledge: Accumulation and Composition in Equatorial Africa." *Journal of African History* 36(1): 91–120.

Kaye, Anthony E. 2009. "The Second Slavery: Modernity in the Nineteenth-Century South and the Atlantic World." *Journal of Southern History* 75(3): 627–50.

Kelly, Kenneth G. 1997. "The Archaeology of African-European Interaction: Investigating the Social Roles of Trade, Traders, and the Use of Space in the Seventeenth and Eighteenth Century Hueda Kingdom, Republic of Benin." *World Archaeology* 28(3): 77–95.

———. 2002. "Indigenous Responses to Colonial Encounters on the West African Coast: Hueda and Dahomey from the Seventeenth through Nineteenth Centuries." In *The Archaeology of Colonialism*. Edited by Claire L. Lyons and John Papadopoulos. Los Angeles, CA: Getty Research Institute, 96–120.

———. 2006. "Preliminary Archaeological Reconnaissance of Sites Related to the Slave Trade Era Along the Upper Rio Pongo, Guinea." *Nyame Akuma* 65: 24–32.

———. 2011. "Archaeological Perspectives on the Atlantic Slave Trade: Contrasts in Time and Space in Benin and Guinea." In *Comparative Dimensions of Slavery in Africa: Archaeology and Memory*. Edited by Paul Lane and Kevin MacDonald, 127–46. Oxford, UK: Oxford University Press.

Kelly, Kenneth G., and Elhadj Ibrahima Fall. 2015. "Employing Archaeology to (Dis)Entangle the Nineteenth-Century Illegal Slave Trade on the Rio Pongo, Guinea." *Atlantic Studies* 12(3): 317–35.

Koger, Larry. 1985. *Black Slaveowners: Free Black Slave Masters in South Carolina, 1790–1860*. Columbia: University of South Carolina Press.

Landers, Jane. 2008. Slavery in the Spanish Caribbean and the Failure of Abolition. *Review: A Journal of the Fernand Braudel Center, Binghamton University.* 31(3): 343–71.

Law, Robin. 1977. "Royal Monopoly and Private Enterprise in the Atlantic Trade: the Case of Dahomey." *Journal of African History* 28(4): 555–77.

———. 1991. *The Slave Coast of West Africa, 1550–1750: The Impact of the Atlantic Slave Trade on an African Society.* Oxford, UK: Clarendon Press.

Lawrence, A. W. 1963. *Trade Castles and Forts of West Africa.* London: Jonathan Cape.

Mark, Peter. 1996. "'Portuguese' Architecture and Luso-African Identity in Senegambia and Guinea, 1730–1890." *History in Africa* 23: 179–96.

———. 1999. "The Evolution of 'Portuguese' Identity: Luso-Africans on the Upper Guinea Coast from the Sixteenth to the Early Nineteenth Century." *Journal of African History* 40: 173–91.

———. 2002. *"Portuguese" Style and Luso-African Identity.* Bloomington: Indiana University Press.

Mayer, Brantz. 1968. *Captain Canot, An African Slaver.* New York: Arno Press.

Mouser, Bruce. 1972. Trade and Politics in the Nunez and Pongo Rivers, 1790–1865. PhD dissertation, Department of History, Bloomington, University of Indiana.

———. 1973. "Trade, Coasters, and Conflict in the Rio Pongo from 1790 to 1808." *Journal of African History* 14(1): 45–64.

———. 1975. "Landlords-Strangers: A Process of Accommodation and Assimilation." *International Journal of African Historical Studies* 8(3): 425–40.

———. 2003. "Continuing British Interest in Coastal Guinea-Conakry and Fuuta Jaloo Highlands (1790–1850)." *Cahiers d'Etudes africaines* XLIII(4): 761–90.

———. 2011. "The Rio Pongo Crisis of 1820 and the Search for a Strategy for the Anti-Slavery Squadron off West Africa." *The Mariner's Mirror* 97(3): 145–62.

———. 2015. "US Slave Trading on the Rio Pongo: Evidence from the Capture and Trial of the Spitfire of New Orleans, 1845." *The Mariner's Mirror* 101(1): 21–37.

Norman, Neil L. 2009. "Hueda (Whydah) Country and Town: Archaeological Perspectives on the Rise and Collapse of an African Atlantic Kingdom." *International Journal of African Historical Studies* 42(3): 387–410.

Pettigrew, William A. 2014. *Freedom's Debt: The Royal African Company and the Politics of the Atlantic Slave Trade, 1672–1752.* Chapel Hill: University of North Carolina Press.

Polanyi, K. 1966. *Dahomey and the Slave Trade: An Analysis of an Archaic Economy.* Seattle: University of Washington Press.

Posnansky, Merrick, and Albert Van Dantzig. 1976. "Fort Ruychaver Rediscovered." *Sankofa* 2: 7–18.

Schafer, Daniel L. 1999. "Family Ties that Bind: Anglo-African Slave Traders in Africa and Florida, John Fraser and His Descendants." *Slavery and Abolition* 20(3): 1–21.

Simmonds, Doig. 1973. "A Note on the Excavations in Cape Coast Castle." *Transactions of the Historical Society of Ghana.* 14(2): 267–69.

Sorry, Charles Emmanuel. 1975. Monographie Historique du Rio Pongo du XVème à la fin du XIXème siècle. Unpublished Mémoire du Diplôme, Faculty of Social Sciences. Conakry, Guinea: Insitut Polytechnique Gamal Abdel Nasser.

Tomich, Dale. 2004. *Through the Prism of Slavery: Labor, Capital, and World Economy.* Lanham, MD: Rowman & Littlefield.

Tomich, Dale, and Michael Zeuske. 2008. "The Second Slavery: Mass Slavery, World Economy and Comparative Microhistories." *Review: A Journal of the Fernand Braudel Center, Binghamton University* 31(3): 91–100.

Wallerstein, Immanuel. 1982[1974]. *Europe and the People without History.* Berkeley: University of California Press.

Chapter 14

Economic and Material Basis of Wildlife Preservation in Early Colonial East Africa

Martin S. Shanguhyia

This chapter examines the material and economic structuring of the creation of wildlife sanctuaries in early colonial East Africa—Kenya, Tanzania, and Uganda—from the 1890s through the 1930s.[1] Between the onset of colonialism in the 1880s and the outbreak of the Great Depression in 1929, wildlife resources played an important role in the economy of these colonial territories. When the Depression began to recede in the mid-1930s, the formal export of wildlife-based products to global markets began to "decline," as colonial administrations in East Africa lost grip of that trade to "poaching" by African hunters. At the same time, Western demand for East African ivory in the industrial centers of Europe and North America also declined, as alternative synthetic materials replaced ivory in Western markets. Up until then, East Africa's wildlife landscapes had a long history of supplying ivory and other game products to local and global economies. The rise of the colonial wildlife preservation movement in the late nineteenth century amplified the economic importance of those landscapes and their wildlife products, the political and cultural dimensions of that movement notwithstanding.

Early colonial East Africa provides an ideal case for analyzing the intersection between wildlife landscapes, politics of Empire, extraction of material commodities, and their distribution to local and global markets. The centrality of East Africa on this issue was defined by the diversity of its fauna, as well as the presence of an influential European settler population—at least in colonial Kenya—whose social and economic interests were inextricably linked to land, forest, and wildlife resources. These interests often ran counter to those of the indigenous communities who, as hunters, traders, farmers, and pastoralists, depended on wildlife landscapes for their survival.

The underlying argument in the chapter is that the push for game reserves in early colonial East Africa had a compelling economic rationale, as colonial administrations sought to utilize those reserves to secure the capitalist base of the colonial states that emerged on this equatorial frontier of emerging European empires. Those administrations initially operated on shoestring budgets and had to identify natural resources of economic value to keep the nascent administrations afloat. Game reserves were a convenient imperial approach to reorganizing East African landscapes to help furnish the emerging colonial states with much needed revenue. This convenience benefited from an already established commercial connection between East African wildlife ecologies with regional and global markets centuries before the onset of colonial rule in the late nineteenth century. Trade in ivory and other game products made a significant contribution to regional and global trade between East African colonies and Asian and European markets. By focusing on the material and economic aspects of preservation of wildlife ecologies in early colonial East Africa, this chapter moves beyond, but does not underestimate the importance of game reserves as cultural landscapes characterized by tensions between Europeans—as agents of imperial power and culture—and Africans—as their subjects. The creation of wildlife sanctuaries was a projection of European culture onto the tropical environment and its indigenous inhabitants. Those sanctuaries inaugurated the social and cultural world of the European hunter in Africa, whom colonial states allowed access into the game reserves as a professional sports hunter. For the British, sport hunting fulfilled the heroism and masculinity of the Victorian Age, as much as the hunt also yielded an economic profit to the hunter through game trophies that found their way into overseas markets and private collections (Mackenzie 1988; Caruthers 1995; Thompson 2015). In this way, wildlife sanctuaries are seen as a manifestation of, or symbol of Western identity in an alien environment, and as landscapes that served the needs of a privileged class of German, British, and other European sport hunters based in Eastern Africa as well as those who visited the region mainly to engage in hunting. The creation of game reserves fit into the broader process of colonial appropriation of land that had previously supported African agriculture, grazing, and hunting and gathering, and in the process undermined the economic bases of the affected communities. Indeed, some scholars have viewed wildlife conservation in East Africa as representing the modernizing, disruptive tendencies of colonial states seeking to promote modern economic development in rural Africa (Neumann 2001).

This chapter focuses on the extractive tendencies of colonial states in East Africa, and their relation to local and global production and flow of natural commodities extracted from wildlife landscapes. Official colonial narratives in these territories made endless connections between wildlife products, licenses, and firearms, on the one hand, and game preservation on the other, so much that interactions with wildlife sanctuaries seem to have been determined by one's ability to access and use "appropriate" or "acceptable" production technologies—means of extraction—and ivory, a product extracted from game sanctuaries.

Game products, as well as licenses and firearms represented a material dimension through which colonial states in the region sought to impose their power and authority on wildlife landscapes. Indeed, some scholars have argued that wildlife conservation as practiced by colonial states was a kind of capitalist mode of production that lays claim to "the intrinsic, or natural, capital game animals," whose value can transform capitalism both at local and global level (Garland 2008, 61–62). A few others hint at this economic value by casting colonial states as agents of modernization that sought to create animal sanctuaries as a means to managing and using African resources sustainably (Gissibil 2016, 9). The sustainability argument notwithstanding, the economic basis of wildlife management lends itself as an obvious motive in early colonial engagement with African fauna.

East Africa's Wildlife Resources: The Precolonial Political Economy

Before the advent of Western Empires in East Africa in the late nineteenth century, local African communities were inextricably connected to wildlife environments. These communities (see fig. 14.1) depended on wildlife resources for subsistence, cultural, political, and economic needs. Game products were extracted through hunting or plundering. The "big men" accumulated and redistributed ivory through trade or as "handouts" to those they sort to build loyal clientele networks. Hunting was also an elaborate institution replete with ritual practices that bestowed privilege, power, and responsibility on professional traditional hunters (Gissibil, 2006, 50–53). In late-nineteenth-century Buganda, hunting elephants for ivory was not just a pastime activity; it also had a political significance. The *Kabaka* (king) used hunting to consolidate his power within the state by expecting chiefs to deliver all ivory from professional hunters to the capital. Hunting was also used as a territorial marker of the *Kabaka*'s influence over the Kingdom's satellite states that offered hunting grounds for elephant tusks. Ivory was also a major medium of commercial exchange for several communities in this Great Lakes region (Twaddle 1993, 14, 117–18).

North of Lake Victoria, aside from Baganda, the Banyoro, Basoga, Lango, Acholi, and Jie communities extracted animal products from the wild to augment their subsistence needs. In Lango and Jie communities in particular, hunting was an important economic and social activity. The Upper Nile was rich in elephants and when ivory emerged as a major commodity in demand in regional and global markets, the Acholi were its key suppliers. Incidences of Egyptian and Sudanese expansion into northern Uganda during the nineteenth century was motivated by the need to access this commodity (Mackenzie 1988, 78).

In the southwestern and southern part of Lake Victoria, the Nyamwezi, Vinza, and Sukuma communities extracted natural resources from their immediate environment, and exchanged commodities ranging from iron hoes, fish, and salt to forest products. An important item the Nyamwezi exported to the East African coast was ivory, which they acquired by hunting or by trade from eastern Congo and Bunyoro in Uganda (Roberts 1970, 39–70). Farther south between Lake Malawi and the East African coast, including northern modern-day Mozambique, hunting supplemented the agricultural diet of communities such as the Yao, Makua, and Lomwe. For the Makua, an ever-increasing demand for ivory in far-flung markets in southern Tanzania and beyond helped reorient their trade to those markets (Alpers 1975, 11). Many of the communities in what became Kenya also depended on wildlife resources for their survival. The Kamba, for instance, were avid hunters that traded their ivory with communities in Tanzania's interior and with the Arabs and the Swahili on the east coast. The Maasai resided in areas endowed with game but hunted mainly to protect their livestock from predators. Around Mount Kenya, the Kikuyu, Embu, and Meru relied on hunting to supplement their agricultural produce, but the need to acquire ivory and other game trophies to be exchanged for products brought there by long distance traders was an option (Ambler 1988, 11–12, 36; Steinhart 2006, 17–41).

The importance of East African ivory in local, regional, and long-distance trade networks prior to colonialism has been accounted for in East African historiography.[2]

The export of ivory to global markets stretches back to classical times. Ivory from the hinterlands of East Africa found its way to ancient Egypt via Nubia along the Nile, and perhaps even into the Roman Empire. Between about 1000 and 1500 AD, Eastern African ivory exported to the Middle East, China, India, and Europe benefited from expansion of the Indian Ocean trade, made possible by commercial voyages by Arab, Persian, and Indian merchants who made frequent contact with the East African coast.

By 1850s, there was a dramatic increase in the value of East African ivory due to a rise in demand in India, China, and Europe. India and China acquired most of this ivory, where it was used in the production of toys, chess and draughts parts, and ornaments, which were in turn exported to European markets. In Europe, ivory-carving centers also benefited from imports of East Africa ivory. Known for its soft texture, East African ivory was in high demand in European industries that produced beauty and entertainment products. In Dieppe, northern France, local producers of ornaments, crucifixes, mathematical instruments, and combs, among other articles, relied on supplies of East African ivory. Consumers of these products were mostly European middle class families that also spent money on entertainment products such as ivory billiard balls and piano keys. In Hamburg, Germany, the Heinrich Adolf Meyer Co. held a monopoly on ivory imported from East Africa between 1840 and 1890, where it was used to produce billiards. However, it was in the United States that this soft ivory was sought in large quantities to feed the ever-increasing demand from industrial capitalism. In Ivoryton, Connecticut, mass production of entertainment and beauty products, especially combs, piano keys, billiard balls, depended on thousands of tons of ivory shipped in annually from Zanzibar. Export of East African ivory into New England lasted into the late 1930s before it faded due to industrial shift to alternative, synthetic material that replaced ivory.

Within East Africa, ivory prices varied from one coastal market to another, but they show a remarkable increase from the 1820s through the 1880s. In Zanzibar, thirty-five pounds of ivory was acquired for 21 dollars in the early 1820s; it appreciated to 140 dollars in 1883, about the time when colonialism commenced in Eastern Africa (Gissibil 2016, 42). For much of the nineteenth century up to about 1890, Zanzibar was the largest market for East African ivory. Zanzibar fed off a well-organized chain of extraction and trade networks that connected this East African metropolis to the ivory landscapes of the interior and the far-flung markets in Asia and Europe. This network involved Africans, Arabs, Indian, and European merchants (Prestholdt 2008). Thus, ivory was the largest valuable wildlife commodity exported from East Africa by the last decade of the nineteenth century.

The commodity was acquired and moved by Arab, African, and some European travelers and sport hunters along distinct caravan and trade routes that connected elephant-rich areas and local markets across the East African interior, with the coastal markets. These routes cut through northwestern and southwestern Lake Victoria; western, central, and southern Tanzania; lower elevations of Mount Kilimanjaro; Maasai country; central Kenya, and the Nyika plateau. Banyoro, Baganda, Basoga, Lango, Kikuyu, Embu, Turkana, Dorobo, Somali, Nyamwezi, Sukuma, Makua, and Yao, among other communities, acquired and traded ivory either within their localities, or with itinerary traders who in turn sold it at coastal markets most notably in Zanzibar and Mombasa. The Kamba, Galla, Swahili, and Arabs were the key long-distance traders who brought the commodity from the interior to those markets (Beachey 1969, viii, 271–72; Gissibil 2016, 42–43; Ambler 1975, 73).

African porters hired by these traders, as well as African slaves, carried the ivory to the coastal markets. From this commercial organization and network, we gain an understanding of how East African wildlife landscapes and their African inhabitants were not isolated local spaces; rather, they were linked to regional and global chain flow of commodities of which ivory was prominent. Local African states and communities, rulers, individual African hunters and traders, professional porters, slaves, and Arabs were key agents in this chain. The advent of European imperialism, European hunters, and colonial administrators toward the end of the nineteenth century added to the dynamic nature of these linkages, though colonial regimes attempted to regulate the chain for commercial gain.

Colonialism, Game Preservation, and Material Extraction

Efforts to preserve wildlife in early colonial East Africa has to be grasped against the foregoing commercial relations that existed between East African wildlife ecologies and world markets in which ivory was a premier commodity. German and British imperial designs in this region were built on these economic relations. The two imperial powers were bearers of Western industrial capitalism, and their expansion into East Africa after 1885 coincided with an ongoing extraction of wildlife resources by local communities and itinerant, often European hunters, and the sale of those resources to near and far markets.

The hunting exploits of European explorers and "sportsmen" in East Africa are well accounted for by historians of British and German Empires (Mackenzie 1988, 147–66). Most of these foreign hunters were Europeans of higher social rank, some who later became influential policy makers in the British and German colonies in East Africa. Their expeditions were in part motivated by the desire for adventure and for scientific research. However, sport hunting was a prime motive for most of these men operating on the emerging frontiers of European Empires in Africa. Lord Delamere, Sir Robert Harvey, Sir John Willoughby, and (later Sir) Frederick J. Jackson are a few of the many members of the British Imperial order who were responsible for institutionalizing the hunt in Eastern Africa. Writing at the turn of the twentieth century, Lord Cranworth, an ardent British sport hunter in East Africa, affirmed that: "The present is the day of the sportsman, of the man of riches, of the 'white hunter' and of the record breaker" (Lord Cranworth 1912, 231–33). Buffalo and rhinoceros horns, among other game products, yielded a fortune for these hunters. East African buffalo horn was assessed to be of superior quality that those from other parts of Africa. "To my mind," Cranworth wrote, "there is no grander trophy" (Lord Cranworth 1912, 257). Some of these hunters, such as Jackson, were later charged with responsibility of preserving wildlife from destruction by the colonial administrations of Kenya and Uganda.

The pursuit of the elephant was much more than hunting for pleasure or for sheer adventure; economic gain was also a key motivation for these hunters. In the late nineteenth century, ivory proved as the most prized commodity for sport hunters who were able to acquire it. Following their hunting expedition in Kenya, Uganda, and Ethiopia, the Hungarian Count Samuel Teleki and the Austrian Ludwig von Höhnel left accounts of seemingly endless stocks of ivory in the Lake Turkana basin. Swahili and Arab long-distant traders who ventured there bought ivory from these communities in exchange for beads and copper, and trekked for hundreds of miles to sell the ivory on the east coast. Ivory was such an important item to Swahili and Arab traders that they were prepared to surrender anything in their possession in exchange for it, so much that they could "pay their way with their last rags of clothing, their ammunition, the iron ramrods of their guns, or even the guns themselves" (Von Hohnel 1968, 185–86; 257). For instance, after a hunting trip in northern Kenya in the late 1890s, Arthur Newmann returned with a considerable amount of ivory that he traded with the Swahili trading caravans. W. D. M. Bell, another accomplished hunter, ventured into the game-rich Karamoja region in eastern Uganda and acquired ivory worth £23,000 (Mackenzie 1988, 152–53). These exploits overlapped with efforts by German and British colonial authorities to implement legislation to create game reserves to protect elephants and other animals in territories that evolved into Tanzania, Kenya, and Uganda.

Expansion of colonial rule into these territories in the 1880s had an immediate and direct impact on the wildlife environments and communities that depended on them (see fig. 14.1). The establishment of imperial jurisdiction ensured the

Figure 14.1. Map of early colonial East Africa. (Redrawn from Peter MacQueen, *In Wildest Africa*, London: George Bell and Sons, 1910)

cooptation into the colonial state economies of all preexisting networks through which African communities had extracted wildlife products and supplied them to local, regional, and global markets before colonial conquest. The game reserve movement reinforced the economic value of wildlife to colonial states as access to wildlife landscapes became highly regulated through colonial legislation. This regulation affected Africans communities that were prior-users of those environments for economic, ritual, and political purposes. Reorganization and transformation of East Africa's wildlife landscapes ensured that colonial states had a monopoly over ivory and other game resources—often not without African contestation.

The idea of game reserves in colonial East Africa originated from growing concerns by pioneer British and German colonial administrators that large African game—particularly elephants, rhinos, and buffaloes—were headed for extinction due to overhunting by African and European hunters. Many of the areas designated as wildlife sanctuaries either were settled by African communities or were hunting grounds for those communities. Colonial officials painted gloomy pictures of wild animals being hunted to extinction and called for urgent remedies. In Tanzania, while German officials pointed at declining wild animals from excessive hunting, they also recognized the economic value of wildlife products to the territory's colonial government. This colony was grafted onto a region that contained rich game habitats and the most extensive precolonial ivory trade routes and markets in East Africa.

The German East Africa Company that was initially charged with administering the territory was keen on profiting from the fortunes it inherited from the pre-colonial order. The Company's attempts to supplant Swahili and Arab ivory traders in the northeastern parts of the territory elicited a violent local rebellion in 1888. Even as the output of ivory started to decline—relative to the decades preceding colonial rule—that commodity continued to dominate exports from Tanzania at the start of the 1890s; only rubber topped all exports. Acquisition of ivory through hunting, tribute, confiscation, looting, and extortion provided the company administration with an important fiscal base for its revenue. The company also rucked up more revenue by levying a tax on tusks destined for export overseas from the coastal markets (Gissibil, 2016: 70–71).

The Company commenced game regulation in Tanzania in 1891 by focusing on the northeastern region that was also the first to come under direct German rule. The 1891 ordinance allowed African hunters to hunt for ivory but only after paying a fee of 500 rupees that only wealthy European hunters could afford. A subsequent ordinance in 1896 allowed Africans with permits to shoot elephants that strayed into their cultivated fields, but excluded them from hunting in game-protected areas. The ordinance also created new wildlife sanctuaries on the slopes of Mount Kilimanjaro and in the vicinities of Rufiji River in central-eastern Tanzania. By the end of the First World War, legislation by the German officials had created almost twenty-five game reserves in Tanzania (Gissibil 2016, 87; Ofcansky 2002, 50). Up until then, German officials succeeded in channeling most of the ivory exports into the colonial economy.

African ivory dealers, usually local chiefs allied to the administration, were sometimes instructed to release their stocks onto the market only when market prices appreciated, thereby enabling the government to reap higher profits from ivory sales. Furthermore, regulating access to game led to careful cropping of animal products mainly for sale. This did not stop, but led to an intensified killing of elephants. The abundance of tusks of lesser weight and size attested to indiscriminate hunting of forbidden herds as well as a decrease in number of mature elephants that had been decimated in the previous decades. The German administration was so dependent on proceeds from ivory that it viewed elephants as what has been termed at a "customs house" (Gissibil 2016, 71–72).

German game preservation policies also led to unintended human-environmental consequences that generated contradictions in the economic objectives of the administration. If protecting wild animals in reserves was intended to secure and tap into the natural wealth of the territory, those reserves led to an increase in certain types of wild animals and bush land infested with tsetse flies. Consequently, trypanosomiasis and nagana were commonplace in northern, western, and south-central parts of Tanzania (Ofcansky 2002, 50–51; Kjekshus 1977, 161–68). These developments debilitated African labor and livestock populations, thereby undermining the primary resources—people and livestock—critical for promoting economic development of the colony.

After Britain took over the territory from Germany at the end of the First World War, a debate emerged among British environmental experts and administrators as to whether wild animals, then closely associated with outbreaks of human and livestock diseases, should be exterminated to save human lives. This issue presented a perpetual dilemma to British officials as increased numbers of wild animals continued to decimate crop fields in African villages. Nonetheless, the British continued to prioritize the wildlife reserve system to protect game. Aside from dealing with the menace of the health problems caused by tsetse fly in relation to game preservation, colonial administrators also saw an economic connection between preserving wild animals and protecting human life and livestock from what the administration regarded as "vermin" or predators. Unless threats posed by game reserves remained unsolved, some officials worried that agriculture, the key sector to which African peasant producers were main contributors, was likely to suffer from animal invasions (Colonial Report on Tanganyika 1921, 52–53). Consequently in 1926, the administration mobilized the help of local communities to prevent what it considered to be "the depredation of marauding elephants and of other game dangerous to life and destructive of crops" in Lindi, Songea, Mahenge, Kilwa, and Tabora districts. Officials attributed the outbreak of famine on the Ilindi Plain in Dodoma to considerable destruction of food crops by elephants (Report of the Administration of Tanganyika Territory 1926, 3). The governor's solution to this economic problem was to recommend a relaxation on the law that prevented African access to firearms that were necessary in shooting elephants and other animals that prayed on food crops in African reserves.

On the extreme, communities that posed challenges to game reserves were evicted on economic grounds. At Gombe near Lake Tanganyika, a community of 500 people that subsisted on fishing and by gathering medicinal plants from a nearby hill country were removed in 1946 to give way to a chimpanzee sanctuary, as the administration felt that this community lacked a substantial tax base for the government. Elsewhere, the Mbulu and Lake Rukwa Game Reserves deliberately enclosed local pastoralist communities, many who responded by killing game that strayed into their grazing areas (Kjekshus 1977, 177). These instances illustrate the extent to which colonial authorities in Tanzania—both German and British—prioritized the game sanctuary movement over efforts to cultivate a coexistence between wild animals and local African communities.

The connection made by colonial authorities between game preservation and economic gain in Tanzania was also evident in Kenya and Uganda. Officials of the Imperial British East Africa (IBEA) Company that was granted a royal charter in the late 1880s to administer these two territories until the mid-1890s recognized the economic importance of ivory and other game products to the colonial economy. Company officials, many who were avid hunters, introduced measures to preserve wildlife in Kenya and Uganda officials. Sir Frederick Jackson, then in charge of Uganda, was likened to Frederick C. Selous, the celebrated sports hunter and trophy collector in South and East Africa in the late nineteenth century. IBEA Company officials virtually depended on wildlife resources for subsistence, personal profit, and to secure the fiscal base of the Uganda and Kenya administrations.[3] Administrators and sport hunters rarely disregarded the economic element from their pursuit of African game in the protected reserves. They sold exotic trophies from the game they hunted to global markets. The company unsuccessfully attempted to monopolize the ivory trade in the interior and coastal markets.

The IBEA Company also levied a 15 percent export duty on ivory at the port of Mombasa. Rhinoceros horns and hippopotamus teeth also fetched a 10 percent duty. This fiscal policy was part of the broader approach to preserve elephants and other large game, but in doing so, it helped the company to meet its administrative expenses. Furthermore, attempts by the Company to levy taxes on ivory twice—at the source in the interior and again at ports of export at the coast—were often resisted by private European commercial companies at coastal locations that sought to stockpile the commodity at a lower prices and disposing them to global markets at a profit (Ofcansky, 2002, 3–4).

British government take-over of Kenya from the IBEA Company in 1895 paved way for the formalization of the colony's game preservation policies. Those policies were the result of sustained pressure from the Foreign Office, and from international efforts aimed at mobilizing all European colonial powers in Africa to protect wild animals in their territories from imminent extermination. For instance, an international conference hosted by the Foreign office in London in 1899 and attended by delegates from Germany, France, Italy, and the Congo Free State signaled Britain's commitment to preserving wildlife in its African territories (Buxton 1902, 117–19). This impetus led to the establishment of the first game sanctuary in Kenya—the Kenia District Reserve—in 1897. Three years later, the Reserve was expanded to create the much larger Southern Reserve, one of the two major reserves in early colonial Kenya located in south-central rural areas inhabited largely by the Kikuyu, Kamba, Maasai, and Taita communities. The other major reserve was the Northern Reserve in the semiarid area—later the Northern Frontier District—largely inhabited by pastoralist communities. These efforts also succeeded largely due to pressure from the Society for the Preservation of the Wild Fauna of the Empire—launched in 1903—and whose officials and members constituted an influential political pressure group that helped promote the idea and practice of game reserves in East Africa (Buxton 1902, 4–15).

In Uganda, the game preservation movement was boosted by concerns from London that "indiscriminate slaughter" of game was likely to lead to extinction of fauna in that territory (Ofcansky 2002, 27). Due to external pressure, Sir Harry Johnston, a renowned hunter and Uganda's Commissioner, pioneered the game sanctuary efforts by setting up the Sugota Game Reserve in 1899, covering southern Lake Rudolf (Turkana) Basin, Lake Baringo, Kamasia, and Elgeyo Plateau, a large area that was part of the Eastern Province of the Uganda Protectorate, but was later transferred to Kenya in 1924. Johnston followed this up with the establishment of elephant reserves in the Budoga Forest in Bunyoro, and in the western portions of Toro Kingdom bordering the Congo Free State. He also tasked African authorities in Buganda, Toro, Bunyoro, and Ankole kingdoms with enforcing harsh game laws that banned their subjects from hunting elephants in the preserved areas (Buxton 1902, 187–88). Agricultural communities opposed these reserves due to an upsurge in game that undermined crop cultivation, leading to conflict between African farmers and wild animals, and tensions between these farmers and the administration for many years.

While agricultural exports continued to form the mainstay of the colonial economy of Uganda and Kenya, state revenue from extraction and sale of ivory directly or indirectly acquired from game reserves remained a significant contribution to government revenue. Official statistics reveal that before ivory exports from Uganda and Kenya started to decline shortly before the outbreak of the First World War, they generated substantial annual revenue in both territories. Between 1901 and 1906, ivory exports from Uganda amounted to £173, 009, though a proportion of this ivory originated from the Belgian Congo (East Africa Protectorate Report, 1905–1906, 14). There is little doubt that domestic ivory supplies contributed a significant proportion, but the largest quantities came from the Belgian Congo as "transit ivory." In 1911, total ivory exported was worth £18,721, of which £3,594 accounted for ivory hunted domestically (Colonial Office Annual Report for Uganda, 1910–1911, 6–8).

Overall, domestic ivory exports from the territory started to decline after 1913, but continued to be an important economic sector for the administration with transit ivory remaining a major source of the commodity. The highest income from ivory registered before the Second World War was in 1937, before registering a fluctuating, mainly decreasing trend in the 1930s (see table 14.1). Reasons for this decline were varied, but poaching, increased restrictions of hunting in protected areas, effective patrol of Uganda's western border with the Belgian Congo, and declining demand of soft ivory by Western industrial manufacturers greatly accounted for it.

Table 14.1. Quantity and Value of Domestic Ivory from Uganda, 1929–1938

Year	Quantity (cwt)	Value (£)
1929	445	26, 477
1930	263	12, 835
1931	—	—
1932	—	—
1933	—	—
1934	453	12, 736
1935	588	18, 440
1936	661	19, 372
1937	666	27, 435
1938	466	14, 602

Source: Figures collated from *Uganda Blue Book.* 1930. Entebbe: Government Printer, p. 132; *Great Britain Uganda Colonial Annual Report, 1938.* London: HMSO, 59.

In Kenya, economic returns from wildlife resources were more evident than elsewhere in East Africa. In 1905, the total value of all exports increased by £59,123 over the previous year, and ivory contributed greatly to the increase. Most of it was shipped to the United States and France. Commercial farming of ostrich and zebra by European settlers also demonstrated "profitable returns to the capitalist" (East Africa Protectorate Report, 1904–1905, 9, 36). Though transit ivory from the Belgian Congo also contributed to proceeds from exported ivory, a larger quantity was derived from within Kenya's wildlife sanctuaries. For instance, of £68,217 of ivory exported in 1906–1907, supplies from the Congo Free State accounted for only £12,362. An upward trend was registered between 1908 and 1910, as ivory helped swell the value of exports from Kenya during 1910 over those of the previous year.[4]

Ivory exports from Kenya began to shrink in quantity and quality after 1912, but like Uganda, they continued to contribute to state revenue. Those exports declined from 33 percent in 1901 to only 4.7 percent in 1912 (East Africa Protectorate Report, 1911–1912, 14, 61), a precipitous decline given those ivory earnings to the individual European hunter and to the government economy was significant in the previous years.

The decline was the result of increased efforts to preserve male elephants by banning the export of cow ivory and tusks weighing less than thirty pounds (East

Africa Protectorate Report, 1910–1911, 12–13). Furthermore, given that hunting regulations denied Africans access to game-protected areas except when permitted to shoot elephants that strayed into their farms, some resorted to illegal hunting and sold the ivory outside government-controlled market channels. The government lost revenue as officials decried the practice as "poaching." The Kenya administration resorted to tracking smuggled tusks and sold it as "confiscated" ivory. Kamba ivory hunters in particular ignored restrictions imposed against hunting in the Southern Reserve and resorted to poaching, prompting their arrest and prosecution under the Game Ordinance, and had their ivory confiscated for sale by the administration (East Africa Protectorate Report, 1911–1912, 62; East Africa Protectorate Report, 1913–1914, 65).

Ivory acquired by this means was smuggled in large quantities over expansive frontiers of the Protectorate with Ethiopia and Italian Somaliland that were challenging to policing. Over-hunting of mature elephants by well-armed sportsmen, or the targeting of stray elephants by African farmers seeking to protect their crops from destruction were also probable reasons for this decline. By 1913, bulls with heavy tasks had become rare due to many years of hunting. Many of these herds had retreated into the far reaches of the Northern Reserve away from the ever-growing human settlements in central and southeastern parts of Kenya, which made poaching and smuggling of ivory easier due to absence of government policing. During and after the First World War, the government derived more proceeds from ivory retrieved from smugglers than that derived from legal hunting. For instance, the administration attributed the relative increase in weight and revenue in ivory exports during 1916 through 1917 to "recovery of a large quantity of buried ivory recovered by the government" (East Africa Protectorate Report, 1916–1917, 6). Acquisition of ivory by this means continued following increased poaching activities in the Northern Game Reserve where the Turkana and Abyssinians—the later crossing into the territory from Ethiopia—made forays to hunt elephants.

Declining profits from wildlife commodities was therefore related to high expenditures incurred in enforcing game preservation. Policing and maintaining the sanctuaries became increasingly expensive shortly before the First World War. Overall, extraction and sale of commodities from East Africa's wildlife landscapes remained important but not significant in the light of predominance of agricultural and mining sectors. When most economies in African colonies took a hit from the Great Depression in the early 1930s, ivory and other game products supplied by sport and commercial legalized hunters provided a cushion to the financial purse of all the East African colonial territories. Britain, India, and especially the United States imported most of this ivory. In 1929, Comstock, Cheney, & Co in Ivoryton, Connecticut, milled about 100,000 tasks in 1929, much of it derived from East African landscapes and exported through Zanzibar, supplemented by supplies from the Belgian Congo and Sudan.[5] Imports declined as from the mid-1930s, following a corresponding decline in the demand for pianos from New England as American consumers shifted to new modes of entertainment, notably the radio, gramophone, and movies. Manufacturers of entertainment products like piano keys turned to plastic as a chief raw material.[6] Even so, ivory became expensive as the high-quality soft pedigree traditionally derived from East Africa became rare from excessive hunting and a commencement of strict colonial conservation campaigns to protect elephant herds.

The Economics of Hunting Licenses and Firearms

Licensing and strict regulation of access and use of firearms were an integral part of game preservation in early colonial East Africa. While focus here is on the economic implications of licenses and firearms, the cultural and political implications of these elements for the colonizers and the colonized must not be overlooked. Licenses and guns were essential tools of colonial domination much as they served as sources of economic benefit linked to extraction of products from wildlife-protected areas.

The game reserve movement offered East Africa's German and British colonial administrations the opportunity to affect gun control laws and to alter human-wildlife relations, and to reinforce the rights of the European, and not the African, to bear firearms. Few, usually designated African game scouts or local chiefs allied to the colonial governments, were allowed possession of certain firearms and could only use them with the governor's permission. In this way, firearm regulations were used not only to impose "order" on wildlife landscapes, but also as a means to reinforcing colonial social and power relations. Hunting and gun licenses proved exorbitant for local communities and also undermined their rights to hunt in areas that belonged to them prior to creation of game sanctuaries. Fees from permits and firearms provided a direct source of income to colonial administrations. Those governments raised revenue mainly by requiring that European sport hunters, colonial officials, and Africans purchase licenses for hunting and for bearing a firearm to be used in hunting.

In Tanzania, the German administration imposed hunting licenses from 1891. European and African nonprofessional hunters were required to acquire hunting permits at 20 and 5 rupees, respectively, while professional hunters paid a flat but hefty fee of 500 rupees. Only those African communities that wished to hunt for subsistence could do so without a license. Over time, the cost of hunting licenses was revised in accordance with game population and the demand for ivory. "Professional" African hunters were usually local chiefs whom the German administrators identified as "great elephant hunters." These individuals, as was the case among the Nyamwezi and Chagga communities, derived their power and influence from their control of hunting grounds and the trade caravan routes that fed ivory into the East African markets in the precolonial period. The administration allowed them to retain hunting rights in their areas in exchange for political loyalty and sharing their ivory hunt with the German administration (Gissibil 2016, 84–85; Buxton 1902, 203). It was an economic measure used by German colonial officials for political motives, as the policy allowed them to create local alliances with powerful African communities while ensuring gradual colonial expansion and control into the interior parts of the territory.

In Uganda, where game preservation elicited a contentious debate between local officials and London because of the likely impact of animal sanctuaries on local communities, hunting licenses appeared quite exorbitant. Early proponents of hunting permits in the territory such as Sir Ernest Berkeley, the commissioner and consul general suggested in 1896 that 1,000 rupees be issued for unrestricted hunting, and 500 rupees for hunting in certain designated districts. These were implemented only after the Foreign Office revised them down to 375 rupees for a sport license and 5 rupees for European settlers and government officials. In 1906, the administration enacted a new ordinance to increase license fees for hunters targeting elephants and other big game. Consequently, special licenses for hunting elephants ranged between 150 and 450 rupees (Ofcansky 2002, 28, 34). Thus, the economic benefit to the state of exacting a fee for hunting in game reserves was evident as proceeds earned helped lessen dependence on London for costs of running the administration.

Strict hunting laws contributed to an increase in elephant population in Uganda, which in turn led to the introduction of licenses for "cropping" elephants. This offered the government an additional source of revenue. Unable to trust the African hunters with firearms and with a special license to protect cultivated fields from wild animals, and convinced that these hunters protected crops with a motive to profit from accumulating ivory, the administration entrusted cropping to European professional hunters at a fixed wage. This strategy failed to prevent crop damages by elephant herds or reduce elephant numbers even as Uganda's colonial treasury earned considerable revenue from the cropping enterprise (Ofcansky 2002, 40). As the price for ivory in regional and global markets declined in the late 1930s, fewer hunters purchased special licenses for hunting elephants. This in turn led to a decline in revenue from the sale of these permits in particular, and in game preservation in general (Annual Report on the Social and Economic Progress of the People of Uganda Protectorate, 1938, 44). The strong push for the protection of elephants after the Second World War, and the transition from game reserves to National Parks where hunting was completely forbidden, may have contributed to that decline.

In Kenya, game laws introduced in the 1890s aimed at attracting wealthy European sportsmen to help cushion the revenue base of the budding state. An ordinance enacted in 1899 catered to these sportsmen and other hunters. It established several fee categories of 375 rupees for sportsmen, and 45 rupees for settlers, itinerant traders, and government officials (Ofcansky, 2002, 9–10). During the fiscal year 1904–1905, two sources of revenue combined for about £14,154 of the total income earned by the colonial government in Kenya; these were hut tax and game licenses. Income from game licenses was even higher for the following year, contributing £7,000 to state revenue due to large numbers of sportsmen that visited the territory. An extra fee was charged for shooting rare animal species. More revenue was derived from £10 licenses issued to European settlers to shoot game on their farms (British East Africa Protectorate Report, 1905–1906, 57–58). In the bid to maximize on this income, and as a way of spreading out hunting to cover as many species of game as possible, the government categorized licenses into eight types for sportsmen, residents, landholders, employees, employers, and special license for the elephant and giraffe (British East Africa Protectorate Report, 1910–1911, 56).

Revenue from hunting licenses in Kenya started to decline after 1913 due to fewer financially able European hunters who visited the Protectorate. The administration lost more revenue to European settlers who, in spite of holding special licenses to shoot game on their estates, leased farms to visiting international hunters for a fee. These hunters were able to obtain a great deal of shooting of different game species and a rich collection of trophies at a cheaper rate than their £50 sportsman's license allowed them (Jensen 1906, 390; British East Africa Protectorate Report

1911–1912, 60–61). Revenue from licenses declined further during the First World War as many residents, both Africans and Europeans, departed for the battlefront. At the beginning of the 1920s, state income from hunting licenses declined to a paltry 1,909, which the governor described as "the lowest figures during the last ten years" (East Africa Protectorate Report 1918–1919, 23). Thenceforth, hunting licenses ceased being major source of revenue as the administration turned toward recovering ivory from smugglers and to transit tusks originating from Tanzania, Uganda, and the Belgian Congo for revenue. Generally, before the First World War, there seem to have been adequate profit earned by the Kenya administration from programs related to game preservation. This is evidenced by the number of pounds spent on those programs and revenue earned per fiscal year between 1904 and 1914 (see table 14.2).

East African early colonial administrations also imposed licenses to regulate access to, and use of firearms as a means of extracting animal products from game reserves. This policy went beyond mere politics of game preservation; rather, through it, the emerging colonial states wished to impose their power of control over the newly conquered African communities. After their overwhelming military subjugation of African communities in imperial wars of conquest, the colonizers wished to maintain the military balance in their favor. Therefore, they imposed strict firearms legislation to prevent the proliferation of guns and gunpowder among the vanquished African communities. The legislation was also in concert with

Table 14.2. Revenue and Expenditure of the Game Department in Kenya, 1904–1914

Year	Revenue (£)	Expenditure (£)
1904–1905	6,223	115
1905–1906	7,013	127
1906–1907	7,060	207
1907–1908	7,560	1,806
1908–1909	6,071	1,459
1909–1910	8,809	2,422
1910–1911	10,666	2,539
1911–1912	7,941	2,788
1912–1913	9,560	3,400
1913–1914	8,529	3,683

Source: Collated from Colonial Office Annual Reports, East Africa Protectorate, 1904–1914.

the 1890 Brussels convention that restricted European sale of modern weapons to Africans. Most important, this policy helped secure financial returns to East Africa's colonial states.

The politics of wildlife preservation were about access to game protected areas. Hunting required a means of extraction, which in turn highlighted to the importance of hunting technologies. Before the advent of guns and colonial influence in many parts of Africa south of the Sahara, the African hunting repertoires were diverse as they were effective and environmentally sustainable. They ranged from traps, snares, pits, poisons, spears, bows, and arrows (Mackenzie 1988, 54–84). The advent of game preservation proscribed the usage of these technologies that British and German colonial officials unfairly blamed for decimation of wild animals and inefficient as hunting tools. The gun, even with its obvious destructive power, attained pride of place in the new hunting regulations. Colonial governments commercialized access to game sanctuaries, as well as the acquisition and use of firearms for hunting by requiring purchase of licenses.

Conclusion

The transformation of East Africa's wildlife landscapes into game sanctuaries from the late nineteenth century was more than a projection of a European imperial hunting culture onto tropical landscapes. It transcended the motive to advance the leisure of a privileged class of European hunters, one whose members took a keen interest in game preservation for social or cultural reasons. Aside from advancing the culture or social interests of the European hunter, the creation of wildlife sanctuaries served to consolidate the capitalist interests of this class and that of British and German imperial states. As specially protected environments, game reserves promoted the cultural and material consumption patterns of a group given to capitalist ethos of Empire.

Furthermore, the project was motivated by localized developments but its impulses reverberated beyond colonial borders, a reflection of broader, global influences. Fears of loss of wildlife in Eastern Africa were expressed in European metropolises, where men of influence with an interest in the natural world supported the "men-on-the-spot" in the colonized territories to effect policies aimed at game preservation. This happened even as wildlife commodities, especially ivory, which had been important in integrating East Africa into global commercial networks before the colonial era, retained their economic importance in the years before the Great Depression. Up until the Depression in the early 1930s, wildlife commodities from the preserved landscapes cushioned the financial base of the colonial states and its auxiliaries, mainly European sport hunters, colonial officials, and foreign traders. The tensions between local communities and colonial administrations over access to wildlife sanctuaries, and over the means of extracting animal resources attested to the economic value of East African wildlife landscapes in the age of imperial capitalism in tropical Africa. Hunting permits and firearms licenses were the cultural and political means of ensuring colonial power over those landscapes. More important, Africans living within those landscapes also engaged in this production process, either directly or from the fringes of the localized global capitalist forces—through poaching, licensed shooting of elephants, and as gun bearers. The game reserve movement of the late nineteenth and early twentieth century was a commodity extraction enterprise that reinforced the supply and consumption of East Africa's natural resources to regional and global markets.

Notes

1. Under German colonization, Tanzania was referred to as German East Africa. Its name was changed to Tanganyika following British takeover at the end of the First World War, and later became the United Republic of Tanzania, following unification with Zanzibar in 1964. Kenya, under the British, was initially referred to as the British East Africa Protectorate, and later, Kenya Colony after 1920. Throughout this chapter, the current names of these countries are adopted: Tanzania, Kenya, and Uganda.

2. Most of the proceeding summary of the global economic importance of East Africa's ivory is drawn from Beachey (1967, 288–89) and Gissibil (2016, 42). Other key works on the subject include: Sheriff (1987); Alpers (1975); Rempel (1998); Mackenzie (1988); and Hakansson (2004).

3. Francis George Hall, a key official of the Company based in Kenya in the early 1890s, narrated in numerous letters to his father, Lieutenant-Colonel Edward Hall, accounts of endless hunting expeditions that provisioned meat to his staff. These expeditions were the root of the Company's conflict with the Kamba and Kikuyu communities. One of Hall's assistants once acquired a grand collection of ivory from a hunting trip to Uganda that included a tusk that he described as "the biggest (194 Ibs.)" he had ever seen, and was subsequently bought as a wedding present for the Duke of York (Letters of Sir Francis George Hall 1894, 182).

4. For details on these trends and statistics, see *East Africa Protectorate. 1908. Colonial Report for 1906–1907.* London: HMSO, 10; *East Africa Protectorate. 1911. Report for 1909–1910.* London: HMSO, 9; *East Africa Protectorate. 1912. Report for 1910–1911.* London: HMSO, 12–13. On more incidents of heavy poaching by the Turkana and Abyssinians in the Northern Reserve, see *East Africa Protectorate. 1921. Colonial Report for 1918–19.* London: HMSO, 23.

5. https://connecticuthistory.org/ivory-cutting-the-rise-and-decline-of-a-connecticut-industry/, accessed August 18, 2017.

6. https://connecticuthistory.org/ivory-cutting-the-rise-and-decline-of-a-connecticut-industry/, accessed August 18, 2017.

Works Cited

Alpers. Edward. 1975. *Ivory and Slaves in East Central Africa.* Berkeley: University of California Press.

Ambler, Charles. 1988. *Kenyan Communities in the Age of Imperialism: The Central Region in the Late Nineteenth Century.* New Haven, CT: Yale University Press.

Annual Report on the Social and Economic Progress of the People of Uganda Protectorate. 1938. London: HMSO.

Beachey, R.W. 1967. "The East African Ivory Trade in the Nineteenth Century." *Journal of African History* 8(2): 269–90.

Buxton, Edward North. 1902. *Two African Trips with Notes and Suggestions on Big Game Preservation in Africa.* London: Edward Stanford.

Carruthers, Jane. 1995. *Kruger National Park.* Natal, South Africa: University of KwaZulu-Natal Press.

Cranworth, Lord. 1912. *A Colony in the Making: Sport and Profit in British East Africa.* London: Macmillan and Co.

Garland, Elizabeth. 2008. "The Elephant in the Room: Confronting the Colonial Character of Wildlife Conservation in Africa. *African Studies Review* 51(3): 51–74.

Gissibil, Bernhard. 2016. *The Nature of German Imperialism: Conservation and the Politics of Wildlife in Colonial East Africa.* New York: Berghahn Books.

Great Britain Colonial Office. Annual Reports for Uganda.

Great Britain Colonial Office. British East Africa Protectorate Reports for 1904–1905; 1905–1906; 1910–1911; 1911–1912; 1913–1914; 1916–1917; 1918–1919.

Hakansson, Thomas N. 2004. "The Human Ecology of World Systems in East Africa: The Impact of the Ivory Trade." *Human Ecology* 561–91.

Jessen, Heinrich Burchard. 1906. *W. N. Macmillan's Expeditions and Big Game Hunting in Sudan, Abyssinia, and British East Africa.* London: Marchant Singer & Co.

https://connecticuthistory.org/ivory-cutting-the-rise-and-decline-of-a-connecticut-industry/ accessed August 18, 2017.

Letters of Francis George Hall Letters. East African Protectorate Letters to Lieutenant-Colonel Edward Hall, January 14, 1894.

Mackenzie, John M. 1988. *The Empire of Nature: Hunting Conservation and British Imperialism*. Manchester: Manchester University Press.

Neumann, P. Roderick. 2001. "Africa's Last 'Wilderness': Reordering Space for Political and Economic Control in Colonial Tanzania." *Africa: Journal of the International African Institute* 71(4): 641–65.

Ofcansky, Thomas P. 2002. *Paradise Lost: A History of Game Preservation in East Africa*. Morgantown: West Virginia University Press.

Prestholdt, Jeremy. 2008. *Domestication of the World: African Consumerism and the Geneologies of Globlization*. Berkeley: University of California Press.

Rempel, Ruth. 1998. "Trade and Transformation: Participation in the Ivory Trade in Late 19th-Century East and Central Africa." *Canadian Journal of Development Studies* 19 (3): 529–52.

Report by His Britannic Majesty's Government to the Council of the League of Nations on the Administration of Tanganyika Territory. 1926. London: HMS Office.

Report by His Britannic Majesty's Government to the Council of the League of Nations on the Administration of Tanganyika Territory. 1923. London: HMS Office.

Roberts, Andrew. 1970. "Nyamwezi Trade." In *Pre-Colonial African Trade: Essays on Trade in Central and Eastern Africa Before 1900*. Edited by Richard Gray and David Birmingham, 39–74. London: Oxford University Press.

Sheriff, Abdul. 1987. *Slaves, Spices, and Ivory in Zanzibar*. London: James Currey.

Steinhart, Edward I. 2006. *Black Poachers White Hunters: A Social History of Hunting in Colonial Kenya*. London: James Currey.

Thompson, Angela. 2015. *Hunting Africa: British Sport, African Knowledge, and the Nature of Empire*. New York: Palgrave Macmillan.

Twaddle, Michael. 1993. *Kakungulu and Creation of Uganda 1868–1928*. Athens, OH: Ohio University Press.

von Hohnel, Ludwig. 1968. *Discovery of Lakes Rudolf and Stephanie: A Narrative of Count Samuel Teleki's Exploring and Hunting Expedition in Eastern Equatorial Africa, 1887–1888*, Vol. II. London: Frank Cass & Co.

Chapter 15

Huge Oceans, Small Comparisons

Danish Enclaves in the Indian and Atlantic Oceans

Mark W. Hauser

The varied political economies of the early modern world and their effects on the engaged populations is not new to conversations in history and social science. Braudel, in his classic *The Mediterranean and the Mediterranean World* (1995), suggests that there are many Mediterraneans and none could be understood independently from what is exterior to these worlds. Rigid adherence to boundaries falsifies the social relations which emerge in and around it. Braudel's insights have been and can be extended to the Atlantic world and especially the slave trade and plantation economies (Blackburn 1997). Sanjay Subramanyam argues that the modern world was formed through a series of connected histories in which "the different sources and roots" brought about "many different forms of meaning it attends" (Subrahmanyam 1997). Importantly such an approach decouples the modern world from a particular European trajectory (Subrahmanyam 2005).

In what follows, I engage in a project of mapping the Danish world. I take as my point of departure an observation that Sidney Mintz made in *Sweetness and Power*—that each object, document, or cartographic representation carries within itself a system of the world. Thinking of the history of the materiality of these crops situates plantations in peripheral and global flows, and is an important avenue for linking physical force with the spread of colonialism and early mercantile networks (Coclanis 1993). But, as Phil McMichael has cautioned, these systems of the world are not prefigured, and the objects, documents, and cartographic representations are not mere residues to be situated within this prefigured world (McMichael 1990). Rather objects, documents, and cartographic features create the world which they map. This is certainly the case of Danish mercantile companies and how they shaped the social relations emerging between the Indian and Atlantic Oceans.

I examine how Danish colonialism created particular landscapes in different parts of the world. In particular, I examine the Danish commercial center, Tranquebar (Tharnamgambadi), in Nagapattinam District, Tamil Nadu and Danish colonial settlements on St. Thomas in the Virgin Islands to make two points (see fig. 15.1). First, distinctions between the Danish West and East Indies are as much a function of administrative categories as a description of capital flows and movements of people. These enclaves were connected through material relations. Second, that

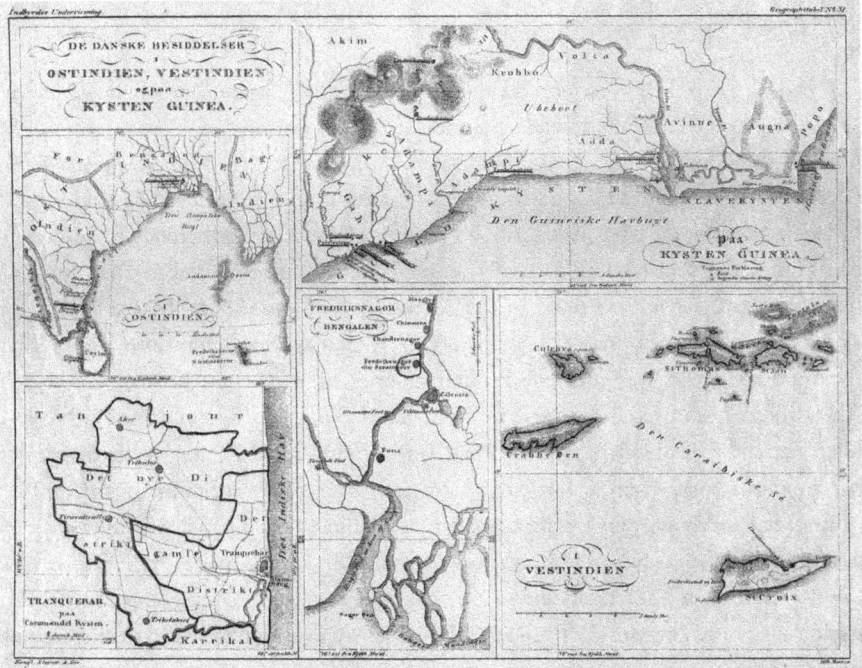

Figure 15.1. Map of the Danish Possessions done in 1828. Counterclockwise beginning in lower-left-hand corner: West Indies (USVI), Gold Coast (Ghana), East Indies (Tranquebar, Fredricksnagar, and Nicobar Islands), Tranquebar (Tamil Nadu) and Fredricksnagar (West Bengal). (KBK Gamle danske besiddelser, Trankebar-0-1825/1 Image 3. Courtesy of the Royal Library, Map Collection, Denmark)

two enclaves implicated in these seemingly distinct regimes were similar in landscape and interaction, despite ostensibly distinct roles. Investigation of changing landscapes associated with the seventeenth- to eighteenth-century imposition of the Danish in the Indian and Atlantic Oceans documents shared and distinct practices by natives and newcomers in relationship to land use, social organization, and commercial engagement.

Two Oceans One System in the Danish Mercantile World

As Philip Stern notes in regard to British Asia and the Atlantic, emphasizing the differences rather than the similarities has shaped historical accounts where development of commerce and empire in each ocean diverges. Despite common agents and commodities flowing between the oceans, the Indian and the Atlantic are often treated as separate bodies of scholarship with their own separate questions that are considered worth asking (2006, 695). For Stern this is unfortunate, because there is a host of ways to integrate both oceans beyond anecdotal accounts that include examination of the ideologies informing engagement with the region, constitution of companies, the methods of the functioning. As such, it becomes the work of political, social, and intellectual histories. This allows us to think more closely about the Danish overseas interests.

Between 1606 and 1794 the Danish crown chartered more than twenty agencies responsible for trade in three regions. Royal Monopolies in trade in the North Atlantic began in 1606, when King Christian the IV granted Copenhagen exclusive rights to trade with Iceland. By 1721, the North Atlantic holdings included Iceland, the Faeroe Islands, Finmark, and Greenland (Feldbæk 1986). The Asian sphere of operation began when the Danish East India Company was chartered in 1616 and Tharangambadi was acquired through lease in 1620 from the Thanjavur (Tanjore) ruler Raghunatha Nayak (Bredsdorff 2009). Over the course of the seventh and eighteenth centuries, the Danish East India Company and its descendants were administered out of Tharangambadi, but included holdings in present day Nicobar, West Bengal, Jakarta, Kerala, and Sulawesi.[1] The Danes only engaged with the mid-Atlantic region, including Africa and the West Indies, in the 1650s. By 1733, its holdings included forts and factories along the Gold Coast, and the islands of St. Thomas, St. John, and St. Croix. While these regions have been traditionally dealt with as distinct constellations, they were interrelated in important ways.

The Danish West Indies

The Danish West India Company was loosely modeled on the Danish East India Company, with many of its key posts being taken up by Dutch nationals. The companies most closely associated with the Atlantic World began with the chartering of the *Glückstadt Guinea* and the Guinea Company of Copenhagen in 1651 and 1656, respectively (Feldbæk 1986, 210). By 1659 key fortified trading posts were seized from Sweden and a structured organization around the slave trade began in 1665, when they first attempted to colonize St. Thomas (DeCorse 1993; Westergaard 1917, 40–41). King Christian the V granted a charter in 1671 for a Danish West India Company (Gøbel 1980). From 1674 onward, there existed a Danish West India-Guinea Company with a monopoly on the trade and a commitment to administer the slave forts on the Gold Coast and to administer the West Indian holdings (Feldbæk 1986, 209). Unlike the East India Company, and in conformity with Danish economic policy, the company's holdings were administered in Copenhagen. Crown Colony status was instituted in 1750, and by 1850 the Danish had sold the Gold Coast possessions to the United Kingdom; in 1917 the Danish West Indies to the United States (Dookhan 1974).

While not a dominant military force, the Danes played important roles during the turbulent eighteenth century. They constituted a wedge between Spanish Puerto Rico, with its dependencies, and Britain's Virgin Islands to the east (Hall 1992). This factor of insular proximity in a patchwork of national properties had important implications for how the Danish West Indies developed both as a free port and as a safe harbor during times of war. For example, after the Seven Years War in 1764, Danish authorities permitted ships of all nations to trade, while maintaining the monopoly between the Danish colonies and Europe (Westergaard 1917, 250). By 1815, all trade restrictions were lifted in St. Thomas and St. John, allowing foreigners equal privileges with those of royal subjects (Armstrong 2003).

The Danish trade was highly profitable.[2] Unlike the Dutch, where gold was 75 percent of the value of exports for West Africa and slaves 13 percent, the exact opposite was true for the Danes. Between 1696 and 1754, the Danish West India-Guinea Company shipped merchandise with a value of 670,000 rix-dollars to the Danish West Indies, and 730,000 rix-dollars to the Gold Coast. The Danish slave trade was threefold. First, there was the Atlantic slave trade importing labor from Africa to the plantations of the DWI. Second, there was also transshipment from St. Thomas and St. John to other colonies. Finally, there was a trade in Caribbean slaves centered around St. Thomas. Svend Green Pedersen estimates that between 1733 and 1807 the Danes exported 50,000 slaves from West Africa (Green-Pedersen 1971). Beyond that St. Thomas acted as a transshipment port for many flags. Pedersen continued to estimate that some 70,000 slaves were involved in the St. Thomas slave trade, thus making it a center of gravity for the company (Green-Pedersen 1975).

While the West India-Guinea Company have been treated as one entity, each region provided different sets of goods and received different sets of goods from Copenhagen. Objects sent to the West African coast included metal ingots, fish hooks, Danish alcohol, brass bangles, and cowries. Textiles comprised nearly 30 percent of cargo sent to the West Indies and nearly 50 percent of the cargo sent to the Gold Coast. Textiles of Indian origin were by far the most popular textile on the Gold Coast (Gøbel 1983, 29). The range of goods sent to the West Indies included military supplies, foodstuffs, textiles, and other goods. From 1702 to 1747, between 70 and 50 percent of the goods were a combination of raw materials like iron, copper, lead, and whale oil, as well as manufactured wares including saws, axes, grindstones appliances, furniture, and apparel. From West Africa, ivory, gold, and humans were taken to the West Indies where the humans would be deboarded and sold. Sugar (in various stages of refinement) and cotton from St. Thomas, along with the African Gold and Ivory, would be shipped to Copenhagen.[3] In addition silver specie acquired through the sale of human cargo purchased in Africa was made available to the European market.

The Danish East Indies

Denmark would be one of several European nations that vied for South Indian trade between the seventeenth and nineteenth centuries. Unlike the Dutch or Portuguese who established more than thirty forts, trading lodges, and plantations on the Malabar and Coromandel Coasts, their engagement was limited to at Tharangambadi on the Coromandel Coast (Diller 1999),[4] which became the company's Asian headquarters. While the Danes had factors in the Bay of Bengal as early as 1670s the Danish colonial presence was formalized in 1755, when the Danish East India Company acquired Serempore and Akhan from the Nawab of Bengal. In the course of the eighteenth century, several attempts were made to establish colonies in the Nicobar Islands. These enclaves remained under company rule until 1775, when all of the company's holdings became a Crown Colony. By 1850, it had sold its Indian possession to the United Kingdom.

While not the dominant mercantile power, the Danes played an important role in the development of Indo-European relations in the region. The Danish Crown chartered the company so that home markets could gain access to tropical commodities such as spices, and Asian trade goods, including cloth and porcelain (Subrahmanyam 1989). Some of the goods included ship stores, domestic cloth for the Chinese market, as well as iron, lead, and copper kept as ballast (Glamann 1960, 116). Miscellaneous items including guns, anchors, barrel hops, nails, and cauldrons were also carried as cargo and ballast. However between 73 and 90 percent of the cargo of East Indiamen traveling from Denmark largely consisted of specie (Glamann 1960: 115). The chain of transactions through which the silver was acquired to mint the specie included a combination of merchants and moneylenders stretching through the Netherlands into mines of New Spain and Peru (Kindleberger 1989).

Tharangambadi was a resource for humans, textiles, and foodstuffs, and a potential market for goods made in other parts of the Danish and Dutch East India companies (Arasaratnam 1986; Raychaudhuri 2013; Struwe 1952). As early as the 1620s, merchants conducted trade with Achim in Sumatra, Bantam in Java, and Macassar in the Celebes in the Indian Ocean (Gøbel 1991, 105). By 1645, trade routes included Porto Novo, Tegnapantam, Pondicherry, and Palicat on the Coromandel Coast, Macassar, Achin, Kedah, Banjamsin, Cherapon, and Japara in present-day Indonesia, Emaldy in Bengal, and Cotiari in present-day Sri Lanka. At the same time, the Danes were in commercial contact with China, the Philippines, and Siam. By 1670, trading itineraries included Pondicherry, Porto Novo, Tondi, Madras, Nagore, Carical, and Nagapatnam on the Coromandel Coast; Malacca and the Sunda Islands; Calicut and Cochin in Malabar; China; and Isle de France. The Danish East India Company also circulated goods within the Indian Ocean. From the region surrounding Tharangambadi, Danes obtained textiles and rice that would be sold throughout the Indian Ocean (Arasaratnam 1986: 103). These would be traded for cloves, sandalwood, pepper, and ginger from Malabar, Sumatra, Java, and the Celebes, and cowry shells in the Isle de France (Gøbel 1991, 51; Heimann 1980; Subrahmanyam 1989).

Goods circulated through the Danish East India Company included salt, rice, and cotton textiles for the Atlantic and Indian Ocean markets (Feldbæk 1986; Glamann 1960), and slaves to fill a variety of roles in the broader Indian Ocean, including domestic service, craft industries, and agricultural labor (Arasaratnam 1995; Carter 2006) (see fig. 15.2). Cloth and rice were generally acquired through country trade from markets near the Danish settlements on the Coromandel Coast (Tharangambadi) and in Bengal (Serempoor) (Feldbæk 1991, 101). As such, the enclave was important to Thanjavur ruler. It bolstered his own political interests with neighboring kingdoms and offset an imbalance of trade and power that had developed between the Portuguese and the local merchants. However, to identify this as a convivial relationship that benefited all would be to elide many of the ruptures and conflicts that did emerge between Thanjavur and the Danes.

Connected Companies

It is scarcely an accident that the spheres of operation had important differences. For example, the Indian Ocean companies were the first to offer a significant departure from late medieval economic circuitries. The Atlantic Ocean enclaves were more

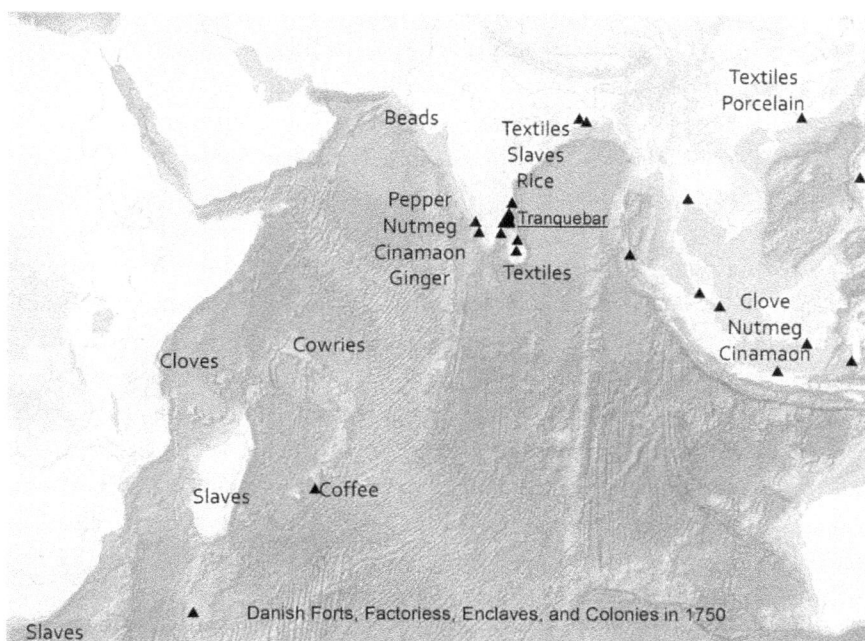

Figure 15.2. Source of goods circulating through the Danish East India Company based on information in Arasaratnam (1995) and Gøbel (1991). (Illustration by Mark W. Hauser)

adaptable because of the distances involved. Add to that the presence of a laboring population that was enslaved meant there was a cost for administering forts and islands that were disproportionately born by the state. But it is important to remember these differences were not born out of preexisting conditions. They were framed largely through the administrative structure of the companies themselves.

The financial correspondence between the spheres of operation was not epiphenomenal. An account book from the *Kommerce Collegiate Journal* reveals that the governor and council in Tharangambadi stood accountable to Kommercekollegiet in Copenhagen. Kommercekollegiet was the central administrative agency for commercial, seafaring, and industry conditions. The cargo enumerated in this document is largely unspoken. That said, it is most likely goods that were making their way to the Atlantic market. It is worth reiterating that return journeys of East India men brought back spices, and trade goods such as porcelain. In addition, cloth and cowries were also obtained from various East Indian ports. These goods would be used directly in the Guinea trade. In addition the cloth and sumptuary goods would be sold to markets in the West Indies. Specie obtained from the West Indies would wind up in Tharangambadi.

One of the commodities circulated to Malaysia and Indonesia from Tharangambadi were Indian slaves from Coromandel Coast (Carter 2006). Commerce in humans was largely managed as private trade among the company's officers. It also could be highly irregular as climatic conditions and harvest dictated the supply that fed the trade. For example, between 1630 and 1631 the monsoon failed to occur (Arasaratnam 1995, 105).The resulting famine meant that the cotton goods exchanged for spices in Macassar were limited. The famine also meant that many farmers sold their children for "a measure of rice to the value of a small coin worth 5 fanum, and the merchants found these could be sold with a large profit in the Sunda Islands" (Bredsdorff 2009, 109). By 1647, 2,000 slaves were being exported form Tharangambadi (Gøbel 2016, 59). By 1732 the Company attempted first to ban the private slave trade and then made the claim on the slave trade and the resulting profit. The initiative was not popular among the Company's officers, who had a secondary income through the slave trade. In 1744, the crown decided that the export of slaves from Tharangambadi should be stopped. This only applied to the company trade, "which was anemic at best. Nevertheless, the purchase of slaves for personal use in the home was still allowed. It was not until 1753 that a general ban on slaves was instituted.

Considerable profits could be made. For example, the Danish soldier Mourids Christensen, who served in Tharangambadi from 1671, documented the price of slaves on the Coromandel coast: 20 dollars for "one fresh groom"; 14–16 dollars for "one beautiful womenfolk"; and "one old womenfolk" could be acquired for 8–9 dollars (Bredsdorff 2009: 149). The corresponding export prices of Indian slaves to Bantam on the Indonesian island of Java was somewhat higher where a "fresh groom" was 40–60 dollars. Between March 14, 1688 and April 1, 1690, the slave trade brought to Tharangambadi 46,071 riks-dollars and four shillings (Larsen 1937). Acche was the most important market (Arasaratnam 1995, 210). In Batavia and Malacca, slaves labored in docks and in shipyards, loading, unloading, repairing, and servicing company vessels. In the Celebes, they labored on nutmeg and clove plantations; while in Sri Lanka, slaves grew food crops, worked as artisans or worked as construction laborers. For example, a group of 500 weavers forced by famine to sell themselves into slavery were able to relocate as a group to Jaffna where they set up a weaving and dying industry (Arasaratnam 1986, 210). Slaves were not only commodities to be circulated in the Indian Ocean, but also were purchased to be servants and laborers. By the mid-eighteenth century Danish activities in India moved away from Tharangambadi toward Bengal.

The itineraries of people and capital link the Danish East and West Indies in important ways. Charles Barrington (see fig. 15.3) was one of the many British

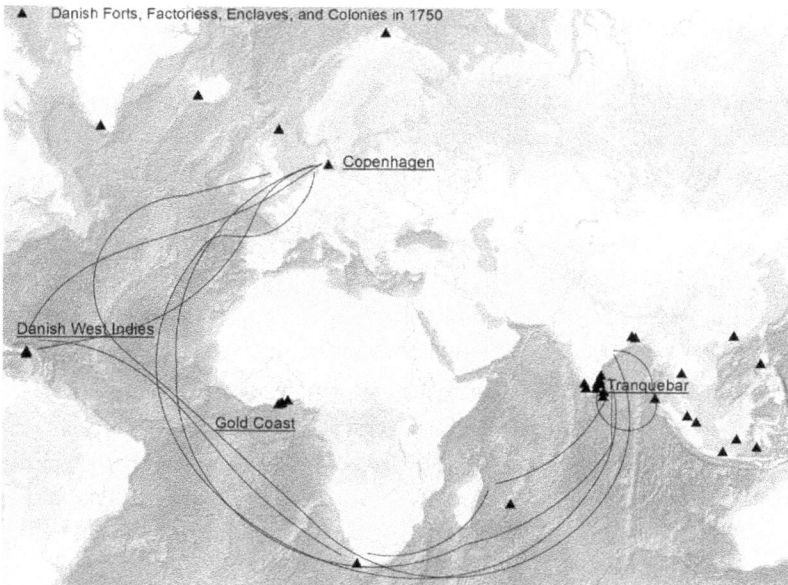

Figure 15.3. The travels of Charles Barrington in 1737, based on information in Banerji (1967) and Boucher (1981). (Illustration by Mark W. Hauser)

sailors and merchants who sought their fortunes with the Danes during the first half of the eighteenth century. After leaving the employ of the London East India Company, he joined the Swedish East India company to lend experience to their fledgling factory at Porto Novo (Banerji 1967). Then, after his failure, he left for Tharangambadi, where he remained until 1735. He later retired to Europe, where he planned to establish himself as a planter on the newly acquired Danish Colony of St. Croix. He approached the Danish West India-Guinea Company to hire the ship *Grevindin af Laurvig*, in order to purchase slaves from Madagascar and return to the West Indies. He never reached St. Thomas, but the vessel did, along with twenty-four slaves (Boucher 1981). Plantations materialized a set of commercial, political, and social relations on which empires and states depended. Commodity cultivation on plantations fueled consumption in imperial metropoles.

Two Danish Enclaves that Rhyme

Despite reactions and contingencies to local conditions, the landscapes of St. Thomas and Tharangambadi rhymed. Although one has generally been described as a plantation landscape and the other a merchant enclave, both had elements of the other. Archaeological engagements with colonialism and landscape in the Atlantic World show how archaeological survey attending to changes in settlement pattern, settlement organization, and household goods, allow insight into changing social roles, land use, and political orientations of communities in the "shatter-zone" of European mercantile engagement and colonialism (Delle 1999; Hauser and Hicks 2007; Kelly 2009; Symanski 2012; Voss 2008). Yet, most Americanist archaeologists' understandings of European expansion come largely from American colonialism (Wilson & Hauser 2016). Recent scholarship demonstrates the importance of a transnational lens that includes colonial holdings in South Asia (Chakrabarti 2003; Dhavalikar 1999; Wilson 2015). Scholars pursuing research on the colonial period have concentrated on fortifications (Lewis 2012; Wilson, Ambekar, & Pande 2013), colonial architecture (Gomes 2011; Hjelm 1987; Rossa & Mendiratta 2008; Shokoohy 2003; Shokoohy & Shokoohy 2010), cemeteries (Brown 2003; Buettner 2006; Scarre & Roberts 2005; Wilkinson 1984), and trade goods (Brooks, et al. 2015; Parthesius, Millar, & Jeffery 2005; Simpson 1980; Subbarayalu 1996). These studies suggest the need for an analysis of landscapes in the wake of European engagement that attends to connected landscapes in the Atlantic World and Indian Ocean.

St. Thomas

St. Thomas was one of the few islands in the last quarter of the seventeenth century that possessed the necessary requirements for colonization (see fig. 15.4). The island had sufficient arable land, a deep-water harbor, and was one of the few islands that had not already been occupied despite early English and Dutch efforts. Like Tharangambadi, Charlotte Amalie subsequently emerged as a cosmopolitan port town. Critically different from Tharangambadi was the near absence of a local population native to the area. To meet this labor force, the first slaves arrived in St. Thomas in the 1670s. In 1715, Westergaard estimates that the population was composed of 547 Europeans, and 3,043 enslaved Africans. In St. Thomas and St. John, Danish, Dutch, English, French, and Spanish were widely spoken, as well as African languages of recently arrived enslaved Africans, and the wide array of Atlantic creole languages. Spatially, Charlotte Amalie consists of the Danish town, the focus of all commercial and company activity. Contiguous thereto along the waterfront, stood the Brandenburgery—that is, the collection of warehouses and

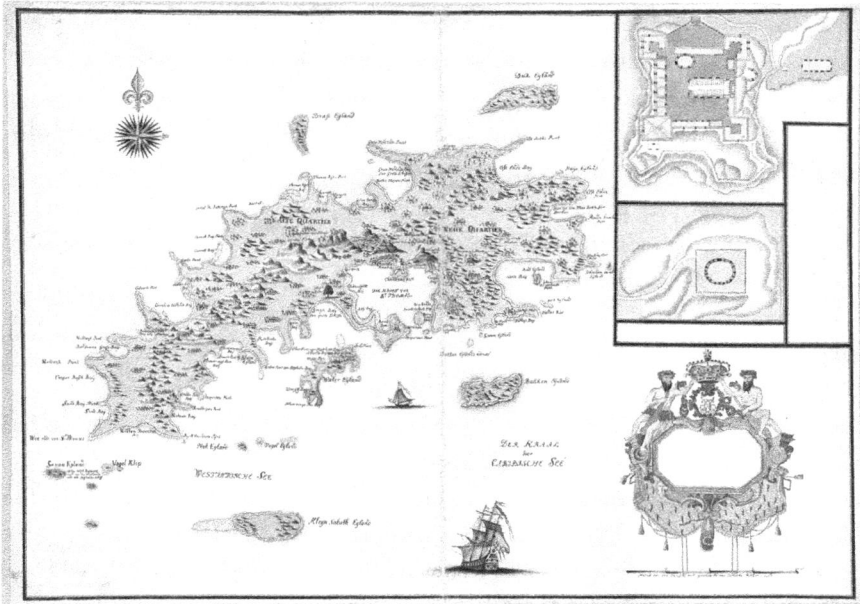

Figure 15.4. *Plan af den Kongel* [Plan of Kongel] showing the locations of ports, plantation settlements, and forts in St. Thomas in 1772. The map depicts the partial use of land for sugar cultivation in the late eighteenth century. (Danske Øe St.Thomas i Vestindien 1772, by Stervboe, Montarques. KBK Ingeniørkorpset Samling XIII, 2, 1. Courtesy of the Royal Library, Map Collection, Denmark)

dwellings leased to the German company. Finally, there was "the negro village," where most of the island's free blacks lived.

Like many neighboring islands, the Danish West Indies was also involved in commodity production. Along with establishing free ports in St. John and St. Thomas for the transshipment of slaves and goods, it had also had the ambition of establishing sugar plantations (Hauser & Armstrong 2012). So, in 1671, along with Charlotte Amalie, some 109 plantations were settled. After some lackluster returns, St. John was officially colonized in 1718. The company established one sugar estate at Coral Bay. After some experimentation the company began refining sugar in Copenhagen in 1729. In 1733, it acquired St. Croix to assure its refinery a steady supply of raw materials. The following year it was granted a monopoly for importing and refining raw sugar in Denmark and Norway (Westergaard 1917).

During the first decades of colonization on St. Thomas, the housing of the original settlers (and their unnamed servants) was provisionally similar. Accommodations were in warehouses and huts built of locally cut timber. The earliest extractive practices required neither a large nor skilled labor force. Sugar, on the other hand, is costly and both labor and equipment intensive. As sugar production expanded and increasing numbers of entrepreneurs arrived on the colony to claim a share of the wealth that sugar was generating, shortages of labor became chronic. This was an intractable fact for all of the colonies. After 1700 sugar production eclipsed all other forms of agriculture, and clear divisions in housing emerged that enabled status and wealth distinctions to be underscored. Enslaved Africans were imported in ever greater numbers, essentially replacing other labor sources and to such an extent that administrators sought legislation to encourage the increase of white servants shipped out to the colony.

Tharangambadi

South India was a node in long-standing and robust trade networks, a site of intensified agriculture, and the location of polities exerting influence on a regional scale. Take for example, the long-term research undertaken through international collaboration in the Thungabadra River Valley. There is a long history of cultivation in South India, beginning as early as the third millennium BC (Krishna & Morrison 2009). In the valley there have been many agricultural transitions involving intensification- some of the most recent occurring in the 18th century (Morrison, et al. 1996). Archaeological examinations of Vijayanagara (destroyed in 1565) have important implications for the commercial, agricultural, and political landscape in which the Danes entered a century later (Lycett & Morrison 2013). The capital city, located in northern Karnataka was a cosmopolitan center of regional and interregional trade networks stretching as far away as Europe, East Africa, China, and Japan (Sinopoli 2003). The extent of its power, in part defined through inscriptions on Stelae, located on the putative borders, extended far to the south (Morrison &Lycett 1997, 220). Temple inscriptions describe actions of the state and the reactions of its subjects in South Arcot, Thanjavur, Chingleput, and Tiruchirapalli districts of Tamil Nadu (Sinopoli 1988).

The Vijayanagara Empire incorporated local and regional deities. This had the effect of elevating local communities they were associated with, and in so doing advancing a dominant ideology of the state. Language and local politics were also mobilized by elites to maintain and advance their own interests (Sinopoli 2000, 394). Non-elites, while being largely defined by geography and occupation, also found ways to mobilize their status within the empire. Weavers and smiths whose craft supplied urban elites with cloth and elite goods experienced economic and social mobility. This enhanced status coincided with some internal differentiation. At the same time different castes could form solidarities that moved beyond occupation and locality on which Vijayanagra's dominant ideology was based. Nine inscriptions, dating between1426 and 1429, describe joint resolutions made between artisans and agricultural producers resisting tax rates imposed on them by Brahmans, local leaders, and imperial elites (Sinopoli, 1998, 170). This is significant for the Atlantic World because, a lot of the methods of governing diversity, found in the overseas holdings of Northern European powers such as Denmark, have parallels, if not antecedents in South India.

It is also important because those living in the twenty-three villages now under Danish control were not new to distant relations of power. Europeans inserted themselves into this political and economic landscape. Unlike the Dutch or Portuguese who established more than thirty forts, trading lodges and plantations in south India, Danish engagement during the study period was limited to Tharangambadi (Brøndsted 1966). Danish efforts there predate their factories in Africa and the West Indies and were strategically located to take advantage of changes in the early modern period and engage with a range of Indian Ocean political and economic actors (Subrahmanyam 1989). A focus on this settlement enables a more thorough documentation of changes in land use, social roles, and commercial arrangements, and allows comparison with similarly studied Danish enclaves in the Caribbean (Armstrong, et al. 2008) and West Africa (DeCorse 1993).

The Thanjavur ruler granted the Danish control of twenty-three villages in 1670—expanding the territory to fifty square miles. The location of Tharangambadi enabled Danes to take advantage of shifting economic and political arrangements on the Coromandel Coast between the seventeenth and eighteenth centuries (Arasaratnam 1986; Gøbel 1991; Subrahmanyam 1989). Attacks on hinterland weaving and market centers during the war between the Marathas and the Mughals meant that trade was disrupted for commercial centers (see fig. 15.5). Consequently, merchants

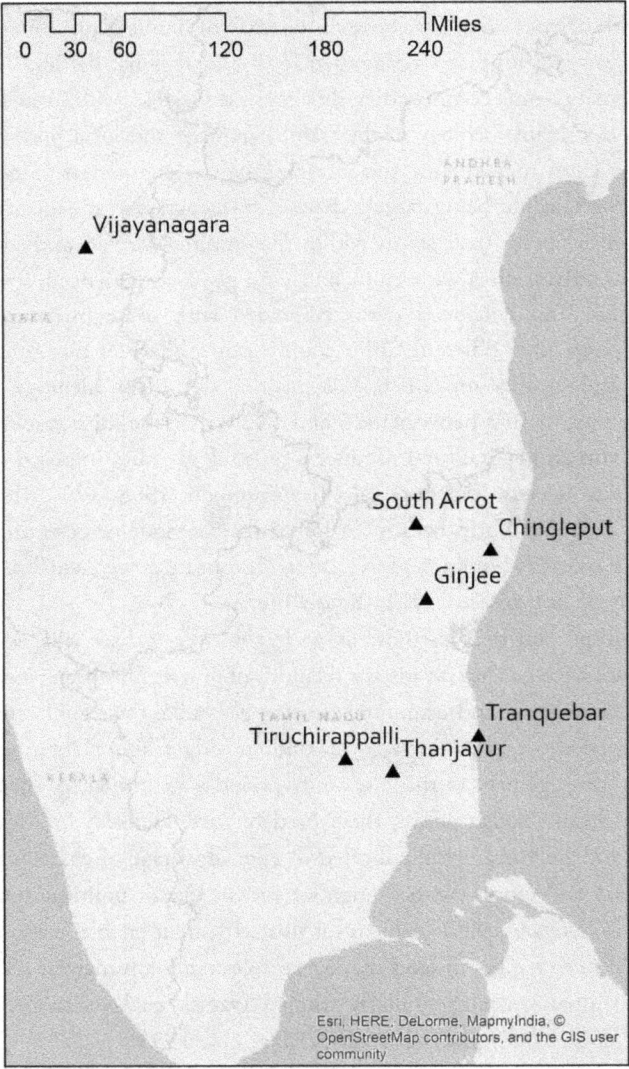

Figure 15.5a. Locations described in the text.

Figure 15.5b. Medieval Fortifications at Ginjee, Tamil Nadu.

Figure 15.5c. Colonial Fortification at Tranquebar (Map and Photographs by Mark W. Hauser)

moved to the south and some Indian European trade centers grew, while others stagnated—independent of the polity that controlled them (Arasaratnam 1986). Additionally, famines affecting the hinterland in the seventeenth and eighteenth centuries, enabled a steady supply of people to feed the Indian ocean slave trade (Gøbel 2016; Larsen 1937).

Studies of the Danish settlement at Tharangambadi have illustrated the potential for a study of landscapes associated with their presence (Højbjerg 1992; Jørgensen 2013; Pedersen 1987). Demographic research utilizing the colonial census has documented changing populations and hierarchy over the course of the seventeenth and eighteenth centuries (Højbjerg 1990; Højbjerg 1992). According to Jan Olafsson who resided there between 1618 and 1622, Tharangambadi was home to Africans, Egyptians, Arabs, Dutch, Danes, English, Javanese, Mollacan, and Portuguese. There were the eighteen villages of varying sizes with a total population of 20,000 people. The largest, Tillali and Poreiar, had respectively 3,307 and 5,172 inhabitants in 1790 (Rasch 1967, 13).[5]

Those living in Tharangambadi and its environs were socially and linguistically diverse, and the Danish presence contributed to changing social dynamics. Tamil-speaking people shaped both commerce and social life (Brimnes 1999). Tharangambadi was an area dominated by the agricultural community of the Vellalas (also Velalars, Vellalars, Vellalas). The Vellalas were landlords and part of the elite caste who patronized the arts during the medieval period (Brimnes 1999, 93). In the town, over one-third of the households were headed by a Vellala, and in the villages they comprised one-third of the population. Other communities included a significant Muslim population, Kavarais and the Paraiyans. The Kavarais (Balija Chetties) were a Telegu-speaking population comprised of traders from the north (present-day Andrah Pradesh and Telagan) who were Tamilized (Brimnes 1999, 106). The Paraiyans were landless laborers who were at the bottom of the social hierarchy. According to Brimmes, their stock rose under company rule (Brimnes 1999, 202–3).

Matthau Seuter's (1678–1757) map (see fig. 15.6) is particularly useful in reconstructing Tharangambadi's landscape. Published circa 1740, the map, including a plan of the settlement and description, was based on illustrations and accounts contained within the Danischen Missionarien series. It nonetheless can be used to understand some of the settlement decisions made before and after Danish colonization. The map depicts the countryside as a bucolic, carefully manicured plantation landscape with rolling fields and rows of trees neatly aligned along country roads.

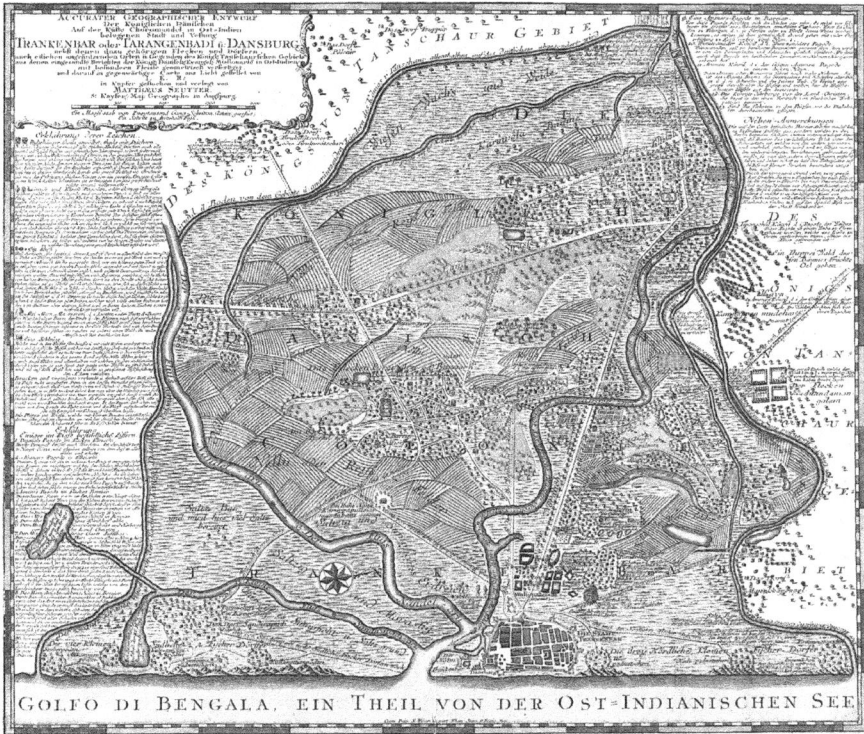

Figure 15.6. *Accuratur Geographischer Entwurf* [Accurate Geographic Design] of Tranquebar in 1730, including the locations of villages, agricultural settlements, and the fort. The map depicts land use, including rice cultivation, irrigation, and the location of and identity of villages. Importantly, the rest houses of the Danish factors are located in Tranquebar's hinterland. (Matthäus Seutter, *KBK Gamle danske besiddelser, Trankebar-0-1730/1-2 Image 2.* Courtesy of the Royal Library, Map Collection, Denmark)

At the time the colonial enclave consisted of over seventy-one square kilometers, encompassing all of the areas of primary economic importance, including fields, kilns, and Danish and local elite residences, and several Indian villages. The positions of the villages and the rest houses were dependent on the location of the fields and roads. Rice fields were given priority for economic reasons, and were located on low-lying, flat strips of fertile soil. Some of the villages are described based on the profession of their inhabitants, such as fishing villages. Others appear to be larger, incorporating the diverse population of the enclave. As identified in the Legend of Sites, the map labels the locations of Hindu Temples ("Pagoden"),

Christian churches, lime kilns, brick kilns, rest houses, and slues gates along the rivers and canals. Land devoted to agriculture includes fields for rice cultivation, different tree species, including coconut palms, and palms for oil. Finally, (Banyan) trees, are denoted as landscape elements of significance.

Notes running along the sides of the Seuter map describe the attributes of the colony in detail. The enclave had 2,407 buildings spread among nineteen villages. In addition, there were 507 buildings in the city of Tharangambadi itself. Importantly smaller hamlets adjoin many larger villages. These villages were spatially separated settlements designated for particular castes, religious groups, and professions. Some settlements distinguished themselves in spatial organization. Take for example settlement 4 (see fig. 15.6). It is identified as the rest house with European gardens. The document goes on to state that inhabitants in the village care for the gardens and provide a portion of rice to the owner Georg Boying.

The representation of settlement organization and the layout of the land are provocative in that in the Atlantic world they might represent an expression of power relations rigid class structure and some land owner's external control over the field laborers provide a means of organizing labor. It could be the villages were deliberately arranged to maintain distinctions. In some cases these settlements and hamlets seem to be reserved for communities linked to religious identity (such as Catholic or Muslim) or profession (such as fishers or Poriyars). In other cases, some hamlets seem to be attached to rest houses of landlords or European owners. In these cases the hamlets appear to be similar to a West Indian planter's spatial criteria for plantation management.

Conclusion

Considering the enclaves in combination highlights a few important similarities. Maps of territory in Tharangambadi and St. Thomas were equally concerned with settlement patterns and settlement organization. Maps allowed company administrators to think about three things: (1) a radical improvement of the predictability and scheduling of harvests; (2) an increased capacity for describing the markets available for Indian Ocean and Atlantic world products, and (3) a growth in the potential maximum size of individual communities in the entire region. It also appears that there were changes in settlement pattern and organization during the course of the eighteenth century that go beyond the ability of maps to capture that change.

That said, in both cases it is surprising to note how limited our understanding is of the overall pattern and timing of demographic change and how households and communities might have dealt with such shifts.

One significant difference is worth noting in the cartographic representations. The 1740 map of Tharangambadi emphasizes several features that go unrecognized in St. Thomas. First, there is a heavy emphasis on the productive resources of the enclave. Highlighted in great detail are the salt pans, rice fields, and coconut palms that were so vital to the East Indian trade. In contrast, the Maps of St. Thomas and St. John are not interested in detailing differences in land use. While there are many potential reasons for this, it does illustrate one important feature. While St. Thomas and St. John have often been depicted as plantation colonies and Tharangambadi as a mercantile colony, it is worth noting that St. Thomas and St. John were as much a mercantile center and Tharangambadi was as much a plantation enclave.

Rather than using formal characteristics as a proxy for attributes internal to historical polities, Subramanyam argues that these historical entities interacted with one another. As such, contrasting outcomes are not the result of attributes internal to entities such as empires or colonies, but reflect "mutually conditioning socioeconomic configurations whose divergent trajectories have decisive implications for the recomposition of land, labor, and technology in each instance" (Tomich 1994, 340). This is an exercise in social relations, rather than a categorical analysis where descriptive statistics somehow how reveal generalizable truths. It is commonly argued that the wider Indian Ocean contained nothing resembling a slave-based plantation system until the later French settlement in Mauritius in the eighteenth century (Vaughan 2005). Investigation of landscapes with the seventeenth to eighteenth centuries imposition of the Danish in the Indian and Atlantic Oceans documents evidence for shared and distinct practices by natives and newcomers in relationship to land use, social organization, and commercial engagement. Skills, practices, and knowledge derived from the Indian Ocean were required to make the plantation mode of production work in the Atlantic.

Notes

1. The Danish East India Company (Østindisk Kompagni) had two iterations—one chartered in 1616 and the second in 1670. In 1730 it was reestablished as Asiatisk Kompagni.

2. Erik Gøobel estimates that in the first half of the eighteenth century, the company shipped 600,000 rix-dollars in goods to Guinea and West Indies, and was able to sell the return cargo for 2 million rix-dollars (Gøbel 1983).

3. According to Erik Gøbel gold and ivory comprised 13 percent of the trade (Gøbel 1983, 31).

4. The Netherlands provided the model and expertise for the founding of this new Danish East India Company in 1616. Dutch promoters and Copenhagen merchants petitioned King Christian the IV in the years leading up to the founding of the company, and its charter closely mirrored the United East India Company's (VOC) organization. Ole Feldbæk has made the point that several articles of the Danish charter were direct translations of the 1602 Dutch charter (1986, 206).

5. In 1730, a Moravian missionary documented 3,000 inhabitants of the fortified town with 100–200 Danish residents. They also estimated that there were 20,000 inhabitants in small villages. By 1790 there were 3,721 people living in Tharangambadi town with a total of 157 Danes, 20 other Europeans, and 62 indo-Portuguese residents (Højbjerg 1990; Pedersen 1987, 3).

Works Cited

Adas, Michael. 1983. "Colonization, Commercial Agriculture, and the Destruction of the Deltaic Rainforests of British Burma in the Late Nineteenth Century." In *Global Deforestation and the Nineteenth Century World Economy*. Edited by Richard P. Tucker and J. F. Richards, 95–110. Durham, NC: Duke University Press.

Arasaratnam, Sinnappah. 1986. *Merchants, Companies, and Commerce on the Coromandel Coast, 1650–1740*. Delhi, India: Oxford University Press.

———. 1995. "Slave Trade in the Indian Ocean in the Seventeenth Century." In *Mariners, Merchants and Oceans: Studies in Maritime History*. Edited by Kuzhippalli Skaria Mathew, 195–208. New Delhi: Manohar. Armstrong, Douglas. 2003. *Creole Transformation from Slavery to Freedom: Historical Archaeology of the East End Community, St. John, Virgin Islands*. Gainesville: University Press of Florida.

Armstrong, Douglas V., Mark Hauser, David W. Knight, and Stephan Lenik. 2008. "Maps, Matricals, and Material Culture: An Archaeological GIS of Late 18th Century Historic Sites on St. John, Danish West Indies." In *GIS in Caribbean Archaeology*. Edited by Basil A. Reid, 99–126. Tuscaloosa: University of Alabama Press.

Banerji, R. N. 1967. "Early Swedish Trade Relation with India." *Proceedings of the Indian History Congress* 29: 74–82.

Beckert, Sven. 2004. "Emancipation and Empire: Reconstructing the Worldwide Web of Cotton Production in the Age of the American Civil War." *American Historical Review* 109(5): 1405–38.

Blackburn, Robin. 1997. *The Making of New World Slavery: From the Baroque to the Modern, 1492–1800*. London: Verso.

Boucher, Maurice. 1981. "An Unexpected Visitor: Charles Barrington at the Cape in 1737." *South African Historical Journal* 13(1): 20–35.

Braudel, Fernand. 1995. *The Mediterranean and the Mediterranean World in the Age of Philip II*, vol. 2. Berkeley: University of California Press.

Bredsdorff, Asta. 2009. *The Trials and Travels of Willem Leyel: An Account of the Danish East India Company in Tranquebar, 1639–48*. Copenhagen: Museum Tusculanum Press.

Brimnes, Niels. 1999. *Constructing the Colonial Encounter: Right and Left Hand castes in Early Colonial South India,* vol. 81. London: Psychology Press.

Brøndsted, Johannes. 1966. *Vore gamle tropekolonier*. Copenhagen: Westermann.

Brooks, Alasdair, Omar Al-Kaabi, Timothy Power, and Peter Sheehan. 2015. "New Objects, Old Trade: 19th- and 20th-Century European Ceramics and Glass in Al Ain, Abu Dhabi, United Arab Emirates."48th Annual Conference on Historical and Underwater Archaeology, Seattle, WA, 2015.

Brown, Rebecca M. 2003. "The Cemeteries and the Suburbs: Patna's Challenges to the Colonial City in South Asia." *Journal of Urban History* 29(2): 151–72.

Buettner, Elizabeth. 2006. "Cemeteries, Public Memory and Raj Nostalgia in Postcolonial Britain and India." *History & Memory* 18(1): 5–42.

Carter, Marina. 2006. "Slavery and Unfree Labour in the Indian Ocean." *History Compass* 4(5): 800–13.

Chakrabarti, Dilip K. 2003. *The Archaeology of European Expansion in India: Gujarat, C. 16th–18th Centuries*. New Delhi: Aryan Books International.

Chaudhuri, Kirti N. 2006. *The Trading World of Asia and the English East India Company: 1660–1760*. Cambridge: Cambridge University Press.

Chaudhury, Sushil, and Michel Morineau. 2007. *Merchants, Companies and Trade: Europe and Asia in the Early Modern Era*. Cambridge University Press.

Coclanis, Peter A. 1993. "Distant Thunder: The Creation of a World Market in Rice and the Transformations It Wrought." *American Historical Review* 98(4): 1050–78.

Davies, Timothy. 2014. "English Private Trade on the West Coast of India, c. 1680–c. 1740." *Itinerario* 38(02): 51–73.

DeCorse, Christopher R. 1993. "The Danes on the Gold Coast: Culture Change and the European Presence." *African Archaeological Review* 11(1): 149–73.

Delle, James A. 1999. "Extending Europe's Grasp: An Archaeological Comparison of Colonial Spatial Processes in Ireland and Jamaica." *Old and New Worlds*. 106–16. Oxford, UK: Oxbow Books.

———. 2014. *The Colonial Caribbean: Landscapes of Power in Jamaica's Plantation System*. Cambridge University Press.

Dhavalikar, Madhukar Keshav. 1999. *Historical Archaeology of India*. New Delhi, India: Books & Books.

Diller, Stephan. 1999. *Die Dänen in Indien, Südostasien und China (1620–1845)*, vol. 8. Otto Harrassowitz Verlag.

Dookhan, Isaac. 1974. *A History of the Virgin Islands of the United States.* Kingston, Jamaica: Canoe Press.

Elliott, John Huxtable. 2007. *Empires of the Atlantic World: Britain and Spain in America, 1492–1830.* New Haven, CT: Yale University Press.

Feldbæk, Ole. 1986. "The Danish Trading Companies of the Seventeenth and Eighteenth Centuries." *Scandinavian Economic History Review* 34(3): 204–18.

———. 1991. "Country Trade under Danish Colours: A Study of Economica and Politics around 1800," In *Asian Trade Routes*, vol. 13. Edited by Karl Reinhold Haellquist, 96–103. London: Curzon Press.

Fihl, Esther, and AR Venkatachalapathy. 2009. "Indo-Danish Cultural Encounters in Tranquebar: Past and Present." *Special Double Issue of Review of Development and Change* 14: 1–2.

Glamann, Kristof. 1960. "The Danish Asiatic Company, 1732–; 1772." *Scandinavian Economic History Review* 8(2): 109–49.

Gøbel, Erik. 1983. "Danish Trade to the West Indies and Guinea, 1671–1754." *Scandinavian Economic History Review* 31(1): 21–49.

———. 1991. "Danish Country Trade Routes in Asian Waters in the Seventeenth and Eighteenth Centuries." In *Asian Trade Routes*, vol. 13. Edited by Karl Reinhold Haellquist, 104–16. London: Curzon Press.

———. 2016. *The Danish Slave Trade and Its Abolition.* Amsterdam, the Netherlands: Brill.

Gomes, Paulo Varela. 2011. *Whitewash, Red Stone: A History of Church Architecture in Goa.* New Delhi: Yoda Press.

Gottmann, Felicia. 2013. "French-Asian Connections: the Compagnies des Indes, Frances's Eastern Trade, and New Directions in Historical Scholarship." *Historical Journal* 56(2): 537–52.

Grafe, Regina. 2011. *Distant Tyranny: Markets, Power, and Backwardness in Spain, 1650–1800.* Princeton, NJ: Princeton University Press.

Grafe, Regina, and Alejandra Irigoin. 2012. "A Stakeholder Empire: The Political Economy of Spanish Imperial Rule in America." *Economic History Review* 65(2): 609–51.

Green-Pedersen, Svend E. 1971. "The scope and Structure of the Danish Negro Slave Trade." *Scandinavian Economic History Review* 19(2): 149–97.

———. 1975. "The History of the Danish Negro Slave Trade, 1733–1807: An Interim Survey Relating in Particular to Its Volume, Structure, Profitability and Abolition." *Revue française d'histoire d'outre-mer* 62(226): 196–220.

Hall, Derek. 2011. "Land Grabs, Land Control, and Southeast Asian Crop Booms." *Journal of Peasant Studies* 38(4): 837–57.

Hall, Neville AT. 1992. *Slave Society in the Danish West Indies: St. Thomas, St. John, and St. Croix.* Aarhus Universitetsforlag.

Hart, Gillian. 2002. "Geography and Development: Development/s beyond Neoliberalism? Power, Culture, Political Economy." *Progress in Human Geography* 26(6): 812–22.

Hartwick, Elaine. 1998. "Geographies of Consumption: A Commodity-Chain approach." *Environment and Planning D: Society and Space* 16(4): 423–37.

Hauser, Mark W. 2008. *An Archaeology of Black Markets: Local Ceramics and Economies in Eighteenth-Century Jamaica.* Gainesville: University Press of Florida.

———. 2011. "Routes and Roots of Empire: Pots, Power, and Slavery in the 18th-Century British Caribbean." *American Anthropologist* 113(3): 431–47.

Hauser, Mark W, and Douglas Armstrong. 2012. "The Archaeology of Not Being Governed: A Counterpoint to a History of Settlement of Two Colonies in the Eastern Caribbean." *Journal of Social Archaeology* 12(3): 310–33.

Hauser, Mark W., and Dan Hicks. 2007. "Colonialism and Landscape: Power, Materiality and Scales of Analysis in Caribbean Historical Archaeology." In *Envisioning Landscape: Situations and Standpoints in Archaeology and Heritage.* Edited by Dan Hicks, Laura McAtackney, and Graham Fairclough, 251–74. Left Coast, Walnut Creek, California.

Heimann, James. 1980. "Small Change and Ballast: Cowry Trade and Usage as an Example of Indian Ocean Economic History." *South Asia: Journal of South Asian Studies* 3(1): 48–69.

Hjelm, Torben. 1987. "Dansborg." *Architectura* 9: 89–121.

Højbjerg, Inger. 1990. Tranquebars Bybefolkningen 1620–1845, University of Copenhagen.

———. 1992. "Tranquebars bybefolkning 1620–1845 i begyndelsen af 1700-tallet." *Handels- og Søfartsmuseet Årbog:* 67–89.

Hughes, Alex, and Suzanne Reimer. 2004. *Geographies of Commodity Chains.* New York: Routledge.

Jørgensen, Helle. 2009. "Whose History? Transnational Cultural Heritage in Tranquebar." *Review of Development and Change* 14(1–2): 227–50.

———. 2013. "Heritage Tourism in Tranquebar: Colonial Nostalgia or Postcolonial Encounter?" *In Scandinavian Colonialism and the Rise of Modernity.* Edited by Magdalena Naum and Jonas M. Nordin, 69–86. New York: Springer.

Kelly, Kenneth. 2009. "Controlling Traders: Slave Coast Strategies at Savi and Ouidah." *Bridging Early Modern Atlantic Worlds: People, Products, and Practices on the Move*: 151–71. New York: Routledge.

Kindleberger, Charles Poor. 1989. *Spenders and Hoarders: The World Distribution of Spanish American Silver, 1550–1750.* Singapore: Institute of Southeast Asian Studies.

Krishna, K. R., and Kathleen D. Morrison. 2009. "History of South Indian Agriculture and Agroecosystems." *South Indian Agroecosystems: Nutrient Dynamics and Productivity.* 1–51. Boca Raton, FL: Brian Walker Press.

Larsen, Kay. 1937. "Danmark Og Slavehandelens Ophævelse." *Historisk Tidsskrift* 10: 106–8.

Lewis, Barry. 2012. "British Assessments of Tipu Sultan's Hill Forts in Northern Mysore, South India, 1802." *International Journal of Historical Archaeology* 16(1): 164–98.

Lycett, Mark T, and Kathleen D Morrison. 2013. "The 'Fall' of Vijayanagara Reconsidered: Political Destruction and Historical Construction in South Indian History 1." *Journal of the Economic and Social History of the Orient* 56(3): 433–70.

McMichael, Philip. 1990. "Incorporating Comparison within a World-Historical Perspective: An Alternative Comparative Method." *American Sociological Review*: 385–97.

Metcalf, Thomas R. 2007. *Imperial Connections: India in the Indian Ocean Arena, 1860–1920*, vol. 4. Berkeley: University of California Press.

Mintz, Sidney W. 1985. *Sweetness and Power: The Place of Sugar in Modern History*. New York: Viking.

Morrison, Kathleen D., Gary M. Feinman, Linda M. Nicholas, Thegn N. Ladefoged, Eva Myrdal-Runebjer, Glenn Davis Stone and Richard Wilk. 1996. "Typological Schemes and Agricultural Change: Beyond Boserup in Precolonial South India." *Current Anthropology* 37(4): 583–608.

Morrison, Kathleen D., and Mark T. Lycett. 1997. "Inscriptions as Artifacts: Precolonial South India and the Analysis of Texts." *Journal of Archaeological Method and Theory* 4(3–4): 215–37.

Nordin, Jonas M. 2016. "The World in a Nutshell: A Historical Archaeology of Early Modern Entanglement of Scandinavia and India Studied through the Life Course of the Danish Nobleman Ove Gjedde, 1594–1660." *Post-Medieval Archaeology*: 1–20.

Parthesius, Robert, Karen Millar, and Bill Jeffery. 2005. "Preliminary Report on the Excavation of the 17th-Century Anglo-Dutch East-Indiaman Avondster in Bay of Galle, Sri Lanka." *International Journal of Nautical Archaeology* 34(2): 216–37.

Pedersen, Karl Peder. 1987. "Landstederne Omkring Tranquebar." *Architectura* 9: 211–15.

Rao, R. S. 1991. "Marine Archaeological Explorations of Tranquebar-Poompuhar Region on Tamil Nadu Coast." *Marine Archaeology* 2: 5–20.

Rasch, Aage. 1967. *Dansk Ostindien 1777–1845*, vol. 7. København.

Raychaudhuri, A. K. 2013. *Jan Company in Coromandel 1605–1690: A Study in the Interrelations of European Commerce and Traditional Economies*. Springer.

Reid, Anthony. 1990. "An 'Age of Commerce' in Southeast Asian History." *Modern Asian Studies* 24(01): 1–30.

Rossa, Walter, and Sidh Mendiratta. 2008. Ghost Towns. Ruined and Disappeared Portuguese Colonial Settlements in Coastal Maharashtra, India: New Research Results. In *61st Annual Meeting of the Society of Architectural Historians*. Cincinnati, OH.

Scarre, Chris, and Judith Roberts. 2005. "The English Cemetery at Surat: Pre-colonial Cultural Encounters in Western India." *Antiquaries Journal* 85(01): 251–91.

Shokoohy, Mehrdad. 2003. *Muslim Architecture of South India: The Sultanate of Ma'bar and the Traditions of the Maritime Settlers on the Malabar and Coromandel Coasts (Tamil Nadu, Kerala and Goa)*. London: Psychology Press.

Shokoohy, Mehrdad, and Natalie H. Shokoohy. 2010. "The Island of Diu, Its Architecture and Historic Remains." *South Asian Studies* 26(2): 161–91.

Simpson, Donald. 1980. "The Treasure in the Vergulde Draeck: A Sample of VOC Bullion Exports in the 17th Century." *The Great Circle* 2(1): 13–17.

Sinopoli, C.M., 1998. Identity and social action among South Indian craft producers of the Vijayanagara period. *Archeological Papers of the American Anthropological Association,* 8(1), pp. 161–172.

Sinopoli, Carla M. 2000. "From the Lion Throne: Political and Social Dynamics of the Vijayanagara Empire." *Journal of the Economic and Social History of the Orient* 43(3): 364–98.

Sinopoli, Carla M. 2003. *The Political Economy of Craft Production Crafting Empire in South India, c. 1350–1650.* Cambridge, UK: Cambridge University Press.

Smith, Neil. 2009. "Nature as Accumulation Strategy." *Socialist Register* 43: 19–41.

Smith, Susan J. 2005. "States, Markets and an Ethic of Care." *Political Geography* 24(1): 1–20.

Stern, Philip J. 2006. "British Asia and British Atlantic: Comparisons and Connections." *William and Mary Quarterly* 63(4): 693–712.

Struwe, Kamma. 1952. *Dansk Ostindien 1732–1776: Tranquebar under kompagnistyre.*

Subbarayalu, Y. 1996. "Chinese Ceramics of Tamilnadu and Kerala Coasts." *Tradition and Archaeology*: 109–14.

Subrahmanyam, Sanjay. 1989. "The Coromandel Trade of the Danish East India Company, 1618–1649." *Scandinavian Economic History Review* 37(1): 41–56.

———. 2002. *The Political Economy of Commerce: Southern India 1500–1650,* vol. 45. Cambridge: Cambridge University Press.

———. 2007. "Holding the World in Balance: The Connected Histories of the Iberian Overseas Empires, 1500–1640." *American Historical Review* 112(5): 1359–85.

———. 2012. *The Portuguese Empire in Asia, 1500–1700: A Political and Economic History.* New York: John Wiley & Sons.

Subramanian, T., and R. Kannan. 2003. *Tarangampadi (Tranquebar) Excavation & Conservation Report, 2001–2002.* Department of Archaeology, Government of Tamilnadu.

Symanski, Luís Cláudio P. 2012. "The Place of Strategy and the Spaces of Tactics: Structures, Artifacts, and Power Relations on Sugar Plantations of West Brazil." *Historical Archaeology* 46(3): 124–48.

Tagliacozzo, Eric. 2009. *Southeast Asia and the Middle East: Islam, Movement, and the Longue Durée.* Stanford, CA: Stanford University Press.

Tomich, Dale. 1994. "Small Islands and Huge Comparisons: Caribbean Plantations, Historical Unevenness, and Capitalist Modernity." *Social Science History*: 339–58.

Vaughan, Megan. 2005. *Creating the Creole Island: Slavery in Eighteenth-Century Mauritius.* Durham, NC: Duke University Press.

Vink, Markus. 2015. *Encounters on the Opposite Coast: The Dutch East India Company and the Nayaka State of Madurai in the Seventeenth Century*. Leiden: Brill.

Voss, Barbara L. 2008. *The Archaeology of Ethnogenesis: Race and Sexuality in Colonial San Francisco*. Berkeley: University of California Press.

Westergaard, Waldemar. 1917. *The Danish West Indies under Company Rule (1671–1754): With a Supplementary Chapter, 1755–1917*, vol. 9. New York: Macmillan.

Wilkinson, Theon. 1984. "British Cemeteries in South Asia: An Aspect of Social History." *Asian Affairs* 15(1): 46–54.

Wilson, Brian. 2015. In the Shadow of the Cathedral: The Production of Urban Landscapes, Human Environment Interaction, and Ruination in Velha Goa during Portuguese Colonial Occupation. PhD. Thesis, Department of Anthropology. University of Chicago.

Wilson, Brian, Abhijit Ambekar, and Rohini Pande. 2013. "Defending the Golden City: Survey and GPS Aided Mapping of the Outer Fortification Wall Surrounding Old Goa." *Man and Environment* 38(1): 90–115.

Wilson, Brian, and Mark W Hauser. 2016. "Toward a South Asian Historical Archaeology." *Historical Archaeology* 50(4): 7–21.

CONTRIBUTORS

Douglas V. Armstrong holds Meredith and Maxwell Professorships at Syracuse University, where he is currently chair of the Anthropology Department, Maxwell School. He is a historical archaeologist specializing in studies of the African Diaspora, GIS, and site preservation in the Caribbean and New York State. The author of several books and monographs and numerous articles, his current research in Barbados explores the shift from small-scale farming to large-scale agro-industrial capital-based sugar production and plantation slavery. His studies in the Caribbean have explored enslavement and transitions to freedom on plantations and in urban port town settings. His research in New York has explored permutations of the Underground Railroad, African American communities, and Harriet Tubman's life in freedom.

Gérard L. Chouin is an associate professor of African History at William & Mary and director of the Medieval and Renaissance Program. His work focuses on societal transformations in pre- and early-modern Atlantic West Africa. His research combines evidence from oral traditions, archival material, travel accounts, and archaeological surveys and excavations. In partnership with Adisa Ogunfolakan at Obafemi Awolowo University of Ile-Ife, he leads the Ife-Sungbo Project, which focuses on the archaeology of southwestern Nigeria. A participant in the ANR-funded project GlobAfrica, he also explores the possible spread of the second plague pandemics in sub-Saharan Africa.

Noa Corcoran-Tadd is a lecturer affiliated with the ERC-Synergy NEXUS1492 project at the Department of World Archaeology, Leiden University. He obtained his PhD in anthropology at Harvard (2017), and is currently developing a new project that explores long-term patterns of connectivity and imperialism in the high-altitude environment of northern Chile. He is the author of several book chapters on Andean archaeology and the archaeology of colonialism, including " 'Is This the Gold that You Eat?' Coins, Entanglement, and Early Colonial Orderings in the Andes (AD 1532–c. 1650)" in *The Archaeology of Entanglement* (2015).

Christopher R. DeCorse (PhD, FSA) is professor and past chair of the Department of Anthropology in the Maxwell School of Citizenship and Public Affairs, Syracuse University. His research interests include African archaeology and history, general anthropology, and archaeology in popular culture. He is currently directing ongoing research projects in coastal Ghana and in Sierra Leone, including work at Elmina, the site of the first and largest European trade-post established in sub-Saharan Africa, and at Bunce Island, the major center of European trade on the African Coast between the Senegambia and coastal Ghana. His principal publications on African archaeology include *An Archaeology of Elmina: Africans and Europeans on the Gold Coast, 1400–1900* and *West Africa during the Atlantic Slave Trade*.

Mark W. Hauser (PhD, FSA) is an associate professor of anthropology at Northwestern University. Mark is an archaeologist and historical anthropologist who specializes in materiality, slavery, and inequality. These key themes intersect in the seventeenth-, eighteenth-, and nineteenth-century Atlantic and Indian Oceans. He has published on these themes in *American Anthropologist, Current Anthropology, Atlantic Studies, Historical Archaeology, Journal of Social Archaeology*, and *International Journal of Historical Archaeology*. He has coedited two books and guest edited one journal issue. He has published one monograph, "An Archaeology of Black Markets." His current research project interrogates environment and slavery on the margins of empire.

Corinne L. Hofman is professor of Caribbean Archaeology at the Faculty of Archaeology, Leiden University. She conducted fieldwork throughout the Caribbean over the past thirty years. Her research is highly multidisciplinary and themes of interest are mobility and exchange, colonial encounters, intercultural dynamics, settlement archaeology, and artifact analyses. Hofman's projects are designed to contribute to the historical awareness and valorization of archaeological heritage. Two recent books are *The Handbook of Caribbean Archaeology* (2013, coedited with W. F. Keegan and R. Rodríguez Ramos) and the *Caribbean before Columbus* (2017, coauthored with W. F. Keegan), both published with Oxford University Press.

Matthew Johnson is an archaeologist specializing in medieval and historical Britain and Europe, 1200–1800 CE. He was educated in the UK at Cambridge, and was then at Durham University, before moving to Southampton in 2004. In 2011, he moved to the United States to take up a professorship in anthropology at Northwestern. Matthew has written on castles, buildings, and landscape. He also writes on theory, and on contemporary cultural issues in archaeology. Matthew has published seven books, including *Archaeological Theory: An Introduction* (Blackwell, third revised edition 2019), *Behind the Castle Gate* (Routledge, 2002), and *Ideas of Landscape* (Blackwell, 2007).

Kenneth G. Kelly is professor of anthropology at the University of South Carolina, where he teaches historical archaeology and African archaeology. Dr. Kelly's research focus has been on developing a transatlantic perspective on the archaeology of the African Diaspora, and its impacts both in West Africa and in the Caribbean, including long-term archaeological research in Bénin, Guinea, Jamaica, Guadeloupe, and Martinique that has been supported by the Fulbright Program, the Wenner Gren Foundation for Anthropological Research, and the French Ministry of Culture. He has published in *American Anthropologist, World Archaeology, Journal of Archaeological Method and Theory, Archéologiques, Journal of Caribbean Archaeology, Atlantic Studies,* and *Ethnohistory.* Dr. Kelly received his PhD in anthropology from UCLA in 1995.

Olanrewaju Blessing Lasisi is a graduate student in the Department of Anthropology at the College of William and Mary. He is a Nigerian with keen interest on West African Archaeology. His ongoing dissertation focuses on the dynamics of power and landscape in Ijebu (Southwestern Nigeria) before and after the Atlantic era. His first publication, "New Light on the Archaeology of Sungbo Eredo" was published in 2016 with David A. Aremu in *Dig It: Flinders Journal of Australian Archaeology.*

George MacDonald is the former director of the Archaeological Survey of Canada, the Canadian Museum of Civilization, the Museum Victoria in Melbourne, Australia, the Burke Museum of Natural History in Seattle, the Bill Reid Gallery in Vancouver, and is the current director of the Bill Reid Centre for Northwest Coast Studies at Simon Fraser University. He is author of over 150 publications on the history, archaeology, and art of the Indigenous peoples of the Northwest Coast of North America, including *Raven's Village: The Myths, Arts & Traditions of Native People from the Pacific Northwest Coast* (1996).

Andrew Martindale is an associate professor of anthropology at the University of British Columbia and the Director of UBC's Laboratory of Archaeology and of the Canadian Archaeological Radiocarbon Database. His research explores the archaeology and history of indigenous peoples of the Northwest Coast of North America.

Guido Pezzarossi is an assistant professor in the Department of Anthropology at the Maxwell School in Syracuse University, where he uses archaeological and archival methods to tell more complicated and different narratives of Maya colonial experiences in highland Guatemala. His interests span postcolonial and indigenous approaches to the archaeology of colonial identities and difference, the archaeology of food, and the economic dynamics of colonization. His current research explores the intersection of postcolonial and new materialist perspectives to analyze the entanglements between capitalism and colonialism, via the analysis of how transformations in labor and economic practices—catalyzed by the violence of colonization—in colonial Guatemala affected the experience of daily life for Maya communities.

Kathryn Sampeck (BA, MA, University of Chicago; PhD Tulane University) is an associate professor of anthropology at Illinois State University. She is also a Non-Residential Fellow at the Hutchins Center for African and African American Research at Harvard University. Her research on the archaeology and ethnohistory of colonialism examines the roles of Native Americans in Mesoamerica and the U.S. Southeast in the cultural history of taste, cultural landscapes, racial ideologies, literacy, money, and commerce in American commodities in the Early Modern world. Her current work includes a study of the social history of chocolate, including contributions in *Substance & Seduction: Ingested Commodities in Early Modern Mesoamerica*, which she coedited with Stacey Schwartzkopf.

Erik R. Seeman is professor of history at the University at Buffalo (SUNY). He is author of *Death in the New World: Cross-Cultural Encounters, 1492–1800* (2010) and coeditor (with Jorge Cañizares-Esguerra) of *The Atlantic in Global History, 1500–2000* (2nd ed., 2018). *Speaking with the Dead in Early America* will be published by the University of Pennsylvania Press in 2019.

Martin S. Shanguhyia is associate professor of African History at Maxwell School of Syracuse University. His most recent publication is *Population, Tradition, and Environmental Control in Colonial Kenya* (University of Rochester Press, 2015). He is currently working on a number of projects focusing on environment-based conflict and conflict-resolution, game preservation, and riverine development initiatives in colonial Kenya.

Thomas E. Tolley is a doctoral candidate in anthropology at Syracuse University with a focus on historical archaeology. He obtained his master's degree (with honors) from Syracuse University in 2002, then worked extensively in cultural resources management across the United States. His experience includes projects from California to New York State, as well serving as the field supervisor for environmental archaeology for the Anglo-American Project in Pompeii, with the University of Bradford, UK. Thomas's current research foci include the mission landscapes and economies of Alta-California, and the developing relationships occurring within broader frontier zones. His publications include *Excavando Los Espiritus: The Holy Cross School Archaeological Project* (2002).

Sage Vanier holds a bachelor's degree in classical archaeology from the University of British Columbia. Her research interests are based in British Columbia's Indigenous history, revolving mainly around the environmental stewardship and management practices of the Tsimshian tribes, of which she is a member.

Christopher Kurt Waters (PhD Syracuse University) is the Postdoctoral Fellow in World Heritage Site Management at the UNESCO World Heritage Site Antigua Naval Dockyard and Related Archaeological Sites in Antigua. His doctoral research focused on the establishment and maintenance of defense policies and fortifications by the colonial Antiguan government in the seventeenth and eighteenth centuries, and the impact that the plantation landscape had on the placement of these defenses.

INDEX

abolitionists, 319

Abu-Leghod, Janet, 4

"The Act for the Better Government of Slaves and Free Negroes" of 1702, 170n4

Acts of Union, 10

adinkra cloth, 192, 193

Africa. *See also* East Africa; West Africa
  African Atlantic economy, 288
  African deathways, 186
  African diaspora, 195
  African settlement patterns, 8
  Amerindian-African-European intercultural dynamics, 67, 69
  Atlantic World and, 9
  chocolate made with African cacao, 126
  enslaved African laborers, 143
  escaped African slaves, 67
  gold and, 286
  importing of enslaved Africans, 360
  material culture of, 196
  slave funerals, African instruments banned at, 188
  sub-Saharan, 5, 300

African Americans, 177
  mortuary customs, 195

African Burial Ground, 177–178, 188, 189, 192
  material culture of, 190

Afro-Portuguese peoples, 311–312, 316

agrarian capitalism, 49

agriculture, 215
  agricultural exports, 337
  communal, 110
  domesticates, 58
  hunting and, 328
  indigenous agro-pastoralist world, 210–211
  land devoted to, 366
  Mesoamerica, agricultural production specialties in, 95
  of Mission San Buenaventura, 237
  pastoral, 40
  predominance of agricultural sector, 339
  root crops, 59
  skilled agricultural labor, 97
  slash-and-burn, 137
  specialized crops, 242
  subsistence, 47

Ajebu, 296

Akan people, 192, 193

Alexcee, Fredee, 263, 265

Alta California, 9, 12, 229, 231, 242
  Catholic Church and, 227
  colonialism and, 228
  credit and, 241
  labor in, 234–235
  maps of, *232*
  trade and, 233

Alvarado, Gonzalo de, 119

Alvarado, Pedro, 88, 89, 119
  Guatemala and, 113
  Tacuscalco and, 115

St. James, Barbados, 131–132
slavery in, 142
sugar and, 134
Barrington, Charles, 357, *357*
Battle of Tacuscalco, 113–114, *114*
Beastal, W. E., 157
Before European Hegemony: The World System A.D. 1250–1350 (Abu-Leghod), 4
Belgian Congo, 337, 338, 340, 343
Bell, W. D. M., 332
Belli, Nyara (queen), 313
Benin City, 297, 298, 299
Berkeley, Ernest, 341
beth haim, 179, 181, 182
Betia, 313, 316, 317
Beynon, William, 263, *265*, 274
Bhabha, Homi K., 86
Bight of Benin, 285, 286, 288, 289
Black Carib, 67
Black Death, 38, 49–50, 290
Blakey, Michael, 190
Bobadilla, Juan de, 122
Bolivia, 214
Bolivian altiplano, 203, 206, 209, 218
botija jar fragments, *214*, 215
bottle glass, 144
Bougainville, Louis Antoine de, 10, *10–11*, 19n12
Bourdaan, Peter, 141
Bouysse-Cassagne, Thérèse, 208
Boying, Georg, 366
Brahmans, 361
Brandenburgery, 359
Braudel, Fernand, 2–3, 7, 28, 241, 275, 349
on cacao, 107
on chocolate, 106
critics of, 49

Brazil, 7
Brenner, Robert, 38
Britain, 28, 309–310. *See also* London
Acts of Union, 10
British Empire, 10, 290–291
colonial forest and wildlife management policies of, 6
English Crown, 42, 43
late medieval house in, *30*
Roman roads in, 33, 48
shipping and, *12*
Britannia (Roman province), 33, *34*, *35*
British Isles, 25, *26*, 28, 46, 49
broad-scale economic models, 7
Browne, Owen, 136
Bruges, 285
Budoga Forest, 337
Buenos Aires, 211
buffalo horns, 331
Buganda, 327
Bunce Island, 309
burial grounds, 196
Jewish, 177–179
in New World, 197
at Ouderkerk, 179
power relations and, 177
burial practices, 60. *See also* coffins
of Amerindians, 62
in Barbados, 186
burial "in the Common," 189
daytime funerals, 187
of Europeans, 62
segregated burials, 189

Caamaño, Jacinto, 271
Cabo Verde, 135
cacao, 12, 97–98, 105
Braudel on, 107
chocolate made with African cacao, 126

IBEA. *See* Imperial British East Africa Company
Iberian lifestyle, 63
Iberian Peninsula, 87
Ife
  long-term chronology of, 295
  Obanta and, 299
Ife-Sungbo Archaeological Project, 290, 295
Ijebu, 290, 292, *293*, 299
  information on, 291
  long-term chronology of, 295
  warrior-kings of, 301n20
Iles de Los, 307, 318
Imago Mundi, 46
Imperial British East Africa Company (IBEA), 335, 336
imperialism, 132, 154, 330
  imperial jurisdiction, 332
  imperial wars of conquest, 343
impermeability, 159
imported diseases, 55
Inca Empire, 55. *See also* Inka Empire
Incan Empire, 5
India, 329, 353, *362*
  Indian European trade centers, 364
  south, 360
Indian Act, 275
Indian Agents, 274
Indian Ocean, 354, 358, 361, 367
  circuits of exchange, 6
Indian Reserves Commissioner, 274
Indian Residential School system, 274–275
Indigenous history, 252
  archaeology and, 253
  Indigenous postcontact history, 256
indigenous peoples, 55
  cultural traditions of, 69

forced movement of indigenous peoples
  in the Caribbean, 62
  in Hispaniola, 61
indigeneity, 5
indigenous agro-pastoralist world, 210–211
indigenous identities, 56
indigenous networks, 63
indigenous social formations, 2
indigenous squatting, 122
indigent poor, 39
Indonesia, 356
industrial capitalism, 49, 329
Industrial Revolution, 25, 153
informal labor (*kajcheo*), 206
Inka Empire, 204, 208, 210
  infrastructural legacy of, 217
intentional cranial modification, 59–60
intercolonial market, 117
interregional connections, 60, 63
interstitial spaces, 211, 215
intimate landscape experience, 109
intraregional networks, *4*
Ireland, 28, *44*
  English Crown's estates in, 42
  pilgrim routes across, 44
Irish Sea, 28, 33, 47
Isle de France, 354
Italian Somaliland, 339
ivory, 325, 353
  confiscated, 339
  decline in, 333
  East Africa and, 328–330
  hunting elephants for, 327–328
  importance of, 331
  in Karamoja region, 332
  Kenya and, 338
  quantity and value of, 338t

www.ingramcontent.com/pod-product-compliance
Lightning Source LLC
Chambersburg PA
CBHW020237290326
41929CB00044B/76